Effective Protection of the Rights of the Accused in the EU Directives

Effective Protection of the Rights of the Accused in the EU Directives

A Computable Approach to Criminal Procedure Law

Edited by

Giuseppe Contissa, Giulia Lasagni, Michele Caianiello and Giovanni Sartor

BRILL
NIJHOFF

LEIDEN | BOSTON

The Project from which this volume originates - CrossJustice project (Grant Agreement number: 847346 – JUST-AG-2018/JUST-JACC-AG-2018 JUST/REC MGA) - was funded by the European Union's Justice Programme (2014–2020).

Funded by
the European Union

The content of this publication represents the views of the authors only and is their sole responsibility. The European Commission does not accept any responsibility for use that may be made of the information it contains.

The Library of Congress Cataloging-in-Publication Data is available online at https://catalog.loc.gov
LC record available at https://lccn.loc.gov/2022002409

Typeface for the Latin, Greek, and Cyrillic scripts: "Brill". See and download: brill.com/brill-typeface.

ISBN 978-90-04-51338-9 (hardback)
ISBN 978-90-04-51339-6 (e-book)

This book is printed on acid-free paper and produced in a sustainable manner.

Contents

PART 3
Comparative and Transnational Analysis

PART 4
Developing a Computable Approach to Defence Rights

Contributors

Anna H. Albrecht
Full Professor of Criminal Law, University of Potsdam, Germany

Marco Billi
PhD Candidate in Legal Informatics, Alma Mater Research Institute for Human-Centered Artificial Intelligence, University of Bologna, Italy

Marin Bonačić
Associate Professor in Criminal Procedure, Faculty of Law, University of Zagreb, Croatia

Marianna Biral
Research Fellow in Criminal Procedure, University of Bologna, Italy

Zoran Burić
Associate Professor in Criminal Procedure, Faculty of Law, University of Zagreb, Croatia

Pedro Caeiro
Associate professor and integrated researcher, Faculty of Law, Univ Coimbra, UCILeR, Portugal

Michele Caianiello
Full Professor in Criminal Procedure, University of Bologna, Italy

Mariavittoria Catanzariti
Research Associate, European University Institute, and Adjunct Professor, LUISS University, Italy

Eleonora Cervellera
PhD Candidate in Criminal Law, University of Paris Nanterre, France

Giuseppe Contissa
Senior Assistant Professor in Legal Informatics, University of Bologna, Italy

Miguel João Costa
Advisor at the Constitutional Court of Portugal; Guest Lecturer and integrated researcher, Faculty of Law, Univ Coimbra, UCILeR, Portugal

Dominika Czerniak
Assistant Professor, Department of Criminal Procedure, Faculty of Law, Administration and Economics, University of Wrocław, Poland

Dorota Czerwińska
Research Assistant & Lecturer, Department of Criminal Procedure, Faculty of Law, Administration and Economics, University of Wrocław, Poland

Luigi Di Caro
Assistant Professor in Computer Science, University of Torino, Italy

Zlata Đurđević
Tenured Professor in Criminal Procedure, Faculty of Law, University of Zagreb, Croatia

Llio Humphreys
Research Fellow in Computer Science, University of Torino, Italy

Elizabeta Ivičević Karas
Full Professor in Criminal Procedure, Faculty of Law, University of Zagreb, Croatia

Wojciech Jasiński
Assistant Professor, Digital Justice Center, Faculty of Law, Administration and Economics, University of Wrocław, Poland

Karolina Kremens
Assistant Professor, Head of Digital Justice Center, Faculty of Law, Administration and Economics, University of Wrocław, Poland

Giulia Lasagni
Junior Assistant Professor in Criminal Procedure, University of Bologna, Italy

Miroslava Manolova
Associate Professor in Criminal Law, Faculty of Law, Department of Criminal Law Studies, Sofia University "St. Kliment Ohridski", Bulgaria

Adriano Martufi
Assistant Professor of Criminal Law and Criminal Procedure, Leiden University, the Netherlands

Rohan Nanda
Assistant Professor in Data Science for Law, University of Maastricht, the Netherlands

Ana-María Neira-Pena
Phd, Contract Professor of Procedural Law, University of A Coruña, Spain

Isadora Neroni Rezende
PhD Candidate in Law, Science and Technology, University of Bologna, Italy

Jannemieke Ouwerkerk
Professor of European Criminal Law, Leiden University, the Netherlands

Raphaële Parizot
Full professor of Criminal Law, University of Paris Nanterre, France

Kelly Pitcher
Assistant Professor of Criminal Law and Criminal Procedure, Leiden University, the Netherlands

Alessandra Santangelo
Research Fellow in Criminal Law, University of Bologna, Italy

Galileo Sartor
Researcher in Legal Informatics, University of Torino, Italy

Giovanni Sartor
Full Professor in Legal Informatics, Alma Mater Research Institute for Human-Centered Artificial Intelligence, University of Bologna, and Part Time Professor in Legal Theory and Legal Informatics, European University, Italy

Anne Schneider
Full Professor of German, European and International Criminal Law, Heinrich-Heine University Düsseldorf, Germany

Emilio Sulis
Research Fellow in Computer Science, University of Torino, Italy

Introduction

Giuseppe Contissa, Giulia Lasagni, Michele Caianiello, and Giovanni Sartor

The protection of fundamental rights for persons accused or suspected of a crime is one of the main aims of the EU policy in the area of criminal justice.

However, the effective implementation of such rights throughout the EU is heavily affected by the highly varying legal frameworks which characterize Member States' regulation on procedural rights in criminal proceedings.

In this context, legal actors often struggle to identify which legislation and therefore which procedural rights are applicable to persons accused or suspected in specific cases, both due to linguistic barriers and peculiarities of different national legal systems.

While we face such challenges in Europe, on a global level the domain of law is also on the brink of a period of fundamental and irreversible change and transformation. Information technologies and computer systems are the main drivers of this change. Increasingly capable machines, operating in support of experts are transforming the way that legal activities and procedures are undertaken. New legal applications and platforms appear, changing the practice of law, specifically by enriching legal texts with computational models of legal reasoning, providing users with automated assessments and explanations of their outcomes with reasons and arguments.

Against this background, the book critically examines the procedural safeguards of the suspect and the accused as recognised by the six EU Procedural Rights Directives: Directive 2010/64/EU of 20 October 2010 on the right to interpretation and translation; Directive 2012/13/EU of 22 May 2012 on the right to information; Directive 2013/48/EU of 22 October 2013 on the right of access to a lawyer and to have a third party informed; Directive (EU) 2016/343 of 9 March 2016 on the presumption of innocence and the right to be present at trial; Directive (EU) 2016/800 of 11 May 2016 on procedural safeguards for juvenile defendants; Directive (EU) 2016/1919 of 26 October 2016 on legal aid.

All these Directives are analyzed both as such and in their practical implementation at the national level. In particular, the volume illustrates the main lacunas in the protection of defence rights in nine EU jurisdictions (Bulgaria, Croatia, France, Germany, Italy, Portugal, Poland, Spain, the Netherlands).

The discussion is carried out with a multi-disciplinary approach, that integrates criminal law and legal informatics analysis.

 | DOI:10.1163/9789004513396_002

The volume thus proposes an innovative perspective on the topic for a twofold reason.

First, the analysis of the shortcomings and obstacles that procedural rights of the Directives meet in their national implementation is carried out through the lenses of legal reasoning and legal informatics. The research adopted a comprehensive approach, consisting in the translation of the EU Procedural Directives, as well as samples of national legislation, into a computable language. This approach allows, through the development of a semi-automated AI platform, to better highlight uncovered deficits of the normative texts, and to enhance comparative analysis among the legal systems.

Secondly, the book proposes a multi-level perspective, since the legal analysis, carried out by highly specialised scholars, tackles both EU law and national legislation, as well as caselaw. Therefore, also the practical implementation of procedural rights will be dealt with in the volume.

Indeed, whereas the existing EU *acquis* establishes common minimum standards on criminal procedural rights, the need to promote their effective and coherent application remains particularly pressing due to the highly fragmented national implementing legislation and relevant case-law.

The volume describes the results of a thirty-month international research project funded by the EU Commission – CrossJustice (https://site.unibo.it/cross-justice/en) – conducted under the supervision of the University of Bologna. The research study counted seven international partners including eminent scholars and researchers in the field of European law and Criminal Procedure, Legal Informatics and Computer Science, as well as private-sector experts working in the field of IT platform development. In particular, the project has resulted in the development of two computer tools, grounded on highly advanced juridical data, collected and uploaded by the legal partners, that provide single case assessments and mass testing outcomes on the EU Procedural Rights Directives (CrossJustice platform, freely accessible at https://www.crossjustice.eu/en/index.html). However, the book goes beyond such specific results, providing a generally applicable and integrated analysis, that results understandable also for readers that are not aware of the CrossJustice project.

The book is composed of four parts.

Part 1, comprising three chapters, serves as a general introduction to the increasing connection between criminal law and technological development. Chapter 1 opens the volume with a general illustration of the most relevant issues emerging from the interaction of criminal procedure rights and Artificial Intelligence technology. Chapter 2 focuses on the development of computable approach to the legal domain, framing this new research field and its potential, in light of the relevant legal and technical challenges. Finally, Chapter 3 expounds on the specific application of a computational approach to the criminal procedure matter, underlining the specificities of the subject and drawing the legal and informatic reasoning approach that may be used to address them.

Part 2 presents nine, concise-but-comprehensive Chapters (4 to 12) of the state of implementation of the six procedural Directives at the national level. It includes legal analyses from Bulgaria, Croatia, France, Germany, Italy, Poland, Portugal, Spain and the Netherlands.[1] The country selection ranges from North to South, from Western to Eastern European States and puts together inquisitorial and accusatorial traditions, allowing a broad representation of EU legal traditions and models.

The examination is innovative and integrated, as it illustrates the state of play of the most significantly critical or successful profiles in the national implementation of the EU standards on criminal procedure safeguards, while taking into account both the legislation and the national case-law. Each analysis, prepared by national experts, highlights the most problematic or significant issues emerging from the specific country context and provides a critical analysis that encompasses both the legislative transposition of the Directives and their concrete implementation. The national analysis, however, does not cover all aspects of implementation or non-implementation of the EU legislation on the matter. Such analysis was carried out in the course of the CrossJustice research, and brought to the drafting of detailed national reports, that are currently available from the webpage of the Project.[2]

Part 3, comprising two Chapters, provides for a comparative and transnational analysis. The comparison of Chapter 13 builds upon the national law chapters of the previous section, as well as findings emerged by the semantic Natural Language Processing analysis, developed thanks to the computational approach previously illustrated. This perspective provides an innovative overview on the harmonization status of the procedural safeguards in criminal proceedings and over the different (and sometimes contradictory) causes that reduces the chances to obtain a uniform level of protections throughout the EU. Chapter 14, on the other side, revolves around the relation between procedural rights and data protection safeguards. It investigates the connections between the data subject's rights under the law enforcement Directive 2016/680 and the rights of information and access laid down by Directive 2012/13,

1 The research also involved two other Member States: Romania and Sweden. The need to complete the volume within the timeframe imposed by the project did not allow us to include those two jurisdictions in the final volume. However, the Country Reports for these national systems can be accessed on the project website.

2 <https://site.unibo.it/cross-justice/en>.

seeking to explore whether individual rights might be improved by the attachment of data protection safeguards.

Finally, Part 4 of our book offers a technical perspective on the computable law approach adopted in the course of the research, based on the development of logic rules and automated reasoning to support the CrossJustice platform and enable the harmonization analysis based on Natural Language Processing techniques. The concepts of knowledge representation, and logic rules, are presented in Chapter 15 and 16, as well as a concrete implementation of a computable approach to defense rights, able to provide the rationale for a specific decision, and to measure the level of harmonization between national and EU law.

The ambitious research Project that resulted in this volume was designed as a multidisciplinary and multilevel study that relied on the collaboration among a private ICT company, researchers in different fields (criminal procedure law, legal informatics, computer science) and legal practitioners coming from several Member States.

Led by the University of Bologna, this study was made possible only by a transnational teamwork, the enthusiasm of whose components deserves our most sincere thanks.

First and foremost, we wish to show our greatest appreciation and gratitude to the many researchers who chose to dedicate their precious time to our research project and brought their boundless enthusiasm and expertise.

As the research, and also this volume, would never have seen the light of day without their hard work and patience in drafting with the project's demanding deadlines, we wish to thank each and every one of our national legal rapporteurs (in alphabetical order per Member State): Miroslava Manolova (Bulgaria), Zlata Đurđević, Zoran Burić, Elizabeta Ivičević Karas and Marin Bonačić (Croatia), Raphaële Parizot and Eleonora Cervellera (France), Anna H. Albrecht and Anne Schneider (Germany), Laura Bartoli, Marianna Biral, Cosimo Emanuele Gatto, Vanessa Maraldi, Irene Milazzo, Isadora Neroni Rezende, Antonio Pugliese, Alessandra Santangelo and Salvo Tesoriero (Italy), Karolina Kremens, Wojciech Jasiński, Dorota Czerwińska and Dominika Czerniak (Poland), Pedro Caeiro and Miguel João Costa (Portugal), Daniel Nitu (Romania), Ana-María Neira-Pena (Spain), Maria Bergström (Sweden), Jannemieke Ouwerkerk, Kelly Pitcher and Adriano Martufi (the Netherlands).

An equally heartful thanks goes to the researchers in the field of legal informatics and computer science, that accepted with patience to share and explain their expertise to criminal lawyers: Luigi Di Caro, Llio Humphreys, Emilio Sulis, Rohan Nanda, Galileo Sartor and Marco Billi.

Research on these topics however is nothing without the capacity to transmitting such knowledge and involving high level academics and practitioners in a transnational debate: For all this, and much more, not less for her constant professional and human support, a special thanks goes to Mariavittoria Catanzariti and to the whole European University Institute in the person of Deirdre Curtin.

Naturally, very little of our research would have been really visible from the outside without the outstanding support of Hristo Konstantinov and his amazing APIS team, who concretely created the CrossJustice Platform, and translated our theoretical debate into a (virtually) tangible tool.

In this regard, we would further like to extend our gratitude to the several stakeholders that, across five Member States, participated to the seminars organized on the topics covered by the Project, testing the CrossJustice platform and providing precious feedbacks for its finalization and development.

We must also extend a wholehearted and special thank you to the wonderful research team, that was the very heart and soul of this research and allowed us to get successfully till the end, surviving among tight deadlines, obscure administrative requirements and a really a lot of work to do (in order of their time in joining the team): Alessandra Santangelo, Galileo Sartor, Marianna Biral and Marco Billi. Our most sincere gratitude goes also to Isadora Neroni Rezende and Antonio Pugliese, without whose tireless efforts this book would have never come to being.

PART 1

Criminal Procedure Law and Technological Development: Toward an Integrated Approach

CHAPTER 1

The Algorithmic (Companion to) Counsel

A Computational Approach to Strengthen the Effectiveness of Defence Rights in Criminal Proceedings

Michele Caianiello

1.1 An Impetuous Development in Twenty Years or So

With some approximation one may affirm that European criminal law, with particular reference to criminal procedure, started to grow just over twenty years ago, following the entry into force of the Treaty of Amsterdam. With the Tampere Council in 1999, the European Union (EU) laid the foundations for the development of judicial cooperation in criminal matters, while at the same time being able to make use of legal instruments, initially Framework Decisions (FD), which until then could not be implemented in criminal matters.[1]

All in all, the path undertaken can be considered a successful story. Within the framework of EU law, the criminal law area has developed rapidly, with a range of new legal sources regulating many different aspects. This has shed new light on the subject as a whole, contributed to the emergence of new methods of study and led to the establishment of new institutional actors, such as the European Public Prosecutor's Office (EPPO).[2] The enterprise started in Tampere has also been consolidated and developed in a crucial way after the entry into force of the Lisbon Treaty. Thanks to it, the Charter of Fundamental Rights (CFREU) has today the same value as the Treaties, thus acknowledging that is an essential mission of the EU to ensure an adequate and effective level of protection of fundamental rights.[3] This is especially important in the criminal matter, where, as well known, restrictions to individual safeguards

1 André Klip, *European Criminal Law. An Integrative Approach* (Intersentia, 2021) 59; Anne Weyembergm, 'History of Cooperation' in Roberto E. Kostoris (ed), *Handbook of European Criminal Procedure* (Springer 2018) 173–197.

2 Lorena Bachmaier Winter (ed), *The European Public Prosecution Office. The Challenges Ahead* (Springer 2018) v-xii; John A. E. Vervaele, 'The European Public Prosecution's Office (EPPO): Introductory Remarks' in Willem Geelhoed, Leendert H. Erkelens, Arjen W. H. Meij (eds), *Shifting Perspectives on the European Public Prosecution Office* (Asser Press 2019) 11–19.

3 Valsamis Mitsilegas, *EU Criminal Law after Lisbon. Rights, Trust, and the Transformation of Justice in Europe* (Hart 2016) 9–11.

 | DOI:10.1163/9789004513396_003

can frequently take place. Furthermore, after Lisbon, the EU can legislate in key areas of criminal justice, both about substantive and procedural profiles, by adopting the traditional sources of the Union's legal order. Thanks to it, the method consolidated under the first Pillar of the former European Community has become a common heritage of EU criminal law.[4]

An essential area regulated by a network of provisions adopted after Lisbon, concerns the protection of individual rights, in particular those of the victim of crimes and of the accused in criminal proceedings. With regard to the latter, the Union constructed a road map that has led a certain harmonisation to the discipline, at supranational level, of the essential aspects of the accused's defence. It seems correct to say that the six procedural Directives adopted by the European legislator in accordance with the Stockholm Programme have laid down *ad hoc* rules for most of the aspects touched upon, in general terms, by Art 6 of the European Convention on Human Rights (ECHR).[5] The unconcealed ambition, in this respect, has been to guarantee an EU statute of the rights of the defence, equally valid both in the horizontal perspective, that is in judicial cooperation between the different Member States, and in the vertical one, in the relationship between the EU criminal justice institutions and the national jurisdictions. It should not be forgotten, in this regard, that, according to Art 41 of the EPPO Regulation, the Directives on the rights of the accused are the main reference also for EPPO, when its investigations interfere with defence rights.[6]

A first conclusion we can draw, therefore, is that the Area of Freedom, Security and Justice (AFSJ), twenty years after its initial development, appears to be vital and capable of projecting its effectiveness in the different dimensions in which EU law traditionally operates. At the same time, precisely because of the wealth of new regulatory sources, it presents numerous aspects, that need to be clarified and standardised in terms of interpretation and application.

4 Klip (n 1) 22–25.

5 Resolution of the Council of 30 November 2009 on a Roadmap for strengthening procedural rights of suspected or accused persons in criminal proceedings (2009/C 295/01), in OJ, 4 December 2009, C 295, then recognized in The Stockholm Programme – An open and secure Europe serving and protecting citizens (2010/C 115/01), in OJ, 4 May 2010, C 115. See André Klip, 'Fair Trial Rights in the European Union: Reconciling Accused and Victims' Rights' in Tommaso Rafaraci and Rosanna Belfiore (eds), *EU Criminal Justice. Fundamental Rights, Transnational Proceedings and the European Public Prosecutor's Office* (Springer 2019) 29.

6 Giulio Illuminati, 'The Protection of Fundamental Rights of the Suspect or Accused in Transnational Proceedings Under the EPPO' in Lorena Bachmaier Winter (ed), *The European Public Prosecution Office* (Springer 2018) 179–199.

1.2 A Complex Legal Framework

The new legal edifice that has been built over two decades is not without flaws, although the positive aspects seem to outweigh the negative ones.

In spite of the passion for the European Union for classical culture and its heritage, it is indeed difficult to adapt the image of the Greek temple, which was used to give the idea of the EU's structure before Lisbon, to describe European criminal law. The typical features of that architecture – its essential structure, its harmony, the balance between fullness and emptiness – seem almost always to be missing in the field under consideration. On the contrary, there is an abundance of redundancies, overlapping regulations and expressions that are as long-winded as they are ill-defined. Remaining within the architectural metaphors, the most appropriate reference would then rather seem that of certain medieval constructions, erected on the foundations of an ancient classical building (such as certain villages in Languedoc or Tuscany constructed inside an ancient Roman theatre).

This is not surprising, of course. Although certainly impetuous in terms of timing and abundant in terms of quantity, the criminal law set of normative provisions within the European Union is more than ever the result of compromises, accelerations followed by sudden setbacks.

One good example concerns the issuing of a harmonised legal system in the law of evidence, and the decision to approve, at last, the EIO Directive. As it is well known, the original plan was to draft a directive with the ambition to establish a single regime for the mutual admission of evidence: However, the final legal product ended up being just an instrument to execute orders to conduct investigations more quickly. Yet, at a deeper analysis, one may discover that, among the EIO provisions, there may be hidden passages which allow, with a little hermeneutical sagacity, a fairly complete European regime of the admission of evidence to be constructed through case law.[7]

Another exemplary case concerns the legal sources approved to prevent potential conflicts of jurisdiction. After a long debate on how to regulate such conflicts, the EU just adopted few provisions allowing an EU body – that is Eurojust – to operate on the mere level of moral suasion.[8] And even when the

7 See on the point Annalisa Mangiaracina, 'A New and Controversial Scenario in the Gathering of Evidence at the European Level: The Proposal for a Directive on the European Investigation Order' (2014) 10 Utrecht Law Review 113; Marcello Daniele, 'Evidence Gathering in the Realm of the European Investigation Order: From National Rules to Global Principles' (2015) 6 New Journal of European Criminal Law 179.

8 This is the case of the Framework Decision on prevention and settlement of conflicts of exercise of jurisdiction in criminal proceedings 2009/948/JHA. See on the topic Michiel

first unitary vertical body, the EPPO, was finally set up, the provisions on jurisdiction regulating the EPPO's action remained so unclear as to raise doubts on whether they are compatible with the principle of the court pre-established by law, proclaimed by the Charter of Fundamental Rights.[9]

Similar considerations apply to the rights of the accused in criminal proceedings, as they have developed within the Union, which are the area of specific interest of the present research. Conceived as part of a unitary and coherent body of law, the 2003 *Green Paper*,[10] they were segmented and approved separately following the entry into force of the Lisbon Treaty, thanks to the political solution promoted through the Stockholm Programme, in order to overcome Member States' political resistance.

In this way, patiently and methodically breaking down the original framework into separate sets of regulations, the European Union has succeeded, in the space of about seven years, in realising its original plan by adopting legal instruments (a set of six Directives)[11] capable of providing an answer to the

Luchtman, 'Choice of forum in an area of freedom, security and justice' (2011) 7 Utrecht law Review 74.

9 Hans-Holger Herrnfeld, 'Choice of forum and case allocation in the Eppo regulation' in Katalin Ligeti, John Vervaele, André Klip and Gavin Robinson (eds), Preventing and Resolving Conflicts of Jurisdiction in EU Criminal Law (OUP 2018) 309; Michiel Luchtman, 'Forum Choice and Judicial Review Under the Eppo's Legislative Framework' in Willem Geelhoed – Leendert H. Erkelens – Arjen W.H. Meij, (eds), *Shifting Perspectives on the European Public Prosecutor's Office* (Asser Press 2019) 155–169; Dominik Brodovski, 'Article 22' in Hans-Holger Herrnfeld, Dominik Brodowsky and Cristoph Burchard (eds), *European Public Prosecutor's Office* (Hart 2021) 383–384.

10 See GREEN PAPER FROM THE COMMISSION. Procedural Safeguards for Suspects and Defendants in Criminal Proceedings throughout the European Union – COM(2003) 75 final <https://eur-lex.europa.eu/LexUriServ/LexUriServ.do?uri=COM:2003:0075:FIN:EN:PDF>.

11 See the following directives: Directive 2010/64/EU of the European Parliament and of the Council of 20 October 2010 on the right to interpretation and translation in criminal proceedings; Directive 2012/13/EU of the European Parliament and of the Council of 22 May 2012 on the right to information in criminal proceedings; Directive 2013/48/EU of the European Parliament and of the Council of 22 October 2013 on the right of access to a lawyer in criminal proceedings and in European arrest warrant proceedings, and on the right to have a third party informed upon deprivation of liberty and to communicate with third persons and with consular authorities while deprived of liberty; Directive (EU) 2016/343 of the European Parliament and of the Council of 9 March 2016 on the strengthening of certain aspects of the presumption of innocence and of the right to be present at the trial in criminal proceedings; Directive (EU) 2016/800 of the European Parliament and of the Council of 11 May 2016 on procedural safeguards for children who are suspects or accused persons in criminal proceedings; Directive (EU) 2016/1919 of the European Parliament and of the Council of 26 October 2016 on legal aid for suspects and accused persons in criminal proceedings and for requested persons in European arrest warrant proceedings.

main problems that the defence may encounter in criminal proceedings (especially if they are transnational in nature, as those where EU law typically comes into play).

As well known, the path taken under the Stockholm Road map to strengthening the protection of defendants' rights has by no means been an easy one. Each Directive has been the subject of a complex and detailed negotiation, which is still clearly visible today in the complex preambles that precede their texts.[12] But a similar impression is also obtained by comparing, in certain cases, the wording of the provisional drafts with those approved in the end: For example, on the subject of remedies for violation of the right to silence, the draft of the Directive on the presumption of innocence originally provided for a far more drastic solution – the exclusion of statements obtained by infringing the defendant's right to silence – whereas, on the contrary, the definitive version just requires, with far less effectiveness, a prudent assessment of statements obtained by infringing or derogating the defendant's right to remain silent.[13]

Thus, although the Directives certainly raise the level of protection of the right of defence within the EU Area of Freedom, Security and Justice, they present quite a few problematic aspects.

In some cases, they contain provisions that are not clear enough, while in others, these are not sufficiently effective:[14] It seems undeniable, it is worth observing incidentally, that almost always the legislator has been careful to use language that would allow, with an adequate hermeneutic will, to adopt even the best possible standard of protection. Moreover, rights sometimes overlap, as in the case of the information to be given to the defendant.[15] Finally, the use of

12 It is rather clear that usually preambles on defendant's rights directives are always careful to pave the way for interpretative solutions that are sufficiently flexible to accommodate the different political impulses promoted by the Member States.

13 See Anneli Soo, '(Effective) Remedies for a Violation of the Right to Counsel During Criminal Proceedings in the European Union: An Empirical Study' (2018) 14 Utrecht Law Review 18. See also Michele Caianiello, 'To Sanction (or not to Sanction) Procedural Flaws at EU Level? A Step forward in the Creation of an EU Criminal Process' (2014) 22 European Journal of Crime, Criminal Law and Criminal Justice 317; André Klip, 'Violations of Defence Rights' Directives' (2018) 26 European Journal of Crime, Criminal Law and Criminal Justice 271.

14 A more detailed analysis of this profiles with regard to the Member States examined in this volume may be found below, in Chapter 13 (Michele Caianiello and Giulia Lasagni, 'Comparative Remarks').

15 In addition to the general provision contained in the Directive on the right to information in criminal proceedings, the other directives usually provide for duty to inform the defendant about the specific right s/he is entitled according to the related legal source. For example, article 10 on the Directive on right of the access to a counsel provide for a

the directives as legal sources, a condition imposed by Art 82 TFEU, always puts the interpreter in front of at least two legal texts: the supranational one, and the national implementing one, which may be partially different from the previous, by exploiting the margins of discretion made available by the directive.[16] Naturally, the complexity may be by far greater when the procedure is transnational and involves several legal systems. In such a case, faced with the European legal source, the interpreter may be forced to consider (and apply) as many national transposition sources as the Member States' jurisdictions involved.

The same phenomenon is bound to occur in the system set up with the EPPO, which will structurally have to deal with cases with a transnational dimension. Although the legislator could choose to unify the legal discipline of rights of the accused, since Art 86 TFEU allows the adoption of a regulation in this field, it preferred referring to the directives already launched by the Stockholm Programme.[17] In this way, practitioners will necessarily have to apply, most time they come across a legal issue, two EU legal texts (the 2017 Regulation, and the specifically Directive concerned), in addition to the national legal provisions transposing the European sources.

As always, eventually, at the peak of the system is the EU Charter of Fundamental Rights, which, as if the level of complexity was not already high enough, by means of a game of cross-references carried out through Arts 52 and 53, transposes the legal precipitate of the European Convention on Human Rights and the common constitutional traditions as elaborated by the jurisdictions of the Member States.

1.3 The Difficult Application of the Established Regulatory System in Practice, with Specific Focus on the Defendant's Fair Trial Rights

The observations made so far suggest that dealing with European criminal law, and in particular with the rights of defence within the framework of the EU legal system, is quite difficult.

---

specific right to information, that it is added and integrates the provisions of the Directive on the right to information in criminal proceedings.

16 See André Klip, 'The Substantive Criminal Law Jurisdiction of the European Public Prosecutor's Office' (2012) 20 European Journal of Crime, Criminal Law and Criminal Justice 367. The issue is even more complex when the matter is regulated by an FD, which is devoid of direct effect, but obliges the court to interpret it accordingly.

17 See Dominik Brodowski, 'Article 41' in Hans-Holger Herrnfeld, Dominik Brodowsky and Cristoph Burchard (n 9) 383–384.

First, the network of rules, as we have seen, is extremely varied. This increases combinatorial possibilities for the interpreter. The difference in legal sources also allows interpreters to make use of various interpretative methods. This aggravates the overall difficulty of making the system predictable *ex ante*.

Such difficulties arise only when applying the general principles to cases, due to the complex interconnection between the two charters of rights (ECHR and CFR).

This statement appears to be confirmed by an analysis, even if not in-depth, of the recent jurisprudence of the European Courts, including both the European Court of Human Rights (ECtHR) and the European Court of Justice (CJEU). Both courts, when confronted in recent years with a case involving both ECHR and EU law, have tried to combine the two levels, justifying the solution adopted in light of supranational law other than the one on which they formally have jurisdiction upon. Thus, for example, in *Ibrahim*,[18] and in *Knox*,[19] the ECtHR arrived at its final decision after considering the relevant EU sources – the Charter and the directives specifically concerned – on the right to a lawyer and on the right to an interpreter and translation of documents respectively (as well as after trying to understand how these sources interact with the national rules of the State involved in the case). The same applies, *mutatis mutandis*, to the case law of the CJEU. If we take into consideration, for example, the judgments issued in *Taricco*[20] and in *DB vs Consob*,[21] we can see how the justification of the decisions adopted by the Luxembourg judges makes consistent reference to ECtHR's case law: in *Taricco*, with reference to the procedural, and not substantive, nature of the rules on limitation periods;[22] in *DB v Consob*, with reference to the identification of the external boundaries (and the intrinsic meaning) of the right to silence, in administrative proceedings having a punitive connotation.[23]

The difficulty of following each step of the reasoning in the above-mentioned decisions makes it clear that the elaboration of legal solutions in the area of European criminal justice, in particular with regard to the rights of defence and fair trial, appears to be highly complex. This realistically implies

18 *Ibrahim and others v UK* App nos 50541/08, 50571/08, 50573/08 and 40351/09 (ECHR, 13 September 2016) §§ 203 ff.

19 *Knox v Italy* App no 76577/13 (ECHR, 24 January 2019) §§ 106 ff.

20 See Case C-105/14, *Taricco and Others* (CJEU, 8 September 2015).

21 See Case C-481/19, *DB v Consob* (CJEU, 2 February 2021).

22 *Taricco* (n 20) § 57.

23 *DB v Consob* (n 21) §§ 39–40.

that, very often, one and the same lawyer does not have all the necessary skills to offer effective defence.

In order to achieve viable solutions, it is required to have a good knowledge of the EU legal level, and at the same time, to have a thorough awareness of the ECtHR jurisprudence developed in this field in the second half of the last century. In addition, it is necessary to have an adequate command of the national system in which the sources are to be applied: if more than one jurisdiction is involved, as likely when the case has a European dimension, it can also be helpful to have some familiarity with national systems other than one's own.

This is an unusual intellectual challenge for modern criminal jurists. It is difficult, for the reasons indicated, to find precedents to refer to, or practices to adapt to the area examined here. This is also due to the fact that, unlike other legal fields, criminal law is characterised by a claim to specificity and strictness, of clear *ex ante* predictability, which does not operate with comparable significance in areas other than the criminal law.

1.4 The Use of AI System to Advance Knowledge and Improve the Effective Protection of Fundamental Rights in the EU Area of Freedom, Security and Justice

To put it simply, the system is extremely complex. It requires multifarious competences, which are not easy to integrate. At the same time, it must guarantee, as an essential reason for legitimacy, high levels of a priori predictability for the citizen, in the name of the principle of legality. This is a task that it is very difficult for an individual to accomplish by her own efforts.

Of course, it may be objected, this kind of cases will usually be handled by a group of jurists, whose background is as varied as the legal sources they have to apply. Thus, there will be justices (and defenders) capable of composing the framework of the European sources, and of the jurisprudences of the relevant supranational Courts, while there also will be other jurists who are trained specifically for the purpose to operate at national level, in which they are experts. In other words, the solution of a European criminal case with a supra- (and trans-) national dimension will in practice always be the result of a team effort, and not of an isolated practitioner.

This objection is certainly well-founded, but it does not solve all problems. On the one hand, although one can certainly speak of teamwork, the solution of the case must ultimately be unitary (and requires an ability to develop an overall view of the legal problems involved at different levels). On the other hand, the very need to work in teams may produce inequalities.

In particular, it may amplify the delta separating the position of the prosecution, which will hopefully be equipped with the necessary personnel resources to face the challenge posed by multilevel criminal justice, from the defence, which will rarely benefit from a comparable set of tools:[24] such as, for example, a pool of defenders able to move in a coordinated way to challenge the case built by the EPPO, across the multiple levels, national and supranational, in which it is organised.

Of course, inequalities may occur also among defendants, and between defendants and victims, depending on how many resources they can deploy to build a team of lawyers capable of dealing with a case of transnational dimensions.

Such gap between private citizens and supranational prosecution agencies, such as the EPPO, is realistically destined to never, or almost never, be closed. But this is the point: Can it be considerably reduced? In this perspective, is it possible to use technology and computational reasoning to make it easier for citizens (and even earlier for legal professionals) to become acquainted and familiar with this new area of law?

The underlying idea of the research is specifically to verify if and how Artificial Intelligence (AI) systems may improve the protection of defendants' fundamental rights, where faced with transnational criminal proceedings in the EU AFSJ area.

Theoretically, it is possible to choose two different ways to test this research question.

The first is to try to build AI systems in order to develop ready-made hermeneutic solutions. In this sense, the operator who has to deal with a transnational EU dimension case has only to enter the relevant data, and try to uncritically follow the solution offered by the algorithm applied by the self-learning machine. This path has recently been theorised in several studies, and is being tested in some areas (usually not including criminal law).[25]

For various reasons, however, this did not seem to us to be the most appropriate direction to take.

24 See in this regard the observations expressed some years ago in Malin Thunberg Schunke, *Whose Responsibility? A Study of Transnational Defence Rights and Mutual Recognition of Judicial Decisions within the EU* (Intersentia 2013) especially at 69 ff.

25 See Antoine Garapon and Jean Lassègue, *Justice digitale* (PUF 2018); Ugo Ruffolo (ed), *XXVI lezioni di diritto dell'intelligenza artificiale. Saggi a margine del ciclo seminariale "Intelligenza Artificiale e diritto"* (Giappichelli 2021).

Firstly, especially in relation to CJEU case law, there is a lack of adequate judicial decisions. In almost all the areas concerned with the defendant's rights – with the possible exception of *ne bis in idem* – interpretative guidelines seem to have been established by the CJEU jurisprudence only on a limited number of issues (not always prominent, by the way).[26] In such a context, the possibility for an AI system to be to come up with solutions within a reasonable timeframe that are actually helpful – ready to use, so to speak – seems somewhat illusory.

In addition, the intention of the research was to improve the knowledge and familiarity of criminal law practitioners, lawyers, magistrates and scholars with this area of law, without necessarily having to provide ready-made practical solutions.

Indeed, the efficiency of the functioning of the judicial system at EU level must be achieved through an improved knowledge of this area of law on the part of practitioners, not by constructing algorithmic calculations that allow the latter to disregard the former. The idea is ultimately to set up a calculation platform that improves knowledge, as an instrumental element for and more conscious (and more uniform) application of the law in the field of individual rights safeguards. By means of more widespread shared knowledge among the various stakeholders of criminal justice, it is possible to achieve a better uniformity and predictability of the system, as well as a more effective protection of the fundamental rights of the accused, even assuming that the written law remains with the flaws that have characterised it so far.

Beyond this, it was also felt that even if an AI system could be devised to provide a ready-made answer, it would hardly be accepted with confidence by the practitioners, since research in this area is still not sufficiently developed and known to legal practitioners.

---

26 It could be argued that ECtHR jurisprudence on the rights of the accused is sufficient to train a learning machine system with an adequate amount of data for the purpose. This consideration is partially correct. It is in fact undeniable that the decisions taken in the field considered by the ECtHR are many, and cover different areas of defence rights.

However, the lack of developed ECJ jurisprudence seemed decisive. Only the EU system has provisions that are directly applicable within the national systems of the member states (if necessary, by disapplying conflicting national legislation). This power of vertical penetration of EU sources gives ECJ case law a potentially very different role from that of the ECtHR. Training the IA system to come up with immediately applicable solutions when it still lacks a numerically significant body of ECJ judgments appeared to be an error of approach. For a brief recollection of the CJEU on the matter of procedural safeguards in criminal proceedings, see below, Chapter 13, Caianiello and Lasagni, 'Comparative Remarks', § 13.3.1.

A different path therefore has been chosen, with the aim to create a platform that would allow integrated knowledge of the different regulatory levels, meaning together supranational and national ones. For both, we tried to transpose and translate into computer language the contents of the statutory provisions and those that can be extrapolated from judicial decisions.[27] Finally, due consideration has also been given to the hermeneutical proposals developed by scholars, which are of significant importance in the field of European criminal justice.

These results can be appreciated using the CrossJustice project's knowledge platform (the Legal Database Module and Advisory Module).[28] This database allows for an integrated set of results. Firstly, it permits to verify the necessary information regarding the rights of the defence of each of the 11 Member States covered by the project. In particular, users of this platform can verify the level of fundamental rights through a specific functionality of the database ("Transposition cross-reference" functionality). Secondly, through a different functionality of the platform (the Advisory Module),[29] it is possible for a legal professional to identify and apply relevant rules of EU and national legislations concerning procedural rights of persons suspected or accused of crimes, both at domestic and cross-border level.[30]

As a result, the practitioner is able, when faced with a criminal legal issue involving the safeguarding of defence rights on a transnational level, to visually have an integrated picture of the different sources. The system also makes it possible to calculate the level of compliance that each legal system, among those taken into consideration, presents with respect to the normative standards required by the European sources (the directives and the Charter of Fundamental Rights). This way, it should be easier for practitioners to decide whether to raise an interpretative prejudicial question before the Court of Justice, so as to fill, hermeneutically, gaps and lacunae that may characterise the protection of a fundamental right at national level, in the event of inadequate transposition of the European source.

27 On which see below, more in details, in particular, Marco Billi, Giuseppe Contissa and Galileo Sartor, Chapter 15, § 15.2 ff, and Luigi Di Caro, Llio Humphreys, Emilio Sulis and Rohan Nanda, Chapter 16, § 16.5 ff.

28 <https://site.unibo.it/cross-justice/en/project-results/tools>.

29 <https://www.crossjustice.eu/en/index.html#crossjustice-platform>.

30 The Module assesses in particular: 1) the level of compliance of national instruments with the EU acquis by highlighting potential gaps in the implementation process, and 2) the compatibility between national frameworks as resulting from the implementation of EU directives.

Actually, with a final effort, the research team also managed to create an AI system (the Reasoning Tool)[31] that provides partial answers, through which a professional can obtain, by entering data and responding to questions on the platform, an initial orientation to help her find the most appropriate solution for her case. This is the closest step to obtaining an algorithmic legal opinion, a choice which, for the reasons set out above, has been deemed as such to be excluded.

The constituent elements of the AI system described so far, which has been implemented in the course of the project, should enable the following results to be achieved (as already noted at least in part in the previous considerations). Firstly, it allows a simultaneous view of the existing sources of protection of fundamental rights and fair trial rights, including case law and scholarly opinions. Secondly, it encourages an integrated view of the different levels of regulation, thanks to which it is possible to identify the areas in which a national system is not compliant (or, conversely, offers a higher level of protection) with the standards laid down at supranational level. Finally, it is able to guide the legal professional in the elaboration of solutions for the concrete case. These solutions remain, for the reasons set out above, within the interpreter's full intellectual autonomy, but are facilitated by the analysis and learning process enabled by the use of data processed by the AI system.

1.5 Bottom-Up Construction of a More Uniform System through the Use of Learning Machines

The objective pursued was to make the legal field of fundamental rights more easily accessible and therefore more predictable, in terms of a priori calculability, as a means of achieving greater harmonisation of national systems (and of this with the supranational level) by means of hermeneutics and application.

Such an approach, if successful, could achieve some significant results.

Firstly it should be able to take into account national normative realities, including the theoretical constructs referred to therein, and better integrate them into the regulatory framework developed at EU level. In turn, this emphasis on the legal cultures of the Member States, which are able to enter into

31 https://legalmachinelab.unibo.it/crossjustice, on which see, below, Billi, Contissa and Sartor (n 27) §15.2.

dialogue with EU law more quickly and in a greater number of cases, should facilitate the identification of common constitutional traditions. This element is often mentioned in EU sources, such as in Art 6(3) TFEU and Art 52 CFR. However, so far, this important component of the European legal edifice has rarely been used to develop new solutions.

Mostly, in fact, recourse to national traditions has been used to stop the effectiveness and pervasiveness of EU law, not so much to expand its scope (and to strengthen its content). An emblematic case to this end is *Taricco*, where recourse to national identity justified the Italian Constitutional Court's choice to oppose the hermeneutic proposal elaborated by the Court of Justice[32] (but not to enhance a new interpretative solution that could have improved the general application of Art 325 TFEU for the whole AFSJ).

Indeed, there are signs that this is about to change soon.

For example, preliminary rulings have already been submitted on the directive on the interpretation of the presumption of innocence aimed at extending the fundamental rights of the accused to the area of pre-trial detention. These solicitations from purely domestic proceedings have the potential to contribute greatly to strengthening the protection of individual rights throughout the AFSJ. A relevant case in this regard is *Milev*,[33] but others have followed (see for instance the case of *RH*).[34] Some analogous indications regard the relationship between the practice of plea bargaining and their compliance with the same directive on the presumption of innocence. A relevant decision, under this regard, was adopted by the CJEU in *AH and others*.[35] In all these cases, national courts have tried to link, in proceedings with purely domestic relevance, the legal provisions of their own law with a European directive. This is done in order to reinforce, or at least to verify, the respect by their legal system of a fundamental right (that of the accused not to be presented as guilty before final conviction in a pre-trial detention decision, in *Milev* and *RH*, and in a guilty

32 Chiara Amalfitano and Oreste Pollicino, 'Two Courts, two Languages? The Taricco Saga Ends on a Worrying Note' (Vervassungsblog, 5 June 2018) <https://verfassungsblog.de/two-courts-two-languages-the-taricco-saga-ends-on-a-worrying-note/>; Valsamis Mitsilegas, 'Judicial dialogue in three silences: Unpacking Taricco' (2018) 9 New Journal of European Criminal Law 38.

33 See Case C-310/18 PPU, *Milev* (CJEU, 19 September 2018) See about the judgment Leandro Mancano, 'The Use of the Charter and Pre-trial Detention in EU Law: Constraints and Possibilities for Better Protection of the Right to Liberty' (2021) 6 European Papers 125 <https://www.europeanpapers.eu/en/europeanforum/charter-and-pretrial-detention-eu-law-constraints-and-possibilities>.

34 See Order in Case C-8/19 *RH* (CJEU, 12 February 2019).

35 See Case C-377/18 *AH and Others* (CJEU, 5 September 2019).

plea decision, in *AH and others*).[36] At the same time, the referral represents an opportunity for the CJEU to promote more effective protection of defence rights.

A case in which the search for a common constitutional tradition was evident was in *DB v Consob*,[37] concerning the presumption of innocence and the right not to be punished for choosing to remain silent in a formally administrative but criminally coloured procedure.

In that case, the preliminary reference of the Italian Constitutional Court, which was followed by a decision of the Court of Justice accepting the prospect of a national referral, very effectively highlighted the search for common ground. The Italian Court, in fact, well pointed out that the right to silence could already be considered part of the right of defence and the presumption of innocence in the light of the text of its own Constitution. However, given the transnational nature of the issue (the sanction for not responding to the administrative authority conducting the investigation had been introduced also in compliance with an EU directive), the Italian Court requested that the CJEU also expressed its opinion on the point, with the aim of reaching a shared view of issue. The decision to opt for a preliminary ruling proved to be well thought out, since the CJEU accepted the perspective of the referring court. The overall result, if one looks at the case as a whole, is that a fundamental right, that of not being punished for choosing not to answer in proceedings of a punitive nature, is now strengthened in two different ways. First, it is protected in a clearer and more unambiguous manner by the CJEU decision. Secondly, it is recognised at supranational level, by enhancing the solicitation coming from the jurisdiction of a Member State (thus enshrining that tradition as part of a

36 In this judgment the ECJ decided that "Article 4(1) of Directive (EU) 2016/343 of the European Parliament and of the Council of 9 March 2016 on the strengthening of certain aspects of the presumption of innocence and of the right to be present at the trial in criminal proceedings must be interpreted as meaning that it does not preclude that an agreement in which the accused person recognises his guilt in exchange for a reduction in sentencing, which must be approved by a national court, expressly mentions as joint perpetrators of the criminal offence in question not only that person but also other accused persons, who have not recognised their guilt and are being prosecuted in separate criminal proceedings, on the condition that that reference is necessary for the categorisation of the legal liability of the person who entered into the agreement and, second, that that same agreement makes it clear that those other persons are being prosecuted in separate criminal proceedings and that their guilt has not been legally established".

37 *DB v Consob* (n 21). See Giulia Lasagni, 'Consob – The Court of Justice on the right to remain silent in criminal matters (and beyond ...)' (*EU Law Live*, 3 November 2021) <https://eulawlive.com/op-ed-consob-the-court-of-justice-on-the-right-to-remain-silent-in-criminal-matters-and-beyond-by-giulia-lasagni/>.

common constitutional heritage). It appears, looking at the cases mentioned so far, that the referring national court is seeking common ground between its own legal system and that of the EU in order to give a new, fuller meaning to the principle of the presumption of innocence.

Ultimately, it is not difficult to discern an attempt, in the references for a preliminary ruling on which the above-mentioned decisions are based, to find a common tradition, which allows the national court to interpret and develop its own system while respecting its identity – at the same time improving at EU level the protection of a certain fundamental right of the individual.

It is not easy to arrange this kind of referrals, as they too often end up being too closely linked to purely internal hermeneutical problems. This limitation is highlighted in particular in the *Milev* case, the most emblematic, because of the importance of the issued involved (the effective judicial review of pre-trial detention orders), of the cases decided by the CJEU of those that can be traced back to this typology.[38]

Against this background, the use of an AI system designed to improve the knowledge of EU law, and its level of integration with individual national systems, could also be of significant help in fostering dialogue between the Courts. In turn, a dialogue on a clearer basis will be able to encourage the development of the doctrine of common traditions which seems to be crucial for the harmonisation of national systems.

Ultimately, the targeted use of the platform should be able to help the creation of a legal reasoning method common to all practitioners in the area at stake, without which no vertical regulatory instrument, adopted by the EU legislator, will be able to produce the desired effects (a more effective and uniform protection of individual rights).

38 Of course, similar methodologies were used in preliminary rulings on other directives. For example, the question of the criminal order, its translation into a language comprehensible to the non-native speaker, and the time allowed for the defence to oppose it: Case C-216/14 *Covaci* (CJEU, 15 October 2015); Case C-278/16 *Sleutjes*, (CJEU, 12 October 2017); Case C-615/18 *UY v Staatsanwaltschaft Offenburg* (CJEU, 14 May 2020). These cases also have similarities in method with those relating to the Directive on the presumption of innocence. They differ, however, for two reasons. On the one hand, they have elements of transnationality (the defendant is a foreign national residing in another EU Member State). On the other hand, the stakes are lower, since the criminal order concerns the payment of a fine, and, in the case of UY, a three-month driving ban (whereas the presumption of innocence decisions concern the legitimacy of a pre-trial detention order and the effects of a conviction for serious offences in a plea-bargaining procedure on co-accused who have not accepted the guilty plea and are tried separately).

1.6 Limits of the Research

The conducted research has some unavoidable limitations.

The first is the use of English as a lingua franca. The problem of languages, in relation to the objective of achieving a better harmonisation of systems, is crucial. Legal reasoning, in fact, is so influenced by the characteristics of the language that expresses it, that it is very often impossible to separate, in its most intimate essence, the legal question from the way in which it is conceived and presented on a linguistic level. The temptation to resort to a single language is frequent, and has even been theorised in some widely circulated studies.[39] However, it seems all in all utopian to achieve linguistic unification, as long as national legal cultures actually continue to be developed into their own autonomous language with a specific identity.

This problem, which has been well known to EU law scholars for a long time, also emerges clearly in the research carried out, in which, due to a practical necessity, the predominant choice was to make general use of English.[40] However, in order to balance the limitations of this decision, an attempt was made to supplement the AI system by implementing official translations of texts in the platform whenever possible (*i.e.* mainly for CJEU judicial decisions and EU normative texts).

A second limitation concerns the number of Member States involved, only 11[41] compared to the 27 that make up the EU. An attempt was made to select countries that would in some way represent the different geographical, legal and cultural areas of the EU, in a fair balance. However, it is clear that the work carried out, although of considerable size, represents only partially the wealth of legal culture that characterises the EU area as a whole. A system that aspired to represent all the national systems of the EU in terms of protecting the rights of the accused in criminal proceedings would require more time and resources.

39 Klip (n 1) 27.

40 Actually, the need to use English as a lingua franca is not only in some respects a limitation, but also a strength. This way, in fact, it is possible to have access to regulations other than those of one's own reference languages.

41 It should also be pointed out that of the 11 systems taken into consideration, only 9 are examined in this volume (Bulgaria, Croatia, France, Germany, Italy, the Netherlands, Poland, Portugal, Spain). All 11 national reports are however published on the CrossJustice website: <https://site.unibo.it/cross-justice/en>, cf. above Introduction.

1.7 Conclusions

The research carried out by the CrossJustice project leads to a number of conclusions.

Among them, a first one, already known, is that the EU legal sources on defendants' rights are developing significant effects on the level of protection of the rights involved, both at national level and within EU law itself. The process of development in this field is still in its infancy, as some institutions are far too recent to constitute an effective benchmark (the reference here goes in particular to the EPPO). There is no doubt, however, that progressively these supranational normative sources will be able to develop a relevant impact in the three dimensions that characterise the AFSJ: That of horizontal judicial cooperation in criminal matters; that of vertical cooperation, between EU institutions and national courts; that of the protection of fundamental rights at a purely or predominantly domestic level. It should also be added that a fourth relevant level concerns the extension of fair trial rights from the criminal sphere *stricto sensu* to the punitive administrative sphere.

The Directives as a whole – as has already happened in the *DB v Consob* case – oblige the Courts, both those of the Member States and the Court of Justice, to take a position on numerous significant aspects of the protection of the accused in matters which lie at the crossroads of these two areas of law: This, in turn, shall be done through a constant cultural dialogue with the case law of the ECtHR.

The second result is that the use of a system of AI for achieving a more effective knowledge of this legal field appears to be significant. It provides an integrated view of the problems, meaning an understanding of the multilevel nature of legal sources and the role played by both judicial decisions and theories developed by scholars. An AI system also makes it easy to identify the level of compliance of a national system with European standards. It also makes it possible to promote faster and more effectively issues related to the identification and transposition of common constitutional traditions, which is in turn a key area for the success of the whole Area of Freedom, Security and Justice.

The third result is that such an AI system helps interpreters to orientate in specific individual cases with a supranational and multilevel dimension, offering first rudimentary solutions (which will then have to be properly developed by practitioners). This implies that the use of AI has a practical problem-solving function, although it leaves the responsibility (and the resolution of the legal issue in its entirety) to the practitioners.

In other words, the assistance of an AI system is objective, in that it aids faster and more integrated knowledge of a complex and multilevel legal system. It is also subjective, in that, by proposing solutions that must then be developed and suitably adapted to the case in question, it acts as a dialectical interlocutor for the jurist. In a nutshell, the selection of the questions (the legal issues) and the final solutions remain firmly in the hands of the jurist. The AI system, however, can play an effective role in helping to identify the problem and, above all, in planning and developing the solution.

The challenge of the contemporary generation of jurists is, as has already been written in other studies, twofold. On the one hand, to help solve the translation problem, *i.e.* to guide the transition of fundamental principles, conceived in a less integrated and non-automated world, into the modern world, characterised by a high level of integration between legal systems and by constant interaction between machines and individuals. On the other hand, to ensure that the ultimate choices on the key decisions to be taken remain in the hands of human beings, exploiting the potential offered by AI systems and machine learning to make legal systems more responsive to people's needs.

CHAPTER 2

How the Law Has Become Computable

Giuseppe Contissa and Giovanni Sartor

2.1 Introduction

In this Chapter we will examine the different ways in which law has progressively merged with computing, through research and applications in legal informatics. The goal is twofold, for on the one hand we want to show that legal informatics builds upon legal premises (content, processes, concepts and theories), and on the other hand our interest is in showing how research in legal informatics can make a contribution to legal studies.

We will distinguish different aspects of the law which have been computationally modelled and different ways in which researchers and developers of computer applications have adressed the law.

To illustrate the perspective from which our endeavor proceeds, it may be useful to start out with a quotation by a scholar who has uniquely combined law, science, and philosophy, namely, Gottfried Wilhelm Leibniz:

> just as the mathematicians have excelled above the other mortals in the logic, i.e., the art of reason, of the necessary, so too the jurists did in the logic of the contingent. Hence, we can learn much from their precepts about complete and half-complete proofs, about presumptions, about conjecturing regarding the meanings of the laws, about contracts and wills, about criminal clues (indicia).[1]
>
> LEIBNIZ 1966

This quote makes it clear that the development of computational models of the law is a bidirectional learning process, in which the law learns from computing, but at the same time computing learns from the law. This idea is born out by the following quote by Thorne McCarty and Edwina Rissland, two leading scholars in AI & law who have observed that the aspects of human

1 Gottfried Wilhelm Leibniz, 'De legum interpretatione, rationibus, applicatione, systemate' in TH. HOBBES. *A dialogue between a philosopher and a student of the Common Laws of England. G. W. LEIBNIZ. Specimen quaestionum philosophicarum ex iure collectarum. De casibus perplexis. Doctrina conditionum. De legum interpretatione.* (Dalloz 1966).

 | DOI:10.1163/9789004513396_004

reasoning most studied by AI (Artificial Intelligence) play a central role in law, such that in the law computer scientists are likely to find interesting models and ideas.

> The law, with its diverse modes of reasoning, provides a rich area for the study of both human and artificial intelligence. The reasoning can involve cases, rules, of text. Cases can be real or hypothetical; rules, well- or ill-formulated; text, free or highly structured. And the reasoning can be deductive, inductive, or analogical. It is a perfect arena in which cognitive scientists and artificial intelligence researchers can merge interests.[2]
>
> MCCARTY and RISSLAND 1987

2.2 The Emergence of Legal Computations

The development of computable models of the law is not the first "fusion" of law and technology. Throughout the history of law, the technologies available at any one time have contributed to determining the locations in which records of the law reside, the way in which legal content is expressed and applied, and the way in which the law governs human behavior.

Before the advent of information technologies, we only had unwritten law, which resides in people's thoughts and actions, linguistic or otherwise, and is elaborated through their natural cognitive endowments (memory, language and action). It includes (1) tacit law (social norms, customs), as well as (2) spoken law (proverbs, parables, commandments, advice). Unwritten law did not disappear when information technologies entered human socieites; rather, it has coexisted in various and changing forms of synthesis and interaction with such technologies (as shared norms and attitudes of acceptance toward legal sources and authorities provide the social foundation on which legal systems rest).

The first information technology applied to the law was handwriting, which made it possible for legal content – regulations, judgments, contracts, etc – to be inscribed on material artifacts (terracotta tablets, wooden tables, papyri, parchment, etc.), so that it could be preserved and transmitted at distance. Subsequently, printing technology became key to the law, enabling legal content to be widely reproduced and distributed, thus reaching a much larger

2 L Thorne McCarty and Edwina L Rissland, 'Series Foreword' in *A.v.d.L Gardner, An Artificial Intelligence Approach to Legal Reasoning* (MIT Press 1987).

number of addressees, and in a short time.[3] By "externalizing" legal content into material artifacts, writing and printing extended the temporal and spatial scope of legal communications, promoting the creation of large and social organizations marked by complex legal systems. However, the legal content stored in such artefacts only becomes operative by being processed by humans, who have to understand and interpret the inscribed legal message so that it can serve as a tool by which to guide their action.

Computational technologies bring a further fundamental change. Thanks to such technologies, externalized legal content can be automatically processed, and in increasingly intensive ways: it become active!

In recent years the ability to automate the law, outside the domain of information retrieval, has greatly increased due to a combination of interlinked socio-technical achievements, providing for the availablity of extensive computer power, huge masses of data, instant communication and data interchanges, and novel AI technologies.

We can indeed distinguish different ways in which the automated processing of legal content can take place:

- Legal texts can be stored in electronic form (in databases or on the Internet) and be automatically retrieved and duplicated.
- Legal rules can be applied semi-automatically or even automatically, based on factual knowledge provided by humans or even obtained by machines, in real or virtual environments.
- Models of the law can be automatically constructed out of legal data, through machine-learning techniques, and can then be applied to new cases to arrive at legal predictions or decisions.

2.3 The Three Waves of Computable Law

In this section we will briefly overview three lines of development in legal computation: retrieval of legal sources, the automated application of formal accounts of the law, and the deployment of machine learning in the legal domain. We speak of three waves to express the idea that there is a logical and temporal sequence to these technological flows that merge with and change legal practice. However, each one of such flows is not displaced by the subsequent ones but rather persists with them in new arrangements combining pre-existing and novel practices.

3 On the influence on printing and other information technologies on the law, see Mireille Hildebrandt, *Smart technologies and the end(s) of law: novel entanglements of law and technology* (Edward Elgar Publishing 2015)

2.3.1 *The First Wave of Computable Law: Legal Sources*

The first wave of computable law, which came in the 1960s, concerned legal sources. We are now used to accessing legal content in digital form, and electronic sources of legal content already have largely replaced traditional paper media (which were predominant even only a few decades ago).

Relative to legal-information retrieval, the first stage of the processing consists in acquiring legal sources in digital form. In the past, paper sources had to be digitized – by human encoders or using scanning technologies – but today more and more legal content is natively available in digital form. These sources are usually preprocessed (which may involve integrating the original documents with metadata, structuring them according to standards, etc.) and then made available to a search engine. The output of the search engine, activated by users' queries, consists in selections of the stored sources served up in a way that fits such queries. Various methods can be used for this purpose, such as Boolean, statistical, or conceptual research.

The use of information-retrieval techniques has had a substantial impact on legal activities, providing legal practitioners with a broader, more accurate, set of legal materials. Some advanced functions are available in commercial systems, such as the relevance ranking of retrieved document, the use of citation networks, conceptual retrieval, and the automated selection of the most relevant fragments of documents (semi-summarization). Further prospects are emerging for making legal documents more easily retrievable and more productively reusable, in particular by using AI techniques for selecting and ranking similar documents and extracting the most significant fragments and arguments.

It may be argued that search tools already influence the way through which the law is understood by legal experts, by making certain materials visible to them rather than others. However, such tools only affect the initial part of legal problem-solving, namely, access to sources. They do not substantially modify the subsequent steps, and in particular those in which norms are interpreted, relevant facts ascertained, and their legal implications determined.

2.3.2 *The Second Wave of Computable Law: Man-made Models of the Law*

The automation of legal reasoning and problem-solving has been a goal of AI from its earliest days. The linguistic structure of legal texts, norms, and arguments has suggested that formal logic can be used to capture legal knowledge – legal rules, cases, facts – and make inferences based on such knowledge.[4]

4 L Karl Branting, 'Data-centric and logic-based models for automated legal problem solving' (2017) 25(1) Artificial Intelligence and Law 5.

2.3.2.1 Rule-Based Systems

Starting from the assumption that legal provisions can usually be represented as rules, and that legal reasoning is based on inferences based on the application of rules to facts,[5] many researchers have focused on developing rule-based systems for the law.

By the 1980s, several projects had implemented working systems based on manually created logical representations of rules, to be processed by a logical-inference engine. Particularly significant among such attempts was the formalization of the British Nationality Act using logic programming,[6] which paved the way for a number of rule-based models of legal domains.

Though logical knowledge can be represented in different ways, using different logical formalisms, the leading approach has consisted in modelling legal knowledge through conditional statements (rules), built using a subset of predicate logic (possibly extended with aspects of defeasibility or probabilistic reasoning). The main components of a rule-based system are (1) a *rule base*, containing the legal rules, and (2) an *inferential engine*, also called *rule interpreter*.[7] The inference engine is the system's reasoning component: it applies legal rules to factual information related to specific cases. Information related to cases may be provided by human users or may be automatically extracted from external databases. Several additional components are usually included. Among the most common are (1) a user interface, making it possible to introduce new facts and rules into the system and to query the system, and (2) a justifier (explanation component), which provides justifications for the conclusions reached by the system, explaining all the reasoning steps.

In order to create a rule-based system, we need a *knowledge representation*, meaning a representation of the law that is *computable*, namely, encoded in formal structures which can be processed by inferential systems. The development of a legal knowledge base usually starts by collecting the relevant legal sources, including statutory laws, case law, legal concepts, doctrine, and expert interviews. The information contained in these sources – or rather the part that is relevant to the function the system is designed to serve – needs to be expressed in a formal language in order for the system's knowledge base to be created. This knowledge-representation activity may be called *legal*

5 Charles Claflin Allen, 'State of Mind in Civil Cases' (1957) Wash. ULQ 223.

6 Marek J Sergot and others, 'The British Nationality Act as a logic program' (1986) 29(5) Communications of the ACM 370.

7 Efraim Turban, J Aronson and Ting-Peng Liang, *Decision Support Systems and Intelligent Systems* (7th ed, Pearson Prentice Hall 2005) 556.

programming, and it is usually carried out by a team including legal experts and logic programmers.

Once the knowledge base has been completed, it can be used to provide fully or partially automated legal analyses or assessments. For this purpose it is also necessary to specify the legal and factual circumstances of the cases to be assessed. This specification can be provided by the system's users or it can be obtained by collection from existing digital sources (e.g., databases maintained by public sector bodies). Relying on the knowledge base and the specifications of facts, the systems assesses such facts according to the law: it may answer a question of legal compliance or qualification or provide other kinds of support for human decision-making. The process is enabled by automated reasoning functionalities (forward and backward rule-chaining, deduction, defeasible reasoning), supported by further functionalities ensuring interaction with the user.

Over the last 30 years, several theoretical issues relating to the representation of legal knowledge have been raised and discussed, including aspects such as isomorphism,[8] deontic positions, and temporal aspects,[9] and how to deal with defeasibility in law.[10]

In particular, it has been noted that logic-based approaches are dogged by a range of difficulties in scaling the logic-based approach to the dimensions of complex, dynamic, real-world legal systems. A first challenge in this regard is how to provide an efficient and verifiable representation of legal texts as logical expressions. In this context, several issues have been identified, among them:

- A computable representation of legal knowledge is an interpretation of the law: only the original source text maintains the legal value. The challenge is how to deal with issues such as ambiguity, vagueness, and conflicting interpretations.
- Not all law can be easily represented as a set of rules: in order to interpret and apply the law, lawyers often take into account the goals pursued by legislators as well as legal values and principles.
- Law is a dynamic system; it changes over time. On the one hand a legal knowledge-based system should represent and reason with the temporal aspect of legal norms, both their external time (concerning a provision's

---

8 TJM Bench-Capon and FP Coenen, 'Isomorphism and legal knowledge based systems' (1992) 1(1) Artificial Intelligence and Law 65.

9 Guido Governatori, Antonino Rotolo and Giovanni Sartor, 'Temporalised normative positions in defeasible logic' (2005).

10 Jaap Hage, 'Law and defeasibility' (2005) Studies in legal logic 7.

lifecycle, namely, its being in force, valid, and effective) and their internal time (the time specified within the norm). On the other hand, legal knowledge bases need to be updated every time the law changes.

– Legal rules can conflict and/or be excluded from being applicable by other rules (defeasible reasoning). The problem here is, for example, how to equip the system with the capability of reasoning about conflicting norms, taking account of the principles of *lex posterior*, *lex specialis,* and *lex superior*.

Other challenges are technical and practical: representing legal texts in computable models is a highly specialized skill, requiring both legal and technical expertise. The process of formalizing legal texts requires a considerable expenditure of resources (time, work) to overcome the difficulties that systems face in scaling up from small prototypes to large applications. Further resources are needed to keep the system up to date.

Some modern approaches and applications have recently been addressing such limitations, providing quasi-natural languages for representing legal knowledge,[11] better interfaces for handling queries and linked data, and powerful explanation functionalities. Many rule-based systems have been developed for the services and facilities provided by the state's administrative apparatus (taxation, social welfare, one-stop shops for enterprises, online legal proceedings, etc.).

Despite the limitations of symbolic approaches, and the recent advent of data-driven approaches, logic keeps playing an important role as a knowledge-representation scheme, capturing both norms and facts. Rule-based systems are also useful in complementing sub-symbolic and data-driven models with reasoning capabilities.[12]

In conclusion, rule-based systems can contribute to the application of the law, especially in the context of government services and functions. However, they provide a simplified analysis of the law, which is appropriate when issues are uncontroversial and speed and accuracy are key. They are less useful for judges and legal experts, who usually focus on controversial cases, where there is an open issue to be addressed, concerning either the facts of a case or the applicable law.

---

11 See for example Robert Kowalski, 'Logical English' (2020) Logic and Practice of Programming (LPOP); and a commercial platform, Oracle Intelligent Advisor, <https://www.oracle.com/cx/service/intelligent-advisor/>.

12 Roberta Calegari, Giovanni Ciatto and Andrea Omicini, 'On the integration of symbolic and sub-symbolic techniques for XAI: A survey' (2020) 14(1) Intelligenza Artificiale; Federico Bianchi, Matteo Palmonari, Pacal Hitzler and Luciano Serafini, 'Complementing logical reasoning with sub-symbolic commonsense' (2019).

2.3.2.2 From Rules to Argumentation-Based Systems

Argumentation plays a central role in the law. In judicial proceedings, each party provides arguments supporting his or her position, and they may conflict with those advanced by the other party. The dispute between parties is usually transferred into the judicial opinion, which takes into account the results of the dispute and determines its output. To convincingly justify a judicial decision in a case, it is not enough to state a single argument: it is instead necessary to establish that the winning argument ought to prevail over all contrary arguments or that the latter have to be rejected on other grounds. Indeed, it has been stated that the problem of defeasibility in the law stems from the existence of arguments both for and against the application of a rule, both of which need to be taken into account in adjudicating the case.[13]

Many frameworks have been developed to capture the dialectical relation between arguments in legal contexts. These frameworks typically make it possible to analyze the interaction between arguments, determining which arguments are justified and wich ones ought to be overruled relative to a set of arguments that may attack one another. Among the frameworks developed in AI & law are those developed by Prakken and Sartor,[14] Gordon,[15] Hage,[16] and Bench-Capon.[17]

Such frameworks have been used to create computer systems that develop justifications for solutions to controversial points, suggest possible arguments, and evaluate the state of each argument in light of the overall argumentative architecture resulting from all the information provided to the system (the arguments, counter-arguments, and meta-arguments that can be constructed with this information and their relationships). The development of such systems has required new languages for representing knowledge, sufficiently expressive to capture the fundamental structures of legal knowledge (rules, rights, cases, principles, values, etc.), as well as new methods of inference, which reproduce the typical steps in legal reasoning (application of rules,

13 Henry Prakken and Giovanni Sartor, 'Law and logic: A review from an argumentation perspective' (2015) 227 Artificial Intelligence 214.

14 Henry Prakken and Giovanni Sartor, 'Argument-based extended logic programming with defeasible priorities' (1997) 7(1–2) Journal of applied non-classical logics 25.

15 Thomas F Gordon and Douglas Walton, 'Legal reasoning with argumentation schemes' (2009) In Proceedings of the 12th international conference on artificial intelligence and law, 137–146.

16 Jaap C Hage, 'Reasoning with rules' in Reasoning with Rules (Springer 1997).

17 Trevor JM Bench-Capon and Paul E Dunne, 'Argumentation in artificial intelligence' (2007) 171 Artificial Intelligence 619.

reference to precedents, teleological reasoning, etc.), and multiple ways to build arguments and organize them.

Argumentation-based systems have not yet been commercially successful in the legal domain. However, they may be useful for legal experts, and in particular lawyers, in preparing, analyzing, and presenting their argument. They may be also useful for judges, helping them to understand the interaction of arguments presented by the parties and to develop their own arguments. Unfortunately, they suffer from some of the problems we have described with regard to rule-based systems, such as the need for humans to provide and update computable representations of all aspects of the law.

2.3.3 *The Third Wave of Computable Law: Data and Machine Learning*

In recent years, a paradigm shift has taken place in AI: the transition from human-made representation of knowledge to machine learning. In machine learning approaches, the computer builds its own model of the domain, applying a learning algorithm to vast datasets. Using this model, the system then generates classifications, evaluations, and predictions for new cases submitted to it. Updating and expanding the dataset automatically improves the model and the system's predictive capabilities.

Three main approaches have been developed in machine learning: (1) supervised learning, in which the system develops its own model on the basis of training sets containing examples of correct answers to previous cases. Once trained, the system will be able to provide correct answers to new cases, taking into account their similarities with past cases; (2) unsupervised learning, where the system autonomously classifies and organizes the input provided during training, identifying relevant patterns; and (3) reinforcement learning, where the system receives feedback for its actions or evaluations (in the form of rewards and penalties), and it learns by itself how to maximize its score in view of the goal to be reached.

In the legal domain, the machine learning approach has led to the development of *legal text analytics*, namely, to the use of natural language processing (NLP) and other computational techniques for automatically extracting meanings (or semantics) from archives of adjudicated cases, contracts, statutes, or other kinds of textual sources containing relevant legal data.

The new data-centric approach in AI has spawned many research initiatives and projects in the legal domain,[18] as well as the creation of a number of legal

18 Daniel Martin Katz, Michael J Bommarito II and Josh Blackman, 'A general approach for predicting the behavior of the Supreme Court of the United States' (2017) 12(4) PloS one e0174698; Nikolaos Aletras and others, 'Predicting judicial decisions of the European

technology companies mostly focused on applications in litigation support.[19] Data-centric applications in the legal domain can be classified into two main areas:[20] document-oriented and case-oriented approaches.

2.3.3.1 Document-Oriented Approaches

Document-oriented approaches are focused on the analysis of individual documents. The main goal of such systems is to extract information, that is, to identify named entities such as places, persons, organizations, dates, and claims, as well as to extract more complex information, such as events and narratives. Automated summarization aims at creating summaries of case facts, decisions, and other legal documents by selecting phrases appropriate to a summary, combining and possibly rephrasing them into a coherent text.[21] The automated parsing of statutory texts aims at the automated conversion of the original, natural-language legislative documents into machine-interpretable rules. Predictive retrieval aims at the the automated selection of legal texts relevant to a certain legal task, such as drafting a new law or deciding a case. Entire corpora of documents can be analyzed to discover correlations, extract implicit information, and organize cross-references between documents and parts of them. Such systems may support the identification and selection of most significant bits of previous cases, and thus facilitate the reuse of portions of previous documents in new ones.

Document-oriented systems may be very useful in legal practice, enabling judges and other legal experts to be more efficient and accurate in doing legal analyses and generating legal documents. They can therefore also improve the quality of legal sources, such as judicial decisions and statutory texts.

2.3.3.2 Case-Oriented Approaches

Case-oriented approaches to legal machine learning typically rely on models extracted from vast sets of cases. They provide aggregate statistical information about such cases, but may also be used to predict specific aspects of new cases, such as their duration, costs, and potential awards or punishments, as well as to calculate the probability that claims, motions, or other pleadings succeed.

Court of Human Rights: A natural language processing perspective' (2016) 2 PeerJ Computer Science e93.

19 The Legal tech list is an extensive database of companies in this area, mantained by the Stanford CodeX Center for Legal Informatics. Available at the following address <https://techindex.law.stanford.edu>.

20 Branting (n 4) 12.

21 See for example Legalrobot, at the website <legalrobot.com>.

The models constructed by such systems embed correlations between (sets of) features of cases on one side and decisions and/or factual forecasts on the other side.

One of the areas of main interest is litigation assistance (i.e., systems providing information to increase the likelihood of success at trial). On the basis of an analysis dealing with factors related to the merit of the case (such as lexical features, events, narratives, and procedural history), but often also on the basis of factors not related to merit (such as the nature of the suit, the attorneys, the venue, the judge, and the parties), such systems can make predictions about the behavior of the parties to a proceeding (e.g., under what conditions a settlement may be accepted) or about the behavior of judges (the decisions they may take).

One of the most successful AI systems combining text analytics with predictive functionalities is IBM's Watson. After having learned the correlation between questions and answers in a certain domain, the system can apply this knowledge to analyze new input questions and generate new possible candidate answers through a broad search across large volumes of content. In this way, Watson can answer a broad range of questions, concerning both general knowledge and specialized domains, by extracting information from vast sets of documents. In the legal domain, IBM Watson technology has been deployed in the ROSS system.[22] ROSS has two main features. The first is the AI Legal Search Engine, which accepts questions in plain English and returns answers based on legislation, case law, and other sources, while also monitoring new materials added to the corpus that may be relevant to a user's previous queries. As users submit new versions of a question, the system forms new links between them and its pre-stored answer. In this way, ROSS learns from user feedback. The second is the Brief Analyzer (EVA), which enables the automated analysis of briefs: the system processes the brief, creating hyperlinks to every case cited in the brief. The system can also check the subsequent history of cited cases and find cases having similar language as the brief.

Other examples of predictive systems for legal advice are Lexmachina,[23] which aims at predicting the behavior of courts, judges, lawyers, and parties in IP Law; Premonition,[24] which focuses on analyzing judicial tendencies and attorneys' performance and outcomes before judges; and Luminance,[25]

---

22 See the website <rossintelligence.com>.

23 See the website <lexmachina.com>.

24 See the website <premonition.ai>.

25 See the website <luminance.com>.

a platform that applies supervised and unsupervised machine learning to the process of document review and enables the automated annotation of legal documents and the detection of possible anomalies.

Systems that correlate the features of new cases with their possible future decisions may enable lawyers to get a sense of their chances of success (possibly reducing litigation), to select or search for aspects of the case that increase their chances of success, and to better develop their arguments. Such systems may also be useful for judges, enabling them to gain a better sense of trends in case law and to see how a possible decision would stand in the context of case law.

A recent innovation is the development of legal applications of cognitive computing.[26] These applications aim at bridging the analysis of legal texts through machine learning with the relevant legal sources and rationales: the portions of texts that contain applicable provisions, judicial holdings and findings of fact; the arguments that justify the proposed conclusions; and the legal and factual reasons in favor or against the proposed outcome. A cognitive computing approach may support judges and other legal experts in investigating and answering legal questions, providing explanations for their legal decisions or assessments, making arguments for and against legal conclusions, and improving predictions about case outcomes.

Cognitive computing in the legal domain can profit from argument mining, which includes a set of techniques and technologies focused on identifying and analyzing argument-related information in text corpora, such as premises and conclusions, relationships between arguments and counterarguments, the substantive strengths or weaknesses of claims, and the rationale for legal decisions.

An example of machine learning that includes elements of cognitive computing is CLAUDETTE (CLAUse DETecTEr),[27] a platform enabling machine learning analysis of consumer contracts and privacy policies. The system combines ML approaches and knowledge-based approaches to deliver explanation functionalities.

26 Kevin D Ashley, *Artificial Intelligence and Legal Analytics: New Tools for Law Practice in the Digital Age* (Cambridge University Press 2017).

27 Marco Lippi, Przemysław Pałka, Giuseppe Contissa, Francesca Lagioia, Hans-Wolfgang Micklitz, Giovanni Sartor, and Paolo Torroni, 'CLAUDETTE: an automated detector of potentially unfair clauses in online terms of service' (2019) 27(2) Artificial Intelligence and Law 117. See also the website <claudette.eui.eu>.

2.4 Towards the Regulation of Computations through Computable Laws

In the previous section we showed how computing has progressively made its way into the legal process, playing an increasingly significant role in the legal process through which legal norms governing human behavior are created, interpreted, and applied. But that is not the only role which computable law can play in the future in our society – equally important is its role in directly governing computations.

Thanks to the advent of AI and the growth of computations and communications, the boundaries between online and offline life break down, and we become seamlessly connected to one another and surrounded by smart, responsive objects, being all progressively integrated into an "infosphere":[28] we work, play, learn, and communicate by symbiotically interacting with computations, and depend on them for most aspects of our social fabric (production, logistics, administration, transportation, communications, services, etc.). As a result, we live in a hyper-connected "onlife" where "artefacts can change states in autonomous ways and can do so by digging into the exponentially growing wealth of data, made increasingly available, accessible and processable."[29] Modern AI entities are an essential enabler for this new social organization, since (unlike earlier mechanical devices) they can engage in complex cognitive tasks and adapt to variable contexts, possibly learning from experience: endowing computational entities with high-level cognitive capacities, AI increases their capacity for diversified and autonomous action, in both the physical world (robotics) and the virtual (digital bots, intelligent agents).

In this context, there is a new need to automate the application and enforcement of law. The infosphere may become an unfriendly and dehumanizing environment, where individuals are subject to persistent surveillance and to determinations over which they have no control, being outsmarted, cheated, and possibly harmed by faulty, illegal, or unethical computations. To avoid such risks, computational entities need to be designed to comply with legal norms, avoid causing harm, respect rights, meet reasonable expectations, and transparently explain their behavior to the individuals concerned. Some early indications that we are in fact moving in this direction can be found in EU legislation.[30] One example is Art. 25 GDPR, containing provisions on "data

28 Luciano Floridi, *The fourth revolution: How the infosphere is reshaping human reality* (OUP Oxford 2014).

29 Luciano Floridi, *The Ethics of Information* (Oxford University Press 2013).

30 Ann Cavoukian, *Privacy by design: leadership, methods, and results' in European Data Protection: Coming of Age* (Springer 2013).

protection by design and by default," namely, measures that have to be taken into account from the start, in the very process of developing and designing products, services, and applications so as to make them compliant with the rights to data protection. Another example is the recent EU proposal for regulating AI,[31] where several provisions cover the design of AI technologies, with measures for governing the data used by AI systems, for example, or measures imposing design constrains designed to ensure the possibility of human oversight.

However, the scale and ubiquity of computations make it impossible for humans to effectively monitor them and anticipate any illegal or unethical behavior: for one thing, the speed of computational entities, and the sheer number of these computations and of their interactions, makes real-time monitoring impossible; and, for another thing, the complexity of their increasingly adaptive and autonomous behaviour, and the diversity of their contexts of deployment make it impossible to specify hard-and-fast constrains at the design stage. If the law is to effectively govern the infosphere, it must be an internal component of computational processes rather than an external constraint on them: legal norms, values, and principles need to be mapped onto, and partially translated into, (a) computable representations of legal information and reasoning that (b) are directly processed by computational entities.

In this context, we need to shift away from an *implicit law-by-design* approach, that is, an approach where systems are designed in such a way as to make illegal behavior more difficult (e.g., regulating the design through legal provisions, technical standards, and guidelines) toward an *explicit law-by-design* approach, where systems are developed to represent law explicitly and to operate effectively on the basis of this knowledge. In fact, the deployment of autonomous and potentially dangerous technologies generates risks, conflicts of interests, and coordination issues that need to be addressed not only by the law (e.g., regulating the design or the use of the technology) but also by those systems themselves at run-time, without direct human intervention.

If we are to meet these two requirements, we will have to act on two fronts, not only creating the socio-technical conditions for the correct design, deployment, and monitoring of law-compliant computations, but also enabling the systems involved to directly apply legal norms and principles, justify their behavior accordingly, and ask for human assistance when needed and feasible. Even when deployed to govern computations, computable law should remain

31 Commission, 'Proposal for a Regulation of the European Parliament and of the Council laying down harmonised rules on Artificial Intelligence (Artificial Intelligence Act) and amending certain Union legislative acts', COM (2021) 206 final

a human enterprise, over which society should maintain full ownership and control: the operation of new AI systems needs to depend on the "joint cognitive" engagement[32] of designers and deployers, whose choices will determine the goals, scope, and limitations of their autonomous action.

32 Christopher D Hollander and Annie S Wu, 'The current state of normative agent-based systems' (2011) 14(2) Journal of Artificial Societies and Social Simulation 6.

CHAPTER 3

Making Criminal Procedure Rights Computable

Giulia Lasagni and Giuseppe Contissa

3.1 An Automated Approach to Procedural Safeguards*

Artificial Intelligence (AI) and algorithms are fundamentally transforming most aspects of human activities, starting with decision-making paradigms.[1]

The criminal matter does not escape this phenomenon; actually, these technologies are a constant feature of current debates on the development of criminal justice policies.[2] Until now, however, this trend has been especially evident with regard to the deployment of investigative tools that aim at supporting the work of law enforcement in crime prevention and repression.[3]

The idea of deploying AI technology to support the role of the defence, on the other side, remains today more at a research or effort stage,[4] often taking

---

* Although the Chapter is a joint reflection of the authors, its drafting is broken down as follows: Contissa, §§ 3.3, 3.4; Lasagni §§ 3.1, 3.2.

1 See, for all, Jack M. Balkin, 'The Three Laws of Robotics in the Age of Big Data' (2017) 78 Ohio St L J 1219; Luciano Floridi, *The 4th Revolution. How the Infosphere Is Reshaping Human Reality* (OUP 2014) 1–24; Mireille Hildebrandt, *Smart Technologies and the End(s) of Law. Novel Entanglements of Law and Technology* (Edward Elgar 2015) 42 ff.

2 Exemplificative the current debate caused by the Commission Proposal on AI (*Proposal for a Regulation of the European Parliament and the Council, laying down Harmonised Rules on Artificial Intelligence* (Artificial Intelligence Act), COM/2021/206 final, Brussels, 21.4.2021), on which see, *eg.*, Vagelis Papakonstantinou and Paul De Hert, 'EU lawmaking in the Artificial Intelligent Age: Act-ification, GDPR mimesis, and regulatory brutality' (*European Law Blog*, 2021) <https://europeanlawblog.eu/2021/07/08/eu-lawmaking-in-the-artificial-intelligent-age-act-ification-gdpr-mimesis-and-regulatory-brutality/> accessed 15 November 2021.

3 Mostly referring to tools aiming at identifying ex ante certain factual profiles of the illegal activity (time and place of commission, type of victims, *eg. PredPol, XLaw* (*Delia*), *CAS, PreCobs, CAPP-PGH, KLB-Operativ*), or the possible occurrence of individual behaviour (typical example: recidivism, *e.g.*, COMPAS, HART, SASSI, LSI-R, PSA …), not to forget the variety of facial recognition technologies.

4 Especially if compared to other fields of law, where the first practical applications of AI judges have already been implemented, see for all the Estonian case (Eric Niller, 'Can AI Be a Fair Judge in Court? Estonia Thinks So' (*Wired*, 25 March 2019)). In recent years, the majority of the most authoritative research carried out in the area of criminal justice have achieved so far an accuracy rate of about 80% (Daniel Martin Katz, Michael J. Bommarito II and Josh Blackman, 'A general approach for predicting the behavior of the Supreme Court

 | DOI:10.1163/9789004513396_005

the form of predictive tools that try to foresee the outcome of judicial decisions, and thus the chances of success of a claim.[5] Nonetheless, the need of a much deeper and productive integration of AI technology in defensive strategies emerges as important at least on a twofold dimension.

First, this appears imperative to give effective meaning to the principle of equality of arms in a context where the prosecution and police services are increasingly making use of AI tools to facilitate and support their activities. In this sense, access to and exploitation of the same technology, even if in different forms, should be ensured to reduce, or at least not to let further increase, the asymmetry between public authorities and private subjects involved in the investigation. Using AI technologies to counterbalance defence prerogatives, therefore, can play a significant role in achieving the fairness of the proceeding.

In practice, this attitude could find application, for example, by the use by defence lawyers of AI tools developed for preventive or repressive purposes also for defensive goals (typical the case of facial recognition tools).[6] Another way could be that of exploiting AI techniques to counter-argue the inculpatory results obtained thanks to automation: For instance by requesting against the automated assessment produced by the accused, a second automated

---

of the United States' (2017) 12(4) PLoS ONE 14 (ca 70,2%); Roger Guimerà and Marta Sales-Pardo, 'Justice Blocks and Predictability of U.S. Supreme Court Votes' (2011) 6(11) PLoS ONE 4 (ca 71 to 83%); Nikolaos Aletras, Dimitrios Tsarapatsanis, Daniel Preoţiuc-Pietro and Vasileios Lampos, 'Predicting Judicial decisions of the European Court of Human Rights: a Natural Language Processing perspective' (2016) PeerJ Comp Sc Op Acc 2 (ca 79%)) which, notwithstanding other considerations, have led to the conclusion that it is "premature at the current time to imagine such systems replacing judges" (Council of Europe, *Study on the Human Rights Dimensions of Automated Data Processing Techniques (in particular algorithms) and Possible Regulatory Implications*, 6 October 2017) 11.

5 In this regard, see the development of a predictive system Brazilian legal judgments concerning damage compensation, illustrated by Isabela Cristina Sabo, Thiago Raulino Dal Pont, Pablo Ernesto Vigneaux Wilton, Aires José Rover and Jomi Fred Hübner, 'Clustering of Brazilian legal judgments about failures in air transport service: an evaluation of different approaches' (2021) Artificial Intelligence and Law; on the development of a platform to support the European Small Claims Procedure, see Marco Giacalone, Francesco Romeo, Giovanni Di Stasio, Fabrizio Corona and Francesco Sacco, 'The Small Claims Analysis Net project' (2019) Jusletter IT.

6 *Eg.* the case of facial recognition software used by the defence to produce an alibi, instead of an inculpatory match, or of risk assessment tools to obtain an assessment of low social dangerousness. Currently, such strategic conducts are still relatively rare and do not necessarily meet the understanding of national courts (see, eg. the rejection of the Italian Supreme Court against the request of the defendant to use a facial recognition tool – SARI – to produce an alibi, Cass. pen., Sez. IV, no. 39731 of 27/09/2019, ECLI:IT:CASS:2019:39731PEN).

assessment issued by a machine created by a different producer, in accordance with the so-called redundancy approach.[7]

Secondly, the empowerment of defence skills (also) thanks to AI technology appears all the more necessary taking into account the complexity of criminal procedure norms within the EU. As known, they indeed result from an often scarcely predictable interaction between EU legislation and jurisprudence, ECtHR decisions and national provisions and case law.[8] Especially in cases of transnational proceedings (*e.g.*, involving EAW, EIO), the understanding of the concrete content of procedural safeguards becomes thus particularly difficult to grasp for all the parties involved, and in particular for the defendant, who usually cannot count on the same structural means of public authorities. This practical lack of timely and economic access to the necessary legal knowledge has a direct, although perhaps difficultly measurable, impact on the effectiveness of defensive strategies and on the awareness that the accused or their lawyer can exercise to design them.

To this end, though, the deployment of AI systems does not have to come from the adoption of so-called "predictive" systems.[9]

In the specific domain of criminal justice, indeed, tools which can "only" provide for a potential solution, for instance by replicating a judicial decision, do not necessarily represent the best advantage that a defendant can derive from AI potentialities. This is due to several reasons, first of all the current structural impossibility of AI systems to be transparent in their decision-making process, whose functioning closely resembles that of a jury (US-style) or of an oracle.[10]

---

7 On the redundancy approach and its potential impact on criminal justice, see Giuseppe Contissa and Giulia Lasagni, 'When it is (also) Algorithms and AI that decide on Criminal Matters: In Search of an Effective Remedy' (28) European Journal of Crime, Criminal Law and Criminal Justice (2020) 288 ff.

8 Cf. above, Michele Caianiello, Chapter 1, § 1.2.

9 Though the term should be used with caution in this domain, cf. Serena Quattrocolo, Speech at the 'Conversazione del 20 ottobre 2020', Processo penale e Intelligenza Artificiale, Position Paper 1, Fondazione Leonardo 2020, 17–18; Michele Caianiello, 'Dangerous Liaisons. Potentialities and risks deriving from the interaction between Artificial Intelligence and preventive justice' (2021) 29 European Journal of Crime, Criminal Law and Criminal Justice 8: "[statistics] cannot tell us with precision anything that concerns the position of a single individual".

10 On the widely debated critical issues of AI "black boxes" see, for all, Jason Millar and Ian Kerr, 'Delegation, Relinquishment, and Responsibility: The Prospect of expert robots' in Ryan Calo, A Michael Froomkin, Ian Kerr (eds), *Robot Law* (Edward Elgar Publishing 2016) 107; Frank Pasquale, *The Black Box Society: The Secret Algorithms That Control Money and Information* (Harvard University Press 2015); Vittorio Manes, 'L'oracolo algoritmico e

At this stage, therefore, it seems more useful for the defence to focus not so much on tools aiming at predicting a specific judicial assessment (*e.g.*, guilty/innocent) but rather on how to exploit AI technology in order to circumvent the practical obstacles that prevent defence lawyers from gathering all necessary elements to have an impact on such a decision.

In other words: AI can already be used today as a support to better understand complex legal bases, overcoming factors such as multilingualism and divergent legal cultures that negatively affect the capacity of defence lawyers to understand the conceptual framework that lies beneath legal notions and textual provisions of other legal systems, even within the EU. This is to say, some forms of AI technology can help the legal operator, first of all the defendant and her defence counsel, to see through the layers of the textual expression and linguistic versions of the legal provisions, getting to the core of the legal notions. This may be obtained, as previously illustrated, by a computable approach to law, which exploits AI as a way to translate legal knowledge and reasoning in a symbolic representation that computers can understand and apply.[11]

Transposing such a computable approach in the field of criminal justice and criminal procedure in particular, is not, however, a straightforward operation.

On one side, criminal procedure is a sector in which legal operators, especially defence lawyers and prosecutors, are in a clear and urgent need for support to overcome the intrinsic obstacles of transnational proceedings illustrated above: use of different languages in the legal bases and case law, scarce access to national legislation (especially if looking for updated English translation), difficulty in retrieving national jurisprudence and in fully understanding the impact of such decisions.

Adopting AI technology can thus speed up such learning process, giving a significant boost to judicial cooperation and effective exercise of defence rights throughout the Union.

This seems especially appropriate in light of the recent beginning of the European Public Prosecutor Office's activities, which will likely increase the chances for such a transnational dimension to emerge before national courts.[12]

---

la giustizia penale: al bivio tra tecnologia e tecnocrazia' in Ugo Ruffolo (ed), *Intelligenza artificiale. Il diritto, i diritti, l'etica* (Giuffrè 2020) 551 ff.

11 Cf. above Giuseppe Contissa and Giovanni Sartor, Chapter 2, § 2.

12 As known, after a long negotiation phase and a preparatory phase, the EPPO became operational on 1 June 2021. Though no proceedings have already been brought before national courts at the time of writing, the preponderant entrance of EU investigations within domestic criminal proceedings is soon to become visible across the 22 Member States which are currently composing the EPPO jurisdiction.

The development and deployment of tools aiming at facilitating the mutual understanding of legal systems and knowledge, and easily accessible by all actors involved in criminal proceedings, such as the CrossJustice platform, meets therefore a clear demand to raise in practice the overall level of fairness of criminal proceedings.

On the other side, criminal procedure law presents a whole series of peculiar features, which make this field especially complex to approach and complicate by far the work of jurists and legal informatics. Such peculiarities deserve therefore to be cautiously examined and carefully addressed to propose a meaningful application of AI technology in the domain of criminal proceedings.

3.2 Different Notions, Different Rules: Procedural Safeguards and the Role of Legal Interpretation

Making criminal procedure law computable, indeed, appears an especially challenging task for a whole series of reasons.

Some of them derive from the specific nature of the subject matter, as such and as they are approached by EU law. Others derive from the application of procedural norms in a transnational dimension. The combination of these two sets of criticism then, further complicates the overall picture.

Concerning the specificity of the matter at stake, a first difficulty emerges with regard to the very procedural nature of the investigated subject.

Most of the legal provisions included in the six EU Directives on defence rights, indeed, do not have a definitory content, but rather require Member States to confer certain rights to specific actors of the proceeding (mainly the suspect and the defendant, and her lawyer, but in some cases also third parties, such as holders of parental responsibilities). As much as this consideration appears obvious for criminal law jurists, dealing with a *procedure*, instead of substantive rights, this opens a whole series of problems under a legal reasoning point of view.

The legal operator (and thus the AI system) first needs indeed to understand what that the specific right is about – a task which already is not always straightforward in the field.

For instance, under the formal label of "right of access to a lawyer" several interpretations may be encompassed, from formalistic approaches that simply require a lawyer to be appointed, to others which instead require her physical presence to certain phases of the proceeding, to legal orders where this is not considered enough, and the role of defence lawyers clearly includes also the power to positively interfere with the performance of certain investigative acts (*e.g.*, by interrupting police interviews).[13]

Other procedural safeguards, on the other side, are especially open to broad and varying interpretations, which encompass multiple profiles, all to be taken into account when it comes to assess the compliance of a legal system with such standards.

Evident, in this sense, is the example of the presumption of innocence, whose notion ranges from rules on the burden of proof, to how the accused should be treated during the proceeding, to the privilege against self-incrimination.

Once identified the meaning(s) of each specific right, the system has then to identify and recognize at which conditions such right shall be conferred to which procedural actor. This logical step, as will be illustrated below, entails in itself a complex and different design of the legal reasoning module.[14]

Other factors of complexity derive from the EU approach to criminal procedural safeguards. As previously illustrated,[15] the use of Directives in this field automatically creates a duplication of legal sources in each Member State.

This phenomenon entrusts the interpreter (and thus also on the AI legal reasoning tool) with a reconstruction operation, which needs to consider the interaction among several types of norms containing procedural safeguards: those included in the Directives; those introduced at the national level as a consequence of the transposition of EU law; and those already established in domestic systems before the entry into force of the Directive, which however cover the same profiles touched upon by the Directives.

The latter can then be further differentiated among: provisions which are amended in the transposition process; provisions which remain formally unchanged, but whose interpretation is amended following the transposition process; and lastly provisions which remain unchanged both formally and in their interpretation, as they are deemed to already guarantee at least the same level of protection required by the Directive.

To further complicate the picture, which provisions fall under this last case, and to which extent, may of course be differently determined, depending on who makes the compliance assessment: Often indeed, the evaluations of national governments (that need to formally address the issue before the

---

13 On this and further examples of divergency in the deployment of procedural safeguards throughout the EU, see the analysis carried out below, in Chapter 13, by Michele Caianiello and Giulia Lasagni.

14 See below, § 3.3.

15 Cf. above Caianiello (n 8), § 1.2.

Commission), courts and legal doctrine do not completely overlap or even clearly contradict with each other.

In this sense, understanding what the concrete level of safeguard of a right is in a given Member States requires a thorough analysis: Not only of provisions explicitly transposing the Directives, but also of forms of indirect or *de facto* implementation, which *per se* are difficult to measure and therefore to be computed.

Other difficulties in making criminal procedure law computable then derive from the need to apply such rules on a transnational dimension.

In this regard, a main role is played by linguistic differences and diverging legal cultures. While differences may at times be found at the EU level among translations in the Member States' languages,[16] more subtle are the cases in which the translation problem overlaps with the co-existence of non-uniform underlying notions, which are expressed by similar wording.

In other words, several are the instances in this matter where misunderstanding may emerge from a seemingly correct translation in national idioms, which however do not correspond under an ontological point of view.

As comparative analysis reveals, egregious is in this sense the case of the term "suspect". While it finds correspondents in all EU languages, its whose substantial notion, and therefore procedural safeguards attached, highly vary depending on the precise identification of which subject falls under that definition, and in which phase of the proceedings.[17]

Finally, (at least) two further considerations contribute to increase the complexity of legal operators and therefore of the supporting AI technology in criminal procedure law.

First, compliance assessment about procedural safeguards usually requires taking a stand about the effectiveness of a right.

This parameter is not easily measurable, and imposes a complex reasoning capacity, in which a crucial role is played by the practical implementation of such right (e.g., case-law, examination of structural organization of the national criminal justice system), in addition to an analysis of the relevant legal framework.

Secondly, any analysis in this domain imposes to take into account the margin of discretion that public authorities (mostly the judge, but to a certain extent also the prosecutor) enjoy in giving application to procedural safeguards. Highly varying from country to country, from court to court, and also changing in time within each jurisdiction, the description of discretionary

16 Cf. Emilio Sulis, Davide Audrito, Luigi Di Caro and Llio Humphreys, CrossJustice Project, Deliverable 3.2, 'Rule ontology, user's guide' <https://site.unibo.it/cross-justice/en> § 9.2.

17 On the specific issue, see below, Caianiello and Lasagni (n 13), § 13.2.1.

powers emerging from open legal clauses poses another substantial challenge in the computational representation of criminal procedure rights.

3.3 From Automated Assessments to Decision Support Systems

Against this background, it is therefore necessary to examine which computational approach seems to be more suitable to the specific field of procedural safeguards.

Research in the domain of legal informatics has brought to the development of a wide number of legal rule-based systems, or legal expert systems.[18] However, as anticipated, almost all of them have been designed with the goal of producing an automated legal assessment, in the form of evaluation of compliance, or prediction of a legal effect.

Such approach has worked in particular for those domains and legal applications having the following features: 1) the legal knowledge is mainly consisting in legal provisions not affected by critical issues of interpretation, with regard in particular to semantic or logic indeterminacy, such as vagueness (involving linguistic fuzziness, namely when it is difficult to attribute a specific meaning to a certain word or expression, in particular "weasel words")[19] or ambiguity (concerning terms and expressions having different meanings, or whose logical connections may be reconstructed in different ways;[20] 2) the goal of the legislator was to provide clear guidance on how to identify a legal consequence, or how to verify legal compliance.

An example of such domains is EU Private International Law. Such legal framework is based on a set of EU regulations, each of them not posing critical interpretative issues concerning vagueness and ambiguity. The complexity in legal reasoning there is rather related to the need to consider a long list of alternative conditions and exceptions, each of them based on further alternative conditions and having their own exceptions.

Thus, the goal of an expert system in such a context would be to provide an assessment (output), on the basis of a set of factual circumstances of the case at hand (input), identifying what the jurisdiction and applicable law are, or whether the identification of a given jurisdiction or applicable law is compliant to the law (namely, a Boolean output consisting in a yes/no statement).

---

18 On this regard, see Contissa and Sartor (n 11), § 2.

19 David Mellinkoff, The language of the law (Wipf and Stock Publishers 2004) 21.

20 Jeremy Waldron, 'Vagueness in law and language: Some philosophical issues' (1994) 82 Cal L Rev 509.

However, as discussed in the previous section, the domain of criminal procedural law, and in particular the specific issues related to procedural safeguards, provide a different and more complex approach to legal reasoning.

In this context, the task of a system would not be limited to making inferences linking premises and conclusions in legal syllogisms, but rather to reason about rights and procedures. Therefore, the pure mechanical deductive reasoning will not be sufficient, but it shall be complemented with other approaches, such as abductive and defeasible reasoning.

In particular, a logic-based abduction allows for hypothetical reasoning, namely the reasoning aimed at determining what are the possible premises that support a hypothetical conclusion. In the context of legal reasoning about procedural rights, the deployment of abduction in the AI system would allow the legal expert to identifying the factual and legal conditions that would make a specific procedural right actionable, in each status of the proceeding.[21]

One important aspect of law, that becomes crucial in the domain of criminal procedural law, is the idea of defeasibility.

Firstly, defeasibility is related to the issues of the representation and reasoning about exceptions: legal concepts must be applied to such a diverse range of instances that they can at best offer a tentative and generic characterization, that shall be supplemented with exceptions. Moreover, issues of defeasibility may also result from the evolution of legal knowledge: after a general rule has been established, exceptions are often provided for those cases where the rule appears to be inadequate: this is the case of the evolution of case law, where general rationes decidendi are often limited by way of distinctions, that is, by way of exceptions introduced for specific contexts. In such cases, judges often leave the original default rule unchanged and add a new, prevailing rule that addresses the specific situations requiring a distinction.

Secondly, defeasibility is concerned with representing and reasoning about conflicts of norms (namely, the issues involving the application of the legal principles of *lex specialis*, *lex superior*, *lex posterior*). On this regard, several computable approaches have been developed to deal with defeasibility, usually combining the capability to treat exceptions as exclusionary rules (namely, rules specifically undercutting other rules),[22] and to reason about temporal aspects with event calculus or other approaches.[23]

---

21 On this regard, see Marco Billi, Giuseppe Contissa and Galileo Sartor, Chapter 15, § 5.

22 Thomas F Gordon, Guido Governatori and Antonino Rotolo, 'Rules and Norms: Requirements for Rule Interchange Languages in the Legal Domain' in Guido Governatori, John Hall and Adrian Paschke (eds), *Rule Interchange and Applications. RuleML 2009. Lecture Notes in Computer Science* (Vol 5858, Springer 2009) 282–296.

23 On this regard, see Billi, Contissa and Sartor (n 21), § 2.

In the domain of criminal procedural law, temporal aspects are relevant not only in connection with defeasibility, but also when reasoning about a legal procedure, and when the representation of a status depends on a timeframe of reference (*i.e.* a status in a time).

In criminal procedure law, a specific issue is how to represent and reason about the timeline according to which procedural safeguards should be recognized. This problem is especially critical in the first phases of the investigations, and even more problematic when temporal issues overlap with semantic issues (such as in the already mentioned case of the term "suspect").[24]

In addition, reasoning about effectiveness of procedural rights (see § 3.2) requires both the support of temporal reasoning, and a model of deontic positions.[25] Only such a combination may indeed enable a reasoning that expresses the idea of rights and corresponding obligations, in a temporal perspective.

Finally, the main goal of an AI system dealing with procedural rights would be to provide a support to human decision-making, in terms of identifying and analysing the content of procedural rights, their shades and implications. Thus, the kind of answers provided by the system would be different than other domains of the law: not a mere assessment or an evaluation of compliance, possibly in Boolean form, but a more open structure of the output, providing a complex and refined insight of the legal matter.[26]

In other words, the role of the AI system would not be (only) to provide a definitive solution to a legal problem, but rather to put the human decision-makers (*e.g.*, judge, prosecutor, defence lawyer, etc.) in the best position to take informed decisions.

Declarative and logical approaches to AI, although recently overshadowed by the rise of sub-symbolic techniques, may relive a new era as they can be exploited in synergy with the latter, mitigating some of their limitations. In particular, logic-based approaches may provide a solution to the issues of explainability and transparency,[27] that in legal systems are preconditions to ensure the protection of the fundamental rights to an effective remedy and to a fair trial.[28]

Explainability and transparency have recently become central in the scientific debate as core principles in the development of AI systems, are also

24 Particularly critical in Poland, see below, Karolina Kremens, Wojciech Jasiński, Dorota Czerwińska and Dominika Czerniak, Chapter 9, § 9.2.

25 On this regard, see below Billi, Contissa and Sartor (n 21), § 2.

26 Idem.

27 Andrew D. Selbst and Solon Barocas, 'The intuitive appeal of explainable machines' (2018) 87 Fordham L Rev 1085.

28 Contissa and Lasagni (n 7) 280.

taken into account by the EU legislators in the recent Regulation proposal on AI. This proposal deals with risks and challenges introduced by the growing use of AI systems and sets out guidelines for the development and marketing of AI applications.[29] Following a risk-based approach, the proposal sets regulatory burdens on AI systems that are likely to pose high risks to fundamental rights and safety, such as in the judicial environment, including transparency and explainability.

The deployment of explanation functionalities is also in line with the most recent supranational standards on the matter. Reference here goes first to the principle "under user control", expressed in the *Ethical Charter on the use AI in judicial systems* published by the Council of Europe. The principle precludes a prescriptive approach of AI systems, but encourages instead solutions aimed at ensuring that users are informed actors and in control of their choices.[30] Secondly, to the *Ethics guidelines for trustworthy AI*, where Human agency (AI allowing human to make informed decisions) and Transparency (AI explaining its decisions) are identified among the key requirements that such systems should meet in order to be deemed trustworthy.[31]

In this perspective, the explanation functionalities are crucial to ensure that the user is in effective conditions to understand the analysis provided by the system. In particular AI systems shall provide ways to explain the rationale behind its assessment, including the factors considered by the system in developing the latter. This output is often as important as its results, namely the final outcome suggested by the system.

3.4 The Lesson for Lawyers, Judges, and Policy Makers

When examining the opportunity to make criminal procedure law computable, a further consideration shall be taken into account.

The legal and technical research aiming at making the procedural rights computable, and at developing AI systems that can support legal experts in developing informed decisions indeed, do not address only defensive needs.

29 See above (n 2).

30 Council of Europe, European Commission for the Efficiency of Justice (CEPEJ) 'European ethical Charter on the use of Artificial Intelligence in judicial systems and their environment' (4 December 2018).

31 Luciano Floridi, 'Establishing the rules for building trustworthy AI' (2019) 1 Nature Machine Intelligence 261.

On the contrary, they can also contribute in a wider manner to the fairness of criminal justice systems as such, under several perspectives.

Under a first point of view, the development of AI tools requires experts to transfer into such systems the distillation of their own legal knowledge and forms of reasoning, giving them a fully explicit formulation. In this way, on one side, experts may simulate the way they would approach hypothetical cases. On the other, AI systems can contribute to the self-awareness of human agents, to the extent that their development and use brings experts to question herself about the nature of law, the components of legal knowledge, the ways in which legal problems are dealt with.

Under a second perspective, AI tools provide a better understating of the law, to the extent that legal analysis supported such technology allows judges to review their past decisions, compare their legal reasoning with the result suggested by the system, with no need of course to adopt those decisions instead of human ones, but considering the former as a further element to consider.

Under a last perspective, the use of AI systems allows for the identification of inconsistencies, conflicts, and gaps in the existing legal frameworks. In this context, not only the symbolic approaches based on logic reasoning are relevant, but also the statistical and sub-symbolic methodology based on Natural Language Processing. This technique, based on AI technology, aims at integrating the analysis of legal language for the identification of unspotted gaps in the legal provisions, where there is a need for clarification of terminology or interpretation.[32] This approach, therefore, may be relevant also for policy makers, to analyse the impact of legislation, and design its future evolution enhancing a right-centred dimension capable to effectively ensure the safeguarding content of procedural rights.

32 On this regard, see below Luigi Di Caro, Llio Humphreys, Emilio Sulis and Rohan Nanda, Chapter 16, § 3.

PART 2

The Implementation of EU Procedural Directives: National Systems Analysis

CHAPTER 4

Bulgaria

"Public References to Guilt" and "Right to be Present at Trial" in Directives 2016/343 and 2016/800 and Bulgarian Law. A Study of the Challenges of the Transposition

Miroslava Manolova

4.1 Introduction

Bulgarian legal framework governing criminal proceedings includes the Bulgarian Constitution, Code of Criminal Procedure (hereinafter "CCP"), other laws and a number of regulations. The fundamental rights of the citizens, also in criminal proceedings, are laid down in the Bulgarian Constitution. The provisions of the Constitution take precedence over other "ordinary" laws whose provisions can be declared unconstitutional by the Bulgarian Constitutional Court. The procedural guarantees for the effective exercise of the rights, in particular in the criminal proceedings, are provided for in CCP. The Code also determines the order for conducting criminal proceedings as well as the competencies of the bodies involved thereto.

Some of the rights as laid down in the six EU Directives under examination[1] are explicitly set out in Bulgarian Constitution. In addition to the *nullum crimen sine lege* principle[2] and the prohibition of torture and cruel, inhumane and degrading treatment,[3] the following rights of the persons involved in criminal proceedings are established at the constitutional level: the right to personal liberty and inviolability and related prohibition of detention, inspection or search or any other interference with the personal inviolability thereof except under terms and according to a procedure established by a law;[4] the

1 Directive 2010/64, Directive 2012/13, Directive 2013/48, Directive 2016/800, Directive 2016/1919 and Directive 2016/343.

2 According to Arti 5(3) of the Constitution, no one may be convicted of any act or omission, which was not criminalized by the law at the time of commission thereof.

3 Under Art 29(1) of the Constitution, no one may be subjected to torture or to cruel, inhuman, or degrading treatment, or to forcible assimilation.

4 Article 30 (1; 2) thereof.

 | DOI:10.1163/9789004513396_006

right to a lawyer;[5] presumption of innocence;[6] the right to a fair trial before the judiciary within the time limit established by a law.[7]

The fundamental rights acknowledgled in criminal proceedings are also guaranteed by the European Convention on Human Rights (ECHR). In this sense, it has to be mentioned that Bulgaria has ratified the Convention in 1992. By virtue of the Constitution, the Convention is part of the Bulgarian law and takes precedence over any conflicting standards of domestic legislation.[8] In the last two decades, significant changes have been made in the Bulgarian legislation in order to ensure the effective exercise of these rights in accordance with the provisions of the ECHR. Many of the standards of the ECHR regarding the rights of the persons in the criminal proceedings have already existed in the domestic law even before entry into force of the six EU procedural Directives.

Besides the Bulgarian Constitution and Code of Criminal Procedure, there are other laws that are part of the legislative criminal justice framework such as the Criminal Code, the Extradition and European Arrest Warrant Act (applicable in the European Arrest Warrant proceedings), the Implementation of Penal Sanctions and Detention in Custody Act (concerning the execution of penalties as well as the legal status of accused persons detained in custody) and the Judiciary System Act (regarding the organisation and the principles of operation of the judicial system bodies).

The Bulgarian Constitution, as well as the Judiciary System Act guarantee the independence of the judiciary.[9] Indeed, according to Art 117(2) of the Constitution, the judiciary shall be independent. In the performance of the

5 Everyone shall have the right to legal counsel as from the moment they are detained or constituted as an accused party. Everyone shall have the right to meet their defence counsel in private. The confidentiality of such communications shall be inviolable (Art 30 (4; 5) thereof).

6 Art 31(3) of the Constitution states that an accused party shall be presumed innocent until otherwise proven by an enforceable sentence.

7 Art 31(1) of the Constitution states that anyone charged with a criminal offence must be brought before the judiciary within the time limit established by a law.

8 Art 5(4) of the Constitution states that any international treaty, which has been ratified according to a procedure established by the Constitution, which has been promulgated, and which has entered into force for the Republic of Bulgaria, shall be part of the domestic law of the land. Any such treaty shall take precedence over any conflicting standards of domestic legislation. For further details in regards the interpretation of this provision see Decision N 7/1992 of the Bulgarian Constitutional Court.

9 Art 1a (1; 2) thereof states that the judiciary is a state authority that protects the rights and legitimate interests of citizens, legal persons and the state and that the judiciary is independent.

functions thereof, all judges, jurors, prosecutors and investigating magistrates (also called "investigators") shall be subservient only to the law.

According to the institutional framework established in Bulgaria, the Prosecutor's Office is part of the judiciary, not the executive. Its structure is in line with that of the courts.[10] It is headed by a Chief Prosecutor, who, according to the Constitution, supervises the legality and methodological guidance of the activities of all prosecutors.[11] Part of the judiciary are the investigating magistrates,[12] who investigate criminal cases in cases explicitly specified in the law.[13]

The Bulgarian judicial system is based on a three-instance trial system. The courts of first instance are the Regional Courts (in cases of minor offences) and the District Courts in cases of more serious crimes.[14] The Sofia City Court has a statute of a district court. The District Courts and the Appellate Courts act as an appellate instance, the Supreme Court of Cassation – as a cassation instance. Only acts of the appellate instance are subject to cassation appeal, and not all of them.[15]

Bulgarian criminal procedure includes two stages: pre-trial proceedings and trial (court) proceedings. Trial proceedings have a central role[16] within the criminal process unlike the pre-trial proceedings, which have a preparatory nature (Art 7 CCP). The pre-trial proceedings are carried out only in publicly actionable criminal cases[17] and can be divided in two stages – investigation and action taken by the prosecutor after the completion of the investigation.[18] The prosecutor is the pre-trial authority who press charges for publicly actionable criminal offences. In discharge of this assignment, the prosecutor directs the

10 See Art 126(1) of the Constitution and Art 136(1) JSA.

11 See Art 126(2) of the Constitution.

12 See Art 128 of the Constitution.

13 These are cases for crimes referred to in Art 194 of the CCP, such as some serious intentional criminal offenses committed by minors; some criminal offenses committed by magistrates, prosecutors, investigators, and other individuals enjoying immunity, members of the Council of Ministers, or civil servants; criminal offenses against the Republic; crimes committed abroad; crimes of factual and legal complexity assigned to them by the head of the respective district prosecutor's office.

14 Art 35 CCP defines the crimes within the jurisdiction of the regional and district court as first instance.

15 See Margarita Chinova and Georgi Mitov, *Short Lecture Course in Criminal Procedure Law*, Ciela, 2021, 34.

16 In the scientific literature, the legal concept of "central role" is criticized as being inappropriate. It points to the place of trial proceedings in criminal process rather than to the main role and importance of this stage. See Idem, 124.

17 The Criminal Code defines most of the offenses as publicly prosecuted, such as those against the Republic, most of the crimes against the person and property, etc.

18 Arts 191 and 192 CCP.

investigation and exercises constant supervision for its lawful and timely conduct. In addition, he/she may personally conduct investigation or undertake separate investigative or other procedural action.[19] In practice, other pre-trial authorities – investigative bodies, carry out the investigation. These are investigators, Ministry of Interior officers appointed at the position of "investigating police officer" and officials of the Customs Agency appointed at the position of "investigating customs inspector" as well as police authorities within the Ministry of Interior and customs authorities within the Customs Agency, in the cases provided for in the Code of Criminal Procedure. In this regard, as already mentioned, the investigators are magistrates unlike the other investigative bodies who are executive authorities. All investigative bodies operate under the guidance and supervision of a prosecutor.

Since the current Code of Criminal Procedure came into force in 2006, the judicial control over pre-trial proceedings has been strengthened. Almost all coercive measures in these proceedings are taken by the court. There are investigative actions (such as the use of special intelligence means, interception and seizure of correspondence, searches and seizures in non-urgent cases) that cannot be carried out without the permission of a court. Besides, most of the acts issued at the pre-trial proceedings can be appealed in court.[20]

After the completion of the investigation, if the prosecutor is persuaded that the necessary evidence for the discovery of the objective truth and for pressing charges before court were collected, that there are no grounds for terminating or suspending the proceedings and non remediable substantial breach of procedural rules has been committed, he/she shall draw up an indictment and submit it to the court.[21] The prosecutor maintains the indictment before the court.

Unlike the pre-trial proceedings, the court proceedings are adversarial. Parties have equal procedural rights, except in the cases specified by the Code.[22] In this regard, the doctrine discusses how the adversarial principle relates to the *ex proprio motu* principle as laid down in Art 107(2) CCP, according to which the court shall collect evidence following requests made by the parties, and of its own motion, whenever this is necessary to the discovery of the objective truth.[23] Some scholars consider that the latter is not inconsistent

19 Art 46 (1; 2) CCP.

20 See Margarita Chinova and Georgi Mitov (n 15), 35.

21 Art 246 CCP.

22 Art 12 CCP. For example, such an exception is the right of the defendant to last plea, which the prosecutor does not have.

23 See Margarita Chinova and Georgi Mitov (n 15), 117.

with the principle of adversariality. The activity of the court to clarify the substance of the case does not derive directly from the principle of adversariality, but is the result of the interaction of several principles of the Bulgarian criminal procedure law, such as those of discovery of the objective truth, of making decisions out of inner conviction, of adversarial nature of the court proceedings etc.[24]

The trial proceedings include five stages. The first stage, called "Submission to court and preparatory actions for examination of the case at a court hearing" has a preparatory nature, i.e. the court does not consider the case on the merits.[25] This stage is mandatory for all criminal cases, including those of a private nature.[26] Competent to hear the case in an operative hearing is the same court that shall hear the case at first instance. The operative hearing is postponed where any of the following does not appear: the prosecutor, the accused party, if his/her appearance is mandatory, the defence counsel.[27]

In the legal literature, the immediate specific task at this stage is defined as the performance of the necessary legal-technical and technical preparatory actions before the beginning of the court hearing at first instance.[28] With changes in the Code of Criminal Procedure from 2017, this task was supplemented (specifically for publicly actionable criminal cases, *i.e.* initiated under an indictment).[29] During this stage, it was envisaged to check whether in the pre-trial proceedings a remediable substantial violation of procedural rules had been committed, which had led to a restriction of the procedural rights of the accused, the victim or his heirs.[30] If such a violation is found, the court

24 See Ivaylo Tsonkov, *Theory and Practice of Criminal Proceedings. Competitiveness in the Light of the European Convention on Human Rights*, Ciela, 2014; Margarita Chinova and Georgi Mitov (n 15), 117–118.

25 See Margarita Chinova and Georgi Mitov (n 15), 425.

26 *Ibidem.*

27 Art 247(d) CCP.

28 See Margarita Chinova and Georgi Mitov (n 15), 425. Therefore, among the issues discussed at the pretrial hearing and which are exhaustively mentioned in the Code of Criminal Procedure, are whether the case is subject to the relevant court, whether there are grounds for termination or suspension of criminal proceedings, whether there are grounds for consideration of the case under special rules, etc. (Art 248(1)).

29 SG, no. 63 of 2017.

30 According to Art 249(4) CCP, a breach of the procedural rules committed in the pre-trial proceedings is substantial and remediable when the following rights of the accused and the victim have been violated: 1. the accused – to learn for what crime he has been involved in this capacity; to give or refuse to give explanations on the accusation; to participate in the proceedings; to have a lawyer and to receive a written or oral translation into a language he understands when he does not speak Bulgarian; 2. the victim or his/her heirs – to be notified of the initiation of the pre-trial proceedings; to be informed

terminates the court proceedings and returns the case to the prosecutor for elimination of the violations.[31] Otherwise, as well as when there are no grounds for termination or suspension of the criminal proceedings, or the case should not be considered under the special rules, the court schedules the case and notifies the persons who appeared.[32]

The other four stages of the trial proceedings are court hearing at the first instance, intermediate appellate review proceedings, cassation proceedings and re-opening of criminal cases. The latter constitutes a procedure for verification of the final sentences and judgements.

4.2 The Implementation of EU Directives: State of Play

As already mentioned above, even before the adoption of the six procedural Directives, it seems that the Bulgarian legislation regulated the rights of the accused in criminal proceedings to an extent that largely corresponds to the standards set in the EU legislation. The national legal framework in this area, as well as the case law, also contain a number of guarantees for the effective exercise of these rights. This is one of the possible explanations why the requirements of only two of the Directives have been explicitly transposed into Bulgarian legislation.

One of them is Directive 2010/64 on the right to interpretation and translation in criminal proceedings. Some of its requirements were established in Bulgarian law even before its official entry into force. However, the most significant changes to fully introduce into Bulgarian legal system the guarantees laid down in the Directive, were made in 2014 at both the legal and regulatory level. Despite these changes, Bulgarian legislation still do not seem in full compliance with the EU standards. This concerns particularly the types of essential documents for which a translation is required and the lack of criteria for determining the qualifications of the interpreters and translators.

The same can be said for Directive 2013/48. In general, even before the entry into force of the Directive, Bulgarian law was overall in compliance with the requirements as set out therein concerning the right of access to a lawyer and to have a third party informed. However, it was necessary the existing legal

---

of his/her rights and to take part in the proceedings; to receive a written translation of the decree for termination or suspension of the criminal proceedings, if he/she does not speak Bulgarian.

31 See Art 249 CCP.

32 See Art 248(5) CCP.

framework to be supplemented, in order to fully guarantee the rights provided for in the Directive.

In this regard, major changes were made in 2019 by the legislator not only in the Code of Criminal Procedure, but also in other laws. Nevertheless, not all the requirements of the Directive have yet been fully transposed. Thus, Bulgarian law still does not sufficiently guarantee the protection against self-incrimination of persons other than accused who, in the course of questioning by the police or by another law enforcement authority, become accused persons. The same could be said for the right to have a third party informed of the detention where the accused is a child as well as the right of access to a lawyer in European arrest warrant proceedings.

In contrast, Bulgarian legislation on the right to information in criminal proceedings largely complies with the standards of Directive 2012/13, albeit without explicit transposition of the latter. However, two of the requirements of the Directive have been either not implemented at all or only partially implemented in Bulgarian law. Here the reference goes respectively to the Letter of Rights on arrest and the Letter of Rights in European Arrest Warrant proceedings.[33]

Among the six directives, Directive 2016/800 is the one, the requirements of which have been implemented only to a minimal extent in Bulgarian law. Although the national legislation even before adoption of the Directive provided for special rules for juvenile accused, aimed at guaranteeing their procedural rights in criminal proceedings, it did not contain all the procedural safeguards as laid down in the Directive. It is no accident that, at the end of 2020, a draft law was submitted to the National Assembly proposing major amendments to the Code of Criminal Procedure for the full transposition of the Directive.[34] However, the proposal has not been adopted yet. Therefore, at present, most of the requirements of the Directive are not implemented at all or only partially in Bulgarian law.

In contrast, regarding the legal aid Bulgarian law largely complies with the standards as set out in Directive 2016/1919. The national legal framework already provided for most of the requirements of this Directive even before its entry into force. Moreover, in some cases Bulgarian law goes even beyond the standards of the Directive.[35] However, one of these standards raises questions

---

33 For more details, see National report on the domestic implementation of the criminal procedural rights of the accused, Sect. 7.6 thereof.

34 See https://parliament.bg/bg/bills/ID/163428/.

35 For more details about such cases, see National report on the domestic implementation of the criminal procedural rights of the accused, Sect. 2, 10.3 and 10.4 thereof.

in the doctrine and in case law, namely the possibility for accused or requested persons to bear part of the costs for legal aid themselves, depending on their financial resources (Recital (8) of the Directive). The application in practice of some of the rules concerning the legal aid is also identified as problematic.[36]

As regards Directive 2016/343, most of its requirements are already *de facto* implemented into Bulgarian law. This mainly concerns the right to be present at the trial and the right to a new trial where the presence of the defendant had not been assured. In contrast, although the presumption of innocence is guaranteed in both the Bulgarian Constitution[37] and Code of Criminal Procedure,[38] certain EU requirements concerning this presumption result only partially transposed. It is about the appropriate measures in the event of a breach of the obligation laid down in Art 4(1) of the Directive not to refer to accused persons as being guilty, in particular, according to public statements made by public authorities. Although Bulgarian law provides for such measures, they do not seem sufficiently effective within the meaning of Art 10 of the Directive.

4.3 Main Critical Profiles in the Legislation and Case Law

This section will examine some aspects of Directives 2016/343 and 2016/800 and the extent to which the relevant national legislation and case law comply with European requirements.[39] This concerns the presumption of innocence, and in particular the public references to guilt, as well as the right of accused persons, including minors, to be present at trial in criminal proceedings. The first issue deserves attention due to the established existence of a systemic problem in our country in light of the numerous convictions against Bulgaria of the European Court of Human Rights for violations of the presumption of innocence. The second is of interest in view of the fact that under Bulgarian law in certain cases the presence of the defendant during the trial is mandatory, *i.e.* it is provided as an obligation and not as a right of the person.

---

36 For more details, see National report on the domestic implementation of the criminal procedural rights of the accused Sect. 10.5 thereof.

37 According to Art 31(3) thereof, an accused party shall be presumed innocent until otherwise proven by an enforceable sentence.

38 Art 16 CCP states that the accused party shall be presumed innocent until the reverse is established by virtue of an effective verdict.

39 Both directives have not been explicitly transposed into Bulgarian law. But unlike the first directive, for the second there is a bill prepared and submitted to the National Assembly at the end of 2020, which brings the Bulgarian legislation in line with its requirements.

4.3.1 *Public References to Guilt*

The requirements of Art 4, Directive 2016/343 regarding the public references to guilt seem partially implemented in Bulgarian legislation. It should be noted, however, that the Bulgarian law contains certain provisions, which seem to introduce the standard of the Directive. Under the Judiciary System Act, the judicial authorities (judges, prosecutors and investigating magistrates) shall discharge the functions thereof impartially (Art 4 thereof).[40] This principle is further developed in the Code of Ethical Behaviour of Bulgarian Magistrates,[41] as well as in the Code of Ethics regarding the conduct the Ministry of Interior civil servants.[42]

Failure to comply with these obligations constitutes a disciplinary violation. In these cases, it is possible to impose a disciplinary sanction on the respective magistrate or employee of the Ministry of Interior – investigating police officer.[43]

---

40 In this regard, the CCP contains separate provisions in which the grounds for dismissal of judges, jurors, prosecutors, investigative bodies are established (Arts 29, 30, 47, 53).

41 The provisions of the Code are applicable to judges, prosecutors and investigating magistrates. The Code states that the magistrate should remain impartial even in cases where society shows strong affinity or antipathy towards participants in proceedings pending before him/her and should decide the case solely on the basis of facts and law. In proceedings pending before him/her, the magistrate should not make public statements or comments, engaging with the final outcome of the case or creating the impression of partiality and prejudice (Arts 2(2) and 2(3) thereof).

42 The provisions of the Code are applicable to the civil servants of the Ministry of Interior, including those acting as investigative bodies in the pre-trial proceedings under the CCP. According to this Code of Ethics, the activities of civil servants shall be carried out in compliance with the ethical principles of conduct, one of which is impartiality, i.e. proper, objective and unbiased performance of their duties, creating conditions of equality between citizens in exercising their powers and avoiding behavior that may be perceived as privilege, bias or prejudice. Furthermore, the civil servant shall follow the principle according to which an accused person shall be presumed innocent until otherwise proven by an enforceable sentence. The civil servant shall perform his/her tasks by following the principles of impartiality and non-discrimination and shall form his/her inner conviction solely on the basis of the facts and data collected by the means offered by the law in any particular case. (Arts 13, 32 and 36 thereof).

43 Art 307(3), p. 3 of the Judiciary System Act states that any act or omission, including a breach of the Code of Ethical Behavior of Bulgarian Magistrates, which damages the prestige of the Judiciary constitutes breaches of discipline for commission of which a disciplinary sanction shall be imposed. Accordingly, the Ministry of Interior Act defines as serious breaches of official discipline for which the disciplinary sanction "dismissal" is imposed any actions incompatible with ethical rules for conduct of the MoI employees, derogating the reputation of the service (Art 203(1), p. 13 of the Ministry of Interior Act).

As regards the press and media, similar provisions concerning the public references to guilt are provided for in Ethical Code of the Bulgarian Media.[44] Arts 2(6)(1) and 2(6)(2) of the Code states that the media shall respect the "presumption of innocence" and will not describe someone as a criminal prior to their conviction. And if the media identify a person as being charged with a crime, it shall also make known the outcome of the trial.

It is true that Bulgarian legislation contains measures which may be classified as a remedy in cases of breach of the obligation established in Art 4(1) of the Directive. Such are, for instance, the right of the accused person to appeal against acts infringing on his/her rights and legal interests,[45] the possibility for the accused person to bring charges and maintain the accusation before court as a private complainant[46] or claims for damages under the Act on the Liability for Damage Incurred by the State and the Municipalities[47] or under the Obligations and Contracts Act, including claims against the media filed under the latter law.[48]

In addition, according to the case law, the prejudice regarding the guilt of the accused constitutes a substantial breach of procedural rules,[49] which leads

---

44 Under the Code, the term "media" includes journalists, editors, producers, publishers and owners of print and electronic media.

45 Art 55(1) CCP.

46 According to Art 147 of the Criminal Code, a person who makes public a disgraceful fact about someone or ascribes to him a crime shall be punished for slander by a fine from BGN three thousand up to seven thousand, as well as by public censure. The perpetrator shall not be punished if the truth of the divulged circumstances or of the ascribed crimes is proved. In these cases, the criminal prosecution is instituted on the basis of a complaint by the victim.

47 According to Art 2(c) thereof, the State shall be liable for any damage inflicted on citizens, which are caused by a sufficiently serious breach of European Union law. In these cases, compensation by the State is owed.

48 The law states that every person must redress the damage he has guiltily caused to another person. In all cases of tort guilt is presumed until proven otherwise. Compensation shall be due for all damage which is a direct and immediate consequence of the tort. It may payable as a lump sum or in regular instalments. A report by the European Union Agency for Fundamental Rights (FRA) of March 2021 on how the rights to be presumed innocent, to remain silent and to be present at trial in criminal proceedings are applied in practice, states that as regards effective remedies, according to the persons interviewed in Bulgaria, it is the civil lawsuit against the media that is the only possibility for the accused, publicly presented as guilty. See FRA Report on Presumption of innocence and related rights – Professional perspectives, https://fra.europa.eu/en/publication/2021/presumption-of-innocence (accessed 20 October 2021).

49 See Judgmenet No. 212/2019 of the Supreme Court of Cassation. The Court accepted that the decision of the Court of Appeal-Burgas, which partially confirmed the conviction of the first instance for a crime committed by the defendant – death caused by negligence while driving a bus, was issued by an illegal panel. It was attended by a judge who was part

to the revocation of the sentence or the decision and the return of the case for reconsideration.[50]

However, despite the existence of the above measures, applicable in cases of a breach of the obligation not to refer to accused persons as being guilty, the question arises whether they are appropriate and constitute a truly effective remedy within the meaning of Art 10(1) of the Directive, especially in cases of violation of the presumption of innocence in public statements of ministers and other public representatives according to Recital (17) of the Directive. The issue acquires special significance in the context of the numerous decisions of the Court of Strasbourg convicting Bulgaria for having violated Art 6(2) of the ECHR, due to public statements by the official authorities, including the Minister of the Interior, the spokesperson of the Prosecutor General, prosecutors, members of parliament, press releases from the police services, etc.[51]

In these cases, the Bulgarian authorities substantiate the thesis that the affected persons could have defended themselves in the criminal proceedings, and after the acquittal to file defamation cases or to file a claim for compensation under the Act on the Liability for Damage Incurred by the State and the Municipalities or the Obligations and Contracts Act. However, the Court

---

of the court panel that exercised judicial control over the decree terminating the criminal proceedings. Thus, according to the Supreme Court, a preliminary opinion on the guilt of the defendant was formed, which is an obstacle for the judges who participated in this control to consider and decide the case on the merits. In another decision No. 14/2020, the Supreme Court of Cassation held that the appellate court, (the Sofia Court of Appeal), had violated the presumption of innocence. The appellate court reclassified the defendant's crime to a lesser one, namely possession of 3.41 marijuana worth BGN 20.46 (approximately EUR 10) and reduced the conditional sentence from one and a half years imprisonment to 6 months imprisonment. However, in its decision the appellate instance accepts that there are no prerequisites for the committed act to be defined as insignificant, i.e. as non-criminal, motivated by the other criminal proceedings against the defendant, for which there was no evidence that it had ended with an effective sentence (it was subsequently terminated by the prosecution). The Supreme Court stated that in this way the appellate court had made an inadmissible negative suggestion that the defendant had participated in a crime in a pending criminal case, thereby violating the presumption of innocence. This constitutes a substantial breach of the procedural rules, which led to a violation of the defendant's procedural rights.

50 Art 354(3), item 2 CCP.

51 See in this context *Stefanov v. Bulgaria*, App no. 26198/13, 2 February 2021; *Alexey Petrov v. Bulgaria*, App no. 30336/10, 30 June 2016; *Gutsanovi v. Bulgaria*, App no. 34529/10, 15 October 2013; *Petrov and Ivanova v. Bulgaria*, App no. 45773/10, 30 June 2016; *Popovi v. Bulgaria*, App no. 39651/11, 9 June 2016; *Slavov v. Bulgaria*, App no. 58500/10, 10 November 2015; *Stoyanov and Others v. Bulgaria*, App no. 55388/10, 30 June 2016; *Toni Kostadinov v. Bulgaria*, App no. 37124/10, 27 April 2015; *Banevi v. Bulgaria*, App no. 25658/19, 12 October 2021.

held that these measures in most cases did not constitute effective domestic remedies.[52]

The numerous convictions against Bulgaria in Strasbourg for violation of the presumption of innocence under Art 6(2) of the ECHR, according to analysts and human rights activists, make the violation of the presumption of innocence in connection with a public reference to guilt in Bulgaria a systemic problem.[53]

Another aspect of this problem is related to the partial transposition in the Bulgarian legislation of the requirements of Art 4(3) of Directive 2016/343. According to this norm, the obligation not to present the accused as guilty does not prevent the public authorities from disseminating publicly information about the criminal proceedings, when this is strictly necessary for reasons related to the criminal investigation or in the public interest. As relevant in this case can be indicated the provision of Art 198 CCP, according to which the materials of the investigation may not be disclosed without the permission of the prosecutor. When necessary, the body of the pre-trial proceedings warns

---

52 See in this context: *Stefanov v. Bulgaria,* cit, §§ 23–24; *Maslarova v. Bulgaria,* App no. 26966/10, 31 January 2019, §§ 35 and 38; *Lolov and Others v. Bulgaria,* App no. 6123/11, 21 May 2019, §§ 43–51; *Banevi v. Bulgaria,* cit, §§ 130–156. The last-mentioned case is on the occasion of a statement made at a press conference in October 2018 by the head of the Specialized Prosecutor's Office (now Chief Prosecutor) and the supervising prosecutor, as well as on the reasons in an order of December 2018 by which the Specialized Criminal Court ruled on the remand in custody of the two applicants (husband and wife accused of participating in an organized criminal group for tax crimes and money laundering). According to the European Court of Human Rights (ECtHR), the words of the two prosecutors to the media go beyond the simple transmission of information about the criminal investigation. In particular, the very slightly nuanced way in which they described the versions in which the investigators worked, the use of terms such as "criminal privatization", "draining" or "boning" to describe the events that led to the closure of the companies in question and their very clear conclusions as to the facts under investigation give the impression that the two applicants were perpetrators of the offenses with which they were charged. Those comments, taken as a whole, therefore undermine the applicants "presumption of innocence". As regards the ruling of the Specialized Criminal Court, the ECtHR held that the reasons for the real danger of the commission of another crime by the two applicants went beyond a simple description of the state of suspicion. According to the Court, they constitute a declaration of their guilt before any decision on the merits of the criminal proceedings against them.

53 See a study of the Center for Legal Initiatives on the state and development of the legal order in our country for the period January – June 2019, published in the Legal Barometer magazine, 115–116, https://legalbarometer.bg/images/ Legal_Barometer_broi_19.pdf. An article from February 2019 by the journalist Mirela Veselinova, https://www.capital.bg/politika_i_ikonomika/bulgaria/2019/02/21/3393932_bulgariia_otnovo_osudena_v_strasburg_zaradi_narushena/ (accessed 20 October 2021) is also dedicated to this problem.

against signature the persons who are present during the actions of the investigation that they cannot disclose without permission the materials of the case and otherwise bear responsibility under Art 360 of the Criminal Code.[54] The provision applies only to the pre-trial proceedings. However, this rule does not correctly transpose the Directive's provision read in conjunction with Recitals (18) and (19) thereof.

In fact, Art 198 CCP allows materials from the pre-trial proceedings to be disclosed after permission of a prosecutor. Recently, this possibility has been used too often by the Prosecutor's Office. However, this situation creates a risk of abuse because, as it depends entirely on the judgment of the relevant prosecutor. The law does not contain the requirements laid down in the Directive, namely public disclosure of such materials could be made only where it is strictly necessary for reasons relating to the criminal investigation or to the public interest. In many of these cases, however, according to representatives of the legal community in Bulgaria, this disclosure by representatives of the Prosecutor's Office violated the presumption of innocence by failing to comply with the standard of Art 4(3) of the Directive.[55]

In this regard, in October 2020 the Supreme Bar Council made a request to the Supreme Court of Cassation for interpretation of Art 198 CCP. The request discusses particularly the practice of the Prosecutor's Office to disclose certain materials from the pre-trial proceedings. In this way, the public, through the media, became aware of excerpts from protocols for interrogation of the accused and witnesses, from telephone conversations made through special intelligence tools and so on. It is emphasized that in all cases the disclosed materials serve the thesis of the Prosecutor's Office, while the accused and their lawyers are prohibited from disclosing the materials of the investigation, including the materials that are in favor of the defence-. According to the Supreme Bar Council, such a practice by representatives of the Prosecutor's Office violates fundamental rights of citizens such as the presumption of innocence, privacy and secrecy of correspondence. The request refers to Art 4 of the Directive, to the European Convention on Human Rights and to the case law of the European Court of Human Rights.

---

54 A person who discloses information of military, economic or other nature, which is no state secret, but the divulgence of which is forbidden by law, an order, or other administrative instruction, shall be punished by deprivation of liberty for up to one year or by probation (Art 360 thereof).

55 In July 2020, sixteen well-known Bulgarian lawyers sent a signal to the European Commission stating that in this way the Bulgarian Prosecutor's Office did not comply with the requirements of the Directive and violated the presumption of innocence.

By Ruling of 15 April 2021, the Supreme Court of Cassation rejected the request as inadmissible.[56] The Court held that it was not a competent body, as it carried out interpretive activity in case of established contradictory or incorrect practice of the courts and not of the Prosecutor's Office. Moreover, the request raised the issue of contradiction of Article 198 CCP with the Bulgarian Constitution, which is within the jurisdiction of the Constitutional Court.

4.3.2 *Right to Be Present at Trial*

Bulgarian law contains provisions, which ensure the right of the accused to appear in person and participate in their trial established by the EU Directives (Art 8, Directive 2016/343 and Art 16, Directive 2016/800). Their right to take part in criminal proceedings, the right to make requests, comments and raise objection, as well as the right to be the last to make statements are explicitly stated in Art 55(1) CCP. In addition, the law provides for rules in cases of re-opening of a criminal case upon request of an individual sentenced in absentia (Arts 423, 425 CCP). These provisions are the same in respect to adults and underage persons.

However, under Bulgarian law, the presence of the accused at the court hearing is mandatory in cases of serious crime accusation.[57] The court may order the accused party to also appear in cases where the presence thereof is not mandatory, if this is necessary for the discovery of the objective truth.[58] Unlike the Code of Criminal Procedure, the Directives provide for the appearance of the accused in person at their trial as a right not as an obligation irrespective of the seriousness of the crime.

Bulgarian law seems to be in compliance with such standards. On the one hand, as stated in the FRA report mentioned above, the defendant's presence at the trial under national law is defined more as a right and only exceptionally as an obligation.[59] On the other hand, the national legislation thus established guarantees in fact the right of the defendant to be present at the trial. Besides, it provides the possibility for the person to defend himself in person, in addition to the defense by a lawyer due to the severity of the crimes. The obligatory

56 See http://www.vks.bg/talkuvatelni-dela-osnk/vks-osnk-tdelo-2020-2-opredelenie.pdf (accessed 19 October 2021).

57 According to Art 93, p. 7 of Criminal Code, "serious crime" is any crime for which the law provides punishment by imprisonment for more than five years, life imprisonment or life imprisonment without substitution.

58 Art 269(1; 2) CCP. For example, such is the case where the presence of the accused is necessary for identification of persons and objects.

59 See FRA's Report on Presumption of innocence and related rights – Professional perspectives, mentioned above in footnote 45, 85–86.

presence of the defendant in these cases also guarantees the protection of the public interest.

It should also be borne in mind that, as far as the requirements of the Directive 2016/343 regarding trials that are hold in the absence of the accused are fully implemented. According to the Code of Criminal Procedure, the case may be tried in the absence of the accused when this will not prevent the disclosure of the objective truth and if the the person has been validly summoned but failed to show good cause for not appearing, and where the procedure under Art 247b(1) CCP has been complied with (Art 269(3) CCP).[60] In all cases where the trial is held in absence of the accused the participation of a lawyer is mandatory (Art 94(1), p. 8 CCP), *i.e.* a lawyer will be appointed if the accused has not retained such one of his/her own and regardless whether such request is made by the accused or not.

According to the case law, failure to summon the accused to the court hearing, regardless of whether his/her participation is obligatory or not, constitutes a substantial breach of procedural rules. This means it is a ground for remit the case to the prosecutor or revocation the sentence and further remit the case to the first instance or the appellate court.[61]

However, the legal literature offers a different approach when it comes to the right to appear in person and participate in the trial of juvenile defendants.[62] Some scholars believe that changes in Bulgarian legislation are needed. In particular, the Code of Criminal Procedure should provide for the right of

---

60 Art 269(3) CCP provides for three more conditions in the presence of which the case may be tried in the absence of the accused: 1) if the person could not be found at the address specified by him, or he has changed his/her address without notifying the respective body; 2) if his/her place of residence in this country is not known and has not been identified after a thorough search; 3) if the person is located outside the boundaries of the Republic of Bulgaria: a) his/her place of residence is not known; b) may not be otherwise summonsed; c) has been validly summonsed, but has failed to specify good reasons for his/her non-appearance.

61 See in this respect Ruling 181/2020 of the District Court-Varna. The Court held that the right of individuals to be present at the trial against them is essential to ensure a fair trial. Their absence during the trial is a ground for a new trial and a new hearing on the merits. Art 8 of Directive 2016/343 states that "reasonable efforts" should be made for the accused to be identified, and such are missing in respect of the defendant in the case. Failure to notify the accused that he is being prosecuted, as well as his non-participation in the pre-trial, respectively in the court proceedings, is a significant procedural violation, which should be eliminated in the pre-trial phase of the process.

62 See in this context Margarita Chinova and Bojan Belejkov, *Necessary measures for the transposition of Directive 2016/800 of the European Parliament and of the Council of 11 May 2016 on procedural guarantees for children suspected or accused in criminal proceedings*, Yearbook of Sofia University "St. Kliment Ohridski ", Faculty of Law, 2019, 86.

the juvenile defendant to explicitly refuse to be present at the hearing and after the court has ruled that his/her presence is of particular importance to justice or in his/her best interests. Only in this way, national regulations will be aligned with Directive 2016/800 and other international instruments in this field.[63]

4.4 Concluding Remarks

In view of the transposition of the six directives, the following should be noted in conclusion.

Only two of the Directives – 2010/64 and 2013/48 –, have been introduced into Bulgarian legislation through explicit amendments. As regards Directive 2016/800, major amendments to the current law were submitted to the Parliament but have not yet been adopted by the legislator. Such an approach can be interpreted as a statement from the public authorities, that Bulgarian legislation largely already complies with the requirements of the other Directives and does not need to be further changed.

The fact that Bulgarian legal framework already and mostly guaranteed the rights as laid down in the six Directives seems to be true, on the one hand. This is predominantly because these rights are also established by the ECHR. And in the last 20 years Bulgarian legislation has undergone significant changes in order to introduce the standards of the ECHR in national criminal proceedings. This is one of the reasons why established case law refers more often to the provisions of the ECHR and the case law of the ECtHR than to the Directives.

On the other hand, however, the above interpretation seems problematic and not applicable to all Directives. Additional changes in Bulgarian law are needed, through which the standards of the six Directives shall be introduced completely and correctly. This consideration concerns, for instance, the already discussed issue about public references to guilt, in particular when public authorities refer to a person in public statements, and the availability of appropriate remedies against such behaviours. Other shortcomings are identified in relation to some of the standards which guarantee the quality of the interpretation and translation, the right to have a third person informed of the detention, especially where the accused is a child, the lack of the Letter

63 *Ibidem.*

of Rights on arrest. The same also can be said for the implementation of the Directives requirements applicable in EAW proceedings.[64]

The introduction of EU standards into national legislation is, in principle, a challenge. This challenge is even greater when it comes to the matter related to the procedural guarantees of the rights of accused persons in criminal proceedings, respectively of the persons requested in the EAW proceedings.

First of all, such implementation should take into account existing national standards, including those which at first sight differ from the standards laid down in the directives, but a more in-depth analysis reveals in fact their compliance with European requirements. A good example in this context is the national legislation discussed above on the right of adult defendants to be present at the trial.

However, a literal transposition of the requirements of the Directives is also problematic. For instance, it can be pointed out the legislator's approach where the derogation from the right of a third party to be notified of the detention, including when the accused is a child (Art 5(3), Directive 2013/48) was implemented in the Bulgarian legislation. This was done without stating the reasons that necessitate such an exception in the national law. This legislator's approach was then severely criticized.[65]

In summary, it can be noted that most of the requirements of the Directives already existed in the Bulgarian legislation and were recognized in the settled case law. The guarantees for the procedural rights of the accused persons in the criminal proceedings, respectively of the requested persons in the EAW proceedings as laid down in the Directives were however strengthened by the changes made in Bulgarian laws to comply with the European legislation. However, further legal amendments still seem to be needed in order to transpose fully and correctly the EU requirements in this area.

64 For more details, see National report on the domestic implementation of the criminal procedural rights of the accused, Sect. 6.3; 6.4; 8.5; 11.2 thereof.

65 Furthermore, the President vetoed the draft law as regards the part relating to these provisions, which was subsequently overturned, and the relevant rules entered into force. According to the grounds of the veto, the adopted legislation does not contain the guarantees for the introduction of such derogations as laid down in the Directive. Therefore, the adopted rules do not guarantee that there will be no cases in which none of the relatives of the accused has been notified of his/her detention. See Decree № 309/2018 г. of the President of the Republic of Bulgaria, https://m.president.bg/bg/cat47/1168/president-veto-zakon-nakazatelen-kodeks.html (accessed 19 October 2021).

CHAPTER 5

Croatia

Implementation of Directives on Procedural Rights for Suspects and Accused Persons: State of Play and Critical Profiles

Zlata Đurđević, Elizabeta Ivičević Karas, Marin Bonačić, and Zoran Burić

5.1 Introduction

This Chapter represents the results of the analysis of the implementation of six EU directives on procedural rights for suspects and accused persons in Croatia. Analysis of Croatian law includes legislation and case law of the Constitutional Court of the Republic of Croatia, the Supreme Court of the Republic of Croatia, the High Criminal Court and some county courts. Only the most important findings of the analysis are represented in this article.[1]

5.2 The Implementation of EU Directives: State of Play

Croatia has implemented all six Directives, not all of them on time. The Directives were implemented explicitly through amendments of the Criminal Procedure Act (CPA), Act on Judicial Cooperation in Criminal Matters with the Member States of the European Union (AJCEU), Juvenile Court Act (JCA) and other laws and regulations. Some Directives were mostly or to a considerable extent implemented *de facto* such as the Directive 2016/343 on presumption of innocence and of the right to be present at the trial and the Directive 2016/800 on procedural safeguards for children.

Directive 2010/64 on the right to interpretation and translation in criminal proceedings was primarily transposed into Croatian law through two

1 The full analysis has been conducted within the project Knowledge, Advisory and Capacity Building Information Tool for Criminal Procedural Rights in Judicial Cooperation (CrossJustice), funded by the European Union's Justice Programme (2014–2020), and it is unpublished.

 | DOI:10.1163/9789004513396_007

amendments of the CPA, which were adopted in 2013.[2] The latter came into force on 15 December 2013 and therefore the provisions of the Directive were transposed with a slight delay.[3] Due to transposition of other directives and to address implementation shortcomings, some provisions of the CPA were amended in 2017.[4] In regard to the European arrest warrant (EAW) procedure, the Directive was transposed through the amendments of the AJCEU in 2017.[5] The Directive was also *de facto* implemented through the Courts' Act,[6] Misdemeanours' Act (MA),[7] and Regulation on permanent court interpreters.[8] Most of the provisions were explicitly transposed and fully implemented. In that regard, the right is guaranteed from the time a person is made aware by the competent authorities that they are suspected or accused of having committed a criminal offence until the conclusion of the proceedings and it also applies in the misdemeanour proceedings. Many new provisions like the ones on the translation of essential documents, the use of communication technology, or the right to challenge a decision on no need for translation and its quality have been introduced.[9]

Directive 2012/13 on the right to information in criminal proceedings has been transposed into Croatian law primarily through the amendments of the CPA which have been adopted in December 2013. These amendments came into force on 15 December 2013, which means that the provisions of the

2 Act amending the Criminal Procedure Act (*Zakon o izmjenama i dopunama Zakona o kaznenom postupku*), Official Gazette No. 56/2013 and Act amending the Criminal Procedure Act (*Zakon o izmjenama i dopunama Zakona o kaznenom postupku*), Official Gazette No. 145/2013.

3 Pursuant to Art. 9(1) of the Directive deadline for the transposition was 27 October 2013.

4 Act amending the Criminal Procedure Act (*Zakon o izmjenama i dopunama Zakona o kaznenom postupku*), Official Gazette No. 70/2017.

5 Act amending the Act on Judicial Cooperation in Criminal Matters with the Member States of the European Union (*Zakon o izmjenama i dopunama Zakona o pravosudnoj suradnji u kaznenim stvarima s državama članicama Europske unije*), Official Gazette No. 102/2017.

6 Courts' Act (*Zakon o sudovima*), Official Gazette No. 28/2013, 33/2015, 82/2016, 67/2018, 126/2019, 130/2020.

7 Misdemeanours' Act (*Prekršajni zakon*), Official Gazette No. 107/07, 39/2013, 157/2013, 110/2015, 70/2017, 118/2018.

8 Regulation on permanent court interpreters (*Pravilnik o stalnim sudskim tumačima*), Official Gazette No. 132/2005, 3/2006, 88/2008, 119/2008.

9 On the implementation of the Directive 2010/64 in Croatian legal system see See Elizabeta Ivičević Karas, Zoran Burić and Marin Bonačić, *Unapređenje procesnih prava osumnjičenika i okrivljenika u kaznenom postupku: pogled kroz prizmu europskih pravnih standarda* (2016) 23 Hrvatski ljetopis za kaznene znanosti i praksu 11, 16–23. See also Martina Bajčić, *Pravo okrivljenika na tumačenje i prevođenje u kaznenom postupku kroz prizmu recentne prakse Europskog suda za ljudska prava i suda EU-a* (2019) 69 Zbornik Pravnog fakulteta u Zagrebu 223, 239–43.

Directive were transposed in time.[10] In relation to the part of its provisions which relate to the EAW proceedings, the Directive has been transposed with the amendments to the AJCEU which have also been adopted in time, in June 2013.[11] Certain legislative shortcomings in relation to the right of the suspected person to be informed, at the earliest stages of police investigation into the criminal offence, of his/her rights and the accusation have been rectified with the amendments of the CPA from 2017. Main challenges in the implementation process related to guaranteeing effective informing of suspects and arrested persons of their rights and the accusation in the earliest stages of criminal proceedings which are dominated by police investigation into the criminal offence.

As concerns Directive 2013/48 on the right of access to a lawyer and to have a third party informed upon deprivation of liberty and to communicate with third persons and with consular authorities while deprived of liberty, the vast majority of its provisions have been transposed and fully implemented in Croatian criminal procedural law. Most provisions of this Directive were transposed with the amendments of the CPA adopted in 2017. The most important change brought by the transposing legislation is the regulation of the interrogation of suspects and arrestees by the police. Before the Directive was transposed, the police were able to conduct informal informative conversations with suspects, without prior instruction on rights and without the right to have a defence counsel.[12] Although the official notes on these informative conversations could not be used as evidence in criminal proceedings, the police could have used them to obtain further evidence, which were derived from the informative conversations. Since the Directive 2013/48 explicitly guarantees the right to defence counsel from the moment of deprivation of liberty, but also before and during any interrogation of a suspect, including the police interrogation, the Croatian legislator had to take significant interventions in the previous legal framework. Thus, a new substantive definition of a suspect was prescribed,[13] and with the regulation of the right to a defence counsel,

10 Pursuant to Art 11(1) of the Directive Member States were obliged to bring into force the laws, regulations and administrative provisions necessary to comply with the Directive by 2 June 2014.

11 Act amending the Act on Judicial Cooperation in Criminal Matters with the Member States of the European Union (*Zakon o izmjenama i dopunama Zakona o pravosudnoj suradnji u kaznenim stvarima s državama članicama Europske unije*), Official Gazette No. 81/2013.

12 Elizabeta Ivičević Karas, *Pomicanje granica prava na branitelja pod utjecajem europskog kaznenog prava* (2015) 22 Hrvatski ljetopis za kazneno pravo i praksu 355, 370–71.

13 *Ibid*, 366.

other fundamental defence rights during the police interrogation were regulated, such as the right to information and the right to remain silent. The audio-video recording of the police interrogation of a suspect and arrestee now may be used as evidence in proceedings.

Directive 2016/343 on the presumption of innocence and of the right to be present at the trial was formally transposed by the 2019 Amendment of the CPA[14] that has introduced only one provision (Art 3(2) CPA) related to the burden of proof while other implementing provisions already existed in the CPA. The analysis of the Croatian law and jurisprudence has revealed the cases of non-compliance, as it will be illustrated further below.

Directive 2016/800 on procedural safeguards for children was transposed into Croatian law through the 2019 amendments of the JCA,[15] Police Duties and Powers Act,[16] and, in regard to the EAW proceedings, through the amendments of the AJCEU.[17] The amendments came into force on 1 January 2020, which means that the Directive was transposed with a delay of almost half a year.[18] These Acts explicitly implemented the provisions of the Directive.[19] However, many provisions of the Directive were *de facto* implemented through already existing provisions of the JCA,[20] CPA, Family Act,[21] MA and Criminal Code.[22] In comparison to other directives, the peculiarity of the transposition of this directive is that many provisions were transposed through regulations that are not laws but administrative acts: Regulation on the admission and treatment of arrestees and detainees and on the Records of detainees in a police detention

14 Act amending the Criminal Procedure Act (*Zakon o izmjenama i dopunama Zakona o kaznenom postupku*), Official Gazette No. 126/2019.

15 Act amending the Juvenile Courts Act (*Zakon o izmjenama i dopunama Zakona o sudovima za mladež*), Official Gazette No. 126/2019.

16 Act amending the Police Duties and Powers Act (*Zakon o izmjenama i dopunama Zakona o policijskim poslovima i ovlastima*), Official Gazette No. 70/2019.

17 Act amending the Police Duties and Powers Act (*Zakon o izmjenama i dopunama Zakona o policijskim poslovima i ovlastima*), Official Gazette No. 70/2019.

18 Pursuant to Art 24 the deadline for transposition was 11 June 2019.

19 For an overview of the implementation in JCA see Ivana Radić, *Implementacija Direktive o postupovnim jamstvima za djecu koja su osumnjičenici ili optuženici u kaznenim postupcima u noveli Zakona o sudovima za mladež* (2020) 27 Hrvatski ljetopis za kaznene znanosti i praksu 571.

20 Juvenile Courts Act (*Zakon o sudovima za mladež*), Official Gazette No. 84/2011, 143/2012, 148/2013, 56/2015, 126/2019.

21 Family Act (*Obiteljski zakon*), Official Gazette No.103/2015, 98/2019.

22 Criminal Code (*Kazneni zakon*), Official Gazette No. 125/2011, 144/2012, 56/2015, 61/2015, 101/2017, 118/2018, 126/2019, 84/2021.

unit,[23] Regulation on the work of expert associates of non-legal profession in matters of juvenile delinquency and criminal law protection of children in the state attorney's offices and the courts[24] and Regulation on Household Order in Prisons for Execution of Detention.[25]

Lastly, Directive 2016/1919 on legal aid for suspects and accused persons in criminal proceedings and for requested persons in European arrest warrant proceedings has been transposed into Croatian law with the 2019 amendments to the CPA[26] and AJCEU.[27] Amendments to the CPA have entered into force on January 1, 2020, and the amendments to the AJCEU on August 1, 2019, both of them after the expiration of the transposition deadline determined in Art. 12(1) of the Directive, May 25, 2019. Main challenge in the implementation process was to guarantee the right to free legal aid for all suspects and accused persons from the earliest stages of criminal procedure – police inquiry into the criminal offence. This has been done by introducing a new institution into the Croatian criminal justice system – provisional legal assistance of a defence attorney at the expense of the budget.

5.3 Main Critical Profiles in the Legislation and Case-law

Shortcomings in the form of partial or incorrect implementation have been detected with regard to all six Directives. The relevant national case law with regard to two Directives (Directive 2016/800 on procedural safeguards for children and Directive 2016/1919 on legal aid) have not been identified and in

23 Regulation on the admission and treatment of arrestees and detainees and on the Records of detainees in a police detention unit (*Pravilnik o prijamu i postupanju s uhićenikom i pritvorenikom te o Evidenciji pritvorenika u pritvorskoj policijskoj jedinici*), Official Gazette No. 88/2009, 78/2014, 123/2016, 50/2019.

24 Regulation on the work of expert associates of non-legal profession in matters of juvenile delinquency and criminal law protection of children in the state attorney's offices and the courts (*Pravilnik o radu stručnih suradnika izvanpravne struke na poslovima delinkvencije mladih i kaznenopravne zaštite djece u državnim odvjetništvima i na sudovima*), Official Gazette No. 22/2013.

25 Regulation on Household Order in Prisons for Execution of Detention (*Pravilnik o kućnom redu u zatvorima za izvršavanje istražnog zatvora*), Official Gazette No. 8/10.

26 Act amending the Criminal Procedure Act (*Zakon o izmjenama i dopunama Zakona o kaznenom postupku*), Official Gazette No. 126/19.

27 Act amending the Act on Judicial Cooperation in Criminal Matters with the Member States of the European Union (*Zakon o izmjenama i dopunama Zakona o pravosudnoj suradnji u kaznenim stvarima s državama članicama Europske unije*), Official Gazette No. 70/2019.

general there are not many judicial decisions referring to such legal acts.[28] The major difficulty to conduct case law research was access to cases as in Croatia the case law of the lower courts is in principle not publicly accessible and even the case law of the Supreme Court is accessible only to a certain extent. The recent data are showing that the number of published decisions on the internet have been continuously reduced in the last years represents only 40% of the Supreme Court decisions.[29]

The analysis which follows is divided into three parts. In the first part, those Directives where the crucial steps in the implementation process are undertaken or are to be undertaken at the level of the case law are presented. In the second part, those Directives where crucial steps in the implementation process are still to be undertaken in the legislation are presented. Finally, the third part deals with a Directive where the crucial part of the implementation process is to be undertaken at the level of training and quality of services assurances.

5.3.1 *The Crucial Role of the Jurisprudence: Directives on the Right to Interpretation and Translation and on the Right of Access to a Lawyer*

The analysis of Directive 2010/64 has shown that some of the provisions are only partially implemented or not implemented at all. In that regard, the requirements regarding the right to interpretation (Art 2) were only partially implemented since there is no specific procedure or mechanism in place to ascertain whether suspected or accused persons speak and understand the language of the criminal proceedings, and whether they need the assistance of an interpreter. It is only partially implemented through the provisions on the obligatory questions about the ethnicity and nationality of the defendant when he/she is interrogated for the first time (Art 272(1) CPA) and the obligation to use interpreter in a case of doubt whether the defendant understands the official language of the court (Art 273(6) CPA).[30]

28 The analysis has included the jurisprudence concluding with April 2021, which has been published and accessible on the web page of the Supreme Court of the Republic of Croatia: https://sudskapraksa.csp.vsrh.hr/home.

29 Viktorija Knežević, *Pravosuđe i javnost: Kako osigurati odgovorno i transparentno sudovanje?*, Okrugli stol Hrvatska akademija znanosti i umjetnosti (HAZU), 15 June 2021.

30 However, in absence of specific procedure or mechanism, the research has shown that there are no problems with it since the main criterion for the decision whether the interpretation or translation is needed is the statement of the suspect or the accused person that he/she does not speak or understand the Croatian language. Elizabeta Ivičević Karas, Zoran Burić and Marin Bonačić, *Prava obrane u različitim stadijima hrvatskog kaznenog*

Another requirement that was only partially implemented is the one that there is no requirement to translate passages of essential documents which are not relevant for the purposes of enabling suspected or accused persons to have knowledge of the case against them (Art 3(4) of the Directive). Art 8(6) CPA provides that the body conducting the proceedings may order that a written translation of a piece of evidence or a part thereof be provided where this is necessary for the exercise of procedural defence rights.[31] The provision mentions only 'evidence', so the other essential documents must therefore be translated in full. Therefore, it can be concluded that the Croatian law sets the higher standards in this regard.

The only requirement that has not been implemented into Croatian law is the one regarding the training, that those responsible for the training of judges, prosecutors and judicial staff involved in criminal proceedings pay special attention to the particularities of communicating with the assistance of an interpreter so as to ensure efficient and effective communication (Art 6 of the Directive). This obligation is not prescribed by any law, and the Judicial Academy, which organizes the training for these groups, did not have any training program on the subject in the last five years.

The importance of case-law for the proper transposition of the directives is perhaps best demonstrated by the Supreme Court Judgment I Kž-Us 52/15-4,[32] which addressed the question of whether a special appeal is allowed against a decision rejecting a defendant's request for translation. Even though the Croatian legislator initially failed to transpose the right to appeal the decision which determines that it is not necessary to translate some documents or their excerpts (Art 3(5) Directive), the Court found that such decision must be subject to review.[33] In relation to other issues, the case-law can be summarized as follows: 1. In the case of foreign nationals, the fact that they live and work in Croatia and are familiar with the Croatian language is not in itself sufficient to establish that they speak or understand the Croatian language to an extent that would not prejudice their rights of defence;[34] 2. The use of *ad hoc* interpreters

postupka: rezultati istraživanja prakse (2016) 23 Hrvatski ljetopis za kaznene znanosti i praksu 509, 543.

31 The phrase 'necessary for the exercise of procedural defence rights' includes the 'passages ... relevant for the purposes of enabling suspected or accused persons to have knowledge of the case against them.'

32 VSRH I Kž-Us 52/15-4, 23 April 2015.

33 See Elizabeta Ivičević Karas, Zoran Burić and Marin Bonačić, *Neka pitanja usklađenosti hrvatskoga kaznenog procesnog prava s direktivama o pravima obrane – analiza sudske prakse* (2020) 27 Hrvatski ljetopis za kaznene znanosti i praksu 543, 564.

34 VSRH, I Kž-Us 22/17-4, 27 April 2017. *Ibid*, 560–62.

instead of permanent court interpreters must be justified by the circumstances of the case and the reasons correspond to those for the use of *ad hoc* experts. In case the *ad hoc* interpreter does not take the oath under Art 280(3) CPA it will not make in itself the testimony of a witness illegal;[35] 3. The defendant has the right to interpretation and translation in cases conducted *in absentia, i.e.* it cannot be a reason for restricting the right to interpretation and translation.[36]

Another case which shows the crucial impact of the jurisprudence in complying with EU standards is that of Directive 2013/48. It is possible to point out two critical profiles in the legislation. The first one concerns the new substantive definition of the suspect.[37] It determines the moment from which defence rights guaranteed by the Directive 2013/48 apply, and that is from the moment in which the 'grounds for suspicion' against a concrete person start to exist and the police or the state attorney take action to clarify that suspicion. Grounds for suspicion must arise from concrete facts or circumstances, in a relation to a particular person.[38] It is necessary to clearly distinguish in each concrete case suspects, on one side, from potential suspects[39] and presumptive witnesses on the other side,[40] since the police cannot conduct informal informative conversations with the former, while it can with the latter. The mixing of these procedural roles undermines the concept based on the introduced substantive definition of the suspect.

A further critical issue in the legislation concerns limitation of the arrestee to communicate freely with a defence counsel. Art 65(2) of the CPA stipulates, in accordance with Art 3(2) of the Directive 2012/48, that the defendant shall be instructed on his/her right to retain defence counsel 'immediately upon his/her arrest or the performance of another act provided for' by the CPA and the CPA does provide a right to defence counsel to arrestee and regulates it in detail. Yet, the possibility to communicate with the defence counsel prior to interrogation is limited to up to 30 minutes, even in the most complex cases. This may constitute an unjustified restriction of the right to access to a lawyer. The right of the arrestee to have a conversation with a defence counsel prior

---

35 VSRH, I Kž 351/16-4, 6 July 2016. Confirmed by VRSH, I Kž 370/2017-10, 26 November 2019; VSRH, III Kr 49/2019-3, 29 May 2019. *Ibid*, 562–63.

36 VSRH I Kž-Us 52/15-4 (n 32). *Ibid*, 565.

37 CPA, Art. 202(2)(1).

38 Zoran Burić and Željko Karas, *Prilog raspravi o dvojbama vezanima uz novu definiciju osumnjičenika i radnju njegova ispitivanja* (2017) 24 Hrvatski ljetopis za kaznene znanosti i praksu 443, 474 and 477.

39 See *ibid*, 477.

40 See Elizabeta Ivičević Karas, Zoran Burić and Marin Bonačić, *Neka pitanja usklađenosti* (n 33) 548–50.

to the interrogation and the time limitation of that right were simultaneously introduced with the legislative amendment in 2013, in the context of enhancing the defence rights, particularly in the pre-trial stage of proceedings.[41] A research conducted in 2016, through interviews and focus groups with practitioners, showed that this limitation has never been used in practice, probably because consultation with defence counsel usually does not last longer than 30 minutes so there is no need to apply this restriction.[42] Therefore, it is not clear why this time limitation was introduced into the CPA since it was obviously not needed in practice.[43]

In the case law, the provisions of national legislation transposing the Directive have been interpreted in several decisions dealing with four separate issues: 1) the moment at which a person acquires the status of the suspect and therefore has the right to be assisted by defence counsel before and during police interrogation,[44] 2) the problem of mixing procedural roles (citizen/suspect),[45] 3) the right to be assisted by a defence counsel during identity parades[46] and 4) the right to be assisted by a defence counsel during home search.[47] The courts in the analysed decisions mainly dealt with the issue of illegal evidence, the regulation of which is left to national laws by the Directive 2013/48. Therefore, the given interpretations concerned mainly domestic law on rather strict exclusionary rules, which were applied in only two cases concerning the identity parades. In the first case, the defendant was provided with a written letter of rights, including the right to counsel, but in the records of identity parade, or in any other record, the defendant did not state whether he waived his rights to defence counsel.[48] This ruling of the Supreme Court is particularly relevant because the CPA, in case of violation of the right to counsel

41 See Zlata Đurđević, *Rekonstrukcija, judicijalizacija, konstitucionalizacija, europeizacija hrvatskog kaznenog postupka V. novelom ZKP/08: prvi dio?* (2013) 20 Hrvatski ljetopis za kazneno pravo i praksu 315, 351. See also Zlata Durđević, *Osvrt na rezultate radne skupine Ministarstva pravosuđa za usklađivanje Zakona o kaznenom postupku s Ustavom Republike Hrvatske* (2013) 20 Hrvatski ljetopis za kazneno pravo i praksu 3, 75.

42 Elizabeta Ivičević Karas, Zoran Burić and Marin Bonačić, *Prava obrane u različitim stadijima* (n 30) 533–34.

43 *Ibid*, 533.

44 VSRH I Kž 716/2018-4, 10 January 2019.

45 VSRH I Kž-Us 88/2018-4, 22 November 2018.

46 VSRH Kžm 13/2018-4, 10 May 2018, ŽS u Puli–Pola Kž-294/17, 8 September 2017, VSRH I Kž 223/17-4, 25 April 2017, VSRH I Kž 389/17-4, 24 August 2017, VSRH I Kž 34/2018-4, 8 March 2018, ŽS u Zagrebu 1 Kž-1211/2017-3, 19 December 2017, ŽS u Zagrebu 7 Kž-155/2019-3, 26 February 2019.

47 VSRH I Kž 251/2020-4, 21 May 2020., VSRH I Kž-Us 149/2017-4, 30 May 2018.

48 VSRH I Kž 34/2018-4 (n 46).

during identity parades, did not provide for *ex lege* illegality of evidence as a procedural sanction, but left the possibility for the identity parade record to be *ex judicio* illegal evidence, in accordance with Article 10(2)(2) of the CPA, if so assessed by the court.[49] Similar reasoning was applied by Zagreb County Court in another case.[50]

The analysis of case law shows that for the proper application of new legal solutions and effective exercise of the right to defence counsel, as well as other defence rights in the earliest stages of the procedure – during police interrogation, it is crucial that the court carefully considers all circumstances of each concrete case. This is especially important in determining: first, the moment at which a person acquires the status of the suspect and therefore has the right to be assisted by defence counsel before and during police interrogation,[51] and second, to consistently apply the rules on the strict distinction between the procedural role of the suspect, with whom the police may not conduct informal informative conversations, and the role of the potential suspect and the presumptive witness, with whom informative conversations are allowed.[52]

5.3.2 *Further Legislative Steps to Be Undertaken*

5.3.2.1 Directive on the Right to Information

Generally speaking, Croatian law is now to a high degree in compliance with the provisions of Directive 2012/13. Still, in the evaluation process, some compliance problems have been identified and they relate to the following provisions of the Directive: Art. 3(1) in its part that relates to the entitlement to free legal advice and the conditions for obtaining such advice in relation to the suspect and the arrested person (it has been fully implemented in relation to the accused); Art. 3(2) because the CPA does not contain a requirement that the letter of rights is written in simple and accessible language nor does it contain a general obligation to take into account specific needs of vulnerable persons when informing them about their rights; Art. 4(3) because there is no information about any possibility, under national law, of challenging the lawfulness of the arrest, obtaining a review of the detention, or making a request for provisional release in the letter of rights to the arrested person or the person in

49 Elizabeta Ivičević Karas, Zoran Burić and Marin Bonačić, *Neka pitanja usklađenosti* (n 33) 552–54.

50 ŽS u Zagrebu 1 Kž-1211/2017-3 (n 46).

51 VSRH I Kž 716/2018-4 (n 44), also VSRH I Kž 161/2019-4, 16 April 2019, see Ivičević Karas, Burić and Bonačić, *Neka pitanja usklađenosti* (n 33) 546–48, 566.

52 VSRH I Kž-Us 88/2018-4 (n 45), also VSRH I Kž-Us 117/2019-4, 29 November 2019, see *ibid*, 548–50, 566.

pre-trial detention; Arts. 4(4) and 5(2) because the letter of rights in Croatia is not drafted in simple and accessible language; Art. 6(4) because Croatian law does not contain a provision which would explicitly or indirectly transpose the obligation to promptly inform the suspect or the accused person of any changes in the information given in accordance with Art 6 of the Directive, where this is necessary to safeguard the fairness of the proceedings; Art 7(1) because the provision of the CPA, which gives the person in pre-trial detention the right to access all the materials which are necessary to effectively challenge the lawfulness of the detention, does not apply to arrested persons or the person in custody; Art 7(4) because Croatian law enables the state attorney and the court to deny the accused not only the rights of access to certain materials of the case, but to the case file in its entirety; Art 9 because no training has been identified.

The main issue which has been identified in the case law is the question at which moment the person acquires the status of the suspect and, in connection to that, the right to be informed of his/her rights and the accusation. In the ruling I Kž 161/2019-4[53] the Supreme Court decided that the person approached by the police did not acquire the status of the suspect at the moment of giving a self-incriminating statement, immediately after being approached by the police (in his statement he claimed that he keeps drugs hidden in a nearby bush), but only after he had, at the initiative of the police, handed over drugs that he has on his person. Since, according to the Supreme Court, it was only then that he acquired the status of the suspect, the police officers acted in accordance with the law by informing him about his rights only thereafter. This position of the Supreme Court has been criticised in the literature for failing to recognize that in the circumstances of the case the person acquired the status of the suspect already at the moment of giving a self-incriminating statement (and not only at the moment of handing over the drugs).[54]

5.3.2.2 Directive on Presumption of Innocence and the Right to Be Present at Trial

Another significant field in which transposition lacunas appear especially problematic is that of Directive 2016/343. Firstly, the privilege against self-incrimination is not stated in the letter of the rights as required by Art 7(2) of the Directive. In cases of criminal offences of penal protection of children (Art. 262/4 CPA) the measure of temporary seizure of written notices of the

53 VSRH I Kž 161/2019-4 (n 51).

54 Elizabeta Ivičević Karas, Zoran Burić and Marin Bonačić, *Neka pitanja usklađenosti* (n 33), 546–48.

defendant to the defence counsel is permitted as an exception to its general prohibition (Art 262(1)(2) CPA). As there are no case-specific reasons when the seizure would apply, this exception violates the right to remain silent and right not to incriminate oneself for a wide range of offences prescribed by Art 113 of the JCA. Then the rule that detention ordered in case of reasonable suspicion that a defendant will destroy evidence or influence witnesses (Art 123(1)(2) CPA) will be abolished if s/he pleads guilty and describes the offence circumstantially and in detail (Art 125(1)(8) CPA) violates the privilege of self-incrimination. It overtly prescribes that if a defendant incriminates him/herself and gives detailed information to the prosecutor how s/he committed the offence s/he will be released from prison. Croatian law does not contain provisions that the exercise by suspects and accused persons of the right to remain silent or of the right not to incriminate oneself shall not be used against them and shall not be considered to be evidence that they have committed the criminal offence concerned as required by Art 7(5). However, they are implied in the right to remain silent and privilege against self-incrimination as confirmed by the Supreme Court case law stating that the defence by silence alone could not have the consequences of determining the danger of tampering with evidence. as ground for detention, and as it is a fundamental defence right the defendant is not obliged to answer questions and there is no measure provided by law for the defendant in such a case.[55]

In line with Art 8(5) if the accused disturbs order or fails to comply with direction of the president of the panel concerning the maintenance of order at trial, the president of the panel shall warn or punish him/her by a fine not exceeding HRK 50,000.00. To punish the accused by fine in this case is an exception in the Croatian criminal proceedings that violates the presumption to be innocent.

The Constitution of the Republic of Croatia guarantees the suspected, accused or indicted person to be present at his/her trial insofar as s/he is at the disposal of the court (Art 29(2)(5)). In the Croatian criminal justice system, the presence of the accused at the trial is not only his/her right (Art 64(1)(9) CPA) but also his/her obligation. It is also the obligation of the competent authorities conducting the criminal proceedings to ensure the presence of the defendant at the trial, as an indispensable element of the fair trial. The criminal trial can

55 VSRH II Kž 428/1999, 12 July 1999. See A. Novokmet, *Pretpostavka okrivljenikove nedužnosti i prijedlog direktive Europskog parlamenta i Vijeća o jačanju određenih vidova te pretpostavke u kaznenom postupku* in Anita Kurtović Mišić and others (eds), *Europeizacija kaznenog prava i zaštita ljudskih prava u kaznenom postupku i postupku izvršenja kaznenopravnih sankcija*, (Pravni fakultet Split 2017), 140.

be fair, justified and legitimate if the defendant is present at the trial and has actual and not only normative right to defend him/herself from the charges. In order to ensure the defendant's presence at the trial the competent authorities can use coercive measures such as compulsory appearance, arrest, bail, pre-trial detention (*e.g.* Art 402(1) CPA). However, the court panel may exceptionally decide that the accused be temporarily removed from the courtroom if the co-accused or witness refuses to give a statement in his/her presence or if the circumstances indicate that they would not tell the truth in the presence of the accused (Art 438 CPA). Taking into account the technological possibilities that exist today that can enable an accused to follow the witness interrogation, this provision violates the defendant's right to be present at the trial.

There is noncompliance with Art 8(2)(b) of the Directive as trial in absence of the accused for a criminal offence punishable by a fine or by imprisonment for a term of up to five years may be held without representation by a defence lawyer and without informing the accused, in due time, of a trial and of the consequences of non-appearance. This applies to the accused who was duly summoned but failed to appear or upon whom the summons could not be served because s/he changed his/her address without having informed the court thereof or where it is evident that s/he is avoiding service of the summons, on condition that his/her presence is not necessary and that prior to the trial s/he was interrogated or responded to the charge (Art 404(5) of the CPA).

As a trial *in absentia*[56] is considered to be contrary to the defendant's right to a fair trial and rights of defence, such as the right to be informed of the accusation, to be heard by the judge and to examine witnesses, the Croatian CPA guarantees a person sentenced in absentia the right to a retrial in his/her presence. So, the provision of Art 483(3) of the CPA gives to the accused tried *in absentia* higher protection than it is required by Art 8(4) of the Directive if she/he is deprived of freedom, as in case of an appeal *in favorem* of the accused, the court shall *ex officio* order the retrial. Under Art 497(3) of the CPA the court will reopen the criminal proceeding if the convicted person or his/her defence counsel file within one year from the day the convicted person found out about the final judgment a request for the reopening of the proceeding specifying the convicted person's address for service and the convicted person promises to comply with the court summons. Under Art 504(2) of the CPA if the trial was held in absence of the defendant (Art 402(3) and (4) CPA), a request for the

56 See Iris Goldner Lang, Zlata Đurđević and Mislav Mataija, *The Constitution of Croatia in the Perspective of European and Global Governance*, in Anneli Albi and Samo Bardutzky (eds), *The Role of National Constitutions in European and Global Governance: Democracy, Rights, the Rule of Law. National Reports* (TMC Asser Press 2019), 1160–62.

reopening of criminal proceedings may also be submitted by the parties and defence, regardless of the presence or absence of the convicted person.

The analysis of case law has indicated two interpretations of the Directive, one related to admissibility of guilty plea final judgment stating the name of the accused as co-perpetrator and the other on the danger of reoffending as ground for detention established on the fact of conducting other criminal proceedings against the same defendant.

The Supreme Court has repeatedly[57] decided in cases where it was undisputed that the guilty plea judgment (judgment based on agreement of the parties) was not made in accordance with Art 4(1) of the Directive and the judgment of the ECJ Case C-377/18 of 5 September 2019, as in the introduction, the ordering part, and the statement of reasons of the judgment, it is not explicitly stated that defendants did not plead guilty, that separate criminal proceedings are being conducted against these persons and that their guilt has not been established in accordance with the law, could be read at the trial and be used as evidence. The reasons given are the following: reading the guilty plea judgment of conviction in the criminal case against the persons mentioned in the factual description of offence in the judgment did not call into the question their presumption of innocence as in respect of guilt and criminal responsibility that judgment applies exclusively to the person found guilty and not to the other persons stated in the factual description; defendants who have not pleaded guilty will be allowed, in separate proceedings against them, to examine in a contradictory proceeding as witnesses the persons who reached and concluded the agreement, and thus to examine and question all those facts relating to the incriminations in relation to which these defendants reached an agreement; the indication of the name and surname of the appellant and the nature of the *tempore criminis* in the operative part of that judgment was necessary solely and exclusively for the purpose of determining the qualification of liability of the defendant who reached and concluded a plea agreement.

As regards the submission of a preliminary question to the ECJ, the Supreme Court expressed its opinion that the Directive does not even address the issues of legality and admissibility of certain evidence, and it is exclusively on the national court to decide completely independently whether the need for an appropriate interpretation of EU law exists in a particular case and the issue of admissibility of evidence is not relevant and crucial to this particular criminal case.

57 VSRH, I Kž Us 26/2020-11, 12 June 2020.

The decision of the Supreme Court is not in line with the Art 4(1) of the Directive and it breaches the presumption of the innocence for the following reasons: a) it is not clear why the judgment based on agreement of the parties is necessary for the analysis and determination of the legal responsibility of the accused person, b) the burden of proof was reversed as the court expressly stated that the accused is allowed to examine in a contradictory proceeding as witnesses the persons who reached and concluded the agreement, and thus to *examine and question all those facts relating to the incriminations in relation to which these defendants reached an agreement*. Therefore, the judgment based on agreement of the parties does not serve only for the categorisation of the legal liability of the person who entered into the agreement but as evidence with regard to the facts that form elements of crime in the judgment that should be disproved and therefore are taken as established. That reverses the burden of proof and violates the presumption of innocence. The burden of proof is on the prosecutor and the incriminating fact in the indictment should be proved by evidence. The factual description of offences for which the witness is convicted in the judgment based on agreement of the parties is not evidence and the prosecutor cannot prove commission of the offence by the accused by the final judgment from another proceeding where the accused did not participate and was not an accused. Additionally in this case it is undisputed that the judgment based on agreement of the parties violates the presumption of innocence as it is not written in line with the ECJ interpretation of the Art 4(1) Directive and according to the Croatian law the court is required to decide on its legality applying the principle of proportionality in line with the article 10(3) of the CPA which was not done.

The other ruling of the Supreme Court[58] that also refused to exclude the ordering part of judgments based on the agreement of the parties, added as a new argument to the claim that it is not illegal evidence in the sense of Art 10(2) CPC as the judgment is drafted in accordance with the relevant provisions of the CPA and illegality of evidence is referred only to the manner of obtaining evidence. However, such a conclusion is incorrect as evidence that is legally obtained can become illegal evidence for reasons that are not related to any irregularities in its obtaining but to its use as evidence at the trial. These are *e.g.* police and state attorney's record on information provided by citizens that can be used as evidence before indictment but not after (Art 86 CPA) and the agreement of the parties if the parties desist from the agreement before the judgment is passed (Art 362 CPA).

58 VSRH, I Kž-Us 122/2020-4, 24 March 2021.

Second issue is whether the detention was justified by the danger of reoffending based on the fact that another criminal proceeding is being conducted against that defendant.[59] The Constitutional Court reiterated that in deciding on the ordering or extension of pre-trial detention the fact that another criminal proceeding is being conducted against the applicant for existence of reasonable suspicion of committing the criminal offense of endangering life and property by generally dangerous act or means and committed precisely to the detriment of the same victim as in the criminal proceedings in question may be taken into account, not as proof of conviction, but as proof that it has been established in other proceedings as well the existence of a reasonable suspicion that that person has committed criminal offenses. Opposite position would lead to unacceptable consequences that the danger of reoffending could not be based on all those parts of the factual substrate of a case about which (parallel) criminal proceedings are still being conducted (only due to the fact that it has been conducted), which may call into question that ground for detention basis. In addition, the fact that the applicant in the second case was found suspicious that he committed another crime reinforces the justification of the prognosis on the existence of the danger or reoffending. This decision of the Constitutional Court can be considered correct and in line with the Directive 2016/343.

5.3.2.3 Directive on Procedural Safeguards for Children

The juvenile criminal law applies in Croatia to children who were under the age of 18 when the offence was committed and who did not reach the age of twenty-three when the jurisdiction of a juvenile court ceases (Art 2, 36 and 48 JCA). However, it must not but can be applied also to so-called young adult perpetrators who were 18 to 21 years of age when they committed offence until they reached twenty-three years of age (Arts 104, 105 and 107 JCA). The provisions excepted from the application to the accused that has reached the age of 18, are also excluded in the Croatian law (Art 48(2) JCA).

The limitation of the scope of the application of the Directive from Art 2(6) is not implemented as the procedural provisions of the Act apply not only before courts having jurisdiction in criminal matters, but also before all other bodies conducting misdemeanour proceedings (for instance tax or customs authorities). The presumption that when the age is uncertain, the offender is a child from Art 3 is not implemented. Art 4(1)(c) introducing obligation to

59 The Supreme Court decision (VSRH II Kž 4/2021-4, 13 January 2021), the High Criminal Court decision (II Kž-97/2021-5, 7 April 2021) and the Constitutional Court decision (U-III-4298/2020, 20 October 2020).

inform a child upon deprivation of liberty in respect of the right to specific treatment during deprivation of liberty, as provided for in Art 12, is not implemented. As concerns Art 6(3)(a), the JCA does not regulate in detail the questioning of the juvenile suspect or defendant, therefore regarding the right to have assistance of a defence counsel before and during the questioning, the provisions of the CPA apply that prescribe that the communication between arrestee and his/her defence counsel may not last for more than thirty minutes (Art 108(3) CPA). Limiting the communication of the arrestee with the defence counsel to up to thirty minutes may constitute an unjustified limitation of the right to access the lawyer.

Art 6(8)(b) was partially implemented as under Art 108.b(1-3) CPA the state attorney may order the police to delay informing (of the arrest) the defence counsel and a member of the arrestee's family, or other person chosen by the arrestee, but it is not required that the criminal proceedings could be 'substantially' jeopardised. Also, there is no explicit obligation for the competent authorities, when applying these provisions, to take the child's best interests into account. Even if the decision may only be taken on a case-by-case basis by the state attorney, it cannot be submitted to judicial review. Yet, the child may only be questioned about circumstances which brought about the notification delay, and not about the criminal offence, so this is not a questioning *stricto sensu*. As regard Art 7(8) there is no other provision that ensures the update of the individual assessment throughout proceedings. In regard to the right to a medical examination, Art 8(5) is not implemented since there is no provision that another medical examination should be carried out where the circumstances so require. The requirement that examination should be as non-invasive as possible (Art 8(1) of the Directive) is also not implemented. However, Art 78(4) JCA stipulates that, where it is necessary for the assessment of the minor's health condition the opinion of a doctor shall be sought, and it could be presumed that such examination would be suggested.

A request that due consideration shall be taken of the age and individual situation of the child when deciding on the deprivation is not implemented. In addition to that, many requirements on the specific treatment in the case of deprivation of liberty (Art 12 of the Directive) are not implemented. In that regard, there is no provision that a child, as a rule, has to be separated from the adult detainees in the police detention unit (Art 12(2) of the Directive). Since the closed prison institutions foreseen by the JCA are not yet established the Regulation on Household Order in Prisons for Execution of Detention does not mention education and training at all, it can be concluded that this right to education and training (Art12(1)(1) of the Directive) are not implemented. For the same reason, the access to programmes that foster the development and the reintegration into society is only partially implemented through the Art. 24(1) Regulation on Household Order in Prisons for Execution of Detention which allows prisoners to work in the prison premises in accordance with the possibilities of the prison, and outside the prison under supervision with the approval of the competent court.[60] There is also no explicit provision that the measures taken should be proportionate and appropriate to the duration of the detention, *i.e.* the exercise of the rights in the Regulation is not connected to the duration of the detention as stated in the Art 12(5)(2) of the Directive. Lastly, the JCA does not implement the requirement that the children who are deprived of liberty can meet with the holder of parental responsibility as soon as possible, where such a meeting is compatible with investigative and operational requirements (Art 12(6) of the Directive). According to the Art 18a(1) of the Regulation on the admission and treatment of arrestees and detainees, the parent, guardian, or professional employee of the social welfare centre must be present during the admission of the juvenile to the detention police unit, but it is not regulated in a form of a meeting with a juvenile.

The requirement that the records of criminal proceedings are not publicly disseminated (Art 14(3) of the Directive) in connection to the protection of privacy, is not implemented. Art 60(1) JCA provides that the inquiries and proceedings against a minor are secret, but competent authority can approve the publishing of the content and course of the proceedings against the minor, but then the name of the minor and other information on the basis of which it may be concluded which minor is involved should not be stated.

All the above examples show that there are a number of provisions of the Directive that have not been implemented in the Croatian legal system. Since the research of the jurisprudence was conducted only four months after the Directive's transposition, no national case law has been identified.

5.3.3 *Critical Issues Related to Training and Quality of Service: Directive on Legal Aid*

In Croatia, the system of legal aid in criminal proceedings is a mixture of three different forms of legal assistance at the expense of the State budget: provisional

60 Marija Pleić and Ivana Radić stated that the non-establishment of closed institutional facilities 'has seriously brought into question the entire concept of the pre-trial detention focussed on the needs and upbringing of the minors'. Marija Pleić and Ivana Radić, *Pre-Trial Detention of Children: European Standards and Croatian Law* (2019) 3 EU and comparative law issues and challenges series (ECLIC) 521, 541. It is also not implemented during police detention, *i.e.* deprivation of liberty other than (pre-trial) detention (Art 12(5)(4) of the Directive).

legal assistance of a defence attorney (provisional legal aid), legal assistance of a defence attorney (legal aid *stricto sensu*), and mandatory defence. Provisional legal aid is a new institution which has been introduced with the transposition of the Directive and it covers the earliest stages of criminal proceedings which are characterized by police inquiries into the criminal offence. After a criminal procedure has been opened against a person (by the decision of the state attorney, who makes such a decision on the basis of information gathered by the police) provisional legal aid may become legal aid *stricto sensu*. The latter form of legal aid applies until the final resolution of criminal proceedings. From the earliest stages of criminal procedure another institution applies – mandatory defence. These are the situations where the law requires that the suspect or the accused is represented by a defence attorney. In those situations, he/she is first called to engage the services of a defence attorney, but if he/she does not do so, a defence attorney shall be appointed to him/her by the court. In the latter situation, the costs of legal representation shall be borne by the State.

Generally speaking, Croatian law is to a high degree in compliance with the provisions of the Directive. Still, there are some shortcomings identified in the evaluation process: restrictive merits test, quality of legal aid services, and the lack of training. First two issues mentioned deserve closer scrutiny.

With regard to the restrictive merits test, its application relates to provisional legal aid for suspects and accused persons who are not deprived of liberty. With regard to provisional legal aid, Croatian law applies a merits test. However, this test is applied differently in relation to the arrested person, on one side, and the suspect and the accused person who are not deprived of liberty, on the other side. As far as the latter category is concerned, the merits test is only fulfilled in relation to criminal offences which are punishable by imprisonment of more than five years. This statutory presumption is contrary to the provisions of the Directive, and it represents an unjustified limitation of the right to legal aid in criminal proceedings.[61]

There are two issues that have a negative impact on the quality of legal aid. The first one is that the legal aid lawyer, who is paid by the State, receives only 30 percent of the remuneration he/she would be entitled to as a chosen lawyer. This leads to a situation where lawyers, especially the most experienced ones, are not motivated to act as legal aid lawyers. The second issue is closely connected with the first one and relates to the fact that there is no specialization required for legal aid lawyers. Any attorney who has the right to practice law

61 Elizabeta Ivičević Karas and Zoran Burić, *Na putu prema transponiranju Direktive o besplatnoj pravnoj pomoći u hrvatski kazneni postupak? Osvrt na Prijedlog osme novele ZKP-a*, (2019) 26 Hrvatski ljetopis za kaznene znanosti i praksu 417, 427–33.

in Croatia can be a legal aid lawyer in criminal proceedings. This leads to situations where attorneys who are not experienced enough in criminal cases act as legal aid lawyers in criminal proceedings. These attorneys can normally not ensure effective defence for the suspect and the accused in criminal proceedings. Both these issues show that, although the legislative provisions which relate to legal aid in criminal proceedings are mostly in line with the provisions of the Directive, there is a lot to be done in order to establish a system of legal aid in criminal proceedings in Croatia.

With regard to the right to legal aid, no national case law has been identified. This may be the result of the fact that the violation of the right to legal aid (unlike the violation of access to a lawyer) is not sanctioned by the most serious procedural sanction – the inadmissibility of the results of the action which has been undertaken in breach of that right.

5.4 Concluding Remarks

From the analysis presented here, it can be concluded that Croatian law has been, even before the procedural rights of suspects and accused persons have been formulated in directives, to some degree compliant with their provisions. If a certain aspect of Croatian criminal procedure that demonstrated significant divergences from European standards had to be identified, it would be the part of the proceedings which is dominated by police work in relation to criminal procedure. These structural deficiencies have finally been rectified in the process of implementation of directives. Of course, this general conclusion does not affect many findings in this study where certain degrees of non-compliance with EU standards have been identified in relation to provisions of all directives included in the research. This study has also shown that in relation to most provisions that require implementation, the adoption of legislative amendments step might be the least problematic one. From the perspective of the implementation, necessary system modifications and adaptations, as well as those that relate to in practice well established attitudes and modes of operation, represent a much bigger challenge in the implementation process.

CHAPTER 6

France

Legal Aid, Juvenile Defendants and Presumption of Innocence – Main Critical Profiles in the Implementation of the Defence Rights Directives

Eleonora Cervellera and Raphaële Parizot

6.1 Introduction

While the dialogue between the Criminal Chamber of the French Court of Cassation and the Court of Justice in the criminal matter has since long focused on subjects like the *ne bis in idem*,[1] or on the thorny question of data retention,[2] no significant interaction can be observed so far with regard to procedural rights in criminal proceedings. Arguably, this is because the state of transposition into French law of the European Directives on the rights of suspects or persons prosecuted in criminal proceedings is considered as generally satisfactory.

The French code of criminal procedure, adopted by a Law of 31 December 1957, has indeed been changed a lot since 1957, in particular under the influence of European Convention of Human Rights and of European Union law.

Historically, the French criminal system is an inquisitorial system. French criminal law procedure is thus traditionally presented as written, secret and non-adversarial. However, this has changed long time ago; today, the preliminary article of the code of criminal procedure provides that "criminal procedure should be fair and adversarial and preserve a balance between the rights of the parties". Now French trial is without doubt oral, public, and, to a certain extent, adversarial. But these remarks apply only for the trial in the strict sense.

On the contrary, the pre-trial phase is always written,[3] secret[4] and rather not adversarial. Accordingly, however, it is necessary to distinguish between the two possible frameworks of the investigation in the French criminal procedure.

1 Crim., 21 October 2020, n°19-81929, C-570/20.

2 Crim., 1st April 2020, n°19-80908, C-339/20.

3 Each act of the investigation must be written in an official report.

4 Art 11 CPP: "Except where the law provides otherwise and subject to the defendant's rights, the inquiry and investigation proceedings are secret".

 | DOI:10.1163/9789004513396_008

On one hand, the *inquiry* (*enquête*), that is the investigation made by judicial police officers under the supervision of the district prosecutor (*procureur de la République*). The latter has a judicial status (magistrate), though without jurisdictional safeguards (he is not an independent magistrate, placed under the supervision of the general prosecutor – *procureur general* – who in turn is under the supervision of the Minister of Justice).[5] [6] The inquiry is actually the common framework for the investigation in France. On the other hand, there is the *judicial investigation* (*instruction*), that is the investigation made by an investigating judge (*juge d'instruction*), who is an independent magistrate. The judicial investigation is required for the most serious offences (*crimes*) and possible for other offences, in particular for complex cases.

Originally, the judicial investigation was the only admitted form of investigation in France. But later on, prosecutors developed a habit of conducting themselves inquiries before deferring them to the investigating judge. This practice was then integrated in the code of criminal procedure and now the inquiry constitutes the commonest form of investigation in the country.

Anyway, the choice of the procedural framework of the investigation has important effects in the perspective of the suspect. If the latter is subjected to a judicial investigation, he is considered as a party and he fully enjoys defence rights.

However, if the person is suspected in an inquiry, she is not considered as a party to the proceeding.

---

5 Art 5 Ordonnance of the 22 December 1958: "Prosecutors are placed under the direction and control of their hierarchical superiors and under the authority of the Minister of Justice. In court, their speech is free".

6 The European Court of Human Rights has taken the view that, owing to their status, public prosecutors in France did not satisfy the requirement of independence from the executive which, according to its well-established case-law, was, like impartiality, one of the guarantees inherent in the autonomous notion of "officer" within the meaning of Art 5(3) (*Moulin v France* App no 37104/06 (ECHR, 23 November 2010) § 57; *Medvedyev v France* App no 3394/03 (ECHR, GC, 29 March 2010)). But the Constitutional Council has expressed disagreement with Strasbourg in a line of cases. In an important judgment published on the 8th of December 2017 (Cons. const., n°2017-680 QPC, 8 December 2017), the Council held that, regarding to the public prosecutor, the principle of independence of the judicial authority (no individual instruction, principle of the opportunity of the prosecution …) was compatible with the powers given to the Government by the Art 20 of the Constitution (« *the Government shall determine and conduct the policy of the Nation* », which includes the power to determine the prosecution policy). This is also the position of the CJEU in the context of the European arrest warrant, see Joined Cases C-566/19 PPU and C-626/19 PPU *JR and YC* (CJUE, 12 December 2019).

For that reason, for a long time, the code of criminal procedure denied these persons defence rights, even where they were under police custody[7] (which can last up to 48 hours, in case of common offences) during the inquiry.[8] Consequently, the suspect has no remedies to challenge decisions made at this time of the procedure.

First of all, under an institutional perspective, national authorities involved in criminal proceedings are the district prosecutor for the inquiry and the investigating judge for the judicial investigation. To strengthen judicial control during this pre-trial stage, Law of 15 June 2000 for the protection of the presumption of innocence[9] created a new judicial institution: the liberties and custody judge (*juge des libertés et de la detention*, JLD), considered as "the judicial authority [which acts as a] guardian of the freedom of the individual". This judge takes all decisions on provisional detention in the judicial investigation and has responsibility for ordering and extending pre-trial detention (*détention provisoire*), according to Art 137-1 CPP. During the inquiry, the "general" police custody (*i.e.* the police custody until 48 hours) can be initiated by the police officer under the supervision of the district prosecutor; on the contrary, the exceptional police custody (over 48 hours and up to 144 hours in case of terrorism) can be triggered only by the JLD. In addition to these judicial authorities of first instance, relevant is also the role of the investigating chamber, which is in charge of all the questions relating to the legality or proportionality of the acts of the pre-trial stage in case of a judicial investigation (without prior preliminary inquiry, or after preliminary inquiry). If there is no judicial investigation, there is no remedy provided for the decisions made in the pre-trial stage. Contesting a breach of rights during the pre-trial stage is thus possible only before the trial judge.

In particular when it comes to the remedies available during the pre-trial stage, the question of criminal procedural rights is actually topical in French law at the moment. In this regard, an evolution can be observed with the gradual "*juridictionnalisation de l'enquête*", *i.e.* the introduction of a judicial control

7 Art 62-2 CPP provides that "the custody is a coercive measure decided by a judicial police officer, under the supervision of the judicial authority, with which a person against whom there exist one or more plausible reasons to suspect that they have committed or attempted to commit a crime or an offence punished with a imprisonment remains at the disposal of the investigators".

8 Duration that can be extended until 6 days in case of terrorism.

9 The law 2000-516 of 15 June 2000 reinforcing the protection of the presumption of innocence significantly reformed criminal justice and profoundly modified the different phases of criminal procedure. The aim was to improve the rights of defendants before the courts and to strengthen victims' rights.

for the inquiry phase. The influence of the European directives explains this development in the legislation, as well as in the French case-law.

6.2 The Implementation of EU Directives: State of Play

An overall analysis of the transposition of each directive into national law has led us to consider that French law is playing the game of transposition, even if not always with fully satisfactory results. First of all, a distinction must be made between the transposed Directives (Directive 2010/64: Right to interpretation and translation in criminal proceedings; Directive 2012/13: Right to information in criminal proceedings; Directive 2013/48: Right of access to a lawyer and to have a third party informed and Directive 2016/800: Procedural safeguards for juvenile defendants), and those that have not been transposed (Directive 2016/1919: Legal aid; Directive 2016/343: Presumption of innocence and of the right to be present at the trial).

6.2.1 *Transposed Directives*

Directive 2010/64 has been transposed into French law by the Law no 2013-711 of 5 August 2013. The code of criminal procedure already foresaw some provisions on the right to interpretation before the implementation of the Directive. But this right was considerably enhanced in 2013 with the law which completely transposed the Directive. The preliminary article of the code of criminal procedure now provides that a suspect or accused person who does not understand French has the right to be assisted by an interpreter throughout the proceedings, including during meetings with his or her lawyer, and to have essential documents translated. The analysis of the relevant legislation leads to the conclusion that transposition has generally been correctly enforced into domestic law. Upon this belief, at least, the Court of Cassation[10] refused to submit a preliminary ruling before the Court of Justice, thus showing the position of the French jurisdiction regarding the state of transposition of this Directive.

Directive 2012/13 has been transposed by the Law no 2014-535 of 27 May 2014. The analysis of the relevant legislation leads to the conclusion that the Directive has globally been correctly transposed into French law. Indeed, also in this regard, the Court of Cassation[11] refused to refer a question to the Court

10 Crim., 12 September 2017, n°17-83874.

11 Crim., 4 October 2016, n°16-8230.

of Justice, once again showing the position of the French jurisdiction regarding the state of transposition of this Directive.

Directive 2013/48 has been transposed in French law by Law no 2014-535 of 27 May 2014, Law no 2016-731 of 3 June 2016, and the Décret no 2016-1455 of 28 October 2016. The analysis of the relevant legislation leads to the conclusion that the Directive has been globally correctly transposed into French law.[12]

According to Art 2 of the Directive, the preliminary Article of the code of criminal procedure provides for that every person suspected or prosecuted "has the right to be informed of charges brought against him and to be legally defended". If the right to be assisted by a lawyer is fully granted in the judicial investigation (according to the Art 80-1, when the investigating judge wants to accuse the person, he puts her under judicial examination and must inform her that she can be assisted by a lawyer) as well as in the trial, the situation is different in the inquiry. There, the right to be assisted by a lawyer is provided only for persons that are suspected of having committed or attempted to commit an offence punished with an imprisonment penalty.

This approach is due to the fact that, in France, full defence rights are bound to the recognition of the role of party, a status that arises in French criminal procedure only with the beginning of the prosecution. During the inquiry, the person is not a party even if suspected. Indeed, French criminal procedure is characterised by three fundamental phases: a first phase of investigation is carried out by the judicial police. Then, on the basis of the evidence gathered, the public prosecutor will decide whether to open an inquiry, which leads to a phase of evidence gathering by a specialised judge, the *juge d'instruction*. Even though criminal proceedings must, in accordance with the preliminary article of the Code of Criminal Procedure, be fair and adversarial while preserving the rights of the parties, the rights granted to the person prosecuted during the inquiry phase are more restricted than at other stages of the proceedings.

In addition to the limitation of the right to access a lawyer, during the inquiry, the suspected has no right to access the materials of the case. The right to be informed, an essential condition for an adversarial proceeding, is only fully effective when the person is prosecuted and therefore has access to the case file. However, during the inquiry phase, a number of rights are recognised and communicated to the person placed in police custody[13] (*e.g.* right to a lawyer, right to an interpreter, right to inform a relative, right to have a medical assistance, right to remain silent …), as well as to the suspect who is heard freely[14]

12 Cf. French national report, 28 ff. <https://site.unibo.it/cross-justice/en>.

13 Art 63-1 Code of criminal procedure.

14 Art 61-1 Code of criminal procedure.

(right to leave the room at any time, right to remain silent, right to a lawyer when the offence is a felony or a misdemeanour punished by imprisonment).

Procedural infringements, however, can only be invoked if the investigation leads to proceedings: therefore, there is no specific remedy if the person remains a suspect (in the inquiry phase) without becoming a party in the investigative phase.

As for the Directive 2016/800, domestic law already provided special rules applicable when a child is suspected or accused in criminal proceedings, in addition to the provisions already applicable for all (adult) suspects.[15] An analysis of the relevant legislation leads to the conclusion that the Directive has been correctly transposed into French law.[16] Regarding the right to a lawyer and the right to have parental responsibility holders informed, the 2019 Law, as some literature points out,[17] "faithfully incorporates the provisions of the directive into national law".[18] In particular, the principle of separation from adults and the right to information and to be accompanied by the holders of parental authority are enshrined in domestic law. Moreover, with the new Law no 2019-222, transposing the Directive, the concept of the best interests of the child has officially been recognised into French juvenile criminal law. Also, the analysis of the case-law and of the legislation shows an increasing attention and protection in the field of juvenile law.[19]

6.2.2 *Non-Transposed Directives*

Concerning the Directives that have not been effectively transposed, they are not perceived as problematic in France, as the French government considered that their standards of protection are already satisfied in the existing

15 *Ordonnance du 2 février 1945 relative à l'enfance délinquante*, repealed and replaced since the 30 September 2021 by the Juvenile Criminal Justice Code – *Code de la justice pénale des mineurs*. The Directive has been transposed by the following texts which have amended some articles of the Ordonnance/Code: Law no 2019-222 of 23 March (Art 94); Law no 2016-1547 of 18 November 2016 (Art 31); Decree no 2019-507 of 24 May 2019.

16 Cf. French national report (n 12), 41 ff.

17 Eudoxie Gallardo, 'L'intérêt supérieur de l'enfant dans la loi du 23 mars 2019 de programmation 2018–2022 et de réforme pour la justice' (2019) Revue de science criminelle et de droit pénal comparé 758 : "La loi de 2019 (…) s'attache à inscrire en droit interne, fidèlement, les dispositions de la directive, tout en prenant acte de la décision du Conseil constitutionnel du 8 février 2019 relative à l'audition libre".

18 At a first reading, it is possible to observe that Art 6-2 of the *Ordonnance* together with Art D. 594-18 and D. 15-6-1 of the Code of Criminal Procedure (now Arts L311-1 to L311-5, D413-3 and D423-4 *Code de la justice pénale des mineurs*) are almost a literal reproduction of Arts 4, 5 and 12 of the Directive.

19 Cf. French national report (n 12), 54 ff.

law. Indeed, the analysis of the relevant internal legislation shows a substantial conformity with the Directives.

Directive 2016/1919, which should have been transposed by 25 May 2019, has not been transposed into national law. However, in the French legal system, a legislation on legal aid already existed before the enactment of the Directive,[20] so the legislator has not considered necessary to transpose it. An analysis of the relevant legislation leads to the conclusion that, despite the lack of transposition, national law is entirely consistent with the Directive.[21]

Directive 2016/343 should have been transposed before the 1st April 2018, but has not been transposed yet and, at the moment, there is no foreseeable project of implementation. An analysis of the relevant legislation leads to the conclusion that several provisions of the Directive are already effectively integrated into French law.[22] Three decisions of the Court of Cassation referring to the Directive also show that the French Supreme Court does not consider national law to be in contradiction with the Directive.[23] Nonetheless, as it will be argued below, some points do remain critical, especially the use of glass boxes and the lack of specific remedies in case of breach of the right to the presumption of innocence.

6.3 Main Critical Profiles in the Legislation and in the Case-law

From the analysis of the transposition of Directives into national law, three points are of outmost interest.

Firstly, it is interesting to examine the state of domestic law regarding directives that have not been transposed. As far as legal aid is concerned, no problem of conformity arises. French law is not only perfectly in line with the Directive, but also provides a scope broader than the European standards. However, more criticism emerges in relation to the presumption of innocence directive.

Secondly, it is interesting to note the increasing attention paid by French legislator to the rights of minors. Beyond the meticulous transposition of the Directive, the case law (especially the *Conseil constitutionnel*), does not

20 Loi n° 91-647 of 10 July 1991 *relative à l'aide juridique* and Décret n°91-1266 du 19 décembre 1991 *portant application de la loi n° 91-647 du 10 juillet 1991 relative à l'aide juridique.*

21 Cf. French national report (n 12), 59 ff.

22 Cf. French national report (n 12) 66 ff.

23 Crim., 11 December 2018, n° 18-85460; Crim., 28 November 2018, n°18-82010; Crim., 10 April 2019, n°18-83053.

hesitate to extend the rights to minors, sometimes even anticipating legislative measures.

Finally, a transversal analysis reveals the absence of specific remedies in case of violation of the rights protected by the Directives: for instance, in the investigation phase no remedies are available at all.

6.3.1 *The Right to Legal Aid*

The French legislator did not feel necessary to explicitly transpose the Directive 2016/1919, considering that the latter was already implemented in national law. As it has been explained,[24] the French approach to the implementation of criminal provisions stemming from Union law is characterised by the intention to make as few changes as possible to the domestic framework. As a result, if all EU standards are considered to be already met in national law, no internal measures will be adopted, as in case of the Directive on legal aid. Beyond what has been formally affirmed by the legislator, the national legislation appears to be effectively compliant, or even more safeguarding than the European standards. Indeed, the scope of legal aid provided by Law no 1-647 of 10 July 1991 is broader than the one enshrined in the Directive.

While the Directive is only addressed to suspected or accused persons, French law has a more general scope of application. This right is indeed granted to any party at any stage of the proceedings. As long as the person concerned has a right to be assisted by a lawyer and is eligible for legal aid (*e.g.* also the victim), legal aid is granted. National law on legal aid is indeed addressed to all "natural persons with insufficient resources to assert their rights in legal proceedings", and not only to the suspected or accused person. Differentiation based on the person's role in the trial (suspect, accused, assisted witness) or on her personal situation (vulnerable person, minor) is only related to less demanding criteria to be considered in order to assess his or her eligibility for legal aid.

On the other hand, in accordance with the Directive, French law applies a means test and a merit test to determine whether legal aid is to be granted. Even in this case, the conditions for receiving legal aid are less strict in French law than in EU legislation.

Firstly, aid is granted only if the person cannot cover the legal fees. The aid may be total or partial according to a means test, the level of which can be

24 Eliette Rubi-Cavagna, 'La transposition des directives de l'Union européenne en droit pénal français' (2019) 1 Archives de politique criminelle 147.

modified at the beginning of each year.[25] As provided for in the Directive, relevant and objective factors are taken into account, such as the income, capital and family situation of the person concerned. According to Art 4 of the Law no 91-647 of 10 July 1991, all resources are to be considered, including those of the spouse and persons usually living at home (unless the action is brought against the applicant for aid). As detailed in Art 5 of the law, movable or immovable property, even if they do not produce any income, are also taken into consideration, but those which could not be sold or pledged without "causing serious trouble to the person concerned" are excluded.

Secondly, aid may be granted only to persons whose action does not appear to be manifestly inadmissible, unfounded *or abusive due in particular to the number of requests, their repeated or systematic nature.*[26] However, the merit test is not required for the defendant, the person with civil liability, the witness, the suspect, the accused person, the condemned person and the person subject to the procedure of *comparution sur reconnaissance préalable de culpabilité.*[27]

In criminal proceedings, the means test provided by the Directive 2016/1919, which is set out in Art 7 of the Law of 10 July 1991, according to which the action "does not appear to be manifestly inadmissible, unfounded or abusive due in particular to the number of requests, their repeated or systematic nature" is not applicable to the defendant, the person with civil liability, the witness, the suspect, the accused or condemned person and the defendant in the procedure of *comparution sur reconnaissance préalable de culpabilité.*

Thus, the exception provided for in national law appears to be broader than the one in the Directive. The latter provides that the merit test shall be deemed to have been met (a) where a suspect or an accused person is brought before a competent court or judge in order to decide on detention at any stage of the proceedings within the scope of the Directive and (b) during detention. On the contrary, in domestic law, the exception concerns the defendant, the person with civil liability, the assisted witness, the person under investigation, the

25 Decree no. 91-1266 of 19 December 1991 implementing Law no. 91-647 of 10 July 1991 on legal aid details the conditions of resources – 1st section of the decree – and the ceiling of resources – Art 98.

26 Conditions in italics have been added by law n°2019-1479 of 28 December 2019.

27 The *comparution sur reconnaissance préalable de culpabilité* (procedure of prior recognition of guilt) is a procedure that enables the author of an offence who recognises the accusations to be tried quickly. This procedure is possible for all offences (not for crimes and contraventions), except those excluded by Art 495-7 of the code of criminal procedure. A penalty is proposed to the offender by the prosecutor. If the offender accepts, the judge validates the decision.

defendant, the accused, the convicted person and the person who is the subject of the proceedings on prior admission of guilt (*comparution sur reconnaissance préalable de culpabilité*). This exception, although certainly including the hypotheses provided for in the Directive, also encompasses other relevant situations.

6.3.2 *Presumption of Innocence*

Concerning the presumption of innocence, although domestic law appears to be globally in line with the Directive 2016/343, some compliance issues do arise.

On the one hand, the regime for the use of glass boxes and the question of compatibility with the presumption of innocence is a source of heated discussion. On the other hand, the absence of a specific remedy for the violation of the presumption of innocence also brings about some criticism. It is indeed difficult to understand why there is no law on the subject, given the jurisprudential debate and the interest of the government on the matter.[28]

Regarding the use of measures of physical restraint that the Directive 2016/343 strictly limits, France legislation provides that "No one may be forced to wear handcuffs or shackles unless he is considered to be a danger to others or himself, or liable to attempt to escape. In either case, all necessary measures compatible with the security requirements must be taken to prevent a person who is handcuffed or shackled from being photographed or filmed" (Art 803 French Code of criminal procedure). Moreover, Art 35ter of the Press Act of 1881[29] punishes with a fine up to 15,000 euros the diffusion without consent of the image of a suspected or accused person with handcuffs or shackles or which is under pre-trial detention.

Regarding more specifically the use of glass boxes, however, there is no specific legal provision, and this point is the most discussed point ; the main criticism regarding the absence of any transposition of the Directive in France. The 3rd of May 2012, the Union of the French lawyers[30] has indeed denounced the national position by a letter addressed to the European Commission. On its part, the Commission answered the 12th of June 2018, indicating that it will analyse the state of the French Law before deciding to trigger an infringement procedure before the Court of Justice (on which process there are still

28 Cf. the report submitted in October 2021 to the Minister of Justice by the working group on the presumption of innocence, Elisabeth Guigou, *La présomption d'innocence: un défi pour l'Etat de droit* (Ministère de la Justice, 2021) < https://www.vie-publique.fr/sites/default/files/rapport/pdf/281978.pdf> accessed 14 November 2021.

29 Loi du 29 juillet 1881 sur la liberté de la presse.

30 Syndicat des avocats de France, SAF.

no updates). The Union also attempted to initiate several procedures against France, lamenting the lack of transposition of the Directive, without any success.

On the 16th of October 2020, the *Conseil d'Etat*,[31] has considered inadmissible the application of the Syndicats des avocats de France (SAF). Firstly, the existing provisions in French law were considered sufficient: the preliminary Article of the French code of criminal procedure provides for a principle of strict necessity for coercive measures that can be accepted only under the control of a judge; Arts 309 and 318 of the code of criminal procedure regarding the hearing before the Assize court provide for that "the president maintains order in court and conducts the proceedings" and that "the accused appears free and only in the company of guards to prevent his escape"; Art 304 of the code embeds the principle of the presumption of innocence in the jurors' oath.[32] Consequently, the president of the court, in application of his power to maintain order, must guarantee the balance between the security of the participants to the trial and the necessity to prevent the accused person from escaping or communicating with third parties, on one hand, and the respect of defence rights on the other hand. The Directive does not prohibit the use of glass boxes as such, and authorises physical restraints in case of necessity. Moreover, the accused person has the possibility to contest a breach of the presumption of innocence by challenging a guilty verdict.

The *Conseil d'Etat* recently reiterated its position and validated the installation of glass boxes.[33] The highest administrative court rejected the appeal against the refusal to abrogate the Decree of 18 August 2016, which specifies the terms and conditions for installing glass boxes in hearing rooms.

Another source of criticism in French law is the lack of specific remedies for breaches of the right to remain silent or not to incriminate oneself.

The right to remain silent (Art 7(1) of the Directive) plays a significant role in many key stages of the procedure. Indeed, throughout the proceedings, the person has the choice "to make a statement, to be interrogated or to remain silent" (Arts 61-1 c. proc. pén. for free interrogation and 63-1 for police custody;

---

31 CE, 16 October 2020, 423954.

32 The Assize Court judges the authors of a crime (the most serious offence *e.g.* homicide). It is composed of judges and citizens drawn by lot (jurors). During the oath taken by the jurors before the court of assizes, the president of the court reminds them that the accused is presumed innocent, and that doubt must benefit him.

33 CE, 21 June 2021 – n° 418694. For an analysis of French case law, voir Raphaële Parizot, 'Box vitrés : feu de tout bois au nom de la présomption d'innocence, note about CE, 16 October 2020, n°423954 et Crim., 18 November 2020, n°20-84893' (2021) Revue de science criminelle et de droit pénal comparé 120.

Art 116 for the investigating judge; Art 328 for the Assize Court). The Criminal Chamber of the *Cour de cassation* has considered that the right to remain silent must be notified even if the legislation does not explicitly foresee it[34] and, at the same time, the Constitutional Council has repeatedly stressed the importance of this right and has censured the provisions of the Code of Criminal Procedure that did not ensure sufficient safeguards in this sense.[35]

The right not to incriminate oneself (Arts 7(2) and (3) of the Directive), on the other side, is not provided for in the code (the only reference to this right can be found in the preliminary article but under a specific formulation: "no decision of guilt can be pronounced against a person on the only basis of declarations made without the assistance of a lawyer").

Similarly, there is no specific provisions for the assessment of statements made by suspects or accused persons, or for evidence obtained in breach of the right to remain silent or the right not to incriminate oneself (Art 10(2)). Nonetheless, the case law has developed the idea, as required by the Directive, that the breach to fundamental rights as defence rights should lead to the exclusion of the evidence.

For instance, jurisprudence recognised a principle of fairness applicable to the search of evidence in relation to the right to remain silent. In this regard, provocation of a criminal offence by police officers is forbidden, as deemed contrary to the privilege against self-incrimination. Following this argument, the Court of Cassation has excluded that police can exploit a fake paedophile network to detect users.[36] This is true, however, only as long as the criminal conduct did not already exist. The privilege, indeed, does not cover the gathering of evidence, when the offence is committed or has already been committed, as long as this process is fair and does not lead the person to incriminate herself.

In respect of Art 7(3), according to an important and relevant case-law,[37] French police has the possibility to elaborate a stratagem in order to gather evidence, as long as this cannot be considered unfair. In the case at issue, a person complained about an attempt of extortion after receiving the threat of a 'sex tape' in which she appeared. To discover the identity of the authors, the

34 Crim., 14 May 2019, n°19-81408; Crim., 8 July 2020, n°19-85954; Crim., 24 February 2021, n°20-86537; Crim., 11 May 2021, n°21-81277; Crim., 26 May 2021, n°20-86382.

35 Cons. const., 4 March 2021, n°2020-886 QPC (art. 396 CPP); Cons. const., 9 April 2021, n°2021-895/901/902/903 QPC (art. 199 CPP); Cons. Const., 30 September 2021, n°2021-935 QPC (art. 145 CPP); Cons. Const., 30 September 2021, n°2021-934 QPC (art. 394 CPP).

36 Cass. crim., 7 February 2007, n° 06-87.753.

37 Assemblée plénière de la Cour de cassation, 9 December 2019, n°18-86767.

public prosecutor authorised a judicial police officer to negotiate by telephone with the suspects, pretending to be the representative of the supposed victim. The question brought before the plenary session of the Court of Cassation was whether and under what conditions public authorities may use a stratagem to obtain evidence of an offence. According to the Court, "the stratagem employed by a public official to establish an offence or identify its perpetrators does not in itself constitute an infringement of the principle of fairness of evidence. The only thing that is prohibited is a stratagem which, by circumventing or abusing a procedural rule, has the object or effect of vitiating the search for evidence by infringing one of the essential rights or fundamental guarantees of the person suspected or prosecuted". Thus, the Court of Cassation appears to be relatively tolerant with police stratagems. Any ploy used by the public authorities to gather evidence of an offence is not in itself an unfair procedure; it only becomes so if a procedural rule is circumvented, thereby infringing the rights of the accused (the rights of the defence).

As for the consequences of the behaviour of the suspect or accused person, French law does not provide for specific rules. When sentencing, there is no obligation to consider, for once, cooperative behaviour of suspects and accused persons. However, according to the principle of personalization of the penalty, the judge can of course take into account the behaviour of the offender during the proceedings. However, except the provision of the preliminary article ("no decision of guilt can be pronounced against a person on the only basis of declarations made without the assistance of a lawyer"), there is nothing in the legislation about the impossibility of using the right to remain silent or not to incriminate oneself against the suspects or accused persons.

6.3.3 *Juvenile Defendants*

Regarding juvenile law, through the analysis of the transposition of the Directive, it should be noted that the legislator, as well as the case law, is paying increasing attention to the rights of minors in criminal proceedings. Among the most important innovations concerning the juvenile law, we must refer to the right for the child to receive the assistance of a lawyer, when he or she is deprived of her liberty or when he or she is heard freely.

Concerning the assistance by a lawyer for minor placed in police custody, the *Loi de modernisation de la justice du XXIe, of 18 November 2016* rewrote Art 4, IV, of the *Ordonnance* of 2 February 1945, now Art L413-9 *Code de la justice pénale des mineurs*. Under the new law, the problem of inconsistency regarding the assistance of the minor from the beginning of police custody is now resolved. From now on, the minor must be assisted by a lawyer. Where the minor has not sought the assistance of a lawyer, this request may also be made by his or her legal representatives. In the absence of a request, the minor will receive a lawyer appointed by the court.

The *Conseil constitutionnel*[38] declared the provisions of the *Ordonnance*, as they were in force in 1984, to be contrary to the Constitution, as they did not provide sufficient guarantees to ensure that the rights of persons in police custody, especially minors, were respected. The declaration took effect on the date of publication of this decision. It is applicable to all cases not definitively decided up to that date. It remained up to the judge to assess the consequences of this declaration of unconstitutionality in the criminal proceedings that gave rise to the reference to the *Conseil constitutionnel*.

Concerning the assistance by a lawyer for minor heard without restrictions of personal liberty, on 8 February 2019, the *Conseil constitutionnel*[39] declared the provisions on free hearings for minors unconstitutional. The causes of the unconstitutionality were identified by the *Conseil* in the absence of a lawyer, the lack of information of legal representatives, the impossibility of requesting a medical examination during the free hearing. Otherwise, instead of providing for the minor to be assisted by a lawyer during this procedure, as it has been the case for police custody since the *Loi n° 2016-1547 du 18 November 2016* (transposing the same 2016 Directive), *Loi n° 2019-222* provides that when the investigation concerns a crime or offence punishable by imprisonment and the minor and his or her legal representative have not appointed a lawyer, the competent authority may appoint one (Art 3-1 of the *Ordonnance* and now Art L412-1 *Code de la justice pénale des mineurs*). The appointment is therefore not automatic, since it is subject to a proportionality test which requires the assistance of the lawyer to be assessed with regard to "the circumstances of the case, the seriousness of the offence, the complexity of the case and the measures likely to be adopted in relation to it, being understood that the best interests of the child always remain a primary consideration". The proportionality test derives from the 2016 Directive, Art 6(6), which precisely prescribes that derogations from the assistance of a lawyer may be made "provided that the right to a fair trial is respected".

There is therefore no obligation for the minor to be assisted by a lawyer during the unrestricted hearing, nor is there any change to Art 4-1 of the *Ordonnance*, which still provides that "the minor being prosecuted" (and not just suspected) is assisted by a lawyer. Art L12-4 of the new *Code de la justice*

38 Cons. const., 16 November 2018, n°2018-744 QPC.

39 Cons. const., 8 February 2019, n°2018-762 QPC.

pénale des mineurs confirms this position providing that a minor who is prosecuted or convicted is assisted by a lawyer.

The case law shows an ever-increasing attention and protection in juvenile justice. The *Conseil constitutionnel* has an important influence, as its decisions often anticipate legislative interventions in this domain or implement current guarantees to measures adopted under a previous regime. On 21 March 2019, two days before the *Loi n° 2019-222* came into force, the *Conseil constitutionnel*[40] deduced for the first time, from the 10th and 11th paragraphs of the Preamble to the 1946 Constitution, the requirement to protect the best interests of the child, imposing that minor present on national territory benefit from the legal protection attached to their age. This decision uses the expression "best interests of the child" for the first time.

Moreover, the necessity to carry out an examination of the child's personality is a fundamental principle recognised by the laws of the Republic laid down by the *Conseil constitutionnel* in 2002, establishing "the need to seek the educational and moral rehabilitation of minors through measures appropriate to their age and personality, ordered by a specialised court or in accordance with appropriate procedures".[41] The analysis of the personality of the child is foreseen by Art 8 of the *Ordonnance* (now Arts L322-1 to L322-7 *Code de la justice pénale des mineurs*), which establishes that the juvenile judge shall take all necessary steps and make all investigations to ascertain the truth and to obtain knowledge of the personality of the juvenile and the appropriate means for his or her rehabilitation. The juvenile judge will collect, through all investigative measures, information relating to the personality and the social and family environment of the juvenile.

The *Cour de cassation*, for its part, has specified the scope of certain provisions in juvenile criminal proceedings. First of all, the *Cour* clarified that the protection of the best interests of the child must always prevent a minor from being unduly considered as an adult. In order to do so, it reminds judges of the strict respect of the conditions and legal guarantees for the use of bone examination and specifies that any doubt must always benefit the minor.[42] If there is any doubt about the individual's age, as provided for in Art 3 of the Directive,[43]

---

40 Cons. const., 21 March 2019, n° 2018-768 QPC.

41 Cons. Const., 29 August 2002, n°2002-461 DC, since reiterated, in particular, on 3 March 2007, n°2007-553 DC; 10 March 2011, n°2011-625 DC; 8 July 2011, n°2011-147 DC; 4 August 2011, n°2011-635 DC.

42 Crim., 11 December 2019, n° 18-84.938.

43 Art 3 of the directive provides that "With regard to point (1) of the first paragraph, where it is uncertain whether a person has reached the age of 18, that person shall be presumed to be a child".

he should therefore be considered a minor and tried by the competent juvenile courts. The specific legislation on juvenile criminal law will apply.

Furthermore, even if the principle of best interests of the child is not explicitly mentioned, the *Cour de cassation* specifies in a recent decision that it is not up to the child to decide the person to whom the police custody measure should be communicated.[44] In the present case, the minor had appointed the head of the household, who was also the alleged victim of the offence, as his legal representative. The Court considered that informing the minor's legal representative, who was also the alleged victim of his violence, did not guarantee the conduct of proceedings that respected the minor's interests. The legal representative must instead be chosen only in the interest of the minor's defence.

The *Cour de cassation* has also specified that the debate for the placement in pre-trial detention must take place in the judge's chambers even if the defendant has reached the age of majority, when the accusation also concerns offences committed when he or she was a minor.[45] The guarantees applicable to minors can therefore be extended to adults, when some of the acts were committed when the person was a minor.

6.3.4 *Remedies*

An overall assessment of domestic law in relation to the Directives also leads to reflect on wider issues to be improved in their spirit. Among these questions, which are common and transversal to several domains, the most important one is probably about remedies.

It is indeed important to stress that French law has almost never provided specific remedies for breaches of rights established by the Directives. Among the few cases where the applicant has a specific remedy, there is the possibility, under Art 23 of the Law no 91-647 of 10 July 1991, that appeals against the decisions of the legal aid office may be made by the person concerned when the benefit of legal aid has been refused, has been granted only partially or has been withdrawn.[46] Another case of specific remedy must be mentioned: the specific civil protection of the presumption of innocence provided by Art 9-1 of the civil code states that "everyone is entitled to the presumption of innocence. When, before any sentence is pronounced, a person is publicly portrayed to be guilty of acts that are subject to an inquest or preliminary judicial

44 Crim., 17 June 2020, n° 20-80.065.

45 Crim., 21 January 2020, n° 19-86.957.

46 Arts 56 to 60 of the Decree provide detailed rules for appeals against the decisions of the offices.

investigation, the judge, even by summary proceedings and without prejudice to the right to recover indemnification for injury suffered, may prescribe any measures, such as the insertion of a correction or the circulation of a communiqué, in order to put an end to the infringement of the presumption of innocence, at the expense of the natural or juridical person responsible for that infringement". However, this remedy is rarely used.[47]

Besides these cases, no specific tools to challenge single decisions exist, but only general remedies, such as those provided by Art 802 of the code of criminal procedure: "In the event of violation of the forms prescribed by law on pain of nullity or failure to observe essential formalities, any court, including the Court of Cassation, which is seized of an application for annulment or which notes such an irregularity of its own motion may pronounce the nullity only when the effect of the latter has been to harm the interests of the party concerned".

It is true that the *Cour de cassation* has developed an important case law based on this provision. For example, on the right to remain silent, the Court considered that the lack of notification of such a right allows "*the* person concerned, in accordance with Art 802 of the Code of Criminal Procedure, from claiming in the course of the proceedings, in the event of the use of statements irregularly collected before the liberty and custody judge, that her interests in the administration of evidence have been prejudiced by the courts ordering a committal for trial or a conviction, in which case the judges must assess the fairness of the proceedings in their entirety".[48]

The question then becomes: does the absence of specific remedies in the legislation bear the risk of making national law non-compliant with European standards?

The issue arises even more strongly because of the lack of possible remedies during the investigation. In this phase, not only there are no specific remedies in case of violation of the rights contained in the Directives, but no remedies are possible at all. Indeed, if the person is suspected in an inquiry, she is not considered as a party. This is because the person had not and has not at her disposal any remedies to challenge decisions at this time of the procedure. An appeal may only be submitted if she becomes accused (and thus a party to the proceedings). Considering the breaches of rights during the judicial investigation (the person is then a party), the remedy is before the investigating chamber. As for breaches of rights during the inquiry, the remedy is before the

47 Cf. Guigou (n 28) 61 ff.

48 Crim., 11 May 2021, n°21-81277.

investigating chamber (only if a judicial investigation is carried out) or before the judge. It is important to stress that there is no specific remedy if the person remains a suspect without becoming accused. However, it is possible to note some progress, especially in what the doctrine calls the "*juridictionnalisation*" of the investigation. Thus, since the law of 23 March 2019, Art 802-2 CPP provides for that "the person who has been the subject of a search or a home visit pursuant to the provisions of this Code and who has not been prosecuted before an investigating or trial court at the earliest six months after the act was carried out may, within one year of the date on which he or she became aware of the measure, apply to the liberty and custody judge to have it annulled".

There is no doubt that this is a progressive step, but it is limited to one act of the procedure: searches. For the rest, no appeal is possible, as long as the person is not prosecuted. The absence of such a remedy may have important consequences, especially since most of the rights protected by those Directives find their natural place in the investigation phase and during the first phase of the proceedings.

6.4 Concluding Remarks

The analysis of the transposition of Directives about procedural rights of suspected or accused persons in criminal proceedings reveals that French law is playing the game of transposition, even if with sometimes uneven results. First of all, a distinction must be made between transposed directives (Directive 2010/64; Directive 2012/13; Directive 2013/48 and Directive 2016/800) and those that have not been transposed (Directive 2016/1919 and Directive 2016/343).

Regarding the Directives that have actually been transposed, a distinction must first be made between those that have been expressly transposed (Directives 2010/64 and 2012/13) and those that have been less explicitly transposed because they are not indicated as such in the title of the law or the heading (Directive 2013/48 and 2016/1919). From a legislative point of view, it would have been preferable the use of explicit transposition, which contributes to simplifying the already complex process of assessing the conformity of domestic law with the Directives. Explicitly transposition can indeed constitute a factor of clarity and intelligibility.

Anyway, the analysis shows that, overall, the national provisions comply to a certain extent with the Directives and meet the expectations of European law.

On one side, however, a careful evaluation of the domestic law in relation to the different Directives allows nonetheless to consider that certain points, often details, are missing in the internal legislation. To give just some examples, as regards the Directive 2010/64 the possibility to a waiver of the right to translation of essential documents (Art 3(8)) has not been transposed in French law. As far as the Directive 2012/13 is concerned, Art 7, that requires to ensure an access at least to all material evidence in possession of the competent authorities, whether for or against suspects or accused persons, has not been transposed. Concerning Directive 2013/48, the impossibility of judicial review in case of temporary derogation from the assistance of a lawyer is contrary to provisions of Art 8(2) of the Directive. However, it should be noted that these aspects are also not very clearly regulated by the Directive either.

On the other side, an overall assessment of domestic law in relation to the Directives also leads to reflect on broader issues to be improved concerning the spirit of the norms; issues which are common and transversal to several domains, like those illustrated about remedies. Indeed, French law does not provide for specific remedies in the event of a breach under the Directive, but only general remedies. Moreover, there is no remedy at all during an inquiry because, at this moment, the suspected person is not considered as a party.

Concerning the Directives that have not been effectively transposed, they are not perceived as problematic in France, since the French government considers that the Directives' provisions have been already included in the pre-existing law. In general, the analysis of the relevant internal legislation shows a substantial conformity with the standards of the Directives. The pre-existing legislation on legal aid in France seems to have an almost larger scope than the Directive 2016/1919, which fully justifies the lack of transposition. Concerning the presumption of innocence, although domestic law appears to be globally in line with the Directive 2016/343, some compliance issues arise. In particular, the regime for the use of glass boxes and the question of compatibility with the presumption of innocence is a source of heated discussion.

From a case law perspective, although there are several judgements in this field, very few decisions explicitly refer to the Directives. This is partly because in the few cases where the *Cour de cassation* reviewed French law in light of EU law, national legislation has come across as being fully compliant.[49] However,

49 See Crim., 4 October 2016, n°16-82309; Crim., 31 January 2017, n°16-84623: the *Cour de cassation* denies to seek a preliminary ruling to the Court of Justice of the European Union considering the Directive of 2012 has been correctly transposed and that there is no breach to the right to defence about the notification of the materials facts and about the access of the entire file. Cf. also Crim., 12 September 2017, n°17-83874: the Court of Cassation notes that the provisions of Directives 2010/64/EU of the European Parliament and of the Council of 20 October 2010 and 2013/48/EU of 22 October 2013 have been transposed into national law by Laws 2013-711 of 5 August 2013, 2014-535 of 27 May 2014 and 2016-731 of 3 June 2016.

this is mainly due to the fact that French practitioners are still relatively unfamiliar with EU law. It is therefore important to raise awareness in France of the importance of the innovative potential of EU standards in an area as sensitive as criminal proceeding.

CHAPTER 7

Germany

Between Laissez-Faire and Literal Regulation – The German Approach to the Implementation of the Directives on Defence Rights

Anna H. Albrecht and Anne Schneider

7.1 Introduction

As one of the founding members of the European Union, Germany has always supported further integration and harmonization of the law, provided that fundamental rights are guaranteed. The implementation of the six Directives on defence rights in criminal proceedings should therefore not have caused any problems. However, the following analysis shows that the German legislator used two different approaches for implementing the Directives, which have both caused friction in German law, as well as shortcomings in the implementation of the Directives.[1]

7.2 The Implementation of EU Directives: State of Play

All EU Directives have been implemented into German law by amendments to existing codifications, primarily the Code of Criminal Procedure (CCP), the Court Constitution Act (CCA) and, when applicable, the Youth Courts Act (YCA). Only two were transposed in time (Directive 2010/64 and 2012/13), the transposition of all others was at least several months after the expiration of the implementation deadline.

Most of the guarantees of the Directives 2010/64 and 2012/13 had previously already been laid down in German law. Thus, the legislator made only minor changes to transpose the Directives, through the Act on Strengthening the Procedural Rights of Defendants in Criminal Proceedings (*Gesetz zur Stärkung der Verfahrensrechte von Beschuldigten im Strafverfahren*).[2] However, the implementation of Directive 2010/64 fell short of the Directive's requirements

1 This chapter is based on a report that was prepared for the CrossJustice project and, in part, contains literally the same passages.

2 Act of 2 July 2013, BGBl. (Federal Law Gazette) 2013 I, 1938 and in effect since 06 July 2013.

 | DOI:10.1163/9789004513396_009

as regards the documents to be translated, whereas the transposition of the 2012 Directive shows minor shortcomings *e.g.* regarding the right to information on the accusation.

When implementing Directive 2013/48 through the Second Act on Strengthening the Procedural Rights of Defendants in Criminal Proceedings (*Zweites Gesetz zur Stärkung der Verfahrensrechte von Beschuldigten im Strafverfahren*),[3] the German legislator again took the view that German law already complied with most requirements of the Directive. Accordingly, there were only minor changes made to the law. Mostly, the transposition laws were convincing but the rules on confidentiality make the implementation partly insufficient.

Many provisions of Directive 2016/800 on the rights of juvenile defendants were explicitly and correctly transposed through the Act on Improving Procedural Guarantees of the Defendant in Criminal Proceedings of Juveniles (*Gesetz zur Stärkung der Verfahrensrechte von Beschuldigten im Jugendstrafverfahren*),[4] leading to substantive changes of the law. However, the transposition of the right of assistance by a lawyer (Art 6), which is one of the crucial guarantees in the Directive, is not completely convincing. In this respect, frictions between the traditional system of defence in German juvenile law and the EU law become apparent.

The implementation of Directive 2016/1919 through the Act on a New Regulation of the Rules on Mandatory Defence (*Gesetz zur Neuregelung des Rechts der notwendigen Verteidigung*)[5] leaves a lot to be desired. Although a merits test, instead of a means test, is allowed by the Directive, the implementation of such rules into the regime of mandatory defence has not been successful.

Lastly, the transposition of Directive 2016/343 has proven to be insufficient, above all because the requirements for the protection of the presumption of innocence have not been implemented in German law, although they had not been laid down previously either. The right to be present, by contrast, had already largely been guaranteed before under German law, which therefore has undergone only minor adjustments in implementation of the Directive through the Act to Strengthen the Right of the Accused to be Present at the Trial (*Gesetz zur Stärkung des Rechts des Angeklagten auf Anwesenheit in der Verhandlung*).[6]

3 Act of 27 August 2017, BGBl. 2017 I, 3295 and in effect since 05 September 2017.

4 Act of 9 December 2019, BGBl. 2019 I, 2146 and in effect since 17 December 2019.

5 Act of 10 December 2019, BGBl. 2019 I, 2128, and in force since 13 December 2019.

6 Act of 17 December 2018, BGBl. 2018 I, 2571, in force since 21 December 2018.

7.3 Main Critical Profiles in the Legislation

The focus of the German legislator when implementing the Directives was to integrate them into existing German law. The German legal system is a civil law system that relies heavily on codifications. All major areas of law are regulated by a code. The advantages of codification are that the applicable law is easier to find for foreign lawyers, and that such a system tends to be more coherent. This makes the integration of supranational law particularly challenging.

Bearing these considerations in mind, it is possible to identify two different approaches to implementing the Directives. With some Directives, the legislator has widely assumed that there was no need for transposition, since the current law already largely met the requirements of the Directives. These are the Directives that provide broad guarantees that are also found in the ECHR (presumption of innocence, right to information, right of access to a lawyer, right to interpretation, Art 6(2), (3), let (a), (c), (e), ECHR).[7] This approach can be called the *laissez-faire approach*.

Other Directives required major amendments to existing law by providing detailed information, although the rights themselves were already accepted in German law. Here, the legislator often stuck to the wording of the Directives, thus creating frictions with existing law. This approach can be called the *literal regulatory approach*.

Both approaches are problematic. The following paragraphs will analyse the two approaches in German implementation laws and show, by means of examples, the problems attached to each of them.

7.3.1 *The Laissez-Faire Approach*

All Directives are based on guarantees that are more or less explicitly laid down in the European Convention on Human Rights (Art 6(1, 3) ECHR). After its ratification, in Germany the guarantees of the Convention have the status of an ordinary statute. According to the settled case-law of the Federal Constitutional Court, however, they influence the interpretation of the fundamental rights and constitutional principles of the Basic Law. The text of the ECHR and the case-law of the ECtHR serve as interpretative aids for determining their content and scope. Thus, within the framework of a methodology-based interpretation, German courts must give priority to an interpretation that is in line with the Convention. They must also take into account the relevant case-law

7 See, e.g., *Cleve v. Germany* App no. 48144/09 (ECHR, 15 January 2015); *Dridi v. Germany* App no. 35778/11 (ECHR, 26 July 2018); *Öztürk v. Germany* App no. 8544/79 (ECHR, 21 February 1984).

of the ECtHR, *i.e.* they must take note of it, include it in the decision-making process and consider it appropriately.[8]

It is therefore not surprising that many rights contained in the Directives were already respected in German law. The legislator's assessment that a change of law was not necessary[9] is correct in many cases. However, a closer look reveals that there are several examples in the implementation law which show that the legislator's *laissez-faire* approach led to wrongful implementation of the Directives and thus to a violation of EU law.

7.3.1.1 Right to Information and Penal Orders

Art 6(3), Directive 2012/13 states an obligation of the Member States to inform the suspect of the criminal offence that they are suspected to have committed and the accusation. The legislator stated that German law already mostly complied with the Directive and made only minor changes to the law.[10] However, in doing so, the problem of penalty orders (sections 407 ff. CCP)[11] was overlooked.

A penalty order imposes a sanction on written application by the public prosecution office without a main hearing. The penalty order may, accordingly, be the first opportunity for the accused to be informed of the accusation against him. Section 410 CCP grants them a two-week period to lodge an objection to the penalty order to defend themself against the accusation, and prevent it from becoming legally binding, bringing about a regular hearing. Section 132 CCP obliges an accused person not residing in Germany to appoint a person authorised to accept service of a penalty order concerning him, with the period for lodging an objection against that order running from the service of that order on that authorised person. Thus, the period to file an objection would be reduced by the time needed by the appointed representative to transmit the penalty order to its addressee. If the order is received by the addressee after the expiration of the period for lodging an objection, it would become final and enforceable even without the knowledge of the addressee.

As the Court of Justice has held in its judgments *Covaci*[12] and *Tranca et al.*[13] the relevant German law must therefore be interpreted in such a way that

---

8 For further details, see the key decision *Görgülü* BVerfGE 111, 307 (German Federal Consitutional Court).

9 See, *e.g.*, BT-Drucks. 17/12578, 7 (legislative materials of the *Bundestag*).

10 BT-Drucks. 17/12578, 8.

11 An English version of the CCP provided by the Ministry is available at <https://www.gesetze-im-internet.de/englisch_stpo/englisch_stpo.html#p2507> accessed 7 November 2021.

12 Case C-216/14 *Covaci* (CJEU, 15 October 2015).

13 Joined Cases C-124/16, C-188/16, C-213/16, 22/03/2017 *Tranca et al.* (CJEU, 22 March 2017).

the addressee of the penalty order is entitled to the full period for lodging an objection from the date on which they receive the penalty order and, if necessary, is to be granted *restitutio in integrum*. In contrast to the otherwise higher requirements for a *restitutio*, the mere knowledge of the penalty order should suffice as a sufficient reason.[14]

However, it follows from this approach that the penalty order would, after expiry of the regular objection period, initially become final and enforceable. In its judgment *UY*,[15] the Court therefore held that the Art 6 precluded a legislation under which a person residing in another Member State, if the person does not comply with an order imposing a driving ban on the person from the date on which that order became final, is subject to a criminal penalty, even though that person had no knowledge of the existence of the order.

This example shows that the German legislator had completely overlooked the problems attached to penalty order proceedings when implementing the Directive.

7.3.1.2 Confidentiality of Lawyer-Client Communication

Art 4 Directive 2013/48 provides for confidentiality between suspects or accused persons and their lawyer. In German law, section 148 CCP is the general rule guaranteeing confidentiality between the defendant and their lawyer. The German legislator saw no need to implement Art 4 further because section 148(1) CCP provided sufficient protection of confidentiality for the purpose of the Directive.[16]

However, this assessment is not completely correct. It is true that section 148(1) CCP, albeit formulated differently, gives sufficient protection of lawyer-client communication. However, section 148(2) CCP provides an exception in terrorist cases: Communication is only allowed if the person agrees to having the communication checked by the court. Such an exception to confidentiality was hinted at in Recital (33) of Directive 2013/48, but it was removed from the text of Art 4. This means that Art 4 does not allow for exceptions. Accordingly, section 148(2) CCP is in breach of Art 4, and therefore not applicable.[17]

---

14 Cf. Thomas Wahl, 'Die EU-Strafverfahrensrechtsrichtlinien vor deutschen Gerichten' (2017) 7 Eucrim 50.

15 Case C-615/18 *UY v Staatsanwaltschaft Offenburg* (CJEU 14 May 2020).

16 BT-Drucks. 18/9534, 15.

17 Anne Schneider, 'Richtlinie 2013/38/EU – III D 18' in Heinrich Grützner, Paul-Günter Pötz, Claus Kreß and Nikolaos Gazeas (eds), *Internationaler Rechtshilfeverkehr in Strafsachen* (40th installment December 2016, C.F.Müller), margin note 67; Thomas Knierim and Anna Oehmichen 'Chapter 17' in Thomas Knierim et al. (eds) *Gesamtes Strafrecht aktuell* (Nomos 2018) margin note 17.

Another problematic constellation is the case that the lawyer is suspected to be involved in the crime. Again, Recital (33) claims that this might be a reason for an exception to the confidentiality rights, but Art 4 does not allow for one. Here, the solution must be to exclude the lawyer as such, which ends confidentiality rights.

Art 4 makes clear that confidentiality must be guaranteed no matter how communication takes place. Section 148 CCP is interpreted in the same way. However, German Law knows several specific investigative measures, *e.g.* for search and seizure (section 94 CCP), telecommunication surveillance (section 100a CCP), covert remote search of internet technology systems (§ 100b CCP) etc. Some of these have special rules on the protection of privileged witnesses, which includes defence lawyers.[18] Sometimes, these special rules offer less protection than section 148 CCP. This is especially true for section 97 CCP, the privilege from seizure. According to the wording of section 97 CCP, written communication between the defendant and their lawyer is excluded from seizure, but only if the lawyer is in possession of the communication.[19] It is generally accepted in German law that this restriction does not apply to the relationship between the accused and the defence lawyer and that communication must also be protected if it is possessed by the defendant by means of applying section 148 CCP.[20] This is also well-established case law.[21] However, this interpretation is not written down in the law and might be difficult to figure out for people who are not familiar with German Criminal Procedure Law. In this respect, the implementation is not transparent.[22]

18 These are sections 81(3), 95(2)2, 97(1-3), 100d(5), 100g(4) and 160a(1) CCP.

19 See section 97(2) CCP: "These restrictions shall only apply if these objects are in the custody of a person entitled to refuse to testify, unless the object concerned is an electronic health card as defined in section 291a of the Fifth Book of the Social Code (*Sozialgesetzbuch V*). The restrictions on seizure shall not apply if certain facts give rise to the suspicion that the person entitled to refuse to testify participated in the offence or in handling stolen data, aiding after the fact, obstructing prosecution or punishment, or handling stolen goods, or if the objects concerned were derived from an offence or have been used or are intended for use in committing an offence or if they emanate from an offence."

20 Matthias Jahn '§ 148'in Jens-Peter Becker et al. (eds) *Löwe-Rosenberg. Kommentar zur Strafprozessordnung*, vol 4 (27th edn, De Gruyter 2021) margin note 26. For more detail, see Sabine Konrad, *Die Beschlagnahme von Verteidigungsunterlagen* (Peter Lang 2000) 241 ff.; Jörg Oesterle, *Die Beschlagnahme anwaltlicher Unterlagen und ihre Bedeutung für die Compliance-Organisation von Unternehmen* (Duncker & Humblot 2016) 194 ff.

21 *E.g.* BVERFG NJW 2002, 1410 (1410); BVERFG StraFo 2015, 61 (63 Rn. 22 ff.); BGH NJW 1973, 2035 (2035).

22 Schneider (n 17) margin note 99; Anne Schneider, *Strafprozessuale Ermittlungsmaßnahmen und Zeugnisverweigerungsrechte* (Mohr Siebeck 2020) 398 ff.

This example shows, again, how the superficial identity of guarantees to be protected has led the German legislator to refrain from amendments that were necessary under EU law. Moreover, the legislator has shown a strong reliance on established case-law and a reluctance to adopt a clarifying provision, especially in the context of lawyer-client confidentiality. Considering that case-law is, in principle, not binding in German law and that the application of this case-law requires in-depth knowledge of German criminal procedure law, this approach falls short of the desired outcome – to improve defence rights in the European Union.

7.3.1.3 Presumption of Innocence

Art. 3(5) of Directive 2016/343 contains provisions on the presumption of innocence. The only explicit formulation of the presumption of innocence in German law can be found in Art 6(2) ECHR. However, it is generally recognised that the presumption of innocence is also enshrined in the Basic Law (*Grundgesetz*, the German Constitution), especially in principle of the rule of law in Article 20(3) BL[23] and presupposed in several provisions, particularly in the CCP. The national legislator, therefore, saw no need for implementation.[24]

As a result, the details of these warranties are not explicitly specified. As the Federal Constitutional Court (*Bundesverfassungsgericht*) states, the presumption of innocence prohibits, in actual criminal proceedings, the imposition of measures on the accused which have the effect of imposing a punishment and treating the accused as guilty in procedural terms, without proof of guilt being established according to the rules of procedure. It also requires proof of guilt to be established in a final judgment before it can be generally invoked against the accused in legal proceedings.[25] The essence of the guarantee therefore concerns the treatment of the accused in criminal proceedings.

However, it must also be taken into account by other public authorities. The presumption of innocence therefore, in accordance with Art 4(1) 1 of the Directive, forbids statements by a public official concerning a person accused of a crime, that reflect the view that the person is guilty before legal proof of guilt has been established.[26] The same results from Art 6(2) ECHR.[27] It is therefore fair to assume that Art 4(1) of the Directive is complied with in the German

23 BVerfGE 19, 342, 347 f.; 35, 311, 320; 74, 358, 369 ff.; 74, 358, 370; 82, 106, 118 ff.; 110, 1, 22 f.; 111, 307, 323 f; BR-Drucks. 384/18, 9 (legislative materials of the *Bundesrat*).

24 BR-Drucks. 384/18, 9, BT-Drucks. 19/446, 9.

25 BVerfGE 35, 311, 320; 74, 358, 369 f.

26 BGH NJW 2016, 3670.

27 *El Kaada v. Germany* App no 2130/10 (ECHR, 12 November 2015).

legal system. In accordance with Art 4(2) of the Directive, in cases of a violation of the presumption of innocence in criminal proceedings, the accused may challenge court decisions with the usual legal remedies, challenge the judge for fear of bias and file a constitutional complaint once all legal remedies have been exhausted. If public communications by courts and authorities violate the presumption of innocence, the person concerned can take action before the administrative courts;[28] in addition, they may claim damages from official liability.[29]

No. 4a of the German directives on Criminal and Administrative Fine Proceedings (*Richtlinien für das Strafverfahren und das Bußgeldverfahren*-RiStBV) instructs the public prosecution office not to unnecessarily expose the accused. This can be understood to also prohibit the presentation of a suspect as being guilty as laid down in Art 5(1) of Directive 2016/343. This should as well follow from the principle of proportionality that is constitutionally anchored in the principle of the rule of law and/or in the fundamental rights laid down in the BL.

It is significant that the only clear provision implementing the Directive is No. 4a RiStBV. Yet, the RiStBV are administrative regulations without legal force, therefore ranking lower than formal statues such as the CCP.

They are issued by the Federal Ministry of Justice and Consumer Protection, are primarily aimed at the public prosecution office and the police and are intended to ensure a uniform approach in the relevant procedures. The lack of clear and binding regulation has several disadvantages: Beyond the obvious essence of the guarantee, it might make the individual specifications appear less susceptible to change. Moreover, it could give rise to the risk that the addressees of the guarantees are not sufficiently aware of the requirements to be observed in their particular situation. Therefore, it is to be doubted that the respective guarantees as laid down in Chapter 2 of the Directive are implemented sufficiently clear and precise.[30]

7.3.1.4 Remedies

All Directives require legal remedies to be in place in case of violations of the procedural rights guaranteed in the Directives.[31] The nature of the remedies is

28 BGH StV 2018, 208.

29 BR-Drucks. 384/18.

30 See also Momme Buchholz, 'Die Selbstbelastungsfreiheit im Lichte der EU-Richtlinie 2016/343 vom 932016' (2018) 19 HRRS 457.

31 See Art. 2(5) Directive 2010/64, Art. 8(2) Directive 2012/13, Art. 12 Directive 2013/48, Art. 10 Directive 2016/343, Art. 19 Directive 2016/800, Art. 8 Directive 2016/1919.

left to the Member States. Accordingly, the German legislator referred to existing legal remedies.

The problem with this approach is that the regulation on legal remedies in criminal procedure law is sketchy and complicated to understand. For instance, the accused may submit an application for a court decision in accordance with section 98(2) 2 CCP in order to review the legality of an investigative measure ordered by the public prosecution office, or of the manner in which a judicial or non-judicial investigatory measure is carried out (*e.g.* in case of a breach of confidentiality). According to its wording, section 98(2) 2 CCP applies only to the seizure. However, case law has moved to by analogy extend the scope of application to other coercive measures including measures already carried out.[32] Any judicial measure issued by a court at first instance or in appeal proceedings can generally be challenged by means of a(n) (immediate) complaint in accordance with section 304 (311) CCP (*e.g.* applicable for mandatory defence). Although the wording of section 304 CCP only refers to judicial decisions, the complaint is admissible against all judicial measures issued by a court at first instance or in appeal proceedings, unless they fall under a statutory exception.

The accused can also lodge an appeal or appeal on points of law, sections 333, 335 CCP. An appeal on points of law will lead to a review of errors of law and only exceptionally includes a hearing. It should be noted that the revision must meet high formal requirements. Pursuant to section 344 (2) sentence 2 CCP, a revision which raises procedural defects must indicate the facts containing the defect. This is interpreted in practice as meaning that the statement of grounds of appeal must state all the facts constituting the procedural defect, so that the appellate court must be able to determine whether the complaint is justified on the basis of the statement of grounds alone. In principle, an appeal on points of law will only be successful if the judgment is based on an error of law, *i.e.* if there is at least the possibility that the outcome would have been different had the proceedings been free of errors of law. However, section 338 CCP contains a list of errors so fundamental, that it is legally presumed that the error has influenced the judgment (so-called absolute revision grounds). The most relevant provision is no. 8, according to which the influence of the error is presumed "if the defence was inadmissibly restricted by an order of the court on a question which is important for the decision". This provision might apply in case of a violation of the defence rights.

---

32 BGHSt 44, 171.

What is lacking in German law is a rule on the admissibility of evidence that has been gathered in violation of the Directives. If the defence rights were violated, *e.g.* if an interpreter or the lawyer was not present at the interrogation of the defendant, the court would have to assess whether the violation of the law leads to the exclusion of this particular piece of evidence. In German law, evidence that was collected illegally is not automatically excluded but only if the violation of fundamental rights outbalances the public interest in prosecution.[33] The outcome of this balancing test is hard to predict for the procedural guarantees contained in the Directives. Therefore, it is unclear under which circumstances evidence that was obtained in breach of the rights contained in the Directive is not admitted in court.

Furthermore, German case law requires the accused or his defence counsel to raise objections to the admission of evidence immediately at the first (or second) instance trial in order not to be precluded from raising them in an appeal on points of law.[34] Even if a violation does lead to the exclusion of the evidence (*e.g.*, violations of the duty to inform the accused *inter alia* about their right to remain silent or violations of the right of access to a lawyer), the defendant can only invoke this on appeal if they or their defence counsel have objected to the use of the statement in the hearing at first instance.

This overview shows that the effectiveness of the legal remedies provided by German law is doubtful. Remedies, apart from appeals against judgements, are far from being clearly regulated. This concerns, for example, the question of which court decisions can be appealed against with an (immediate) complaint. Nor is it apparent from the legislation in the CCP that, by analogous application of section 98(2) sentence 2 CCP, a court decision can be sought with regard to the manner in which certain investigative measures are carried out. The same is true for the need to object to the admissibility of evidence, which is not written down in the Code of Criminal Procedure but is the result of case-law. Finally, it is always difficult to predict in which cases evidence that was collected illegally will be excluded.

All these inconsistencies make the implementation of the rules on remedies unconvincing.

7.3.2 *The Literal Regulatory Approach*

While it was possible to refrain from adopting new legal provisions in some cases, some guarantees required a change of law. In these cases, the legislator

33 Sabine Gleß 'Germany: Balancing the truth against protected constitutional interests' in Stephen C. Thaman (ed) *Exclusionary rules in Comparative Law* (Springer 2013) 113, 166 ff.

34 BGHSt 38, 214, 225; BGH NJW 1997, 2893.

often stuck close to the wording of the Directive. In principle, this approach is the safe option and worked fine in most cases. However, a close orientation on the wording of the Directive sometimes has to the opposite effect when the meaning of a word differs in the context of supranational and national law. The following examples focus on problematic implementations.

7.3.2.1 Translation of Documents

Art 3, Directive 2010/64 contains a right to have essential documents translated. This article was transposed in section 187(2) CCA.[35]

Although section 187 CCA mostly takes up the wording of Art 3, it has been criticized severely in German academic writings. One point of criticism is that the concept of "judgment" as used in the Directive is to be understood broadly, whereas German law limits the obligation to translate to judgments in the strict sense. This obligation would therefore not cover decisions terminating proceedings apart from judgments in the narrow sense, especially '*Beschlüsse*',[36] which *e.g.* are issued under section 206a Code of Criminal Procedure, if a final obstacle to proceedings becomes apparent after the opening of the main proceedings but before the main hearing is held. A corresponding obligation is indeed laid down in No. 181(2) RiStBV, as mentioned, however, just an administrative regulation. Therefore, an interpretation in line with the Directive is suggested, which is based on the concept of essentiality and focuses on the meaning of the individual document.[37]

It is also objected that the right to translation is limited to non-appealable judgments. The German legislator considers this to be in conformity with the Directive, as the temporal scope of application of the Directive as set out in Art 2(1) only extends to the conclusion of the proceedings.[38] However, this

---

35 Section 187(2) CCA: "As a rule, a written translation of orders involving deprivation of liberty as well as of bills of indictment, penal orders and non-binding judgments shall be necessary for the exercise of the rights under the law of criminal procedure of an accused who does not have a command of the German language. An excerpted written translation shall be sufficient if the rights of the accused under the law of criminal procedure are thereby safeguarded. The written translation shall be made available to the accused without delay. An oral translation of the documents or an oral summary of the content of the documents may be substituted for a written translation if the rights of the accused under the law of criminal procedure are thereby safeguarded. As a rule, this can be assumed if the accused has defence counsel."

36 Mustafa Oğlakcıoğlu, '§ 187 GVG' in Christoph Knauer (ed) *Münchener Kommentar zur StPO*, vol 3 (2018) margin number 18.

37 ibid. margin number 19; Anne Schneider, 'Der Anspruch des Beschuldigten auf schriftliche Übersetzung wesentlicher Unterlagen' (2017) 35 StV 379, 383 ff.

38 BT-Drucks. 17/12578, 11.

understanding is too narrow. In European law the right of appeal is not to be understood technically and can also cover extraordinary legal remedies.[39] Moreover, the German system, according to which judgments can become final before the defendant has been served a written version, is peculiar and probably not what the EU legislator planned for.[40] The temporal scope of application of the Directive thus extends beyond the force of law; the defendant must therefore also be able to demand a translation of final judgments, which is why the German law and case-law falls short of the protection guaranteed by the Directive.

The presumption in section 187(2) 5 CCA, that the procedural rights of the accused are also safeguarded in the case of a mere oral translation or oral summary of the contents of the documents if the accused has a defence counsel, misunderstands Art 3(7) of the Directive and considerably restricts the protection intended in it. The legislator assumed that, as a rule, consultation with the defence counsel already enabled an accused without sufficient command of the language to exercise their rights of defence and sufficiently ensured a fair trial; it would also avoid delaying the proceedings by providing a written translation of the judgment after the written grounds of the judgment have been drafted. An exception was to be made when the accused had a legitimate interest in a written translation which they could express by requesting it.[41] This deviation from the Directive is rightly considerably criticised in the literature. Section 187(2) 5 CCA reverses the relationship of rule and exception as laid down in Art 3(7) of the Directive. Also, the defence counsel usually does not have sufficient factual knowledge to compensate for the loss of information due to the limited translation. Furthermore, it is not compatible with the fact that the accused has a right to translation of even the communication with the defence counsel. Finally, the shift to the lawyer is also contrary to the principle that the translation should be free of charge regardless of the outcome of the proceedings.[42]

This example shows that the legislator cannot be careful enough when relying on the wording of the Directive. The notion of 'judgment' and the reference

---

39 Schneider (n 37) 380 ff.; approvingly Helmut Frister, '§ 187 GVG' in Jürgen Wolter (ed) *Systematischer Kommentar zur Strafprozessordnung*, vol 9 (2016) margin number 11; Oğlakcıoğlu, (n 37) margin number 18.

40 Schneider (n 37) 381.

41 BT-Drucks. 17/12578, 12.

42 Ulrich Eisenberg, 'Gesetz zur Stärkung der Verfahrensrechte Beschuldigter im Strafverfahren« – Bedeutung und Unzuträglichkeiten' (2015) 10 JR 442, 445; Oğlakcıoğlu (n 37) margin number 19; Schneider (n 37) 382.

to the 'conclusions of proceedings' should have been interpreted in the context of EU law, not in the national context. Moreover, the structure of the exceptions was changed when they were integrated into German law which leads to partial incompatibility with the Directive.

7.3.2.2 Right to Legal Aid and Mandatory Defence

Art 4 Directive 2016/1919 contains the crucial guarantee on legal aid in criminal proceedings. According to Art. 4(2) of the Directive, Member States are free to apply either a means test, or a merits test. German law has always based the rules on mandatory defence purely on a merits test, and the legislator saw no need to change the existing system completely.

German law contains a list of cases in which mandatory defence is called for in section 140(1) CCP. Apart from this list, there is also an open clause for mandatory defence in section 140(2) CCP that is modelled on Art 4(4) of the Directive. This clause can serve as a catch-all element to cover situations that are missing from the list of section 140(1) CCP. The German legislator has changed section 141 CCP in order to make it compatible with the requirements of Art. 4(5) of the Directive. Nonetheless, in doing so, the system of mandatory defence was changed distinctly. Section 141(1) CCP makes the appointment of a lawyer dependent on an application by the defendant. This is at odds with the paternalistic approach of the CCP to provide mandatory defence and also a useless formality because the authorities are obliged to grant the application.[43] In effect, the need for an application (which can be oral) might even prevent the effective exercise of a right. It has been pointed out in literature that the German implementation blends the right of access to a lawyer and the right to legal aid, thus rendering the former less effective than prescribed.[44]

Section 141(2) CCP states a number of cases in which the lawyer must be appointed *ex officio*. These include the situations referred to by Art 4(4) let. a) and b), Directive 2016/1919, in which the merits test must lead to legal aid according to the Directive. However, the German provision knows some exceptions to this rule: In case of an arrest warrant, an application by the defendant is required (section 141(2) sentence 2 CCP). It is also allowed to refrain from appointing a lawyer in case of placement in an institution (section 141(2) No. 2), if the proceedings will be dispensed with soon and no intrusive investigative measures were adopted. Moreover, section 141(2) No. 3 makes the appointment

43 Anke Müller-Jacobsen, 'Das neue Recht der notwendigen Verteidigung' (2020) NJW 575, 579.

44 Albert Spitzer, 'Das Gesetz zur Neuregelung der notwendigen Verteidigung aus europarechtlicher Sicht' (2020) StV 418, 421.

dependent on the ability to defend oneself, although the Directive uses the term 'interests of justice' (Art 4(4)). These exceptions are commonly regarded to be contrary to the Directive in literature.[45]

German law has introduced another exception to section 141(2) CCP in a new section 141a CCP. This exception is based on Art 3(6) of Directive 2013/48. However, it has been rightly pointed out that exceptions under this norm must apply to both mandatory and elected defence, whereas section 141a only applies to mandatory defence.[46] Accordingly, this provision does not comply with the Directive either.

All in all, the transposition of the key guarantee of the Directive has not been executed successfully. This is because the German legislator wanted to keep its system of mandatory defence at all costs and refrained from developing a new coherent system of legal aid. On EU level, ithad been controversially discussed between Member States whether the Directive should follow a means or merits test, due to the fact that the Member States are obliged to fund legal aid. Allowing both options was a compromise that has led the German legislator to believe that substantial change of the German system was not necessary. The result is a law that will give rise to much case-law in the near future.

7.3.2.3 Right of Access to a Lawyer in Juvenile Proceedings

The YCA refers to the rules of the CCP, so the right of access to a lawyer as provided for criminal defendants in general applies to juvenile defendants, too. However, Art 6(2) of the Directive requires the Member States to make sure that children are assisted by a lawyer. This is understood to mean that mandatory defence is required.[47] The same is true for Art 6(3), which provides assistance by a lawyer at certain points in time. In German literature, it has indeed been argued that this is the general principle that the Directive follows and that German law (*i.e.* section 140(2) CCP) must be interpreted that way.[48] Nonetheless, there is no provision in German law claiming that children must always be assisted by a lawyer. Section 68 YCA does prescribe mandatory defence in more cases than for adults, but there is no general rule on

45 Hans Meyer-Mews, 'Umsetzung der EU-Richtlinie über Prozesskostenhilfe im Strafverfahren' (2019) ZRP 5, 6 ff.; Müller-Jacobsen (n 43) 576.

46 Müller-Jacobsen (n 43) 577; Sven Schoeller, 'Das neue Recht der Pflichtverteidigung – richtlinienkonformer und praktikabler Prozesskostenhilfeersatz?' (2019) StV 190, 195; Albert Spitzer (n 44) 422.

47 BT-Drucks. 19/13837, 24; Stefanie Bock, 'Schutz von Kindern und Jugendlichen im europäisierten Strafverfahren: Zur Kinderrechtsrichtlinie der EU und ihrer Umsetzung ins deutsche Recht' (2019) StV 508, 513.

48 Stefanie Bock (n 47)513.

mandatory defence for children. In this respect, the implementation thus seems to be insufficient.

Art 2(6) of the Directive also requires the child's assistance by a lawyer if deprivation of liberty might be imposed as a sanction. This requirement has been transposed in section 68 No. 5 YCA: Mandatory defence is necessary if 'the imposition of a youth sentence, the suspension of a youth sentence or the ordering of placement in a psychiatric hospital or in a detention center are expected'. However, the transposition is not complete. Juvenile law knows – beside the 'youth sentence', which is an imprisonment sentence – another sanction that deprives the juvenile of liberty, so-called 'youth detention' (*Jugendarrest*, see section 16 YCA). Because youth detention is a deprivation of liberty, it should have been included in the catalogue of section 68 No. 5 YCA.[49]

The German legislator also decided to make use of the possibility to provide an exception to mandatory defence in section 68b YCA. This provision mirrors Art 6(8) of the Directive. Still, it has been criticized in German literature as being too vague.[50] Moreover, the rule only applies to mandatory defence attorneys, not chosen defence attorneys, a situation which is in breach of the Directive.

Again, this example shows that it is challenging to implement EU law in an existing legal system that is based on different premises. The inclusion of the rights in the law on mandatory defence does not take sufficiently into account that the EU rights apply to both mandatory and elected defence lawyer. The example of section 68b YCA illustrates the difference between EU directives and national law: while the former needs implementation and can be vague, the latter must be more precise.

7.4 Main Critical Profiles in the Case-law

The relevant case law of the courts tends towards the *laissez-faire* approach. In line with the continental tradition, courts are mainly oriented towards national law. Insofar as national law required no or at most minimal adaptations to the Directives, courts in general do not refer to the Directives at all. For the rest, they as a rule still rely on the previously established case law on the assumption that it already corresponded to the level of protection provided by the Directives and did not need to be revised. In few decisions, direct references to

49 Ibid 513 fn. 68.

50 Ibid 513.

the Directives can be found; however, they primarily serve as supportive argumentation. As a result, insufficient transposition of the Directives is perpetuated also in case law.

This trend can be exemplified in relation to the right to translation as laid down in Art 3, Directive 2010/64. In 2018 the Federal Court of Justice (*Bundesgerichtshof* – *BGH*) confirmed that German law did not entail a right to a translation of the final and absolute judgment. Section 187(2) 1 CCA only provided for a right to the translation of decisions that are not final and absolute. Neither was there any need to interpret the provision in conformity with the Directive. The translation should enable the defendant to exercise their procedural rights. This would no longer be possible after the judgement had become final. The fact that the sentenced person considered an application for retrial (*Wiederaufnahme*), or a constitutional complaint (*Verfassungsbeschwerde*) was not sufficient, since these were not legal remedies, also in the sense of EU law. For the same reasons, it was not possible to base the claim directly on the Directive.[51] The BGH also ruled that, in accordance with section 187 (2) 5 CCA, a written translation of a judgment was in principle not required if the defendant, who is not fluent in German, had the assistance of a defence counsel. Since the defence counsel knows the written judgment and the defendant can consult it with them – if necessary, with the participation of an interpreter – an effective defence was sufficiently guaranteed.[52]

In few cases, however, national courts of first instance have referred cases to the CJEU for preliminary rulings with regards to the right to translation as laid down in Art 3 of Directive 2010/64 and the right to be informed of the accusation in accordance with Art 2, 3(1), let (c) and 6(1) and (3) of Directive 2012/13, resulting in the judgments *Covaci, Tranca et al.*, and *UY* (mentioned above), as well as *Sleutjes*.[53]

Furthermore, in case of Directives 2016/800 and 2016/1919, courts have undertaken or at least discussed direct application. After the deadline for transposing Directive 2016/800 had expired, two courts pointed out that the Directive had become directly applicable and interpreted the right to mandatory defence for juveniles accordingly. Therefore, a lawyer was appointed in the

---

51 BGHSt 63, 192, 195 ff. ECLI:DE:BGH:2018:130918B1STR320.17.0; see also BGH, 4 StR 51/17, decision of 4 october 2018, ECLI:DE:BGH:2018:041018B4STR51.17.0; BGH, 3 StR 519/18, decision of 7 december 2020, ECLI:DE:BGH:2020:071220B3STR519.18.0.

52 BGH, 4 StR 506/17, Decision of 22 January 2018, ECLI:DE:BGH:2018:220118B4STR506.17.0; see also BGHSt 63, 192, 201 ff. ECLI:DE:BGH:2018:130918B1STR320.17.0; BGHSt 64, 283 ff, ECLI:DE:BGH:2020:180220B3STR430.19.0.

53 C-278/16 *Sleutjes* (CJEU, 12 October 2017).

pre-trial phase[54] and in a case in which the defendant could be sentenced to a probationary prison sentence,[55] although German law originally would not have considered the cases to be ones of mandatory defence.

A similar question arose with regard to Directive 2016/1919. In the case at stake, the public prosecution office wanted to have a mandatory lawyer appointed for the defendant before their first examination based on Art 4 (5) of the Directive. The BGH rejected this approach because the Directive was not clear and precise enough to be immediately applicable, particularly, because Member States could choose whether they wanted to apply a means or a merits test.[56] This assessment was shared by another court.[57] However, the LG Chemnitz based the appointment of a lawyer on Art 4(4), Directive 2016/1919, which amounts to direct application of the Directive, although the court did not explain the dogmatic background.[58] The Chamber Court (*Kammergericht Berlin*) also considered the Directive to be directly applicable.[59]

The BGH even rejected an interpretation of the national law in light of the Directive (*richtlinienkonforme Auslegung*) in this decision. The court argued that legal aid, meaning financial funding of legal representation, and mandatory defence as it was understood in German law were fundamentally different; therefore an interpretation of German law by having recourse to the Directive was not possible. Only one court accepted this reasoning for the interpretation of national law.[60] The majority of courts, on the other side, did interpret national law referring to the Directive, *e.g.* in extradition cases[61] or when deciding on appointing a mandatory lawyer.[62]

Such orientation towards European Directives can also be observed in relation to the question of whether a mandatory lawyer can be appointed retroactively, *i.e.* after the (investigative) proceedings have ended. The majority of courts have pointed out that such a retroactive appointment in cases in which

54 AG Freiburg BeckRS 2019, 19711.

55 LG Chemnitz StV 2019, 601.

56 BGH, order of 04.06.2019 – 1 BGs 170/19 <Entscheidungen: Andere Gerichte: RiLI 2016/1919, Umsetzung, Anwendung im nationalen Recht / BGH, Beschl. v. 04.06.2019 – 1 BGs 170/19 – Burhoff online> accessed 7 November 2021. The court had jurisdiction in first instance because it was a case of espionage.

57 LG Frankfurt BeckRS 2020, 7595.

58 LG Chemnitz BeckRS 2019, 19698.

59 KG BeckRS 2019, 18928.

60 LG Frankfurt BeckRS 2020, 7595.

61 OLG München BeckRS 2019, 12699; OLG München BeckRS 2019, 10914.

62 AG Freiburg BeckRS 2019, 19711. See also LG Chemnitz BeckRS 2019, 19698.

the defendant was not responsible for the delay would fit better with the purpose of the Directive and the German transposition law.[63]

Overall, it appears that the BGH, in particular, is rather reluctant to delve into the contents of the Directives, while the lower courts tend to be more open in this respect. In many cases, the BGH correctly assumes that national law complies with the guarantees of the Directives. For the rest, restraints may be explained by the fact that, in accordance with its task of harmonising jurisprudence, the court wants to avoid frictions and contradictions in national law. In some aspects, however, this comes at the cost that the national level of protections falls short of the Directives' guarantees.

7.5 Concluding Remarks

The predominant assumption of the legislator as well as the jurisprudence that the guarantees of the Directives had already been safeguarded by national statutory or case-law before the transposition has shown to be well justified. At the same time, however, the analysis indicates that this confidence could stand in the way of adequate implementation in those areas where national law fell short of the Directives' guarantees.

It can be assumed that the legislator wanted to avoid what they considered to be unnecessary substantial revisions which could cause friction in the concerted regulatory framework and would render the previous case-law and maybe even discussion in the scientific legal community void. This caution in changing the existing legal framework also explains why German courts are mostly guided by national law, former case-law and the legislative will and rarely explicitly refer to Directives or refer cases to the CJEU, even where this would be appropriate. In other cases, such as the largely non-legislated presumption of innocence, the legislator may simply have shied away from the effort of a legal establishment. Even where the legislator has decided in favour of a more detailed implementation of the Directives' guarantees, the insistence on the previous national system has caused difficulties, *e.g.* leading to an odd mixture of rules that are shaped by differing concepts of mandatory defence and legal aid in transposition of Directive 2016/1919.

In summary, it can be stated that the guarantees of the Directives were already largely part of the essence of the rights of the accused as laid down

---

63 LG Mannheim BeckRS 2020, 4792; LG Passau BeckRS 2020, 7551; LG Bonn BeckRS 2020, 7166; LG Nürnberg-Fürth BeckRS 2020, 10878; LG Aurich BeckRS 2020, 10940; LG Hechingen BeckRS 2020, 14359; divergent OLG Hamburg BeckRS 2020, 27077.

in German legislation and recognized in practice, although the EU legislation are to some extent more detailed. Along with the amendments introduced in implementation of the Directives, their transposition took place to a very large extent. It seems quite possible that minor transposition deficits will be eliminated by amendments to the legislation or its interpretation in conformity with the Directives. But it remains doubtful if the legislator will undertake larger schemes to explicitly implement, for example, the provisions on the presumption of innocence or in the legislation on legal remedies. If the German legislator does so, it would be better to adopt a *tabula rasa* approach instead of making piecemeal changes to existing provisions.

CHAPTER 8

Italy

Minimalistic Transposition and Substantial Protection in the Implementation of the EU Defence Rights Directives

Marianna Biral, Isadora Neroni Rezende, and Alessandra Santangelo

8.1 Introduction

This Chapter aims to offer an overall glimpse of the implementation of the six EU Directives on criminal defence rights in Italy.[1] It is arguably an ambitious task: The topic has manifold and complex implications, too vast to be exhaustively dealt with in this venue. From a methodological perspective, this work implied an investigation of both legislative sources and jurisprudential decisions, with the aim of providing a picture of the Italian framework as comprehensive as possible. In addition, the findings here presented are the result of an extensive, two-years long research conducted by a pool of national legal experts in the framework of the CrossJustice project.[2] Thus, acknowledging the practical limitations of this contribution, its primary objective will be that of conveying the most significant trends in the Italian way of approaching the implementation issues brought by the enactment of the EU Directives.

To this end, Section 8.2 first summarizes the state of play in the transposition of the six EU Directives on defence rights in criminal proceedings. At a first glance, the analysis will present an overall satisfactory situation in the country. Italy seems indeed fairly advanced in the implementation path, with only Directive 2016/800 being left uncovered by formal transposition. At a closer examination, however, gaps in legislation emerge, revealing a pattern of minimalistic implementation of EU safeguards. Whether this is the result of a "naïve", or rather protective, attitude of the Italian legislator, it remains to be seen.

---

1 While this work is the result of a joint research carried out by the three Authors, Marianna Biral is the author of § 8.2, Isadora Neroni Rezende of §§ 8.1 and 8.4 and Alessandra Santangelo of §§ 8.3 and 8.5.

2 The Authors are extremely grateful to the UNIBO team of researchers that co-participated in the drafting of the Italian national report: Laura Bartoli, Cosimo Emanuele Gatto, Giulia Lasagni, Vanessa Maraldi, Irene Milazzo, Antonio Pugliese.

 | DOI:10.1163/9789004513396_010

Against this backdrop, Section 8.3 then focuses on the active role of the jurisprudence in the implementation of the Directives. This overview highlights the growing importance of case law, as a legal source, in defining the concrete standards of protection for defendants in criminal proceedings. This will allow to take notice of a global trend in the Italian system towards the use of substantial approaches and case-by-case assessments, likely due to the increasing impact exercised by legal orders more oriented towards a pragmatic approach.[3]

Keeping the focus on substantial issues, Section 8.4 brings attention to problems undermining the effectiveness of various defence rights laid down in the Directives. The quality of professional services provided for in the proceedings, as well as the efficiency of judicial remedies in the Italian system, will be put under scrutiny. Again, trends similar to those previously illustrated will resurface. In this domain, for instance, the Italian legislator simply chose to rely on the pre-existent regime of procedural nullities, leaving several situations uncovered by bespoke solutions. Also in such a context, thus, judge-made solutions are de facto gaining significant relevance.

Finally, Section 8.5 summarizes the main findings and closes the Chapter with some final considerations on recently adopted instruments and current legislative proposals, which may mark a shift in the attitude of the Italian institutions to the matter of EU-derived criminal procedural safeguards.

8.2 The Implementation of EU Directives: State of Play

The approach undertaken by the legislator towards the transposition of the Directives on the procedural rights of suspected and accused persons adopted so far has been quite minimalistic. Deeming the national system to be overall compliant with the standards established therein, the legislative framework has indeed been subjected only to minor amendments. This left the judiciary to take charge for the opportune adjustments, at the interpretative level, to the pre-existing legislation.[4]

---

3 On this topic, see Roberto E. Kostoris, 'European Law and Criminal Justice' in Roberto E. Kostoris (ed) *Handbook of European Criminal Procedure* (Springer 2018) 58-60; Vittorio Manes and Michele Caianiello, *Introduzione al diritto penale europeo* (Giappichelli 2020) 59 ff.; Michele Caianiello, *Premesse per una teoria del pregiudizio effettivo nelle invalidità processuali penali* (BUP 2012) 131–168; Vittorio Manes, *Il giudice nel labirinto* (Dike Giuridica 2012).

4 This aspect will be examined in depth in § 8.3.

The greatest diligence has been devoted to the implementation of Directive 2010/64, which has been subjected to a two-step transposition. The first step dated back to the 2014 (Legislative Decree no. 32, of March 4, 2014), and the second one was pursued in 2016 by the Legislative Decree no. 129, of June 23, 2016. This over-sensitivity on the part of the legislator is probably due to the fact that the field in question has been the first to be homogeneously ruled by the European Union; besides, it should be considered that, until EU institutions turned the spotlight on the rights to interpretation and translation, scarce attention had been devoted to the matter at the domestic level. This has stimulated a proactive approach,[5] which has nevertheless led to an incomplete alignment to European standards. On the bright side, it should be mentioned: the acknowledgement of the right to translation as separate and independent from the right to interpretation (Art 143(2) CCP); the obligation to translate a number of acts of the proceedings (Art 143(3) CCP);[6] the fact that waiving the right to translation of procedural acts by the accused is deemed admissible only where the person is informed about the consequences of this choice, having previously consulted a lawyer (Art 51-*bis* disp. att. CCP); the express recognition of the right to linguistic assistance where the accused, who is under arrest or subjected to precautionary detention, meets her defence counsel (Art 104(4-*bis*) CCP); the fact that costs for interpretation and translation shall be borne by the State, regardless from the outcome of the proceedings (until the transposition of the Directive, free assistance of interpreters and translators was acknowledged by the law, but disregarded in practice; the entry into force of Legislative Decree no. 32/2014 contributed to render this right effective). Moving to the gaps in the implementation, inconsistencies are to be detected, in particular, in relation to the quality of the service provided by interpreters and translators.[7] The fact that quality is scarcely ensured in practice has a considerable – negative – impact on the fulfillment of the right to

5 Which has been addressed as 'the opening of new and important perspectives for the rule of law'. Silvio Sau, 'Art 143', in Giulio Illuminati and Livia Giuliani (eds), *Commentario breve al codice di procedura penale* (3rd edn, Wolters Kluwer Cedam 2020) 512.

6 In particular, notice of investigation, notice of the right to defence, the decision ordering personal precautionary measures, notice of the conclusion of preliminary investigations, decrees ordering the preliminary hearing and decrees of summons for trial, judgements and criminal decrees of conviction shall be translated. Besides these acts which shall be translated in any case, translation may be provided for those other acts which are deemed to be essential for the accused in order to state her case (Art 143(3) CCP). As for the erratic findings of the case-law on what is deemed to be an essential document, see later § 8.3.

7 For a detailed account on this, see § 8.4.

interpretation and translation, at risk of becoming 'theoretical' and 'illusory', to put it in ECtHR's terms.[8]

Directive 2012/13 has been transposed into the Italian legal system by Legislative Decree no. 101 of July 1, 2014. National transposition mostly focused on the information about procedural safeguards, the crucial intervention concerning the duty to serve the Letter of Rights (Art 4 Directive) to suspects or accused persons deprived of liberty (Arts 293(1) and 386(1) CCP) or subjected to surrender procedure (Art 12 Law no. 69/2005 implementing the Framework Decision on the European Arrest Warrant). In order to ensure better compliance with such informative obligation, judicial oversight has been accordingly introduced (Arts 294(1-*bis*) and 391(2) CCP). Only minor changes were made instead in relation to the right to be informed about the accusation, and no amendments occurred as for the right to access the file.[9]

In general terms, national provisions on the right to information within criminal proceedings fully implement the Directive, either directly, on the basis of the interventions stimulated by the adoption of the European text, or indirectly, on the basis of the pre-existent legislation. Also, courts have played a crucial role in this sense. Meaningful is the case of the duty to inform the accused about the modification of the legal qualification of the fact. Not explicitly provided for by the law, this right has been progressively acknowledged by the Italian jurisprudence following the landmark decision *Drassich v Italy* (2007) by the European Court of Human Rights.[10] Even though a few critical issues remain, as for the scope,[11] timing[12] and form[13] of the guarantees enshrined by the European legislator, the overall picture is satisfactory.

---

8 In literature, see Mitja Gialuz, 'L'assistenza linguistica nel processo penale: un meta-diritto fondamentale tra paradigma europeo e prassi italiana' (Wolters Kluwer/Cedam 2018) 149 ff.

9 For a comprehensive overview on the Legislative Decree no. 101/2014, see Stefano Ciampi, 'Diritto all'informazione nei procedimenti penali: il recepimento low profile della direttiva 2012/13/UE da parte del D.L.gs 1° luglio 2014 no. 101' (2014) Dir. pen. cont. <https://archiviodpc.dirittopenaleuomo.org/upload/1411391808CIAMPI%202014a.pdf> accessed 8 November 2021.

10 *Drassich v Italy* App no 25575/04 (ECHR, 11 December 2007). A synthetic account of the evolution of the Italian jurisprudence is contained in Alberto Camon and others, 'Fondamenti di procedura penale' (2nd edn, Wolters Kluwer Cedam 2020) 633 ff.

11 In case of investigative questioning of the suspect on the part of the police (acting on her own motion), it is not foreseen that the suspect shall be informed about the criminal act she is accused of having committed (Art 350(1) CCP).

12 With the exception of the right to silence, the information about the other rights of the accused shall be bestowed only during the pre-trial phase.

13 The requirement of a 'clear and precise' information is prescribed not in each and every occasion the suspect or accused person shall be given notice of her procedural rights, but

Directive 2013/48 has been transposed into the Italian system by the Legislative Decree no. 184, of September 15, 2016. Since the right to access a lawyer was already guaranteed in the Italian framework – under some aspects to a degree even higher than that of the European standards[14] – also in this case the legislator limited its intervention to minimal profiles. These substantially consisted in: the inclusion of the informal identification or line-up (Art 364(1) CCP) among the investigative acts requiring the appointment and assistance of the lawyer; in relation to European Arrest Warrants proceedings, the establishment of the duty for the executing authority to inform the requested person about the possibility to appoint a lawyer in the Issuing State (Art 9(5-*bis*) Law no. 69, of April 22, 2005).[15]

The overall evaluation on the implementation of this Directive is therefore positive. Only some minor shortcomings can be detected in the *law-in-action*. For example, with regard to derogations to the right to access a lawyer (Arts 3(6) and 8 of the Directive), the requirement of an in-depth motivation, based on the specificities of the case, is sometimes disregarded in practice. In interpreting Art 104(3) and (4) CCP,[16] indeed, the case-law tends to infer the risk of adverse consequences for a correct and positive evolution of the criminal proceedings (Art 6(3)(b) of the Directive) and, in particular, the risk of arranged depositions between co-accused, from the seriousness of the offence at stake and from the fact that more than one person is charged for it.[17]

---

only when an arrest, a temporary detention or a precautionary measure are applied (Arts 386(1) and 293(1) CCP).

14 First of all, legal assistance is mandatory in Italy, even in proceedings for minor offences (the defence is understanded as an inviolable right). This means that self-defence is not admitted and, therefore, if the accused has not appointed a retained lawyer a court-appointed one shall be provided (Art 97 CCP). Besides, the right to have the lawyer present during questioning (Art 3(3)(b) of the Directive) is subjected to special protection where the questioning is executed (as a direct or a delegated action) by the police (Arts 350(3) and 370(1) CCP). In this case, unlike the case of a questioning accomplished by the Public Prosecutor (where the absence of the lawyer is admissible and perfectly tolerated, provided that the accused have been informed about her rights) the presence of the defence counsel is prescribed under penalty of nullity of the investigative act.

15 It has to be noted however that no mention has been made by the legislator concerning the duty to inform the issuing authority of the lack of an appointed lawyer in that issuing State, nor of the will of the requested person to proceed in this regard. In this sense, therefore, Art 10 of the Directive cannot be considered exhaustively transposed into the Italian system.

16 This provision allows the deferment of the exercise of the right to consult a lawyer where the defendant is placed under precautionary measure or arrested or temporarily detained.

17 Cass. pen., Sez. III, no. 30196, 8/03/2018, rv. 273756-01; Cass. pen., Sez. VI, no. 1941, 21/10/2009, rv. 245806-01.

The approval of the Legislative Decree implementing the Directive 2016/343 is very recent, dating back to November 8, 2021.[18] The core of the legislative act – which introduced minimal changes to the pre-existent legislation, with the explicit transposition of Arts 3, 4 and 10 of the Directive only – is devoted to setting a code of conduct for public authorities in situations where they are called to give information about the ongoing criminal proceedings. The objective pursued by the legislator is to stop the tendency to present the defendant as being guilty before her culpability is definitely established and, therefore, avoid the vicious cycles that might be generated where incautious words of the public authorities are spread and often emphasized by the press.[19] In this sense, the possibility for Prosecutors to hold press-conferences has been limited[20] and strictly regulated as for the type and mode of information being conveyed (Art 5 Legislative Decree no. 106, of February 20, 2006). Besides, it has been ruled that interim decisions adopted by judicial authorities shall avoid terms suggesting the defendant to be responsible for the alleged criminal conduct. Should the prohibition be violated, the accused has the right to ask for a correction of the given statement (Art 115-*bis* CCP). Although some (mainly representatives of the judiciary) have depicted this reform as an embargo for investigating authorities, the intervention has been generally warmly welcomed, as a long-awaited way to achieve the end of misrepresentation of justice on screens.

The other aspects of the presumption of innocence dealt with in Directive 2016/343 have not been addressed by the Legislative Decree, on the assumption that the Italian framework was already compliant with the European standards. This is generally true, even though some lacunas remain. This is the case, for instance, of the privilege against self-incrimination, whose level of protection finds full recognition only inside the realm of criminal proceedings *stricto sensu*. The Grand Chamber of the Court of Justice has recently stated that the right at issue should be applied also in proceedings which may lead to the imposition of administrative sanctions of a criminal nature.[21] In this sense, the Legislative Decree has represented a wasted opportunity to provide

18 Legislative Decree no. 188 of November 8, 2021.

19 Nello Rossi, 'Il diritto a non essere "additato" come colpevole prima del giudizio. La direttiva UE e il decreto legislativo in itinere' (2021) *Quest. Giustizia* <https://www.questionegiustizia.it/articolo/il-diritto-a-non-essere-additato-come-colpevole-prima-del-giudizio> accessed 8 November 2021.

20 They can be held only in case there is a strong public interest towards the case. Otherwise, public authorities shall convey information about criminal proceedings only through official public statements.

21 C-481/19 of 2 February 2021. The case will be analyzed later. See § 8.3.

a coherent and systematic regime for the right to silence within administrative (but substantially punitive) proceedings.[22]

Against this background, Directive 2016/800 is the only piece of EU legislation here examined that has not been transposed (yet). At a first glance, this does not cause particular gaps in terms of protection. Within the Italian system, in fact, the features of the 'fair trial for children' are fairly recognized. A special statute of guarantees is in force for juvenile defendants, independent and autonomous from that applying to adults, and tailored to the special needs of minors.[23] In this sense, it can be said that the pillar of the Directive, i.e. the acknowledgement of the inadequacy of ordinary rules for children, whose personality is under development, is firmly rooted at the national level. Moreover, looking at the specific safeguards enshrined by the European legislator, the overall picture is reassuring, especially in relation to the right to information (Art 4), the right to have the holder of parental responsibility informed about the proceedings and its developing (Art 5), the right to individual assessment (Art 7), the necessary expertise of the authorities that, at different levels and bearing different responsibilities, get in touch with the minor along the proceedings (Art 20).

On second thought, however, some negative notes emerge. The first is related to the duty to audiovisual recording of the questioning conducted by investigating authorities (Art 9) which, as things stand, receives no implementation at the national level, even indirectly.[24]

The second concerns legal assistance (Art 6). Within the Directive, there are some indicators suggesting that the standard established in relation to the

22 Reference goes to the substantial definition of criminal matter, also known as 'Engel doctrine', first developed by the ECtHR (*Engel and o. v The Netherlands* App no 5100/71 (ECHR, 8 June 1976)), and more recently, applied also by the Court of Justice since the Bonda decision (Case C-489/10 *Łukasz Marcin Bonda* (CJEU, 5 June 2012) §§ 36–46) and more recently confirmed also with regard to some Italian cases (Case C-524/15 *Luca Menci* (CJEU, 20 March 2018) §§ 26–33; Case C-537/16 *Garlsson Real Estate SA and o. v CONSOB* (CJEU, 20 March 2018) §§ 28–35; Join Cases C-596/16 and C-597/16, *Enzo Di Puma v CONSOB* and *CONSOB v Antonio Zecca* (CJEU, 20 March 2018) § 38).

23 Reference goes to the Presidential Decree no. 448, of September 22, 1988. For what is not specifically provided by this law, the precepts of the CCP are to be applied, but only at the condition they are 'suitable' and adequate to the peculiar features of the proceedings against minors (Art 1 Presidential Decree no. 448/1988). For an analysis of the fundamental traits of the criminal proceedings against children, see Adonella Presutti, 'Evoluzione e caratteri fondanti del sistema', in Marta Bargis (ed), *Procedura penale minorile* (3rd edn, Giappichelli 2019) 32 ff.

24 The only provision providing for audiovisual recording of the questioning is Art 141 disp. att. CCP which applies only in case the (adult or underage) defendant is detained.

right to access to a lawyer for children may be higher than the one provided for adults. In particular, Recital (27) affirms that, where the Directive provides the assistance by a lawyer during questioning '*a lawyer should be present*' [emphasis added]. Besides, Art 6(7) provides that 'where the child is to be assisted by a lawyer [...] but no lawyer is present, the competent authorities shall postpone the questioning of the child, or other investigative or evidence-gathering acts [...] for a reasonable period of time in order to allow for the arrival of the lawyer, or, where the child has not nominated a lawyer, to arrange a lawyer for the child'. These wording seems to require an additional level of protection for juvenile defendants, namely, requesting the necessary presence of a defence counsel during her questioning. If this interpretative reconstruction were founded, a gap in the Italian legislation may be detected, since the assistance of the lawyer is not mandatory for children, as well as for adults, during questionings conducted by the prosecutor.[25] In this sense, should a piece of legislation aimed at implementing the Directive be adopted, it would be advisable for the legislator to foster this aspect of the right to legal assistance.

Still on a *de lege ferenda* perspective, but from another angle, some missteps and errors shall be avoided in the future implementation of Directive 2016/800. In this sense, particular caution should be exercised in the transposition of the provisions regulating derogations to the right to access a lawyer.[26] Indeed, since Art 6(6) of the Directive sets vague conditions allowing for some exceptions to this right, a blind implementation could lead to a watering down of the essence of the guarantee at issue. Besides, in this context the interest of the child assumes an ambiguous significance, with potentially adverse reflections on the effectivity and coherence of the safeguards established for juvenile defendants.

Art 6(6) of the Directive states that 'provided that this complies with the right to a fair trial', Member States may derogate from paragraph 3 where

25 While questionings carried out by the police pursuant to Art 350 and 370(1) CCP foresee the mandatory presence of the lawyer, that is not the case for those conducted by the Public Prosecutor. The questioning of the suspect by the Public Prosecutor is regulated by Art 364 CPP, which requires the court-appointed or the retained lawyer to be informed at least 24 hours before the hour set for the questioning. However, the provision also indicates that the lawyer has only a right to be present during the activities, thereby implying that his or her presence is not necessary for the validity of the act. If the lawyer has been duly informed and he or she chooses not to appear, the questioning can be regularly performed without his or her presence.

26 See Glauco Giostra, 'Dall'Unione europea la prima direttiva sui diritti dei minori indagati o imputati' (2016) Il Penalista, <https://ilpenalista.it/articoli/news/dall-unione-europea-la-prima-direttiva-sui-diritti-dei-minori-indagati-o-imputati> accessed 8 November 2021.

assistance by a lawyer is not proportionate in the light of the circumstances of the case, taking into account the seriousness of the alleged criminal offence, the complexity of the case and the measures that could be taken in respect of such an offence, it being understood that *the child's best interests shall always be a primary consideration* [emphasis added]. Should such clause be intended to weigh in favour of the assistance of the lawyer, it does not really affect the balancing test entailed by the disposition (and, therefore, is substantially useless). This leads to the conclusion that the meaning of the clause probably goes in the opposite direction, implying that in some circumstances legal assistance does not constitute the best interest of the child since public authorities – judge, Public Prosecutor and social services – are in charge for the rehabilitation of the minor. If that is the case, however, the implication is that the criminal proceedings against minors is seen not only and not so much as a method for the ascertainment of criminal acts, but as a rehabilitative instrument. But if the function of the criminal proceedings is not to ascertain criminal liabilities but to ensure a rehabilitation opportunity to the accused, fair trial guarantees lose their sense and the core of the presumption of innocence is endangered.

In sum, to ensure a proper implementation of Directive 2016/800, a fairly pondered intervention of the legislator seems opportune. What has to be avoided is protracting and exacerbating some misunderstandings concerning the best interest of the child clause. A superficial approach, indeed, might collide on one side with the presumption of innocence and, on the other, with the nature of criminal proceedings that, even against juveniles, remain first and foremost an instrument for the ascertainment of criminal liability, rather than means of rehabilitation.

Directive 2016/1919 on legal aid has been transposed by the Legislative Decree no. 24, of March 7, 2019. Even in this case the intervention of the legislator has been minimal,[27] since the European guarantees in this field received already ample recognition within the Italian system. The roots of the acknowledgement of legal aid in the national framework should be traced in Art 24 of the Constitution. Given that defence has to be effective, it follows that the State shall pay for legal assistance in situations where the defendant is not in the

27 Substantially amounting to the extension of the rules on legal aid to proceedings for the execution of a European Arrest Warrant (Art 75(2-*bis*) Presidential Decree no. 115/2002). On the importance of such amendment for the effective acknowledgement of the right to 'dual defence' within the EAW proceedings, see Francesca Dri, 'Vizi e virtù dell'attuazione della direttiva 2016/1919/UE sul patrocinio a spese dello Stato: una prima lettura' (2019) 5 Proc. pen. giust. 1214 ff.

condition to do it himself.[28] It is noteworthy that this principle receives a firm and convinced protection – which goes even further what is prescribed at the European level[29] – as it applies not only to the accused but also to other private parties, in some cases even regardless of the economic situation of the concerned person (Art 74 Presidential Decree no. 115, of May 30, 2002). Moreover, the benefit covers also legal services provided by the expert witness (Art 102 Presidential Decree no. 115/2002) and private investigator (Art 104 Presidential Decree no. 115/2002) eventually appointed by the party.

Against this backdrop, however a substantial deficiency of the Italian system has to be addressed. In accordance with Art 76 Presidential Decree no. 115/2002, legal aid is available to anyone who has an income taxable resulting the last declaration, not exceeding euros 11.746, 68. The threshold is clearly too low to guarantee a satisfactory protection.

Besides, there are other aspects, related to how legal aid functions in practice, that reinforce the impression that Italian system falls short of the European prescriptions. They include: untimely access to State funds; delays in the payment of the wages of lawyers providing legal aid services; and the absence of specific trainings to the personnel entitled of deciding the admission to legal aid. All these issues are neglected by the Legislative Decree, with the consequence that the right to receive legal assistance free of charge is (and continues being) pretentiously affirmed, but substantially denied in everyday judiciary life.[30]

8.3 Main Critical Profiles in Legislation and the Role of National Courts in Implementing the Defence Rights' Directives

Examining the transposition of the EU Procedural Rights Directives, it has been clear from the outset that domestic courts play an essential role for – at

---

28 In accordance with Art 76 Presidential Decree no. 115/2002 legal aid is available to anyone who has an income taxable resulting the last declaration, not exceeding euros 11.746, 68. The person concerned who is in this income condition may apply for legal aid at any stage of the proceedings and the application is decided by the judge proceeding at the time.

29 See Art 2 of the Directive.

30 Marta Bargis, 'L'attuazione della direttiva (UE) 2016/1919 nei procedimenti di esecuzione del mandato di arresto europeo fra scelte positive e lacune strutturali' (2019) 11 Sist. pen. 68 ff; Dri (n 27) 1223 ff; Elisa Grisonich, 'L'attuazione della direttiva 2016/1919/UE: un timido intervento in materia di patrocinio a spese dello Stato' (2019) 5 Riv. trim. dir. pen. cont. 225 ff.

least – a threefold reason. This Section considers such aspects, through a selection of relevant judicial cases, analysing the standard of implementation of procedural safeguards and evaluating the forthcoming evolution in the relationship between the national and the European dimension.

First, the substantial approach often applied by national judges has fostered the protection of fundamental rights whenever the national legislator implemented the EU Directives only partially, or via extremely general drafts.[31] Furthermore, the domestic Courts' involvement has helped to correctly allocate the necessary resources and to respect a reasonable duration of criminal proceedings, avoiding the exploitation of European provisions to circumvent effective trials.[32]

However, the *law-in-action* has sometimes incurred in serious inconsistencies which have risked jeopardising the protection of procedural guarantees put forward by the European legislator. What might appear to be a paradox vanishes if one pushes the analysis 'behind the appearances': in fact, the tolerance towards incomplete or ineffective implementation by national legislation conferred – as an inevitable outcome – a relevant amount of discretion to the judiciary, undermining legal certainty and individual autonomy.

On top of that, the Italian Constitutional Court has been crucial in determining not only the boundaries between national and European competences but also in identifying the exact thresholds to be met by criminal procedural rights.[33]

As for the first aspect – mentioning some relevant cases – the partial legislative implementation of Art 7 of the Directive on procedural safeguards for

31 In this perspective, in fact, it is useful to highlight that 'although the aim of the Directive has been to establish minimum standards, in essence they have introduced a series of binding norms which are designed to ensure the respect of human rights and which must be interpreted broadly in order for their practical effectiveness to be ensured': Valsamis Mitsilegas, *EU Criminal Law after Lisbon* (Bloomsbury 2016) 175. See also Case C-216/14 *Criminal Proceedings v Gavril Covaci* [2015] EU C 2015 305, Opinion of AG Bot, §§ 74 and 100.

32 In this light, the national judges excluded that the right to interpretation and translation applied in a case where the accused claimed not to comprehend the language, but he had personally appointed his lawyer, he had confirmed that he could understand the language during the first questioning – as emerged from official reports – and had personally submitted the application before the Court of Cassation: Cass. pen., Sez. II, no. 8094, 04/02/2016, rv. 266238-01.

33 As for the so called 'Taricco saga', see Vittorio Manes 'Taricco Endgame' in Valsamis Mitsilegas, Alberto Di Martino and Leandro Mancano (eds), *The Court of Justice and European Criminal Law* (Bloomsbury 2016) 188 ff.

children[34] required domestic Courts to take action to ensure a constant direct observation of the child's behavior throughout the proceedings. Despite the absence of specific written indications,[35] national scholars observe that the right has been ensured in practice, fulfilling 'in action' the legislative gaps and protecting the vulnerable person involved.[36] Moreover, in relation to Art 2(1) of the Directive on the right to interpretation and translation,[37] the national legislator directly summons the judiciary[38] stating that 'knowledge of the Italian language shall be assessed by the judicial authority', as well as 'knowledge of the Italian language by Italian citizens shall be presumed unless proven otherwise'.[39] In this regard, the judicial interpretation has recognized that the understanding of the Italian language[40] could emerge from procedural acts signed by the accused or from personal unequivocal declarations.[41] Thus, while judicial authorities retain the power to assess, on a case-by-case basis, the knowledge and understanding of the relevant language, no automatisms apply, not even when the person involved is a foreign citizen.[42] Similarly, as far as the Directive on legal aid is concerned,[43] national judges have excluded that the revocation of benefits might automatically derive

34 Directive 2016/800/EU of the European Parliament and of the Council of 11 May 2016 on procedural safeguards for children who are suspects or accused persons in criminal proceedings [2016] *OJ L132*.

35 In particular, Art 9, decree no. 448 of 1988, regulates minors' individual assessment but does not necessary entitle experts or qualified personal as, instead, imposed by Art 7 (7), Directive on procedural safeguards for children.

36 Camon (n 10) 991 ff.

37 Directive 2010/64/EU of the European Parliament and of the Council of 20 October 2010 on the right to interpretation and translation in criminal proceedings [2010] *OJ L280*.

38 Art 143(4) CCP.

39 Ibid. On the issue, see Cass. pen., Sez. F., 04 September 2014, 44016, rv. 260997-01, where the judges pointed out that the assessment on the accused's language knowledge represented a substantial evaluation to be completed by the national Tribunals or Appeal Courts rather than by the Court of Cassation.

40 Considering the right to interpretation and translation, the Constitutional Court has identified the guarantee's rationale in allowing a conscious and effective involvement of the accused or suspect within the criminal proceeding in order to fulfil the right to defence and fair trial: Const court 6 July 2007, 254.

41 In this perspective, Cass. pen., Sez. II, 31 January 2017, 7913, rv. 269505-01.

42 The guarantee is not to be applied if the accused never claimed difficulties in comprehending the language during the proceeding: Cass. pen., Sez. II, 19 June 2018, 30379, rv. 273246-01.

43 Directive 2016/1919/EU of the European Parliament and of the Council of 26 October 2016 on legal aid for suspects and accused persons in criminal proceedings and for requested persons in European arrest warrant proceedings [2016] *OJ L297*.

from an untruthful self-certification on the possession of the legal requirements whether the subject's income does not exceed the thresholds established by the law.[44]

In brief, the balance between the need to ensure effective trials and sufficient protection for the procedural safeguards largely depends on the national judges' substantial evaluation. In this regard, the most troublesome task for the judiciary appears to be, on the one hand, to remedy by interpretation to some imprecise provisions left by the national legislator, and, on the other hand, to hinder formalistic approaches that could undermine the goals pursued by the EU with the procedural Directives.

Notwithstanding the special efforts of national judges, the drafting of legislative implementation has implied relevant inconsistencies whenever the judiciary has not been able to reach a common perspective and, rather, it has developed contrasting interpretations.[45] In this light, a serious issue has emerged considering the lack of specific remedies able to face the violation of EU procedural safeguards (see *infra*, § 8.4). Indeed, where national case law offers inconsistent interpretations, avoiding discriminations and strengthening effective levels of protection have gradually become more arduous goals to achieve. In fact, if interpretative solutions are not uniform, fair warning and legitimate expectations on the respect of minimum standards of protection risk being undermined. In other words, a cooperative attitude of the national legislator – correctly and attentively reacting towards European provisions – seems crucial not only to grant the necessary safeguards but also to shift from the judiciary the liability for decisions that are rather addressed to the Parliament.

Lastly, while ordinary judges have been playing a fundamental function in granting *de facto* the procedural safeguards, it is necessary to highlight the essential role fulfilled by the Constitutional Court[46] in fostering cooperation between the national and the European level. An emblematic example has

---

44 Cass. pen., Sez. Un., 19 December 2019, 14723, rv. 278871 – 01. Sharing the same approach, the national judges also allowed the applicant to demonstrate her income suffered a sudden and relevant decreasing which entitled her of legal aid, despite a declaration higher than the legislative standards: Cass. pen., Sez. IV, 4 September 2019, 37007.

45 This is the case for the definition of 'essential documents' under Art 143 (4) CCP: see, in particular, Cass. pen., Sez. I., 10 January 2018, 40733, rv. 274531-01 and Cass. pen., Sez. I, 28 January 2020, 8591, rv. 278364-01.

46 As for the role of the Courts in the 'history of a power struggle for the right to determine what punishment is and who should decide', see Lucia Zedner, 'Penal subversions: When is a punishment not punishment, who decides and on what grounds?' (2016) Theor Criminol 11 ff.

been provided by the preliminary reference that the Italian constitutional judges have recently brought before the Court of Justice, aiming to clarify the scope of the right to remain silent[47] in relation to sanctions which are labelled administrative but are, rather, criminal in nature.[48] Thus, where sanctions of a criminal nature are involved, the proceedings before the National Companies and Stock Exchange Commission (CONSOB) shall comply with the guarantees enshrined for natural persons by Article 47[49] and Article 48 of the EU Charter of Fundamental Rights.[50] As a result, the privilege against self-incrimination is to be applied beyond the boundaries of 'traditional' criminal proceedings,[51] enlarging the *rationale* of the procedural right.[52] Following this ruling, the Constitutional Court has declared unlawful those national provisions allowing to sanction natural persons who remain silent against self-incriminating requests from Consob or Banca d'Italia.[53]

---

47 Considering the interconnections among the right to remain silent and the failure to cooperate with the competent authorities, André Klip, *European Criminal Law. An Integrative Approach* (Intersentia 2021) 328. As for a recent overview on the Italian discipline, see Diletta Marchesi and Michele Panzavolta, 'Keep silence for yourself: The protection of the right to silence in the Italian criminal justice system' (2021) 12 NJECL 367 ff.

48 Const court 10 May 2019, 117. As for a general overview on the Italian partial implementation of the '*matière pénale*' doctrine when 'basic fair trial rights' are involved, see Michele Caianiello, 'Conclusive remarks antifraud investigations and respect for fundamental rights faced with the challenge of e-evidence and digital devices', in Michele Caianiello and Alberto Camon (eds), *Digital Forensic Evidence* (Cedam 2021) 248.

49 For a deep analysis, see Kathleen Gutman 'Article 47: The Right to an Effective Remedy and to Fair Trial' in Michal Bobek and Jeremias Adams-Prassl (eds) *The EU Charter of Fundamental Rights in the Member States* (HP, 2020) 371 ff.

50 Case 481/19 *DB v Consob* [2021] ECLI C 2021 84.

51 Ibid, stating the judges that 'in the light of the right to silence enshrined in the second paragraph of Article 47 and in Article 48 of the Charter, of Article 14(3) of Directive 2003/6 and of Article 30(1)(b) of Regulation No 596/2014, it is necessary further to ascertain whether those provisions of secondary EU legislation lend themselves to an interpretation which is consistent with that right to silence, in that they do not require penalties to be imposed on natural persons for refusing to provide the competent authority under that directive or that regulation with answers which might establish their liability for an offence that is punishable by administrative sanctions of a criminal nature, or their criminal liability'.

52 See Thomas Wahl, 'CJEU Delivers Landmark Judgment on Right to Silence in Administrative (Punitive) Proceedings' (2021) Eucrim <https://eucrim.eu/news/cjeu-delivers-landmark-judgment-on-right-to-silence-in-administrative-punitive-proceedings/> accessed 11 November 2021.

53 Const court 30 April 2021, 84.

On the one hand, therefore, such an interaction between national and European courts strengthens the process of integration,[54] identifying the Constitutional Court as the point of junction between the two jurisdictions. On the other hand, however, the Italian legal order has – once again – discharged a serious amount of responsibility on the judiciary, required to satisfy 'in action' the European standards of protection.

8.4 (Continues): The Effectiveness of Defence Rights

When looking at how defence rights are implemented *in action* by criminal justice actors, another issue to be considered is their effectiveness. In criminal proceedings, this question may indeed emerge in a twofold manner. Firstly, there may be a problem of the quality of the services provided by different experts that are called to intervene in the proceedings. Secondly, also the effectiveness of judicial remedies available in the legal system may sometimes be questioned.[55] As far as the Italian framework is concerned, both aspects gain relevance in assessing the effectiveness of the rights granted by the six Directives.

8.4.1 *Quality and Training*

The effectiveness of the right to interpretation and translation is highly dependent on the training of professionals providing such services. In this regard, despite the high standards of accuracy demanded by the Directive,[56] the Italian framework appears quite bleak. While the rights at stake are fully recognised in the legislation and case law,[57] the institutional setting is still quite lacking in ensuring high-quality linguistic assistance for the suspect or accused person.[58] Specifically, Italian law is absolutely silent on the qualifications that

---

54 On the issue, see Francesco Viganò, 'Supremacy of EU Law vs. (Constitutional) National Identity: A New Challenge for the Court of Justice from the ItalianConstitutional Court' (2017) EuCLR 103.

55 On the effectiveness of defence rights in criminal proceedings, see Silvia Allegrezza and Valentina Covolo, *Effective Defence Rights in Criminal Proceedings. A European and Comparative Study on Judicial Remedies* (CEDAM 2018).

56 See Arts 2(8), 5 and 3(9) Directive 2010/64.

57 Cass. pen., Sez. V, no. 4929/2006.

58 Marta Bargis, 'L'assistenza linguistica per l'imputato: Dalla direttiva europea 64/2010 nuovi inputs alla tutela fra teoria e prassi' in Marta Bargis (ed) *Studi in ricordo di Gabriella Aimonetto* (CEDAM 2013) 114.

the interpreter or translator must have to be admitted as an expert in the proceedings.

Two subsequent Legislative Decrees have amended the CCP, mandating the creation of experts registries for interpreters and translators.[59] Despite these novelties, however, the Italian legislator did not intervene on the kind of training and accreditation that professionals need to have to be inserted in those lists. Thus, far from establishing proper registries, as required by Art 5(2) of the Directive, the legislator opted for a watered-down approach that left unaltered the previous state of play.

The responsibility to decide on who may be qualified to act as an interpreter is then entirely left to legal professionals, giving them too much leeway in determining the criteria to enrol in the experts' lists and be called upon participating in the proceedings. Indeed, the requirements highly vary across Courts. In addition, people listed in these "registries" cannot usually cover with their expertise all languages that are actually needed in most trials. That is why the Clerk's Offices also keep unofficial registries of lesser-known languages and dialects, spoken by the most common immigrant nationalities in the country. No qualification is asked to apply to those registries; only a self-declaration of knowledge of the language and ready availability to participate in the proceedings.

The widespread lack of training and accreditation of interpreters in Italy may have worrying consequences on the defendants, as empirical studies have shown.[60]

Another issue affecting the quality of interpreting services is the unbelievably low sums that court professionals are paid for their performance. These are indeed set out by a Law no. 319 of 1980, which appears obsolete nowadays: with such lower wages,[61] it appears difficult to attract more trained interpreters to the domain.

Similar issues have emerged in the implementation of the Directive 2016/1919 on legal aid. Compared to the Directive 2010/64, criteria to be enrolled in the bespoke registries legal aid defence lawyers are at least established at the national level.[62] However, this does not seem to be enough to consider the

59 See Arts 67(2) and 67-bis disp. att. CCP, as amended and introduced, respectively, by the Legislative Decree no. 32/2014 and 126/2016.

60 Christopher John Garwood, 'Court interpreting in Italy. The daily violation of a fundamental human right' (2012) 17 Interpreters Newsletter 173.

61 Ibid 179. Remuneration is calculated using *vacazioni* (period of two hours spent in court). The first *vacazione* is paid € 14.68 and the subsequent are paid € 8.15 each, for a maximum of four *vacazioni* per day even if the interpreter works more than eight hours.

62 Art 80 d.P.R. no 115/2002.

domestic framework compliant with the quality standards set out by Art 7 of the Directive. Indeed, the possession of an adequate expertise is simply ascertained by the lawyer based on a self-declaration, while a common professional training is not foreseen. Also, no specific training is provided for the judicial authorities involved in the decision of granting legal aid, which at times can lead to an inconsistent interpretation of the criteria of access to legal aid at the national level.[63] Finally, in this case as well, the quality of services offered can be highly affected by the poor remuneration conditions of legal aid defence lawyers. In fact, these are remunerated far less than retained lawyers, and they can sometimes wait years to receive their due compensation.[64]

Issues of quality and training may also affect the effectiveness of the children's defence rights in criminal proceedings. In such sensitive contexts, professionals involved in the proceedings clearly need to have a bespoke expertise in juvenile matters. While this requirement is usually satisfied in the domestic framework,[65] a few critical aspects remain. For instance, Art 9 of the Decree no. 448/1988 does not demand that the individual assessment of the personality and background of the child should necessarily be performed by experts or qualified professionals, as provided by Art 7(7) of the Directive 2016/800. The provision accepts instead that such assessment may be based only on the statements of her parents or of other persons closely involved in her life. While Art 9 is only partially compliant with the Directive, legal scholars have also observed that, in practice, individual assessments are nearly always made by the Ministry of Justice's experts of the juvenile services that first come in contact with the child.[66] Thus, this legal gap does not seem to be that impactful in the concrete level of protection of the right at stake. Moreover, similarly to what has been pointed out in the case of legal aid, no specific training is foreseen for *all* the lawyers participating in juvenile proceedings.[67] This kind

63 Consiglio Nazionale Forense, 'Ipotesi di modifica del D.P.R. 30 maggio 2002, n. 115 Testo unico delle disposizioni legislative e regolamentari in materia di spese di giustizia' (18 April 2018) 5 <https://www.consiglionazionaleforense.it/documents/25901/425930/Patrocinio+a+spese+dello++Stato+-+ARTICOLATO.pdf/1911c3e8-58f4-42b5-ad6a-228d319aa380> accessed 26 October 2021.

64 Fair Trials International, 'The Practical Operatation of Legal Aid in the EU' (July 2012) 5 <https://www.fairtrials.org/wp-content/uploads/2012/09/Legal_Aid_Report.pdf> accessed 26 October 2021.

65 See, e.g., Art 2 Royal Law Decree no. 1404/1934 (establishing a specialized judge for juvenile matters).

66 Camon (n 10) 974.

67 Cfr. art 16, Law of 31 December 2012, no. 247 defining the regime applicable to the legal profession (*Nuova disciplina dell'ordinamento della professione forense*), and the subsequent Legislative Decree of 30 January 2015, no. 6 as well as the National Bar Counsel,

of specific training is only provided for the lawyers authorized by the Council of the Bar Association to take the office of public defenders. No specific training, instead, is required for retained lawyers who are directly appointed by the defendant.

8.4.2 *Effective Judicial Remedies*

In the transposition of the six Directives, a common *fil rouge* can be detected in the choices of the Italian legislator: the reliance on the pre-existent regime of nullities for procedural sanctioning of defence rights' violations. Although most of the Directive's provisions on sanctions were subject to a *de facto* implementation, some of them would have probably deserved more attention by the legislator.[68]

In some cases, the issue lies in the total lack of a bespoke remedy in the national system, where the violation at stake does not fall in the general hypotheses of nullity foreseen at Art 178 CCP. For instance, no specific remedy is available if information rights are provided in a language that is spoken by the suspect or accused person, but not substantially understood by the latter (e.g. because of technical wording used). Also, no sanction has been set out for a violation of the right to medical examination;[69] breaches of this obligation can be invoked before judicial authorities only if they amount to a violation of Art 3 ECHR, which leaves uncovered less serious hypotheses of violation. Finally, effective remedies may not be available if the legislator did not acknowledge the different level of protection granted by the Directives in similar situations. That is the case of the right to access to a lawyer in questionings performed by the Prosecutor. As suggested above, the wording of Directive 2016/800 seems to indicate that presence of the lawyer is mandatory for juvenile defendants, while according to Directive 2013/48 adults retain only a right to have the lawyer present during the act.[70] Despite this potential difference in the EU standard of protection, the Italian legislator left unaltered the pre-existing legislation, where the rules on legal assistance during questionings provided for adults are simply extended to child defendants. In case of violations,

---

Regolamento per la tenuta e l'aggiornamento dell'elenco unico nazionale degli avvocati iscritti negli albi disponibili ad assumere le difese di ufficio of 12 July 2019, as amended on 20 March 2020.

68 See on this topic Michele Caianiello, 'To Sanction (or not to Sanction) Procedural Flaws at EU Level? A Step forward in the Creation of an EU Criminal Process' (2014) 22 European Journal of Crime, Criminal Law and Criminal Justice 317.

69 See Art 8 Directive 2016/800.

70 See *retro* § 8.2.

therefore, available remedies in Italian law may not be enough to ensure the effectivity of the right to access to a lawyer for juvenile defendants questioned by the Prosecutor. Indeed, if under the CCP the absence of the lawyer in such instances might well result in an absolute nullity, detectable until the end of the proceedings, the current regime only foresees the remedy of a nullity of intermediate nature, which can be rectified in much shorter timeframes.

In other cases, a more insidious problem arises, that is where the domestic framework provides for a remedy, which could be potentially ineffective in practice. For instance, Arts 99 and 113(1) of the DPR 115/2002 establish the conditions to lodge and appeal against the decisions rejecting the admission to legal aid. Even if this remedy is formally compliant with the Directive, it is affected by critical issues undermining its effectiveness. Among these, we could mention: the excessive shortness of the deadline to lodge the appeal (i.e. twenty days); the fact that claimants cannot benefit from the legal aid regime for this procedure; the lack of a suspensive effect of the appeal.[71]

Finally, the effectiveness of remedies in the Italian system could be sometimes undermined by the very structure of the internal regime of procedural nullities. According to the legislative technique chosen indeed, nullities can be classified in *general* and *special* ones. General nullities are detailed in Art 178 CCP and identify broad situations that give rise to sanctions of potentially different nature (e.g. intermediate and absolute nullities). Special nullities instead are provided for in bespoke CCP provisions and almost always give rise to relative nullities. The problem may arise when the interpreter is left with enough margin of freedom to label one specific situation as affected by either one or another kind of nullity.[72] In juvenile proceedings, this may happen with regard to decisions taken without prior individual assessment. While part of the doctrine holds that such decisions are affected by an intermediate nullity (Art 178(1)(c) CCP), others think that a relative nullity pursuant to Art 125(3) CCP is at stake.[73] Against this backdrop, a persistent lack of clarity of the applicable regime may make uncertain the situation of the defendant so as to the available remedies and the timeframes to make use of them.

71 Even though the ECtHR has recently clarified that the lack of a suspensive effect does not necessarily undermine the effectiveness of a remedy. See, e.g., *Umoru v Italy* App no 37442/19 (ECHR, 8 June 2020) §43.

72 This is not a novel issue in the Italian case law, as highlighted by Caianiello (n 3) 35 ff.

73 Part of the scholarship holds that the nullity of Art 125(3) CPP only applies to decisions graphically lacking any motivation, while others think that logical deficiencies of motivations should be associated with one of the cases to lodge an appeal before the Court of Cassation (Art 606(1)(e) CPP). See Camon (n 10), 235.

8.5 Concluding Remarks

The analysis of the national implementation of the Defence Rights' Directives provides a relevant benchmark to assess both the standard of effectiveness recognised to fair trial, and the current attitude the Italian system embraced towards judicial cooperation within the criminal sphere. In particular, the minimalistic approach traditionally adopted by the Italian legislator has paved the way for the judiciary to enlarge the procedural safeguards and meet the European minimum requirements.[74] Besides, the relevant function played by the *law-in-action* has fostered a permanent dialogue with European Courts, pursuing common standards of protection whenever afflictive sanctions are to be envisaged.[75] In this perspective, the state of play tends to depict a positive scenario, identifying efficient judge-made remedies capable of facing legislative gaps or shortcomings (see *retro*, § 8.2).

However, the growing involvement of domestic case law has brought about relevant inconsistencies in several fields, undermining legal certainty and individual autonomy. On the one hand, stemming from the cautious approach endorsed by the Italian Parliament, some controversial issues have received contradictory, or rather conflicting, judge-made solutions (see *retro*, § 8.3); on the other, the lack of specific provisions implied the quality assessment of professional services as well as the development of specific trainings to be significantly neglected or inaccurate (see *retro*, § 8.4). Thus, the effectiveness of defence rights has not always been ensured: the reliance on pre-existent regimes of nullities for procedural remedies has undermined the required levels of protections in several hypotheses which would have demanded specific solutions provided by the law (see *retro*, § 8.4).

In this context, the recent legislative initiatives on the privilege against self-incrimination[76] and on the development of a more efficient criminal justice[77] detain a peculiar importance. In particular, the Italian Parliament has recently adopted a proactive attitude, granting specific remedies against penal

74 Examining the considerable scope and level of protection adopted by European laws although the Lisbon Treaty conferred 'competence to legislate in the form of minimum rules', Valsamis Mitsilegas, 'The European Union and the Rights of Individuals in Criminal Proceedings' in Darryl K. Brown, Jenia I. Turner and Bettina Weisser (eds), *The Oxford Handbook of Criminal Process* (OUP 2019) 128.

75 Hence, 'in a legal culture of liberal criminal law that is firmly committed to the legality principle and devoted to fair trial and judicial review, there is little space for the exercise of punitive powers without a solid Constitutional backgroud', see Allegrezza (n 55) 26.

76 The legislative decree is dated back on November 5, 2021: see *retro*, § 2.

77 Law no. 134/2021.

populism and mass-media trials (see *retro*, § 8.2), as well as recommending substantial and procedural instruments to be envisaged in order to curb the duration of criminal proceedings, underpin alternatives to custody and implement the efficient flow of criminal justice. The question is whether the legislator's involvement represents an isolated occurrence or, rather, the beginning of a new process, prioritising these aspects.[78] A hint could be found in the fact that the Constitutional Court has endorsed the procedural guarantees[79] as a prominent trigger to pinpoint the relationship among the primacy of European provisions and the boundaries forged by constitutional national identity (see *retro*, § 8.3).[80] In this view, even judicial cooperation is experiencing a progressive centralisation:[81] the implementation of procedural safeguards has become an interesting spotlight to ascertain the common standards of protection for fundamental rights[82] as well as to assess the unstable balance among national and European actors.[83]

78 On the contrary, as for the defence rights crisis before the European Court of Human Rights, see Michele Caianiello, 'Criminal Process faced with the Challenges of Scientific and Technological Development' (2019) EJCCL & CJ 270 ff.

79 In this perspective, see the dialogue between the Court of Justice and the Italian Constitutional Court on the implementation of the presumption of innocence: *retro*, § 3. As for a general overview on the approximation of Procedural Law, see Kai Ambos, *European Criminal Law* (CUP 2018) 414.

80 On this issue, see Antonio Ruggeri, '"Dialogue" Between European and National Courts, in the Pursuit of the Strongest Protection of Fundamental Rights (with Specific Regard to Criminal and Procedural Law)' in Stefano Ruggeri (ed), *Human Rights in European Criminal Law. New Developments in European Legislation and Case Law after the Lisbon Treaty* (Springer 2015) 9 ff.

81 Considering the latest judgements of the Constitutional Court on the primacy of EU law, in fact, it has been observed that 'these decisions should not be seen as a dangerous step back or a *souverainiste* turning point, but they are actually a consequence of the latest developments in the process of supranational constitutionalisation': Giuseppe Martinico and Giorgio Repetto, 'Fundamental Rights and Constitutional Duels in Europe: An Italian Perspective on Case 269/2017 of the Italian Constitutional Court and Its Aftermath' (2019) EuConst 732. For a broad analysis on the role played by the Constitutional Court in the criminal sphere, see Vittorio Manes, 'Some Lessons from the Taricco Saga' (2018) NJECL 12 ff.

82 As for 'the influences and challenges of EU law as a driving force for national trial procedure reforms', see Helmut Satzger and Frank Zimmermann, 'Challenges of Trial Procedure Reform' in Darryl K. Brown, Jenia I. Turner and Bettina Weisser (eds), *The Oxford Handbook of Criminal Process* (OUP 2019) 633 ff.

83 Analysing 'how to strike a balance, in terms of judicial cooperation, between sovereignty and supranationality': Daniele Gallo, 'Challenging EU constitutional law: the Italian Constitutional Court's new stance on direct effect and the preliminary reference procedure' (2019) Eur Law J 434 ff.

CHAPTER 9

Poland

There and Back Again. A Struggle with Transposition of EU Directives

Karolina Kremens, Wojciech Jasiński, Dorota Czerwińska, and Dominika Czerniak

9.1 Introduction

The effective approximation of the legal orders of EU Member States in criminal law implies their obligation to adjust domestic legal regimes to minimum standards derived from EU law. The process of harmonisation of Polish criminal law has started with the implementation of the EAW Framework Decision, with the aim to enhance the mutual trust between the States becoming the very basis of the existence of transborder instruments in criminal proceedings. While the obligation to implement the EAW was imposed on Poland a bit later than on some other EU Member States due to its date of accession to the EU, it did not run without problems.[1] This shows that from the beginning Poland, similarly as other EU Member States, struggled with the proper implementation of EU laws into the domestic legal system.

This Chapter focuses on the level of implementation in the Polish legal system of six EU Directives concerning protection of the rights of suspects and accused persons in criminal proceedings. It identifies the lacunas and flaws in the transposition process and analyses the reasons standing behind the failure to properly implement this important piece of EU legislation into the Polish legal system. Although there are noticeable differences in the number and gravity of shortcomings that refer to each of the analysed Directives, some general points regarding transposition can certainly be made. Some deficiencies are of a structural character, negatively affecting the transposition of several Directives for the same reason, while others appear only in a specific context of transposition of a given Directive. The latter are numerous in number, and

1 See: The practice of the European arrest warrant in Poland as an issuing country. Country report, HFPC, 8–13.

 | DOI:10.1163/9789004513396_011

they are impossible to all be addressed in this chapter.[2] On the other hand, the most important structural deficiencies can be narrowed down to three. The first concerns the improper understanding of the term 'suspect' used in the EU Directives, bringing major consequences for the effective guarantees of the right of access to a lawyer and the right to legal aid. The second relates to the lack of individual assessment of the particular needs of vulnerable suspects or accused persons and lack of adequate protection of their rights at the domestic level. The third structural deficiency concerns the growing problem of the deterioration of the quality of implementation process in Poland during the past seven years.

The main conclusion of the chapter is that the transposition of EU Directives concerning the rights of suspects and accused persons is generally far from satisfactory and does not provide for their effective protection. Therefore, immediate legislative actions are necessary to remedy the situation. However, since there is a far-reaching and disturbing regress in the transposition process that can be observed in recent years, the prospects for significant improvement to happen soon are not very high.

The Chapter has been divided into three parts. Section 9.2 outlines the overall assessment of the implementation of the six EU Directives in question showing general problems concerning the identification of laws that are deemed to transpose EU law into the Polish system. Section 9.3 is devoted to the analysis of the three structural problems affecting the implementation, as mentioned above. Finally, Section 9.4 focuses on the case law from Polish courts concerning the standard of EU Directives. The Chapter ends with concluding remarks, and brings the views on possible further steps in the implementation of EU Directives for the near future.

9.2 The Implementation of EU Directives: State of Play

The general inquiry into the transposition process in Poland reveals the lack of identifiable uniform course of action in the case of each analysed Directive. It seems to be rather a combination of random factors, including current political needs of the governing majority, that determine how the Directives are implemented to the domestic legal order. Directive 2010/64 and Directive 2012/13 have been almost fully transposed, which may be a result of the formerly

2 The complex and detailed analysis of transposition into Polish law of all rights of suspects and accused persons that stem from EU Directives can be accessed through the project website.

present positive attitude towards Europeanisation processes and the enhancement of human rights protection. On the other side, national law only partially meets the standard resulting from Directive 2016/343. As for Directives 2013/48 and 2016/800 the core rights provided by them are not transposed, and in the case of Directive 2016/1919 there has not even been any legislative effort taken to implement it. In consequence, Polish law provides for an inconsistent framework in which the lack of certain rights intersects with properly designed guarantees.

Directive 2010/64 may be considered as relatively well transposed. Notwithstanding the systemic deficiency of the Polish Code of Criminal Procedure (hereinafter: k.p.k.)[3] that influences the applicability of the right to translation and interpretation at an early stage of a criminal process,[4] there are other minor lacunas in its transposition. This concerns the absence of procedure of ascertaining the capacity of the suspect or accused person to speak and understand the language of proceedings as well as the lack of specific measures allowing the quality of interpretation or translation to be challenged. In addition, the implementation of the right to an interpreter's assistance in communication between suspect or accused person and her/his defence counsel is also deficient, since the domestic provisions do not offer any guidance on how to apply such assistance.

In case of Directive 2012/13 the shortcomings in transposition are also considerably minor. There is no provision in Polish law that directly guarantees that the particular needs of vulnerable suspects or accused persons in relation to their right to information will be taken into consideration. In the case of arrest or detention the transposition of the right to information is not full, as the notification about the right to legal aid and the conditions for obtaining it and the right to access a case file are incomplete or missing. Additionally, the relevant k.p.k. provisions allow the prosecutor or other investigating authority to deny access to some documents, such as witness depositions, essential to challenging the lawfulness of the arrest or detention. There is also no judicial review over decisions to refuse access to case files issued by an investigating authority other than the prosecutor.

On the contrary, the transposition of Directive 2013/48 is seriously flawed.[5] The most important deficiency stems from a lack of access to a lawyer to the

---

3 *Kodeks postępowania karnego* of 6 June 1997, Dziennik Ustaw 1997, nr 89, poz. 555 with amendments.

4 See Sect. 9.3.1.

5 See *e.g.* the Statement of the Polish Ombudsman to the Minister of Justice of 5 June 2017 concerning lack of implementation of Directive 2013/48 (II.5150.9.2014) <https://www.rpo.gov.pl/sites/default/files/Wystąpienie%20do%20Ministra%20Sprawiedliwości%20w%20sprawie%20prawa%20osoby%20zatrzymanej%20do%20pomocy%20prawnej.pdf>accessed

extent provided in the Directive for suspects to whom charges were not officially presented. The right to contact a lawyer before the first interrogation is also not fully guaranteed in k.p.k. Pursuant to Article 301 k.p.k. the suspect may demand that her/his interrogation is conducted in the presence of a defence attorney, but failure of the attorney to appear does not impede the course of proceedings and the questioning may continue. In addition, the privileged lawyer–client communication is not sufficiently protected, since during the first fourteen days of detention a prosecutor may decide that it is supervised, which can seriously undermine the effectiveness of the defence in the proceedings as a whole. Moreover, the decision to supervise the privileged communication is not subjected to judicial review. Yet some other rights guaranteed in Directive 2013/48 are correctly transposed. That refers to the right to have a third person informed of the deprivation of liberty, the right to communicate with consular authorities as well as the right to communicate, while deprived of liberty, with third persons. Nonetheless in the latter case it might be questioned whether the implementation is full, since there are no domestic provisions related to the communication with third persons of the arrestee.

Accordingly, the transposition of Directive 2016/1919 into the Polish legal system must also be evaluated as flawed, since a suspect to whom charges were not officially presented is not offered a right to legal aid to the extent demanded by EU law. The obligation to organise an effective legal aid system of sufficient quality was not explicitly transposed. Considering the low remuneration paid to lawyers appointed as legal aid, as well as the lack of any dedicated procedures allowing the quality of their service to be verified, the transposition of these requirements seems deficient. That does not need to mean that the legal aid services themselves function ineffectively. But there is no formal mechanism to verify that issue. Directive 2016/1919 has also not been transposed when considering particular needs of vulnerable suspects, accused persons and requested persons. The Polish law provides for mandatory defence if the suspect or accused person is under 18 years old, deaf, mute, blind or suffered from a mental disorder at the time of committing the alleged offence and is unable to participate in proceedings or reasonably defend herself. However,

---

2 November 2021. This was repeated on 4 July 2018 <https://www.rpo.gov.pl/sites/default/files/Wystąpienie%20RPO%20do%20Prezesa%20Rady%20Ministrów%20ws.%20wprowadzenia%20dyrektywy%20gwarantującej%20m.in_.%20prawo%20zatrzymanego%20do%20adwokata.pdf,> accessed 2 November 2021; and 14 July 2021 (II.5150.2.2021.MH) https://bip.brpo.gov.pl/sites/default/files/Pismo_RPO_Reynders_(jez_angielski)_14.07.2021.pdf accessed 2 November 2021.

apart from these situations the particular needs of vulnerable suspects, accused persons and requested persons are not formally recognised.

The transposition of Directive 2016/343 is incomplete for other reasons. First, the measures to ensure that suspects and accused persons are not presented as being guilty, in court or in public, using measures of physical restraint, have not been introduced in Polish law. The right to remain silent and the right not to incriminate oneself are also not fully transposed, due to the structural problem with the divergence in understanding of the word 'suspect' in EU and Polish law.[6] As a result, the right to remain silent and the right not to incriminate oneself are not fully guaranteed to suspects to whom charges were not officially presented. The right to be present at trial is also incorrectly transposed and it is also doubtful that the implementation of the burden of proof standard is correct. Since domestic provisions in the vast majority of criminal cases allow for the absence of the prosecutor at trial, the burden of proof is *de facto* shifted onto the court, which might be perceived as contrary to Art 6(1), Directive 2016/343.

Finally, the rights provided in Directive 2016/800 have not been transposed to the Polish legal system almost entirely. This lack of implementation has been openly criticised,[7] and although the relevant amendment has even been drafted by the government,[8] it has not so far been enacted. The main deficiency of the existing domestic provisions stems from the adoption of the definition of a child under Polish criminal law that does not include those who are 17- to 18-year-olds. The Polish law refers the term 'minor' only to those aged 15 to 17 years-old and not to those are 17- to 18-year-olds. This leaves the latter group entirely without the special level of protection demanded by the Directive also for them. Other core rights provided by the Directive are also overlooked. This refers to the right to information of children suspected or accused of

6 See Sect. 3.1.

7 Cf. the Opinion of Ombudsman to Minister of Justice of 11 March 2019, II.510.820.2018II.510.820.2018.MM; https://bip.brpo.gov.pl/sites/default/files/Wyst%C4%85pienie%20do%20Minístra%20Sprawiedliwo%C5%9Bci%20w%20sprawie%20dyrektywy%20o%20gwarancjach%20procesowych%20dla%20dzieci%20b%C4%99d%C4%85cych%20podejrzanymi%20lub%20oskar%C5%BConymi.pdf, accessed 2 November 2021; Maciej Fingas, 'Podmiot odpowiedzialności rodzicielskiej w procesie karnym – wybrane zagadnienia implementacji dyrektywy 2016/800' (2019) 11 Europejski Przegląd Sądowy 11.

8 The draft of the Act on amendment of the CCP and other acts (U31) <https://legislacja.rcl.gov.pl/docs//2/12338566/12722226/12722227/dokument468012.pdf> accessed 2 November 2021. The drafted law also aims at transposing Directive 2011/93/EU of the European Parliament and of the Council of 13 December 2011 on combating the sexual abuse and sexual exploitation of children and child pornography and replacing Council Framework Decision 2004/68/JHA.

committing a criminal offence as well as the holder of parental responsibility. Likewise, an important tool aiming at the identification of particular needs of suspects and accused persons under 18 years old, namely the right to an individual assessment, has been not implemented. In the cases of other provisions, referring to the protection of children's privacy, audio-visual recording of their questioning, special treatment during deprivation of liberty and a right of the child to be accompanied by the holder of parental responsibility during the proceedings, the implementation is also only partial.

9.3 Main Critical Profiles in the Legislation

As mentioned in Section 9.1, the legislative efforts taken by Polish authorities to transpose EU Directives are not satisfactory. There are numerous deficiencies that can be identified. Three of them, however, are of crucial importance. They will be discussed below.

9.3.1 *The Improper Interpretation of the Term 'Suspect'*

The most important structural problem affecting the transposition of almost all analysed EU Directives is the understanding of the word 'suspect' as used within them. Contrary to the uniform views expressed in the legal doctrine,[9] Polish authorities continuously equate the term 'suspect' used in the Directives with the Polish equivalent used in the k.p.k. (*podejrzany*). This is not only erroneous, but also affects in a disturbing way the desired application of the rights granted to the suspect at the very early stage of criminal proceedings. This misconception demands a broader explanation.

Polish law provides for a formal procedure by which the person is preliminarily charged with a crime (Art 313 k.p.k.). This takes place by issuing a formal charging decision against her/him, promulgating it, which is followed by

9 Sławomir Steinborn, 'Status osoby podejrzanej w procesie karnym z perspektywy Konstytucji RP: (uwagi de lege lata i de lege ferenda)' in Piotr Kardas, Tomasz Sroka, Włodzimierz Wróbel (eds) *Państwo prawa i prawo karne: księga jubileuszowa profesora Andrzeja Zolla, t. 2,* (Wolters Kluwer 2012) 1781–1801; Sławomir Steinborn, Małgorzata Wąsek-Wiaderek 'Moment uzyskania statusu biernej strony postępowania karnego z perspektywy konstytucyjnej i międzynarodowej' in Beata T. Bieńskowska, Hanna Gajewska-Kraczkowska, Maria Rogacka-Rzewnicka (eds) *Wokół gwarancji współczesnego procesu karnego. Księga jubileuszowa profesora Piotra Kruszyńskiego* (Wolters Kluwer 2019) 429–456; Andrzej Sakowicz, *The Right to Silence in the EU Directive 2016/343 on the Strengthening of Certain Aspects of the Presumption of Innocence from the Perspective of Polish Criminal Proceedings,* 41 Review of European and Comparative Law 55, <https://czasopisma.kul.pl/recl/article/view/6155> accessed 2 November 2021.

mandatory interrogation, unless the person has fled. In theory, the investigative authorities are obliged to bring charges as soon as they have sufficient evidence indicating the crime was committed by a specific person. Delaying formal charging is impermissible. Only if the charges are formally presented does the individual gain the status of *podejrzany* and becomes a party to the proceedings with a possibility of fully exercising defence rights. This procedure was primarily introduced to guarantee the suspect the proper and complete information about the content of the charges as adopted against her/him by the investigating authority.[10] Yet, it resulted in setting a formal point in time from which the individual can fully enjoy her defence rights. As a consequence, Polish law makes a very strict distinction between the status of *podejrzany* and *osoba podejrzana*.[11] The former term has been normatively defined as a person regarding whom a decision initially charging a person with a crime has been issued, or who, without the issuance of such a decision, has been informed about charges in connection with the initiation of the person's interrogation in such capacity (Art 71 § 1 k.p.k.). Conversely, the latter term has no legal definition, although it is understood as referring to a person who is in fact suspected of committing a crime, but who has not yet been initially charged with an offence.[12] And only a person presented with preliminary charges is provided with defence rights including the right to information, right of access to the case file, right of access to a defence counsel, as well as right to legal aid. Moreover, even the right not to incriminate oneself is formally attributed in k.p.k. only to *podejrzany*. Accordingly, *osoba podejrzana*, because of the lack of a formal preliminary charging procedure launched against her, remains unprotected by the same set of rights.[13] Only when *osoba podejrzana* is arrested will some rights be granted to her. Paradoxically, the situation of such a person becomes better when she is arrested, since at least she gains an enforceable right of access to a lawyer, the right to remain silent, the right to information and the right to be assisted by an interpreter (Arts 245 § 1 and 244 § 2 k.p.k.). An important deficiency in the legal protection of *osoba podejrzana* is also visible when she is willing to appoint a professional counsel. Such a counsel does

---

10 Janusz Tylman and Tomasz Grzegorczyk, *Postępowanie karne* (Lexis Nexis 2014) 669.

11 See more broadly on the preliminary charging process and the status of *podejrzany* and *osoba podejrzana* in: Doris De Vocht, 'Poland' in Ed Cape, Zaza Namoradze, Robert Smith, Taru Spronken (eds) *Effective Criminal Defence in Europe* (Intersentia 2010) 435; Wojciech Jasiński and Karolina Kremens, *Criminal Law in Poland* (Wolters Kluwer 2019) 221–222.

12 Wojciech Jasiński and Karolina Kremens, *Criminal Law in Poland* (Wolters Kluwer 2019) 202.

13 Karolina Kremens, *Powers of the Prosecutor in Criminal Investigation. A Comparative Approach* (Routledge 2021) 223.

not have a status of defence counsel and the right to appoint her is subject to the prosecutor's approval based on whether the procedural interests of *osoba podejrzana* so requires. Refusal is not subject to judicial review.[14]

The lack of adequate protection of the individual before the preliminary charging takes place has been criticised in the literature for many years.[15] Moreover, the Polish Constitution confers the right to defend oneself to anyone against whom the criminal proceedings are conducted (Art 42(2) of the Polish Constitution), which also includes a person before her/his formal designation as *podejrzany*. Therefore, the formalistic approach as adopted in the k.p.k. does not even comply with the constitutional standard. And in the context of the standards provided by the EU Directives this issue becomes particularly problematic.

The EU Directives use the term 'suspect', which is indeed directly translated into Polish as *podejrzany*. This seems to be the primary cause of this very serious misinterpretation of to whom the rights guaranteed in EU Directives are granted. A *podejrzany* under Polish law is indeed guaranteed the rights provided for a suspect by the EU Directives, while an *osoba podejrzana* (which is typically and naturally translated from Polish as 'suspected person'), who also remains within the scope of protection of EU Directives, is not given the same status, despite the criminal investigation already being directed against her/him.

This literal translation of the term 'suspect' supported the claim of the Polish authorities that the implementation of the EU Directives has been successful. The government even went so far as to assert that the implementation was unnecessary since Polish law provided a sufficient standard of protection for *podejrzany* before the EU Directives were even adopted.[16] Although this belief has been undermined by the Polish Ombudsman, who addressed the

14 Art 87 § 2 k.p.k.

15 See *e.g.* Feliks Prusak, 'Faktycznie podejrzany w procesie karnym' (1971) 3 Palestra 32; Andrzej Murzynowski 'Faktyczny podejrzany w postępowaniu przygotowawczym' (1971) 10 Palestra 36; Sławomir Steinborn, 'Status osoby podejrzanej w procesie karnym z perspektywy Konstytucji RP (uwagi de lege lata i de lege ferenda)' in Piotr Kardas, Tomasz Sroka, Włodzimierz Wróbel (eds), *Państwo prawa i prawo karne. Księga jubileuszowa Profesora Andrzeja Zolla* (Wolters Kluwer 2012) 1781; Ryszard A. Stefański, 'Prawo do obrony osoby podejrzanej' in Tomasz Grzegorczyk, Jacek Izydorczyk, Ryszard Olszewski (eds), *Z problematyki funkcji procesu karnego* (Wolters Kluwer 2013) 305; Andrzej Sakowicz, *Prawo do milczenia w polskim procesie karnym* (Temida2 2019) 236.

16 See for example the answer of the Minister of Justice of 14 August 2019 in response to the Intervention No. 32684 filed by the Member of the Polish Parliament concerning the lack of transposition to Polish law the Directive 2016/1919 <https://www.sejm.gov.pl/Sejm8.nsf/InterpelacjaTresc.xsp?key=BF7HE5> accessed 2 November 2021.

government on numerous occasions indicating the improper implementation of the Directives,[17] the Ministry of Justice has refused to admit that Polish law demands corrections to embrace *osoba podejrzana* with the desired protection. Because the government has been made aware of who should be covered by the minimum standard of the EU Directives and why the term 'suspect' should also cover *osoba podejrzana,*[18] the erroneous interpretation should be considered as intentional.

Therefore, it must be argued that to assume the proper and full implementation of the EU Directives in Poland the guarantees provided for the suspect should be extended to those individuals who were targeted by the criminal justice authorities through such measures as arrest or search but were not yet preliminarily charged with a crime. Whether it is done simply by attaching these rights to *osoba podejrzana* or by revoking the formal determination of a suspect under Polish law is less important. The bottom line is that at this point in Poland a great number of individuals against whom an investigation is being conducted are deprived of the rights that EU Directives provide them with.

Hence, since the Polish government deliberately refuses to take into account the fundamental difference between the meaning of 'suspect' in EU and Polish law, the transposition of the majority of a suspect's rights into Polish law is only partial, as it offers no protection to suspects (in the European meaning of the word) to whom charges were not officially presented (*e.g.* a person arrested by the police under suspicion of committing an offence). That is an

---

17 See *e.g.* the Statement of the Polish Ombudsman to the Minister of Justice of 5 June 2017 concerning lack of implementation of Directive 2013/48 (II.5150.9.2014) <https://www.rpo.gov.pl/sites/default/files/Wystąpienie%20do%20Ministra%20Sprawiedliwości%20w%20sprawie%20prawa%20osoby%20zatrzymanej%20do%20pomocy%20prawnej.pdf> accessed 2 November 2021. This was repeated on 4 July 2018 <https://www.rpo.gov.pl/sites/default/files/Wystąpienie%20RPO%20do%20Prezesa%20Rady%20Ministrów%20ws.%20wprowadzenia%20dyrektywy%20gwarantującej%20m.in_.%20prawo%20zatrzymanego%20do%20adwokata.pdf> accessed 2 November 2021.

18 See also other works publicly presenting similar arguments, for example by the Chief Justice of the Polish Supreme Court – Pierwszy Prezes Sądu Najwyższego, Uwagi o stwierdzonych nieprawidłowościach i lukach w prawie, Warszawa 2017, 86–88 <http://www.sn.pl/osadzienajwyzszym/Uwagi_PPSN_luki_w_prawie/luki-w-prawie-2017.pdf> accessed 2 November 2021; Helsinki Foundation on Human Rights – Wzmacnianie praw osób podejrzanych i oskarżonych. Rola krajowych instytucji ochrony praw człowieka, Warszawa 2019, 54 <https://www.hfhr.pl/wp-content/uploads/2020/04/Wzmacnianie-praw-os%C3%B3b-podejrzanych-i-oskar%C5%BConych-NHRI-krajowy-web.pdf> accessed 2 November 2021; Barbara Grabowska-Moroz (ed), *Prawo dostępu do obrońcy w świetle prawa europejskiego* (Warszawa 2018) <https://www.hfhr.pl/wp-content/uploads/2018/05/Prawo-dostępu-do-obroncy-w-swietle-prawa-UE-20180410.pdf> accessed 2 November 2021.

issue in relation to suspects' rights granted by Directives 2010/64 (in respect of the right to translation and interpretation), 2013/48 (in respect of the right of access to a lawyer), 2016/800 (in respect of the right of access to legal aid), 2016/1919 (again in respect of the right of access to a lawyer) as well as Directive 2016/343 (in respect to the right to remain silent and the right not to incriminate oneself).

9.3.2 *Neglecting Particular Needs of Vulnerable Suspects*

The second structural deficiency in the transposition process refers to the lack of the explicit implementation of the Directives' provisions referring to particular needs of vulnerable suspects or accused persons. This issue is emphasised in the context of the right to information (Directive 2012/13), the right of access to a lawyer (Directive 2013/48) and the right to legal aid (Directive 2016/1919). Moreover, in the case of the right to interpretation (Directive 2010/64), particular needs of persons with hearing or speech impediments should be acknowledged. A variety of specific measures, including individual assessment, are also included in Directive 2016/800. This clearly indicates how important that issue is for the EU lawmakers.

The concept of vulnerable suspects is not explicitly defined in EU Directives. However, the European Commission emphasised that states shall 'foresee a presumption of vulnerability in particular for persons with serious psychological, intellectual, physical or sensory impairments, or mental illness or cognitive disorders, hindering them to understand and effectively participate in the proceedings', as well as for children.[19] It is the duty of the criminal justice authorities in each case to identify the particular needs and adjust their actions to the cognitive abilities of the suspect or accused. This applies to effective access to a lawyer, medical assistance, the right to information as well as the respect for the right to privacy and non-discrimination.[20]

Unfortunately, Polish law does not provide for any specific measures aiming at acknowledging the particular needs of vulnerable suspects, nor are there any policies adopted to safeguard the effectiveness of their rights. The procedural provisions fail to even recognise the need for such protection and individual assessment.[21] Isolated rights have been awarded only to some of the categories of persons belonging to this group. One of the rare examples

19 Commission Recommendation of 27 November 2013 on procedural safeguards for vulnerable persons suspected or accused in criminal proceedings, OJ 2013/C 378/02, 8–10.

20 Points 8 to 10 of the Commission Recommendation of 27 November 2013.

21 Cf. Monika Zbrojewska, Amadeusz Małolepszy, 'Obiektywna podatność podejrzanego na pokrzywdzenie w procesie karnym' (2014) 5 Przegląd Sądowy 63.

of recognition of such needs is the mechanism of mandatory defence as provided by Art 79 §§ 1-2 k.p.k. It applies to blind, deaf or mute persons, persons under the age of 18, as well as those whose mental state raises doubts as to their sanity during the supposedly criminal act or ability to participate reasonably in the proceedings. The mandatory defence also applies when the court deems it necessary due to other reasons. However, there are no statutory guidelines pertaining to the interpretation of this clause. Moreover, no mechanisms were introduced to assess the particular needs of persons who do not fit into the catalogue included in Art 79 § 1 k.p.k., leaving it entirely to the discretion of the procedural authorities.

9.3.3 *Setback in the Quality of the Transposition Process*

The analysis of the transposition process regarding the analysed EU Directives reveals that its quality is deteriorating. The first two adopted EU Directives (2010/64 and 2012/13) were relatively correctly implemented into the Polish legal system. However, in the case of the other four Directives enacted later, the transposition was seriously flawed or even non-existent. This may be considered as resulting mainly from the current Polish authorities' approach of being highly reluctant to accept EU standards and the necessity of their implementation in the domestic legal system. For the past six years, the Polish Ombudsman and various NGOs have addressed the Ministry of Justice and the Prime Minister on numerous occasions underlining the pressing need for introducing effective access to defence counsel for suspects.[22] These notifications have been continuously ignored, and no legislative actions have been undertaken.

Another problematic factor is the lack of a transparent and uniform procedure for adopting amendments resulting from the transposition of EU standards into the Polish legal system. The draft laws and transcripts of parliamentary works on the implementation of EU Directives do not offer comprehensive and convincing justification regarding the choice of adopted measures.

22 The latest statement by the Ombudsman of 14 July 2021 (II.5150.2.2021.MH), <https://bip.brpo.gov.pl/sites/default/files/Pismo_RPO_Reynders_(jez_angielski)_14.07.2021.pdf> accessed 2 November 2021. See also <https://bip.brpo.gov.pl/pl/content/ms-nie-odpowiada-na-wystapienia-rpo-ws-kontaktu-z-obronca-juz-od-samego-zatrzymania-marcin> accessed 3 November 2021. See also regarding the Opinion of Ombudsman to Minister of Justice of 11 March 2019 concerning the lack of transposition of Directive 2016/800 (II.510.820.2018II.510.820.2018.MM) <https://www.rpo.gov.pl/sites/default/files/Wystąpienie%20do%20Ministra%20Sprawiedliwości%20w%20sprawie%20dyrektywy%200%20gwarancjach%20procesowych%20dla%20dzieci%20będących%20podejrzanymi%20lub%20oskarżonymi.pdf> accessed 2 November 2021.

Only in the case of a draft act amending k.p.k. implementing the Directives 2010/64 and 2012/13[23] was this condition met. The need for transposition of other Directives was either erroneously denied or the transposition itself was not preceded by a comprehensive justification attached to the bill presented by the government. Instead, in the case of Directives 2013/48 and 2016/343 a footnote was added to k.p.k. indicating the transposition. It is not, however, at all clear through which provisions of the Code the process was accomplished. As for Directives 2016/800 and 2016/1919, neither k.p.k. nor any other statute provided for them.

More recently, another severe backslide in the transposition of the Directives can be noticed. Some provisions that were either directly or indirectly implementing the Directives have been revoked. A good example may be the right of a detained person to access the case file derived from Directive 2012/13. It was fully transposed until 14 April 2016. On that date, however, the Polish law was amended and significant restrictions on access to the case file by a suspect were introduced contrary to Article 7(1) of Directive 2012/13. Likewise, one of the most recent amendments of k.p.k., which was introduced at the end of 2019, has provided for a possibility of conducting a trial during a justified absence of an accused willing to participate at trial (Art 378a k.p.k.), which is incompatible with the standard established by *Directive* 2016/343. All this together adds up to a sad picture of gradual distancing of Poland from EU standards in criminal matters.

9.4 Main Critical Profiles in the Case Law

The analysis of the case law of Polish courts in criminal cases indicates that direct references to the EU Directives in question appear only incidentally, similarly to their direct application. So far there are no studies that identify the causes behind such inaction. Several factors might be perceived as relevant, namely the relatively short time since Polish accession to the EU (17 years), a low level of awareness of Polish judges with regard to EU law in general, and the lack of proper training, especially for those judges who were not trained in EU law during their legal education.[24] Rather vague provisions offered by EU

23 *Act of 27 September 2013 on the amendment of CCP and other acts* (Dziennik Ustaw 2013, poz. 1247) – hereinafter: Act of 27 September 2013.

24 A similar problem has been reported on the poor use of EU law by Polish judges in cases concerning the transfer of prisoners among EU Member States which results from a lack of specialisation of judges in transnational criminal cases – cf. Agnieszka Frąckowiak-Adamska, Wojciech Jasiński, Karolina Kremens, 'Polish report' in Tony Marguery (ed),

law might also be considered a reason why courts are reluctant to base their decisions on the Directives directly. However, since none of the Directives were fully and properly transposed to Polish law, the burden of protecting the rights of the accused in practice rests upon the courts. They should adopt an interpretation of national regulations that ensures the effectiveness of EU law, and if the EU regulations meet the criteria of direct effectiveness, they shall apply the relevant provisions of the Directives.[25]

There are only a few examples of such an approach. One is the judgment of the Court of Appeal in Wrocław[26] addressing the *in dubio pro reo* rule as derived from Art 6 of Directive 2016/343. The Court of Appeal deciding on the case of involuntary manslaughter referred directly to this provision and ruled that it is not its obligation to verify whether doubts as to the facts of the case that appeared during trial could be eliminated or not, even though the national law stipulates that only doubts that cannot be eliminated should benefit the accused (Art 5 k.p.k.).

Another illustration of courts' activity in the direct application of the EU Directives can be a broader recognition of the category of suspects particularly vulnerable to harm than in terms of mandatory representation by the counsel.[27] However, such recognition and the procedural faults regarding particularly vulnerable suspects' rights often does not affect the final decision unfavourably for the accused.[28]

Also, the ruling of the Court of Appeal in Gdańsk of 8 April 2020[29] may be treated as another example of direct application of the EU Directives. The

Mutual trust under pressure, the transferring of sentenced persons in the EU: transfer of judgments of conviction in the European Union and the respect for individual's fundamental rights (Wolf Legal Publishers 2018) 310–311.

25 Hanna Kuczyńska, 'Bezpośrednie stosowanie dyrektywy UE w sprawach karnych. Skutki braku implementacji dyrektywy UE' in Jerzy Skorupka, Dominika Czerniak (eds), *Europejskie gwarancje prawidłowego wymiaru sprawiedliwości w sprawach karnych* (C.H. Beck 2021) 73–107.

26 Judgment of the Court of Appeal in Wrocław of 15 May 2019, II AKa 131/19, LEX no. 2704602. English summary <https://crossjustice.eu/LegalDB/Doc/CourtAct/6761732/13> accessed 2 October 2021.

27 The judgment of the Supreme Court of 4 April 2013, III KK 327/12, OSNKW 2013, nr 7, poz. 60. See also: the Judgment of the Court of Appeal in Wrocław of 28 July 2018, II AKa 169/18, LEX no. 2532130; the judgment of the Supreme Court of 27 June 2017, II KK 82/17, LEX no. 2338030, English summary <https://crossjustice.eu/LegalDB/Doc/CourtAct/6761761/14> accessed 2 November 2021.

28 See: the Judgment of the Court of Appeal in Katowice of 29 November 2018 r., II AKa 171/18; LEX no. 2690783. English summary <https://crossjustice.eu/LegalDB/Doc/CourtAct/6761480/12> accessed 2 November 2021.

29 II Akz 207/20 – unpublished.

case concerned the decision on detention on remand that was imposed on the individual based on witnesses' testimonies withheld by the prosecutor from the defence. This was done based on domestic provisions allowing for such restrain in a situation in which the life, health or liberty of the witness might be endangered. The Court of Appeal quashed the decision underlying the violation of the defence's rights to access the documents. This right, as guaranteed by Article 7(1) of Directive 2012/13, was considered as essential to effectively challenge the lawfulness of detention and resulted in denying the right of the prosecution to restrict such access. Therefore, the Court stated that the national provision allowing the recordings of witnesses' testimonies to be withheld from the defence should not be applied.

9.5 Concluding Remarks

The transposition of the EU Directives concerning rights of suspects and accused persons in criminal proceedings into Polish law is far from satisfactory. The Directives have been transposed to different extents, but none have been implemented fully. While in the case of the transposition of Directives 2010/64 and 2012/13 shortcomings are limited, the acknowledgement of EU standards stemming from all other Directives encountered many more difficulties. This results in providing only partial protection of the rights of suspects and accused persons under Polish law. Particularly disturbing is the reluctance or even hostility of the government and parliamentary majority towards adjusting national laws to the binding European standards of procedural fairness. Unfortunately, this is accompanied by a low level of awareness and engagement in safeguarding EU defence rights standards on the courts' part, which raises doubts as to whether the lacunas in the implementation will be, where possible, corrected in practice. Thus, the insufficient level of protection of the suspects and accused persons continues to be an important problem in Polish criminal proceedings both on a statutory and practical level.

The lacunas in the transposition of the Directives are of both a structural and incidental character. Certainly, the most important structural problem is the insufficient protection of suspects' rights at the early stage of criminal investigation stemming from improper interpretation by Polish lawmakers of the term 'suspect' used in the EU Directives. Yet the incidental errors, if taken separately, could be considered as relatively minor flaws, and be fixed easily. This applies for example to clarification of the catalogue of documents delivered to the accused with a translation or introduction of procedures challenging the quality of interpretation and translation. However, there are no signs of legislative activity in this sense.

Sadly, the research also shows that since 2016 the level of transposition of the EU Directives in Poland is not only not improving but even deteriorating. Several recent amendments of the k.p.k. only deepened the inconsistencies between the EU and domestic legal orders. This concerns for example access to the case file during the proceedings concerning pre-trial detention (Arts 156 § 5a, and 250 § 2b k.p.k.) and insufficient guarantee of personal participation of the defendant at trial (Art 378a k.p.k.). Thus, the phenomenon of the 'de-implementation' of EU Directives can be observed. This alarming tendency has not gone unnoticed. The Polish Ombudsman and NGOs consequently draw lawmakers' attention to the shortcomings of implementation concerning Directives 2012/13, 2013/48, 2016/343 and 2016/800. The failure in the case of the last Directive is known to the government since it has been working on a draft of an appropriate amending act for almost a year. Moreover, the flaws in the implementation of Directives 2016/343 and 2013/48 have already been noticed by the European Commission, and the Polish government has been called on to provide explanations.[30] This situation demands the introduction of immediate and effective remedy actions.

Yet hopes that the situation will change soon should not be too high. The reluctant or even hostile attitude of the Polish government towards the EU and the primacy of EU law could be seen in the past years on numerous occasions, particularly regarding the judiciary. The most recent Polish Constitutional Court judgment of 7 October 2021 finding the provisions of TEU incompatible with the Polish Constitution on multiple counts[31] is probably the most striking example of such an attitude. This has a very negative impact not only on the implementation of EU standards regarding defence rights in Poland, but also on the ability to cooperate with other countries within the area of freedom,

---

30 The European Commission's information of 18 February 2021 on key decisions regarding the infringements of EU law <https://ec.europa.eu/commission/presscorner/detail/pl/inf_21_441> accessed 2 November 2021. The European Commission noticed lack of implementation of Article 4 of the Directive 2016/343. The European Commission's information of 15 July 2021 on key decisions regarding the infringements of EU law <https://ec.europa.eu/commission/presscorner/detail/pl/inf_21_3440> accessed 2 November 2021.

31 Decision of the Polish Constitutional Court of 7 October 2021, K 3/21 <https://trybunal.gov.pl/postepowanie-i-orzeczenia/wyroki/art/11662-ocena-zgodnosci-z-konstytucja-rp-wybranych-przepisow-traktatu-o-unii-europejskiej> accessed 2 November 2021. See Jakub Jaraczewski, 'Gazing into the Abyss. The K 3/21 decision of the Polish Constitutional Tribunal' (*Verfassungsblog.de* 12 October 2021) <https://verfassungsblog.de/gazing-into-the-abyss/> accessed 2 November 2021.

security and justice. The lack of respect for EU law has already resulted in the ability of Polish courts to provide a fair trial for requested persons under the EAW procedure being challenged.[32] Certainly, the dominating Eurosceptic narrative of the governing majority in Poland is not a friendly environment for introducing necessary correction in the transposition of the EU Directives. Therefore, regrettably, it is hard to expect that Polish law will fully implement the EU standards of protection of defence rights in criminal proceedings in the near future.

32 See Judgment of the CJEU of 25 July 2018, C-216/18 PPU *The Minister for Justice and Equality v. LM*. Cf. Agnieszka Frąckowiak-Adamska, Mutual trust and independence of the judiciary after the CJEU judgment in LM – new era or business as usual?, EU Law Analysis Blog (15 August 2018), http://eulawanalysis.blogspot.com/2018/08/mutual-trust-and-independence-of.html (accessed: 2 November 2019) and A Frąckowiak-Adamska, 'Drawing Red Lines with No (Significant) Bites: Why an Individual Test Is Not Appropriate in the LM Case' in Armin von Bogdandy, Piotr Bogdanowicz, Iris Canor, Christoph Grabenwarter, Maciej Taborowski, Matthias Schmidt (eds) *Defending Checks and Balances in EU Member States Taking Stock of Europe's Actions,* Springer 2021, 443-454.

CHAPTER 10

Portugal

The Implementation of the Directives on Procedural Rights in Law and Practice

Miguel João Costa and Pedro Caeiro

10.1 Introduction

The traditional view in the legal literature is that Portugal pursues a humanistic approach to penal matters,[1] having been among the first countries to abolish the death penalty and life imprisonment.[2] Moreover, Portuguese criminal procedure, in its fundamental tenets, was forged in antagonism towards the criminal procedure of the dictatorship that governed the country from 1926 to 1974. The authoritarian nature of the regime was imprinted in the (former) 1929 Code of Criminal Procedure (CCP), which established an inquisitorial procedure, reserved few decisions of impact on fundamental rights in the pre-trial stages to independent authorities (judges) and subjected political crimes to special rules which engrained evident violations of basic individual freedoms.[3]

The 1987 CCP[4] (which is still in force, with several amendments) established an accusatorial system, conferred ample defence rights to defendants and

1 For a critique of the traditional view, see José Manuel Merêa Pizarro Beleza, 'A pena de prisão, a reforma das cadeias e o *Ensayo sobre o Plano mais Conveniente para a Fundação das Cadêas* (Notas para a história do direito penal vintista)', in Manuel da Costa Andrade, José de Faria Costa, Anabela Miranda Rodrigues, Maria João Antunes (eds) *Liber Discipulorum para Jorge de Figueiredo Dias* (Coimbra Editora 2003) 365 f. The traditional view might also be at odds with the high imprisonment rate in Portugal, the average length of imprisonment and the significant increase of prison population over the past decade – the third biggest in the 49 prison administrations of the Council of Europe – in stark contrast with the vast majority of the remaining member states (see Marcelo F. Aebi and Mélanie M. Tiago, *Prisons and Prisoners in Europe 2020: Key Findings of the SPACE I report*, Series UNILCRIM 2021/1, Strasbourg and Lausanne: Updated on 29 June 2021, respectively at 2, 13, 24).

2 Which in turn would soon reflect on extradition treaties with States that applied such penalties: see *v.g.* Art 2 of the Extradition Treaty of 1892 between Portugal and Great Britain.

3 In further detail, see Pedro Caeiro and Miguel João Costa, 'Portugal' in Katalin Ligeti (ed), *Toward a Prosecutor for the European Union. Vol. 1: A Comparative Analysis* (Hart Publishing 2012), 540 f.

4 Enacted by the Decree-Law no. 78/87 of 17 February.

 | DOI:10.1163/9789004513396_012

entrusted to judges the power to order or validate measures with a significant impact on fundamental rights. Adopted in an atmosphere of rupture with the former regime, the original version of the new CCP, heavily concerned with individual rights, did not yet reflect the trend – which was already in course in other European countries – of enhancing State capacity against terrorism and organised crime.

It was only in the 1990s and onwards that such a trend reached Portuguese criminal procedure, in reaction to overly lengthy criminal proceedings that many perceived to be the result of excessive individual guarantees. Nevertheless – and in spite of an increasing populist stance that propounds a further enhancement of State punitive power, with a correlative constriction of individual liberties –, the CCP remains a body of norms broadly concerned with individual guarantees.

This – rather than a concern about the effectiveness of the criminal justice system – may help to explain why the Portuguese legislator, the courts and even the legal scholarship (normally more critical than the former) tend not to adhere lightly to the idea that national standards fall short of those that are being considered ideal by supra-national organisations in which Portugal is integrated, such as the EU.

There is, for instance, no visible resistance to the implementation and application of EU legislation on mutual recognition. The national statute on the EAW transposed all grounds for non-execution provided for in this Framework Decision (the mandatory ones as mandatory, the optional ones as discretionary), which suggests that no evaluation whatsoever was carried out by the national legislator as to whether all the optional grounds were indeed necessary or desirable in the light of the Portuguese legal tradition and political interests.[5] Likewise, judicial decisions refusing to execute EAWs are rare: grounds for non-execution are only relatively seldom deemed applicable by the courts, and EAWs are usually executed in the name of mutual trust.[6]

There are, of course, differences of many sorts between harmonisation and mutual recognition legal instruments. The latter apply vis-à-vis other Member States (MS), whereas the former affect national legal systems rather transversally. Mutual recognition is generally an alternative to a classic international

5 See further in Miguel João Costa, *Extradition Law: Reviewing Grounds for Refusal from the Classic Paradigm to Mutual Recognition and Beyond* (Brill | Nijhoff 2019) 180 f., and ulterior references.

6 See *ibid.*

law device, and hence its transposition generally requires enacting an autonomous statute, which necessarily originates case law on 'European' law. In contrast, harmonisation impacts on rules developed and intended to apply at the internal level, and therefore it tends to require the modification of longstanding legal instruments, developed domestically in the course of time in an unconstrained manner. This serves to state that some difference in attitude regarding mutual recognition and harmonisation legal instruments is understandable and in fact normal.

However, in the Portuguese legal system this dichotomy is somewhat overstated. The difference in commitment to mutual recognition and to harmonisation is particularly unfounded when we consider that harmonisation of procedural rules is preordained to reinforcing the former.[7] The exception are those cases where a directive touches upon issues regarding which there already was a debate at the internal level as to whether or not the existing rules were adequate, as it is notably the case with trials *in absentia*.[8] Such cases suggest that there is critical mass concerned with safeguarding procedural rights and resisting against rising penal populism; but somehow this critical mass seems to be less energetic when the parameter of control is heteronomous – *i.e.*, when the movement towards higher standards of individual protection does not originate internally, as an exercise of self-improvement, but is instead commanded by an external entity, in the case the European legislator.

These considerations may help to explain why – as expounded in further detail throughout this Chapter – the Portuguese legislator has enacted so few amendments and additions to existing norms while implementing the Directives on procedural rights; and why, consequently, there are so many cases in which it is at least doubtful that they have been fully implemented. But it may also contribute to explain why, notwithstanding, that does not really translate into a serious deficit of procedural rights in Portugal.

7 Art 82(2)(b) TFUE states that the rights of individuals in criminal procedure may be harmonised by the European Parliament and the Council "[*t*]*o the extent necessary to facilitate mutual recognition*"; see also Pedro Caeiro, 'Introduction (Or: Every Criminal Procedure Starts with a Bill of Rights)' in Pedro Caeiro (ed), *A Agenda da União Europeia sobre os Direitos e Garantias da Defesa em Processo Penal: A 'Segunda Vaga' e o seu Previsível Impacto sobre o Direito Português / The European Union Agenda on Procedural Safeguards for Suspects or Accused Persons: the "second wave" and its predictable impact on Portuguese law* (UCILeR 2015) 13 f.

8 See *infra*, 10.4.3.2.

10.2 General Characterisation of the Portuguese Criminal Procedure: Key Constitutional Provisions

Art 20 of the Constitution[9] provides that everyone has the right to access the law and the courts with a view to obtaining protection of their rights and legally protected interests, and that fruition of this right may not be hindered by lack of economic means.[10] Moreover, it guarantees the right to legal information and counselling.

Regarding criminal proceedings specifically, the key provisions are, firstly, Art 27, according to which, as a principle, a person may only be deprived of liberty in result of a judicial decision determining him/her to be either criminally liable or dangerous.[11] Secondly, Art 28, which sets the conditions in which a person may be placed in pre-trial custody. Thirdly, Art 31, on *habeas corpus*. Lastly, Art 32, the main constitutional provision on procedural rights.

Art 32 establishes that criminal proceedings must comply with defence rights, including the right to appeal.[12] It enshrines the presumption of innocence – and therewith also *in dubio pro reo* and *nemo tenetur* –,[13] as well as the right not to be tried *in absentia* (albeit with important exceptions),[14] and the right to challenge inculpatory allegations. It entitles defendants to be assisted by an attorney of their choice and commands the law to specify the acts and phases where assistance is mandatory. Finally, it enshrines the principle of the legal judge (*juge naturel*) and it provides that investigative measures of impact to fundamental rights must be ordered or at least authorised by a judge.

Regarding transnational mechanisms, the provision of more direct relevance is Art 33, which addresses extradition and expulsion, but Art 32 also has

9 Enacted through the Decree of 10 April 1976.

10 An analysis of the Portuguese criminal procedure from a transnational perspective is provided in Miguel João Costa and Pedro Caeiro, 'Country Report Portugal', in Martin Böse, Maria Bröcker and Anne Schneider (eds), *Judicial Protection in Transnational Criminal Proceedings* (Springer 2021) 271 f., followed closely in this paragraph.

11 A criminal penalty cannot be applied in the absence of guilt/blameworthiness, but the perpetration of a criminal act together with the criminal dangerousness of the offender may lead to the application of a security measure.

12 While defence rights generally receive ample constitutional protection, the right to appeal is enclosed within somewhat narrow confines (see esp. Art 400 CCP), although there is a slight tendency to expand it in more recent times (see the ruling of the Constitutional Court no. 429/2016).

13 The latter, which in turn comprises the right to remain silent, has also been broadened recently, namely concerning the intersections between tax and criminal investigations: see the ruling no. 298/2019.

14 See *e.g.*, the ruling of the Constitutional Court no. 366/2018.

some implicit application here, since the Constitutional Court tends to equate criminal procedural law to extradition proceedings[15] (save for those rights and principles which are specific to the ascertainment of criminal liability, such as presumption of innocence).

10.2.1 *The Concept of* 'Arguido' (*Defendant*)

It is also crucial to explain the concept of '*arguido*'. In Portugal the suspect as such has few specific procedural rights or duties. These emerge only with the formal designation as '*arguido*', which is, therefore, a procedural act of utmost relevance for the individual.

Arts 57 ff. CPP establish the procedural acts and moments in which such a designation must take place: it is, for instance, mandatory in certain cases where a person is to provide statements before a judicial authority or the criminal police; and at any rate it must take place as soon as a person is prosecuted or the optional phase of instruction (in which the person may be indicted) has been requested.[16] Moreover, if a founded suspicion emerges in the course of an interrogation that the person has committed an offence, the authorities shall suspend it immediately and designate him/her as an *arguido*. Finally, under certain conditions, the concerned person him/herself may request such a designation. Thus, a person may obtain this procedural status in a rather wide number of hypotheses which meet those required by the EU Directives. This will carry the immediate emergence of some duties, but it will carry mainly the emergence of a wide set of rights.

On one side, an *arguido* has the *right*:[17] (a) to be present in all procedural acts of direct concern to him/her; (b) to be heard; (c) to be informed of the acts which are imputed to him/her; (d) to remain silent; (e) to appoint a lawyer or request that one be appointed to him/her; (f) to be assisted by a defence lawyer in every procedural act in which s/he takes part, and, if arrested, to communicate with him/her in private; (g) to intervene in the investigation phases of the procedure, *e.g.* by providing evidence or requesting that investigative measures be adopted; (h) to be informed of the rights springing from this status; (i) (if s/he is under 18 years old) to be accompanied in any procedural act that s/he is to attend by the persons who exercise parental responsibilities over him/her, by his/her legal representative or a person who holds his/her factual guardianship, or if need be, by another adequate person indicated by him/her

15 See *e.g.* the ruling of the Constitutional Court no. 54/87.

16 See further below, 10.2.2.

17 See Art 61(1) CCP.

and agreed to by the judicial authority; and (j) to appeal the decisions that personally affect him/her.

On the other side, an *arguido* has the duty:[18] (a) to be present before a judge, a public prosecutor or a police officer, where imposed by law and upon being regularly convened to do so; (b) to be truthful on his/her identity; (c) to be subjected to investigative measures aimed at evidence-gathering, and to coercive measures and patrimonial warrants aimed, *inter alia*, at securing his/her presence at trial; and (d) to be subjected to a peculiar coercive measure named 'statement of identity and residence', which involves a duty not to change residence or absent oneself for more than five days without notifying the authorities, failure to comply with which may legitimise a trial *in absentia*.

10.2.2 *Phases of the Criminal Procedure and Institutional Framework: Overview*

In Portugal, the common criminal procedure[19] starts with the investigation of the offence in the inquiry (*inquérito*), which ends with a decision (usually by the public prosecution) whether or not to prosecute. Such decision can be challenged by the *arguido* or the *assistente*[20] before a judge of instruction (*juiz de instrução*), in which case the (optional) phase of instruction will take place, with a judicial assessment of the decision taken at the end of the inquiry. If the procedure is to continue, then a trial (*julgamento*) will follow,[21] and after that, possibly, a phase of appeal (*recurso*).

The authorities involved in criminal proceedings are mainly the criminal police (*órgãos de polícia criminal*), the public prosecution (*Ministério Público*) and judges (*juízes*) or courts (*tribunais*).

The public prosecution directs the inquiry, with the assistance of the police acting under its supervision and functional (but not hierarchical) dependence. Its activity is based on a principle of objectivity ('*à charge et à décharge*') and on the procedural principle of legality. It enjoys institutional and functional autonomy vis-à-vis the executive branch and cannot be instructed to act or not to act in a certain manner, which warrants the classification of 'judicial

18 Art 61(6) CCP.

19 In more detail, see Pedro Caeiro and Miguel João Costa (n 3) 540 f.; Maria João Antunes, *Direito Processual Penal* (Almedina 2021).

20 The *assistente* usually is the holder of the interests especially protected by the violated norm (in most cases, the victim). The designation of a person as an *assistente* (always at his/her own request) carries the emergence of certain rights and duties which would not otherwise emerge, in terms similar to those expounded in relation to the *arguido*.

21 Unless certain exceptional cases in which the judge presiding over the trial phase decides otherwise upon receiving the file (see Art 311 CCP: *saneamento do processo*).

authority', placing it closer to the judicial function *stricto sensu* than to the administrative function.[22]

The judge of instruction directs the phase of instruction (also with the assistance of the criminal police under his/her direct supervision and functional dependence), but also plays a central role in the (preceding) phase of inquiry, as a '*juge des libertés*' who is competent for executing or at least ordering or authorising the investigative measures of more impact to fundamental rights.

Trials run before a (single-judge, three-judge or jury) court. Judicial decisions and judgments can be appealed to a High Court, the Supreme Court of Justice or the Constitutional Court, save where the law provides otherwise. Where a different authority orders, authorises or validates a procedural measure (notably the public prosecution, during the inquiry), there is no *direct* judicial review of the measure, as the public prosecution has autonomy to direct this phase, but its validity can be challenged before a judge at the instruction or later at trial.

10.3 The Implementation of EU Directives: Brief State of Play

To the exception of the Directive 2016/800, on juvenile defendants, Portugal did not enact new legislation with a view to transposing the Directives on procedural rights, as existing legislation was deemed to ensure full compliance. This, in turn, seems to reflect on two levels. On the one hand, and in contrast with EU instruments that have been explicitly transposed (notably, on mutual recognition), the Directives received very scarce attention in the literature.[23] Likewise, case law only seldom makes explicit reference to the Directives – and often only to evince the view that their norms were covered by pre-existing national norms –, and even more seldom does it engage in actual reflection on the correspondence between the former and the latter, and on the interplay between EU law and national law more generally.

In the following section we present a critical analysis of the state of play concerning the implementation of each Directive, with particular emphasis on some problematic issues and reference to the most noteworthy case law.[24]

22 See Jorge de Figueiredo Dias, 'Nótulas sobre temas de direito judiciário (penal)' (1995) 127 *Revista de Legislação e Jurisprudência* 354 f., and *ibid.* (1995) 128, 8 f.

23 To our knowledge, the sole work wholly dedicated to the EU agenda on procedural rights published in Portugal is Pedro Caeiro (n 7).

24 Unless stated otherwise, the translation of the excerpts of case law and provisions of the Portuguese legal system contained in this report is unofficial; the responsibility for its accurateness lies with the authors of this report.

Sections 5 and 6 then summarise the main critical profiles in the legislation and case law concerning the Directives as a whole.

Apart from Directive 2016/1919, on legal aid, problems have been identified in relation to all the Directives. The transposition deficit is, in some cases, merely partial. In other cases, there are provisions that lack transposition entirely.

10.4 Main Critical Profiles in the Legislation and in the Case-law

Since practically no specific legislation was enacted in Portugal with a view to transposing the Directives (save for the one on juvenile defendants), it is only natural that significant problems exist. They exist in all the Directives (save for the one on legal aid), and they take the shape either of actual implementation gaps (whether complete or only partial), or, in the best scenario, of serious doubts as to whether a given provision has been implemented (thus allowing for different interpretations, causing legal uncertainty).

The issues found in the implementation of the Directives can be divided into four main groups, based on the number and the intensity of the problems raised: (i) few and not particularly serious (Directive 2012/13 on information); (ii) many but not particularly serious (Directive 2016/800 on juvenile defendants);[25] (iii) few but serious (Directive 2010/64 on interpretation and translation and Directive 2016/343 on presumption of innocence and *in absentia*); (iv) many and some of them serious (Directive 2013/48 on access to a lawyer *et al.*).

From the case law assessed for the purposes of this research,[26] very few rulings refer explicitly to the Directives,[27] and usually only to evince the view that they were already covered by national norms. Nevertheless, some of them were issued in 2019 or later,[28] which suggests increasing attention towards the Directives.

The right to interpretation and translation is among the procedural rights regarding which more case law can be identified as relevant for implementation

---

25 The fact that the problems detected in relation to this Directive are not very serious can be explained precisely by the fact that specific legislation was enacted (although one would also have expected this to lead to a narrower number of problems).

26 *Sc.*, 80 rulings, proffered by the Constitutional Court, the Supreme Court of Justice and High Courts, added by a ruling of an Administrative Court and a Recommendation by the Ombudsman.

27 *Sc.*, only 14.

28 *Sc.*, 9.

analysis purposes, and the Directive 2010/64/EU is probably the one which has received more explicit references. This should be due in part to the fact that it is the oldest of the six Directives. Another explanation might be that the cases where those rights are called into play are inherently cases with an international element: the defendant is not Portuguese and is often a citizen of another Member State. This might increase the willingness of the courts to refer to EU legislation. Similar considerations apply to some issues regulated in the Directive 2016/343, notably the right to be present at the trial, when the defendant has fled to another country.

At the other end of the spectrum are Directives 2016/800 and 2016/1919. As noted, the scarcity of case law on procedural rights of young offenders may be seen to express some disregard for the specificities of this class of defendants, which would be concerning, but may also be a consequence of few criminal procedures being carried out against them, which would be positive phenomenon. As for legal aid, the scarcity of case law is consistent with the view upheld in this paper, that national rules are theoretically sound (even if, largely in consequence of shortage of funds, this might not translate into practical effectivity).

Be that as it may, considering that the implementation of the Directives relies heavily on pre-existing norms, we find it crucial for national courts to engage in critical assessment more frequently and profoundly.

10.4.1 *Few and Not Particularly Serious Implementation Issues: Directive 2012/13*

Regarding the rights enshrined in Directive 2012/13, our view is that most, but not all its norms have sufficient backing in previous legislation. The main problems identified relate to Art 4(2)(a), (c) and (d), on the Letter of Rights to be provided upon arrest.

Different procedural subjects are entitled to obtain information in criminal proceedings, but this right is particularly important for the targeted person. Therefore, it is one of those rights that emerges immediately upon the designation as an *arguido*, and it is even more important when deprivation of liberty is involved, with Art 27(4) of the Constitution establishing that "any person who is deprived of liberty must be immediately informed in an understandable manner of the reasons of his/her arrest, imprisonment or detention, as well as of his/her rights".[29]

---

29 The Constitutional Court has reinforced different dimensions of the right to information, *v.g.* in rulings no. 121/97, no. 416/2003, and no. 417/2003.

However, the letter of rights regulated in Art 4 of the Directive cannot be deemed fully implemented. While defendants must be informed of the rights to which they are entitled, the only rights that authorities are required to proactively provide information about are those listed in Art 61 CCP[30] or in other specific provisions, and these do *not* include the information mentioned in Art 4(2)(a) (right of access to the materials of the case) and (d) (maximum number of hours or days for which suspects or accused persons may be deprived of liberty before being brought to a judicial authority). The same applies to Art 4(2)(c) of the Directive (information about the right of access to urgent medical assistance), although several provisions do exist that carry a duty to provide medical care to defendants, arrested persons and inmates.

Case law only seldom refers explicitly to this Directive. One ruling worthy of reference is that of the High Court of Coimbra of 05-02-2014, case 174/13.0GAVZL-A.C2, where it held that, during an inquiry which is under secrecy of justice, consultation of the elements of the file is subject to certain constraints: during the term for which a defendant has the possibility to appeal against a decision placing him/her in pre-trial custody, the investigation judge may – although it may *only* –, based on Art 194 CCP, deny access to certain elements (even if they have served as grounds for applying pre-trial custody) when this might seriously jeopardise the investigation, or render it impossible to discover the truth, or create a risk to life, limb or freedom of any procedural participant or of the victim. The defendant had invoked Directive 2012/13, but the Court held that Recital 32 and Art 7(4) allow for that kind of restriction, and therefore national law was fully compliant with the Directive in that respect.

In turn, the High Court of Évora (in a ruling further analysed *infra*, 10.4.3.1) addressed the Directive on the right to information and made a negative assessment of its implementation into national law. It held that Art 3 requires that the defendant be informed of the right to interpretation and translation – a right which is not contained in Art 61 CCP.[31] The Letter of Rights on arrest regulated in Art 4 of the Directive – the Court held – simply does not exist in Portugal and, in the case of a defendant whom the authorities were unsure understood Portuguese and did not care to confirm so, the Directive would require them to actively ascertain whether or not that is true. In case of doubt, they should appoint an interpreter. Positive obligations imposed on those authorities – the Court proceeded – carry the revocation of any norms of national law, present or future, that are contrary to what is provided for in Directives establishing an

30 See *supra*, 10.2.1.

31 Which, as noted above (see *id.*), lists the (main) rights of the defendant.

imperative common regime. Moreover, the Court held that this Directive *has direct effect* in Portugal (in the terms further explained below, *id.*).

However, in a ruling of 23-04-2020, case 18/20.7JELSB-B.L1-9, the High Court of Lisbon vehemently points in a direction opposite to that of the High Court of Évora. While noting that Directive 2012/13 (as well as Directive 2013/48) had not been explicitly transposed, the Court held that they lack direct effect, as they 'do not have a binding character' (*sic*), in contrast with Regulations and Decisions. Nevertheless – the Court added –, they do have *indirect effects*. That is, they are subject to the principle of harmonious interpretation (as ruled by the CJEU in 10-04-1984, *Sabine von Colson and Elisabeth Kamann v. Land Nordrhein-Westfalen*, and numerous other subsequently). This applies to Directives that: (i) have not been transposed but should have; (ii) have been deficiently transposed; or (iii) have not been explicitly transposed because national law already provided for the rights at issue. In the case, the CCP, together with Art 7 of the Directive 2012/13, already provides for a right to access 'essential elements', this being a very wide concept that includes any element which is relevant for the defence (or the prosecution), whether incriminating or exculpatory. And all such elements must be provided to suspects, accused persons, *inter alia*, at the latest before a competent judicial authority is called upon to decide on the legality of the arrest or imprisonment (under Art 5(4) ECHR), and in due time, so as to allow for the effective exercise of the right to judicial review of the arrest or imprisonment. On a different but related note, the Court of Lisbon also held that 'the intervention of the CJEU for ascertaining in preliminary ruling the validity and the interpretation of acts adopted by the EU must or can only be required in the case of binding acts, such as Regulations and Decisions, not of acts such as Directives, Recommendations and Opinions'. Thus, it decided not to make use of the mechanism.

In our view, the distinction drawn by the High Court of Lisbon, according to which the power/duty to refer a matter to the CJEU for a preliminary ruling concerning the validity or interpretation of EU legal instruments applies only to acts of a binding nature, is not fully accurate: the CJEU has already ruled in several judgments that it has jurisdiction to interpret non-binding acts in preliminary reference procedures.[32] But even more surprising – and plainly wrong – is the conclusion of the Court that directives are not 'binding acts' to the effects of such procedures.

32 Case C-322/88 *Grimaldi* [1989] ECR 4407, paras 7–9; Case C-188/91, *Deutsche Shell AG v Hauptzollamt Hamburg-Harburg* [1993] ECR I-00363 paras 18–19.

More generally, although it may be exaggerated to conclude that there is a very high level of implementation deficit of Directives 2010/64 and 2012/13, there is no reason either to hold Portuguese law fully compliant.

10.4.2 *Numerous but Not Particularly Serious Implementation Issues: Directive 2016/800*

Unlike all other Directives, Directive 2016/800 was explicitly transposed through an amendment – the 33rd – of the CCP, effected by Law no. 33/2019, of 22 May (shortly before the transposition term: 11 June 2019). The most important amendment introduced by this statute was carried out in Art 61(1), the key provision that lists the fundamental rights of defendants. The statute added one provision (i) – which will be referred to throughout this Section –, according to which:

> Unless the law provides otherwise, the defendant has, at all stages of the criminal procedure, the right: (…) If he/she is a minor [under 18 years old], to be accompanied in any procedural act by the persons who exercise parental responsibilities over him/her, by his/her legal representative or by a person who holds his/her factual guardianship, or yet, if the former cannot be reached or when and insofar as special circumstances concerning his/her best interest so command, by another adequate person indicated by him/her and agreed to by the competent judicial authority.

Even so, not every provision in this Directive is fully implemented. There are issues, firstly, with Art 2 (3), as Portuguese law does not explicitly provide that the rights and guarantees established for minors shall still apply if they subsequently reach the age of 18, and the application of such rights and guarantees is appropriate in the light of all the circumstances of the case, including the maturity and vulnerability of the person concerned; also with Art 5 (3), on the information to be provided to the holder of parental responsibility, a measure that finds no equivalence in national law; nor do Art 7(4)(a), which commands authorities to determine whether any specific measure should be taken to the benefit of the minor, or Art 8(2), which provides that the results of the medical examination be taken into account when determining the capacity of the child to be subject to questioning and other procedural measures. As for Art 8(5), the General Regulation of Prison Facilities regulates the "*initial clinical evaluation*", and other provisions are concerned with subsequent evaluations,[33] but there

33 See Arts 53 ff.

is no obligation to assess whether a re-evaluation is needed, as required by the Directive.

Many issues concerning this Directive stem from the lack of national provisions specifically designed to safeguard the rights and interests of minors. General provisions applicable to all defendants are sufficient to secure compliance with several norms in this Directive, yet the absence of specific focus on minors inevitably carries some discrepancy. That is not only the case of Art 8, already mentioned, but also, for instance, of Art 10, on limitation of deprivation of liberty, Art 11, on alternative measures, Art 12(1), which as a principle requires detained children to be held separately from adults; and Art 14(4), on the protection of privacy.[34] No national provision is in place, either, transposing Art 15(3), which requires that in case of modification of circumstances the child be given the right to be accompanied by the holder of parental responsibility during the remaining court hearings. Finally, this lack of specific focus on minors also prevents compliance with Art 20, on training to be provided to the staff of law enforcement agencies and detention facilities: as far as it was possible to establish, such training measures have no clear resonance in the Portuguese legal system.[35]

In conclusion, although new legislation was enacted to transpose this Directive, several deficiencies can still be identified.[36] Thus, further intervention by the legislator is necessary.

As for case law, very few rulings could be identified as meaningful, and even fewer proved useful for clarifying the doubts about the extent of implementation, which is worrying, as it may express some disregard for the specificities of this class of defendants. On the optimistic side, it might be a consequence of few criminal procedures being carried out against young offenders, whether because (in proportion) they commit less offences or because they are less often prosecuted. In any event, this Directive has been enacted more recently than other Directives, and it is possible that we will see a rise in the number of decisions addressing it.

---

34 There is a regulatory framework for the media (*v.g.*, Art 14(2)(g) of the Statute of the Journalist (Law no. 1/99, of 1 January) and Art 8 of the Deontological Code of the Journalist), but it is unclear whether it suffices "*to achieve the objectives*" of the Directive on privacy protection (the latter is not even an actual legal instrument).

35 In this direction, see also Ana Rita Alfaiate (with the collaboration of Helena Moniz), 'Commentary on the Proposal for a Directive of the European Parliament and of the Council on procedural safeguards for children suspected or accused in criminal proceedings', in Pedro Caeiro (n 7) 55.

36 See also *ibid*, 47 f., writing prior to the enactment of the Directive.

10.4.3 *Few but Serious Implementation Issues*

10.4.3.1 Directive 2010/64

Most of the norms of Directive 2010/64 are sufficiently covered by previous legislation, notably by Art 92 CCP,[37] which provides, *inter alia*, that, if a person intervening in the criminal procedure does not know or is not fluent in Portuguese, he/she must be appointed a suitable interpreter, free of charge, even if the authority presiding over the act or any of the subjects of the procedure happen to know the language in which that person expresses him/herself; failure to comply with this imposition carries that any evidence thereby obtained (notably, the statements made by the defendant) is null and cannot be used. It also provides that an interpreter is appointed whenever it is necessary to translate a document that is written in a foreign language and has not been subject to authenticated translation. In turn, Art 93 contains rules on the right to interpretation for persons with a hearing or speech impediment. The right to interpretation and translation is not even one of those rights to which only an *arguido* is entitled, but rather it applies to any other individual intervening in the criminal procedure.

However, not all the norms of the Directive are implemented, notably those concerned with the quality of interpretation and translation, and with the control of such quality. Not that there are no provisions concerned with these issues: for instance, Art 153 (3) CCP establishes that an interpreter may be replaced if he/she is "*performing in a careless manner the duties that have been assigned to him/her*";[38] Art 47 (1) CCP prohibits certain individuals from participating in procedural acts due to the existence of relevant doubts as to their impartiality; and Art 91 (2) CCP requires interpreters to swear an oath that they will faithfully carry out their functions (save for interpreters who are civil servants and intervene in the procedure in the exercise of their duties). These provisions do contribute to the quality of the activity of the interpreter or translator, but they seem insufficient to meet the *mechanisms* envisioned in the Directive for controlling the need for, and the quality of the interpretation or translation. Similar considerations apply to the norms on the training of judges, prosecutors and judicial staff.

Indeed, the register(s) of independent translators / interpreters prescribed in Art 5 (2), and the training prescribed in Art 6, do not seem to have been implemented. This raises legitimate doubts about the quality of interpretation and translation being provided in Portugal at present, and about whether any "*special attention*" is given to the "*particularities*" of the cases that involve

37 Regarding EAW proceedings, see especially Arts 17 and 34 LEAW.

38 These provisions refer to expert witnesses, but apply to interpreters *ex vi* Art 92(8) CCP.

interpretation. Moreover, interpretation and translation in judicial proceedings may be considered as not well-paid, which does not contribute to increasing quality, and no differentiation is even made depending on the language.[39]

This is one of the Directives regarding which more case law has been identified as relevant, but the general view of the judges is that Portuguese law already provides sufficiently for the rights at issue. Diverging case law has however been issued by the High Court of Évora, in a ruling of 20-12-2018, case 55/2017.9GBLGS.E1. The Court held that Directive 2010/64/EU and Directive 2012/13/EU *have direct effect* in Portugal (respectively, since 28-10-2013 and 02-06-2014), based on the case law of the CJEU according to which a Directive which has not been (or has been wrongly) transposed may produce direct effect in certain circumstances. Most notably, the Court held that Portuguese law blatantly fails to secure the standards imposed by those Directives, and that Art 92 CCP is a poor provision which commands the appointment of an interpreter to the defendant and little more than this. This led the Court to conclude that the Portuguese State was over-confident to find that no transposition was required. More specifically, the Court held that the Directive is clear in establishing a catalogue of acts that must be translated, which includes written translation of all essential documents, whereas no norm exists in the CCP providing for such a catalogue, and in fact not even the minimum situations required by the Directive are provided for, leading to a situation where, in practice, translation is in most cases *systematically excluded*. Thus, the Court concluded that the Directive is directly applicable, and that, consequently, Portuguese courts must conclude that as a general rule translation must be made of "*any decision depriving a person of his liberty, any charge or indictment, and any judgment*", added by the cases mentioned in Art 3 (3) of the Directive.

In our view, the stance taken by this High Court is somewhat overstated. Most rights contained in the Directive spring from pre-existing national rules, notably from Arts 92 and 93 CPP. And while it is true that Portuguese law makes no differentiation between essential and non-essential documents, it does establish a dichotomy that carries largely equivalent effects, namely between documents whose translation is necessary or unnecessary. Thus, if the translation of a document is deemed necessary, it must be officially ordered – and if it is not, the defendant may request so, and appeal a decision that refuses to order the translation.[40]

---

39 See Art 17(2) of the Decree-Law no. 34/2008, of 26 February and Table IV attached thereto.

40 Also Sandra Oliveira e Silva, 'The right to interpretation and translation in Criminal Proceedings: the situation in Portugal' in Rui Sousa-Silva, Rita Faria, Núria Gavaldà and Belinda Maia (eds), *Bridging the Gap(s) between Language and the Law – Proceedings of the*

Nevertheless, this case law draws attention to the fact that Portuguese norms on translation / interpretation might not rise up to the ambitious standards set by the Directive, and that official transposition would have avoided ambiguities that now rest entirely with the courts to solve.[41] At the very least, it has the merit of dealing openly with the transposition of the Directive into the Portuguese legal system, a discussion which has no equivalence regarding the other Directives.

10.4.3.2 Directive 2016/343

Presumption of innocence is a key principle of Portuguese criminal procedure, and it comprises *in dubio pro reo*, the right to silence and *nemo tenetur* more broadly.[42] The presence of the defendant at the trial is also an important principle.[43] Nevertheless, our view is again that important norms of the Directive do not have sufficient backing in existing legislation.

That is the case, to begin with, of Art 4(1) and (2), on public references to guilt. Art 343(2) CCP provides that at the trial hearing the court shall hear the defendant "*without expressing any opinion or making any comment that allow for inferring a judgement on his/her guilt*", but there is no provision clearly prohibiting authorities from issuing public references to guilt to the extent envisaged by the Directive. Some norms establish a general duty on judges, prosecutors and different police bodies not to make public statements or comments concerning criminal proceedings in which they intervene,[44] and there are also substantive and procedural norms aimed at preventing public disclosure of information concerning ongoing investigations,[45] but they are more

---

3rd European Conference of the International Association of Forensic Linguists (Faculdade de Letras da Universidade do Porto 2012) 96 f. <https://ler.letras.up.pt/uploads/ficheiros/13605.pdf>, asserting that, "despite some omissions, the Portuguese legislation accomplishes the minimum standards outlined in the Directive".

41 The latter aspect is emphasised by Júlio Barbosa e Silva, 'A Directiva 2010/64/UE do Parlamento Europeu e do Conselho, de 20 de Outubro de 2010, relativa ao direito à interpretação e tradução em processo penal', (2018) *Julgar Online* 48 f. (esp.) <http://julgar.pt/a-directiva-201064ue-do-parlamento-europeu-e-do-conselho-de-20-de-outubro-de-2010-relativa-ao-direito-a-interpretacao-e-traducao-em-processo-penal/>, noting that this is particularly regrettable given that Portugal was one of the MSs that promoted the adoption of this Directive.

42 See esp. Art 32(2) of the Constitution.

43 See esp. Art 32(6) of the Constitution, and Arts 113, 312 f. and 332 f. CPP.

44 See Art 12(1) of Law no. 21/85 (on judges), Art 84(1) of Law no. 47/86 (on public prosecutors), Art 13(2) of Law no. 37/2008 (on the Judiciary Police), Art 12 of Decree-Law no. 297/2009 (on the National Republican Guard), and Art 14(1) and (2) of Decree-Law no. 243/2015 (on the Public Security Police).

45 See, notably, Arts 86 f. CCP, and Art 371 of the Penal Code.

concerned with the *public interest* in maintaining the functioning of the justice system secret up to a given procedural moment than with the *individual right* to be presumed innocent (even if the latter collaterally benefits from that). Similar problems affect Art 5(1), on the presentation of suspects and accused persons.

The most contentious issue, however, relates to Art 8(2)(a) and (4), on the right to be present at the trial, and Art 9, on the right to a new trial in case of a trial *in absentia*. There is significant internal debate about their implementation, in contrast with most issues concerning the other Directives, which is probably due to the fact that there was already a debate as to the sufficiency of the guarantees established in national law before the enactment of the Directive.

By providing that the presence of the defendant can only be dispensed with if his/her rights are duly safeguarded, the Constitution may be deemed to enshrine a general right of the defendant to be present at trial. Moreover, the Constitutional Court has delivered case law conditioning the validity of trials *in absentia*.[46] In Portuguese law, the defendant has a specific duty to provide the authorities with truthful information about his/her identity and place of residence ('statement of identity and residence').[47] In the course of the procedure all notifications will be sent to that residence and the defendant is explicitly informed that: (i) notifications will be sent by regular mail to that address; (ii) he/she has a duty not to change residence without reporting it to the authorities; and (iii) failure to comply with such a duty may entail being tried *in absentia*. At the outset of the trial, the judge notifies the defendant and his/her attorney of the date of the hearing, and also designates an alternative date, in case the hearing (as scheduled for the first date) has to be postponed. This notification is effected through regular mail to the said address, and it is not necessary for the defendant to sign a reception form: the notification is *presumed* to have been received on the 5th day following that in which it was deposited in the mailbox. If a duly notified defendant does not attend trial in due time, the hearing will only be adjourned if the court deems his/her presence at the beginning of the hearing absolutely *indispensable* for ascertaining the truth of the facts; otherwise, trial may take place *in absentia*. In sum: particular circumstances aside,[48] the sole condition for a defendant to be tried *in absentia* is that he/she was *notified of the date of the trial by regular mail*.

---

46 See *e.g.* the judgments no. 465/2004 and no. 206/2006.

47 Arts 61(6)(c) and 196 CCP.

48 *E.g.*, age, serious illness, residence abroad (see Arts 117(2) to (4), 333(2) and (4), and 333(2) and (4) CCP).

This means that it is possible that a defendant is unaware that his/her trial is going to take place or even that it has already taken place – which might fall short of the standards envisaged in the Directive. The debate on whether or not the domestic regime complies with the Directive boils down to the interpretation of the Directive's requirement that the defendant "*has been informed*": if it is construed in the sense that the defendant must get *actual knowledge* of the trial date, then national law falls short of the standard; if, on the contrary, it is construed in a normative sense (encompassing an *implicit presumption*), then the Directive can be deemed implemented, at least in part.[49]

This model of notification through regular mail was adopted in reaction to what was perceived as a serious problem of delay in the completion of criminal procedures due to difficulties in notifying defendants – who would often refuse to sign the reception form in order to avoid being properly notified –, and, in our view, it is not proscribed by the Directive. However, the Directive does seem to require for the defendant to be at least given the possibility to rebut the presumption that he/she was informed of the date of the trial and to prove that the non-receipt of the notification was not imputable to him/her.[50] By not acknowledging this possibility, national law will, therefore, be failing to meet the minimum standards set out by the Directive.

The other problem is that Portuguese law does not provide for a right to a new trial. It does enable defendants who were tried *in absentia* to appeal,[51] but it does not afford a "*fresh determination of the merits of the case, including examination of new evidence*". Those appeals consist of a review, by a High Court, of the decision taken by a court of first instance, namely an evaluation

49 Strong doubts were also voiced by Maria João Antunes and Joana Fernandes Costa, 'Commentary on the Proposal for a Directive on the presumption of innocence and the right to be present at trial in criminal proceedings', in Pedro Caeiro (n 7) 42. However, this analysis was based on a Proposal that differed significantly from the final, enacted version. The 2013 Proposal by the Commission (CELEX:52013PC0821) admitted a trial *in absentia* only where the defendant or accused "was summoned in person and thereby informed of the scheduled date and place of the trial, or by other means actually received official information of the scheduled date and place of that trial in such a manner that it was unequivocally established that he/she was aware of the scheduled trial (…)". Taking as a reference the Directive itself, a positive implementation assessment is upheld *v.g.* by João Miguel Cabral, 'Da validação dos julgamentos *in absentia* em face do mandado de detenção europeu' (2020) 30 *Revista Portuguesa de Ciência Criminal* 97 f. In contrast, Bárbara Churro, *Julgamento na Ausência – Contributo para uma revisão do regime do Código de Processo Penal à luz da Directiva (UE) 2016/343* (Almedina 2020) 134 *et passim*, upholds that the Portuguese legal system is not fully compliant.

50 This view is therefore close to that defended by Bárbara Churro (n 49) 134.

51 And in more protective terms than for other defendants: see Art 334(6) and (7) CCP.

of possible mistakes. Such re-evaluation may focus on legal as well as factual issues, but by no means does it amount to a retrial.[52] In order for Portuguese law to comply with the Directive, appeals before the High Courts would, in our view, have to admit significantly wider possibilities to produce new evidence.

The case law on the multiple refractions of the presumption of innocence and on the right to be present at the trial is abundant, but references to the Directive are scant. An exception is the decision of the High Court of Oporto of 10-12-2019, case 195/18.7PTPRT.P1, on *nemo tenetur* and blood alcohol tests, where the Court referred to the ECtHR and to the Directive 2016/343 while determining the circumstances where the privilege against self-incrimination should prevail over conflicting public interests – though in the situation at hand it concluded in the negative.

10.4.4 *Numerous and Serious Implementation Issues: Directive 2013/48*

Directive 2013/48 is, in our view, the one with the poorest implementation level. Many of the issues are not serious, but they are numerous. They concern: Art 3 (2) (a) and (b), on the procedural moments and acts in or as of which the person concerned should be provided with access to a lawyer; Art 3 (3) (a), Art 5 (3) and (4), Art 8 (1) (c), on the issue of temporary derogation of rights, which seems to conflict with the national provision according to which, in cases of terrorism and violent or highly organised criminality, the arrested person, prior to the first judicial interrogation, may be prevented from communicating with anyone, save for the lawyer; Art 7 (2), on the right to be visited by consular authorities, to converse and correspond with them and to have legal representation arranged for by them; Art 9, concerning waiver of rights; and Art 10 (4) and (5), on the duty of the executing MS in EAW proceedings to inform requested persons that they have the right to appoint a lawyer in the issuing MS, and to inform the issuing MS when requested persons wish to exercise the right to appoint a lawyer there.

The fundamental issue concerns the cases and conditions in which access to a lawyer is required by the Directive. Art 64 CCP entitles defendants to a *right* of access to a lawyer in all the cases listed in Art 3(2) of the Directive, and

52 The court of appeal may command the court of first instance to 'renew the evidence' that had been produced (Art 430 CCP), but such a possibility is exceptional. The request for extraordinary revision (*recurso de revisão*, Arts 449 f. CCP) also leads to an extensive re-evaluation of the case, but it is not concerned with trials *in absentia*. Similar considerations apply as well to the possibility of 'resending the file for a new trial' (*reenvio do processo para novo julgamento*), Arts 426 and 426-A CCP.

assistance by a lawyer is *mandatory* in many of these cases, but not in *all* of them; and Art 3(2) of the Directive may plausibly be interpreted as requiring the defendant, not simply to be given a right, but to be *actively provided* with "access to a lawyer". If not, then Portuguese law is fully compliant; but if so, then only the cases covered by Art 64 CPP respond to the command of the Directive.[53] Art 3(2)(a) would be implemented only regarding interrogations by judicial authorities, but not by the police,[54] and Art 3(2)(b) too would only be partially implemented, for if the police is to proceed to the identification of a suspect, this person has the possibility to contact a person of trust, but the presence of the lawyer is not in fact required.

As for the confidentiality of client-attorney communications, it receives sufficiently wide protection in Portuguese law. However, regarding the right to communicate with consular authorities, there is no provision explicitly and specifically establishing that suspects or accused persons who are arrested have the right to be visited by their consular authorities or the right to converse and correspond with them.

Likewise, there is an issue concerning the temporary derogation of rights. Art 143(4) CCP provides that, in cases of terrorism and violent or highly organised criminality, the public prosecution may order that the arrested person, prior to his/her first judicial interrogation, does not communicate with anyone, except for his/her lawyer. This provision requires no further condition (*e.g.*, an assessment of the actual danger to the investigation or to third parties) than the circumstance that the case concerns terrorism or violent/highly organised crime. A Report by the Commission of the Portuguese Parliament on Constitutional Issues, Rights and Guarantees, concerning the proposal that would eventually result in the Directive 2013/48/UE, remarks that the provision of the Directive may be seen as "*excessive*", considering that "*the special gravity of such cases and the complexity of their investigation may justify a restriction of the rights of*

53 It is the interpretation defended in Miguel João Costa, 'Commentary on the Proposal for a Directive of the European Parliament and of the Council on Provisional Legal Aid for Suspects or Accused Persons Deprived of Liberty and Legal Aid in European Arrest Warrant Proceedings', in Pedro Caeiro (n 7) 61 f.

54 One of the reasons why the presence of a lawyer in interrogations by the police is not mandatory is that such statements cannot serve as evidence later in trial, unless the defendant him/herself so requests (Art 357(1)(b) CCP). In fact, making the presence of a lawyer mandatory in interrogations by the police might be regarded by the Portuguese legislator as an invitation to admit those statements as evidence, which ironically would represent a compression of fundamental rights, whereas the aim of the Directive is obviously the opposite.

the arrested person".[55] Be that as it may, the fact is that Portuguese law does not, at present, comply with the Directive on this particular point.

Problems exist also with regard to EAW proceedings. Of course, any person arrested pursuant to an EAW has the right to be assisted by a lawyer. Nevertheless, Art 10(4) of the Directive is, at best, only partially implemented, for there is no explicit provision imposing on Portuguese authorities, as executing authorities, a duty to inform requested persons, without undue delay after them being arrested, that they have the right to appoint a lawyer in the issuing MS. If a lawyer does come to be appointed in the issuing MS, then his/her role will naturally include assistance, information and advice to the lawyer in the executing MS, but there is no explicit provision on this either.

This Directive has received even less explicit reference in Portuguese case law than the former, which is particularly bewildering, considering that the implementation problems are numerous.

10.4.5 *A High Level of Implementation: Directive 2016/1919*

Directive 2016/1919 is, in our view, the sole Directive of the agenda that can be considered as fully implemented. The Constitution provides for a right to legal aid,[56] which is concretised in the Law on Access to the Law and the Courts.[57] The legal framework on legal aid engrains two fundamental ideas: on the one hand, that the State should bear the costs of legal assistance not only when the defendant is in a situation of financial hardship, but also when he/she chose to be assisted by a State-appointed lawyer and is ultimately acquitted (which in fact seems to be even more protective than the Directive);[58] on the other hand, a defendant who seeks support without being eligible shall be penalised for such a behaviour.

The very few problems that were detected (notably Art 5, on legal aid in EAW proceedings) originate in the defective implementation of Directive 2013/48, on access to a lawyer, to which this Directive is closely related. Thus, access to a lawyer is the context where such problems should be primarily addressed.

---

55 Ofício n.º 30/XII/1ª CACDLG/2014, sobre a Proposta relativa ao apoio judiciário (COM(2013) 824 final), <www.parlamento.pt> 6.

56 Art 20.

57 Law no. 34/2004, of 29 July, further concretised by Art 3 of Ordinance no. 10/2008. This Law applies also to EAW proceedings: see Commission of the Portuguese Parliament on Constitutional Issues, Rights and Guarantees, Ofício n.º 30/XII/1ª (CACDLG/2014) <www.parlamento.pt> 11–12, concerning the proposal that would result in the Directive 2013/48/UE.

58 See Art 64(4) CCP.

Apart from that, existing problems are of a *practical* character: arguably, the funding of the system is insufficient, which undermines its effectiveness. As a consequence, only persons who clearly cannot bear the costs of their involvement in a criminal procedure are covered, meaning that there is a number of individuals who face significant economic difficulties but are not entitled to legal aid. Thus, the positive assessment of the implementation of the Directive on legal aid does not concomitantly embody a positive assessment of the *functioning* of the Portuguese system of access to the law and to the courts globally considered.

Only six rulings could be identified as relevant for Directive 2016/1919, which concurs to the view that the national legal aid system, while sound in theory, may be lacking the desired practical effectiveness. There is, nevertheless, some case law by the Constitutional Court which reflects the importance of the right to legal aid.[59]

10.5 Concluding Remarks

In light of the above, we can conclude that the enactment of the Directives has been met with insufficient legislative action and narrow case law in the Portuguese legal system. Moreover, as far as was possible to ascertain, there are no ongoing legislative reforms or pending cases that touch meaningfully upon these matters, although a new amendment of the CCP has been enacted by the Law no. 94/2021, of 21 December.

It is important to emphasise that this does not necessarily mean that there is a deficit of procedural rights in Portugal. For historical reasons, and until recently, national criminal procedure has been more concerned with protecting fundamental rights than with enhancing crime control.[60] Consequently, most of the European provisions were covered by already existing domestic norms. This may explain why the legislator, the courts and the literature have been paying little attention to the Directives.

Nevertheless, the fact that Portuguese criminal procedural law may be considered satisfactory or even good is not a reason not to remain open to the ambitious goals being set by the EU in this realm.

59 *V.g.*, rulings no. 353/2017 and no. 242/2018.
60 Recall *supra*, 1.

CHAPTER 11

Spain

The Transposition of Directives on Criminal Procedural Rights into National Law

Ana-María Neira-Pena

11.1 Introduction

This Chapter analyzes how the Spanish legal system is being adapted to the six European Directives on guarantees for the accused in criminal proceedings. Some of the Directives, despite the fact that the deadline for their transposition has largely elapsed, have not been expressly transposed by the Spanish legislator, as is the case of the Directive on the presumption of innocence or the Directive on the rights of the minor accused in criminal proceedings. On other occasions, even though the legislator has reformed domestic legislation to formally transpose the Directives, certain gaps and deficiencies can still be observed in the national implementation. In some other cases, deficiencies come from the judicial interpretation, which does not apply national rules in accordance with European standards, despite having an adequate legislative basis for doing so.

The purpose of this Chapter is to examine, on the one hand, the transposition at the legislative level, emphasizing some of the gaps detected, but also the advances that the transposition of the European standard have brought, where national implementation has gone even beyond EU requirements. On the other hand, it analyzes the way in which judicial interpretation has served, at times, to fill the gaps in the legislation and, at others, to anticipate the lack of express transposition through an application of national rules in accordance with the spirit of the Directives.

Throughout the Chapter the dominant jurisprudence and current legislation are analyzed, without forgetting the Draft of the new Criminal Procedural Law which, if approved, would represent a comprehensive reform of the Spanish criminal procedure. This new legal act will necessarily have to integrate European standards when regulating the rights and safeguards for suspects and accused persons in criminal proceedings. The prohibition of regression should also be respected, so that the incorporation of the European standard

 | DOI:10.1163/9789004513396_013

does not mean, in any case, a lowering of the level of national safeguards, which, in relation to certain rights, is more demanding than the European one.

11.2 The Implementation of EU Directives: State of Play

The state of adaptation of the Spanish legal system to the various Directives on criminal procedural rights for the accused is uneven, despite the fact that the deadline for transposition has largely expired for all of them.

Directives 2010/64, 2012/13, and 2013/48 have been transposed into the legal system, although not without some delays and shortcomings in certain cases. Directive 2016/1919 has been the last to be transposed and was incorporated into the Spanish legal system in 2018. The deadline for its transposition was respected, probably because it was easy to integrate these rules into our legal system, which already enshrined a high level of protection of the right to legal aid, even higher than that provided for in the Directive. The four abovementioned Directives have been transposed through the amendment of three pre-existing domestic laws: Criminal Procedural Act of 1882; Law 1/1996, of January 10, on legal aid and Law 23/2014, of November 20, on mutual recognition of criminal decisions in the European Union.[1]

On the contrary, the other two Directives (2016/343 and 2016/800) have not been implemented yet. Moreover, there are no proposals for their incorporation into the Spanish legal system so far. In particular, the need to transpose Directive 2016/343 has gone practically unnoticed.[2] However, it is possible to find numerous references to this Directive in judgments relating to the presumption of innocence, the *in dubio pro reo* principle or the privilege against self-incrimination. On the other side, Directive 2016/800 not only has not been transposed, but it is also difficult to find references to it in case law. Therefore, this Directive, although it does not find relevant contradictions in the current

1 The Judgment of the Constitutional Court No. 13/2017, of January 20 anticipated the transposition of Directive 2012/13. It stated that, since the deadline had expired, Spanish judicial bodies were obliged to interpret their domestic law in light of the Directive.

2 See, among others: Miguel Rodríguez-Piñero y Bravo-Ferrer, 'La Directiva (UE) 2016/343 y el derecho a la presunción de inocencia' (2016) 8750 Diario La Ley; Alicia González Monge, 'La presunción de inocencia en la Unión Europea: Directiva 2016/343 del Parlamento Europeo y del consejo de 9 de marzo de 2016 por la que se refuerzan en el proceso penal determinados aspectos de la presunción de inocencia y el derecho a estar presente en el juicio' (2016) 39 Revista General de Derecho Europeo; María Luisa Villamarín López, 'La Directiva Europea 2016/343, de 9 de marzo, sobre presunción de inocencia y el derecho a estar presente en el juicio' (2017) 3 InDret 1, 39.

Spanish system, has so far gone unnoticed not only in legislation, but also in case law (perhaps because it is the most recent).

It is therefore evident that, despite a good level of implementation, the Spanish legislation will have to continue to make progress in the incorporation of European standards about procedural safeguards, fully adapting its national legal system to the obligations stemming from the aforementioned Directives. In this sense, the Draft Bill of the new Criminal Procedural Act, currently being processed, may be a good opportunity to complete this process of adaptation.[3]

Furthermore, it will be necessary to make a special effort with regard to the training of those agents in charge of its application, particularly police, prosecutorial and judicial authorities, who are ultimately responsible for ensuring respect for the rights enshrined in the European regulation. As will be discussed below, shortcomings in implementation are often due to the judicial interpretation of the laws and their practical application rather than to the content and wording of the transposing legal acts.

11.3 Main Critical Profiles in the Legislation

Indeed, as far as legislative adaptation is concerned, it can be observed that in Spain, like in other Member States, sometimes approaches to the transposition of Directives follow a minimalistic approach, trying to change as little as possible, instead of taking advantage of the opportunity of the legal amendments to carry out more complete, rigorous and systematic legislative reforms.[4]

Of all the aspects that critically came to light thanks to the need to comply with the European standards established in the six Procedural Directives, a few emerged as especially relevant in the Spanish system. A first one concerns the many profiles that, despite lack of transposition, remain unaddressed with regard to the presumption of innocence.

On the contrary, in some cases the impact of the Directives had a clear positive effect on the domestic system. This is the case, for instance, of the reform of the "incommunicado" regime, brought by the transposition of Directive 2013/48. A last profile worth mentioning, eventually, concerns the attitude of the Spanish legislator who, in the transposition process, took in many

3 See the text at <https://www.mjusticia.gob.es/es/AreaTematica/ActividadLegislativa/Documents/210126%20ANTEPROYECTO%20LECRIM%202020%20INFORMACION%20PUBLICA%20%281%29.pdf>.

4 Michele Caianiello, 'Dal terzo pilastro ai nuovi strumenti: diritti fondamentali, Road Map e l'impatto delle nuove direttive' (2015) 4 Diritto Penale Contemporaneo 70, 78.

instances the chance to amend criminal procedural rules also beyond what strictly required by the EU standards, providing in certain cases for a higher level of protection.

11.3.1 *Lacunas in the Presumption of Innocence*

Under a certain perspective, the implementation of Directive 2016/343 was considered unnecessary in Spain because of its vague provisions, mostly referring to general principles, such as the *in dubio pro reo*, or fundamental rights already included in the Spanish Constitution, such as the presumption of innocence or the right to remain silent.[5]

However, some of the aspects included in the Directive do not find a detailed regulation in the Spanish legal system.

As for the presumption of innocence, despite the fact that Spain recognizes this right at the constitutional level (Art 24(2) Spanish Constitution), there is a lack of a legal configuration of the right, which details, as the Directive does: what is its temporal scope of application (Art 2 Directive 2016/343); what is its content and its implications (Arts 3, 4 and 5); how it affects issues such as the distribution of the burden of proof in criminal proceedings (Art 6); and, especially, how it interrelates with the right to silence of the accused (Art 7). In this sense, I agree with Guerrero Palomares when he states that neither in our Constitution, nor in our procedural laws there is a definition or a legal-positive construction of the content, contours and attributes of the presumption of innocence.[6] Many domestic provisions simply proclaim this right, without detailing its material content and implications.

Against this background, some aspects can be highlighted, that need to be reviewed in the light of the Directive.

Firstly, the application of the presumption of innocence, as a rule of treatment (Art 2 Directive 2016/343), is not protected in our national legal system, neither at the legislative, nor at the jurisprudential level. In this sense, the lack of express normative provisions, together with the lack of practical application in the case law, fuels the arbitrariness in the application of this fundamental right to the phases prior to the oral trial.[7]

---

5 Some scholars, as Coral Arangüena Fanego early warned of the risk that States might not see the need to review their existing national legislation due to the imprecise content of the European standard. See Coral Arangüena Fanego, 'Las Directivas europeas de armonización de garantías procesales de investigados y acusados. Su implementación en el Derecho español' (2019) 1 Revista de Estudios europeos 5, 24.

6 Guerrero Palomares, '¿Es necesaria la transposición de la Directiva 343/2016, de 9 marzo en materia de presunción de inocencia?' (2019) 1 Revista de Estudios Europeos 164, 166.

7 Ibid 170.

Secondly, the provisions relating to the so-called *extraprocedural dimension* of the presumption of innocence (Arts 4 and 5 Directive 2016/343) are not reflected neither in the Criminal Procedural Act, nor in other national rules.[8] On this profile, the Directive prohibits public authorities, including judicial ones in their *interim* decisions, to make statements referring to the suspect or accused as guilty, and prevents the latter from being presented so through the application of physical restraints, such as handcuffs, glass booths, cages or shackles, except when the use of such means is necessary for security reasons (Recital (20) of the Directive). In Spain, however, there is no legal rule regulating public references to the guilt of the accused person by authorities or public officials. Nor is there any regulation that limits the mediatic treatment of certain criminal cases, especially those with a high profile, or that determines to what extent, how or by whom the media should be informed of the proceedings *sub iudice*.[9]

In addition, sanctions established for disclosing secret or confidential data of an ongoing judicial investigation (Art 301 Criminal Procedural Act) do not make any reference to the presumption of innocence. On the contrary, they rather serve other purposes, such as guaranteeing the success of the investigation or the privacy of the persons involved in the process, among others. Likewise, there is a lack of legal provisions regulating the public exhibition of detainees. In this regard, the way in which suspects or accused persons are usually presented to the public, often appearing handcuffed and/or covering their faces with their hands or with certain objects is not respectful of the Directive.[10]

---

8 The draft of the new Criminal Procedural Act, however, does regulate this aspect of the right in Art 7.2.

9 Cf. Pablo García Molina, 'La transposición de la Directiva (UE) 2016/343 en lo que respecta al reforzamiento en el proceso penal de determinados aspectos extraprocesales de la presunción de inocencia' (2018) 9300 Diario La Ley 1, 13.

10 And this, despite the fact that the Spanish Attorney General's Office in the Instruction 3/2009, of December 23, on the control of the manner in which the detention is to be carried out, 11–13, indicates that both the detention and the transfer must be carried out in such a way as to guarantee respect for the dignity of the detainee, adopting the appropriate precautions to protect the persons transferred from the curiosity of the public and from any type of publicity, as well as avoiding, as far as possible, that they appear handcuffed or shackled in front of photographers and television cameras. The problem lies, surely, not so much in what the law indicates, but in the usual police practices. Thus, although the law does not regulate the issue in detail, it states that "[t]he arrest and provisional detention must be carried out in the manner that least harms the person, reputation and assets of the detainee or prisoner" (Art 520.1 Criminal Procedural Act). This precept is surely insufficient, especially because of its protectionist orientation towards other legal rights – dignity, honor, property- which have nothing to do with the presumption of innocence.

11.3.1.2 Loopholes in Juvenile Legislation

On a different subject matter, despite the lack of express transposition of the Directive 2016/800, the Organic Law 5/2000, of January 12, regulating the criminal liability of minors, complemented by the provisions of the Criminal Procedural Act (applicable in all matters not expressly regulated for minors), is generally respectful of the provisions of the Directive, without any relevant contradictions being detected. Spanish legislation and case law is generally safeguarding, limiting punitive measures (especially custodial measures) via the principle of proportionality and adapting the measures to the particular needs of the minor. However, in light of the very detailed and meticulous nature of the Directive, certain legal adjustments are required for a complete adaptation of the Spanish legal system[11]. It is striking that, despite the expiration of the deadline for transposition of the Directive, this aspect has gone rather unnoticed, not only by the legislator, but also by the Courts.

To start with, it should be clarified that in the Organic Law regulating the criminal liability of minors there are no legal provisions that directly contradicts the content of Directive 2016/800. This fact could lead to the temptation of considering that the current legislation, if interpreted by the judges in accordance with the letter and spirit of the Directive, would be sufficient to comply with the minimum standard imposed by the European regulations.

However, interpreted in accordance with the Directive 2016/343, it could serve to banish certain practices that do not respect the right to the presumption of innocence. Equally relevant on this point could be the provision of the Criminal Procedural Act, according to which [n]o extraordinary security measure shall be taken against the detainee or prisoner except in the case of disobedience, violence or rebellion, or when she has attempted or made preparations to escape. In any case, a more precise legal provision on the use of handcuffs or other means of physical coercion would be desirable. Additionally, as indicated by Pablo García Molina (n 9), another obstacle to the effective realization of the rights of detainees in terms of avoiding their public exposure could derive from the fact that police headquarters do not have an independent entrance hidden from the eyes of the public for police vans, an architectural adaptation that would require a specific budget allocation.

11 Among others, it would be necessary to at least reform the following points: periodical rewiew of the individual assessment of minors; the right of minors to be fully informed of all the rights to which they are entitled, as well as the right of the holder of parental responsibility to receive the same information; the system of substitution of the holder of parental responsibility by another adult of the minor's choice in cases of conflict of interests; periodic review of detention as a precautionary measure depriving of liberty, among others (On aspects in need of tranpostion regarding Directive 2016/800, see Esther Pillado González, "Implicaciones de la Directiva (UE) 2016/800, relativa a las garantías procesales de los menores sospechosos o acusados en los procesos penales, en la Ley de responsabilidad penal del menor" [2019], 48 Revista General de Derecho europeo, 59).

And it is possible that this is the reason that has led the legislator not to make any concrete proposal for its transposition.[12] Although the principle of conforming interpretation that must guide the actions of the Courts can serve as a temporary and provisional solution until the Directive is transposed, case law, given its own casuistic and mutable nature, does not seem an ideal way to generate the trust and confidence that is sought with the legislative harmonization at the European Union level.

The transposition of the Directive 2016/800 should also serve to eradicate certain judicial practices contrary to its letter and spirit. Thus, for example, the possibility, even endorsed by the Constitutional Court,[13] of exempting the minor investigated from being present at the trial. A position that, in addition to being incompatible with the rights of information and defense of the minor, would clash with the need to carry out an individual assessment of the minor at the earliest possible stage of the proceedings (Art 7(5), Directive 2016/800).[14]

11.3.2 *Reform of the Incommunicado Regime*

The transposition of Directive 2013/48 represented in Spain a crucial occasion to improve the regime of *incommunicado* detention, that is the situation in which a detainee or remand prisoner may be subject in exceptional cases, in order to avoid contact with the persons with whom she would ordinarily be entitled to communicate while in custody.

In particular, restrictions on communication with third parties may be justified by the urgent need to avoid serious consequences that could endanger the life, liberty or physical integrity of a person, or to avoid seriously compromising criminal proceedings (Art 509 Criminal Procedural Act),[15] cases in which it could even be justified to deprive the detainee of the right to a private and confidential interview with her lawyer (Art 527(1)(c) Criminal Procedural Act).

Already before the advent of the Directive, however, Spanish legislation on the matter was more safeguarding than European legislation in certain

12 It should be noted, however, that the scientific doctrine does not agree with this lack of need for transposition: Arangüena Fanego (n 5) 29; Jorge Jiménez Martín, 'Garantías procesales de los menores sospechosos o acusados en el proceso penal: cuestiones derivadas de la directiva 2016/800/UE, de 11 de mayo' in Coral Arangüena Fanego and De Hoyos Sancho (eds), *Garantías procesales de investigados y acusados. Situación actual en el ámbito de la Unión Europea* (Tirant Lo Blanch 2018) 177–200; Pillado González (n 11) 59, 97.

13 Judgment of the Constitutional Court No. 146/2012, of July 5 (8th Legal Basis).

14 Arangüena Fanego (n 5) 9.

15 The cases in which it is possible to order incommunicado detention are the same as those provided for in Art 5(3) of Directive 2013/48.

aspects. For example, according to the Spanish legislation, the right of access to a lawyer is never suspended, not even for the *incommunicado* detainee, who is only deprived of the right to freely choose her own lawyer. In this case, indeed, a lawyer is always assigned to her from the public defender's office.

The *incommunicado* detainee may also be deprived of the right to communicate with all or some of the persons with whom she has the right to do so, except with the judicial authority, the Public Prosecutor's Office and the Forensic Doctor. Nonetheless, according to Spanish regulation, the detainee held *incommunicado* shall always retain the right to have the fact and place of her arrest communicated to certain third parties, even when the latter are not allowed to communicate with her (Art 520(2)(e) Criminal Procedural Act),[16] with no exceptions. In this way, the existence of secret detentions – not clearly prohibited in Directive 2013/48 – is prevented, in line with the requirements of international treaties on the subject matter.[17]

The reform triggered by the Directive's transposition improved the previous regime on *incommunicado* detention, by specifying the grounds for this regime and the manner in which the detainee's or prisoner's rights of communication may be restricted.

In particular, the national regime of *incommunicado* detention has been modified and ostensibly improved, by establishing that it is for a judge to determine what specific restrictions of rights are necessary and proportionate to apply to the detainee or prisoner held *incommunicado*. This decision should now also express the reasons justifying each of the adopted restrictions (Art 527(2) Criminal Procedural Act).

The reform, however, did not exhaust all criticalities of this sensitive regime. Probably the most controversial aspect is the maintenance of Art 520 bis(2), Criminal Procedural Act, which allows to apply *incommunicado* detention for crimes committed by persons integrated or related to armed gangs or terrorist

16 This Article includes a right – not subject to restriction in cases of incommunicado detention as provided in Art 527(1) Criminal Procedural Act – consisting of the fact that the family member or person that the detainee wishes, without undue delay, is made aware of his deprivation of liberty and the place of custody in which s/he is at all times. Foreigners will have the right to have the above circumstances communicated to the consular office of their country.

17 See, *e.g.*, Art 6 of the Convention against Torture and Other Cruel, Inhuman or Degrading Treatment or Punishment adopted and opened for signature, ratification and accession by General Assembly resolution 39/46 of 10 December 1984.

or rebel individuals, regardless of the concurrence of the circumstances provided in Art 509 Criminal Procedural Act (*i.e.* in cases of urgent need to avoid serious consequences that could endanger the life, liberty or physical integrity of a person, or urgent need for immediate action by the investigating judges to avoid seriously compromising the criminal process). This provision, indeed, seems to be in contradiction with Art 8(1)(c) of the Directive, according to which derogations shall not be exclusively based on the type or the seriousness of the alleged offense.[18]

11.3.3 *Transposition as a Way to Go beyond the European Standards of Protection*

The levels of protection provided by the Spanish legal system in relation to certain rights, such as the right to legal assistance, legal aid or the right to be present at trial, are sometimes more demanding than those provided for in European legislation. In many cases, therefore, the implementation of the Directives provided the legislator a significant chance to increase the level of protection of fundamental rights even beyond the minimum level required by EU standards.

For instance, although not directly imposed by Directive 2013/48, the following reform was used to reduce the time for the *ex officio* appointment of a lawyer. Specifically, the period of time available to the appointed lawyer to go to the detention center was brought from eight to three hours (Art 520(5) Criminal Procedural Act). In this way, the generic formula indicating that legal assistance must be provided *without undue delay* becomes in Spanish legislation a specific requirement, subject to control.

Relevant is also the case of the transposition of Directive 2016/1919. Despite the fact that legal assistance is not always mandatory in Spanish law, during

---

18 Judicial interpretation is also not in line with the Directive 2013/48 on this point. In fact, in the case of terrorist offenses, given the seriousness of the offense, the Constitutional Court holds that the legislator in Art 520-bis 2 of the Criminal Procedural Act makes a prior weighing of the need for incommunicado detention in these cases, which exempts further reasoning about the need for the measure to achieve the purpose that legitimizes it, since it can be stated in these crimes in a generic way in terms of high probability and regardless of the circumstances of the person subjected to incommunicado detention, given the nature of the crime under investigation and the knowledge of the way terrorist organizations operate, the decision is justified (3rd Legal Basis of the Judgment of the Constitutional Court No. 127/2000 and 5th Legal Basis of the Judgment of the Constitutional Court No. 7/2004). In the same line, the Judgment of the Supreme Court No. 1665/2000, of October 26, 2000, highlights the terrorist context of the detention as a sufficient argument for the adoption of the measure of incommunicado detention (1st Legal Basis).

the legislative process implementing the Directive, the scope of legal aid was extended to all cases in which the accused can prove insufficient economic resources. These might be cases of minor offenses, in which legal assistance is optional for the accused, but the latter still decides to exercise her right of access to a lawyer. The right is then granted, provided that the competent court or tribunal authorizes the request, taking into consideration the nature of the offense and the personal circumstances of the applicant for legal aid.[19] On this point, it can be seen how, once again, the transposition has served as an opportunity to improve the level of domestic protection of the right, beyond what expressly required by Directive 2016/1919.[20]

11.3.4 *Main Critical Profiles in the Case Law*

Although a legislative framework mostly compliant with the EU standards, at the jurisprudential level, many are the shortcomings in the practical implementation of the rights enshrined by the six Procedural Directives.

A significant example in this sense may be observed with regard to the rights to interpretation and translation. In this domain, the most worrisome profiles certainly emerge, on the one hand, regarding the confusion of the Spanish courts about the distinction between the rights of translation and interpretation. Most case law, indeed, considers that when the defendant is assisted by an interpreter, the written translation of certain essential documents is dispensable.[21] With regard to the right to written translation of certain documents, it is also unacceptable how broadly the possibility of replacing the translation of documents with an oral summary of their content is being interpreted by Courts, despite the fact this is provided only as an exception both in Art 3(7), Directive 2010/64 and in the Spanish Criminal Procedural Act (Art 123(3)).[22]

---

19 Art 6.3 a) Law 1/1996, of January 10, on Legal Aid.

20 Which leaves the door open to deny legal aid on grounds of the merits of the case, the low seriousness of the criminal offense, the simplicity of the case or the leniency of the possible sanction.

21 See, *e.g.*, Judgment of the Provincial High Court of Madrid No. 750/2016, of December 13; Judgment of the Provincial High Court of Barcelona No. 283/2017, of March 24.
This problem seems to be fixed in Art 51(h) of the Preliminary Draft of the Criminal Procedural Act, where the translation of essential documents is set up as an inalienable character.

22 Cf. Judgment of the Provincial High Court of Madrid No. 750/2016, of December 13 (in relation to the indictment); Judgment of the Provincial High Court of Barcelona No. 283/2017, of March 24 (in relation to the sentence). *Compare* the analysis made by Clara Fernández Carron, *El derecho a interpretación y a traducción en los procesos penales* (Tirant Lo Blanch 2017) 104–105.

Another problematic issue regarding the judicial interpretation of procedural safeguards concerns the assessment over the need to appoint an interpreter or to order translation of documents. According to Directive 2010/64, indeed, the key element in determining the status of beneficiary of translation and/or interpretation rights is that the defendant does not speak or understand the language used in the proceedings.[23] The case law of the Spanish Courts is consistent with this standard.[24] A significant problem, however, remains with regard to the substantial absence of a mechanism to assess *ex officio* the level of understanding of the language by the defendant. Despite the fact that the law in principle allows the judge to act *ex officio* (Art 125(1) Criminal Procedural Act), in practice judges perform this assessment only if the defendant requests the assistance of an interpreter or the translation of a document. This implies a clear inversion of the burden of proof,[25] according to which it is up to the accused to prove the lack of sufficient linguistic skills.[26] Unless corrected during the legislative procedure, this problem will remain also in the Preliminary Draft of the new Criminal Procedural Act, if approved in its current version.[27]

Critical appears also the possibility to challenge *ex post* problems about the quality of the interpretation or translation. In this regard, the Criminal Procedural Act merely provides that if the Court, the Judge or the Public Prosecutor's Office, *ex officio* or at the request of a party, considers that the translation or interpretation did not offer sufficient guarantees of accuracy, the Judge may order the necessary evaluation to be carried out and, if necessary, also order the appointment of a new translator or interpreter (Art 124(3) Criminal Procedural Act). In practice, however, this control *a posteriori* results very difficult.

---

23 See Judgment of the Constitutional Court No. 181/1994, of June 20, 1994.

24 See, e.g., Judgment of the Constitutional Court No. 181/1994, of June 20, 1994.

25 See the Judgment of the Provincial High Court of Barcelona of November 13, 2000; the Judgment of the Provincial High Court of Segovia of November 9, 2011; Judgment of the Provincial High Court of Barcelona No. 471/2017, of June 7.

26 As indicated by Manuel López Jara, 'La modificación de la Ley de Enjuiciamiento Criminal en materia de derechos y garantías procesales: los derechos a la traducción e interpretación y a la información en el proceso penal' (2015) 8540 Diario La Ley 1, 5, each of the authorities involved in each moment of the process should determine the lack of knowledge of the language. Furthermore, doubts on this point should be resolved in favor of the appointment of an interpreter or translator.

27 Anteproyecto de Ley de Enjuiciamiento Criminal <https://www.mjusticia.gob.es/es/AreaTematica/ActividadLegislativa/Documents/210126%20ANTEPROYECTO%20LECRIM%202020%20INFORMACION%20PUBLICA%20%281%29.pdf> accessed 9 November 2021.

Despite the fact that Art 123(2) of the Criminal Procedural Act states that the general rule must be the simultaneous interpretation of the proceedings, indeed, in practice a different rule is applied. In absence of simultaneous translation booths and adequate technical means at the disposal of the Courts to perform simultaneous translation, what has taken over is the technique of so-called "whispered interpretation". According to it, the interpreter translates live the proceedings in a low voice into the ear of the accused, just after the interventions of the different parties heard in the proceedings. In this context, and in spite of technological advances,[28] it seems however complicated to have a reliable record of such whispered conversation; obviously, this also makes it extremely difficult to successfully challenge errors in the translation or the insufficient quality of the interpretation.[29]

Moreover, it is a consolidated doctrine of the Supreme Court that such deficiencies or mistakes in translation are only relevant if they cause material defenselessness, which in practice greatly limits the challenges regarding the poor quality of the interpretation of the oral proceedings.[30]

On a different level, Spanish case law on the right of access to a lawyer holds that such legal assistance must be effective and must be respected in the different phases of the procedure, resulting null and void any action in which the detainee collaborates with the investigation (*e.g.* consenting to the search of her home or giving indubitable biological remains for DNA testing) without the presence of her lawyer.[31]

A field where the role of judicial interpretation has a major relevance Spain also concerns the rights enshrined by Directive 2016/343, not expressly transposed into the Spanish legal system.

For instance, the incorporation of the principle of *in dubio pro reo* as part of the content of the right to the presumption of innocence (Art 6(2)) clashes with the current and reiterated doctrine of the Spanish Supreme Court on the matter.[32] The jurisprudential doctrine that separates the *in dubio pro reo*

---

28 The law does provide for audio-visual or, alternatively, written documentation of the interpretation of oral proceedings. See Art 123(6) Criminal Procedural Act.

29 Fernández Carron (n 21) 86–88.

30 Among others, see Judgment of the Supreme Court No. 70/2019, of February 7.

31 See Judgment of the Supreme Court No. 547/2017, of July 12 (concerning home searches); Judgment of the Supreme Court No. 11/2017, of January 19 (concerning DNA samples collection).

32 For this purpose, it is relevant the judgment of the Supreme Court No. 549/2018, of November 13, which collects a consolidated jurisprudence of the Supreme Court according to which the principle *in dubio pro reo* is not part of the right to the presumption of innocence. In fact, this decision refers to Supreme Court case law, reiterated since the

principle from the presumption of innocence shall thus be reviewed in light of the Directive, especially insofar as the separation between them limits the possibility of appealing violations of the referred principle.[33] Indeed, Art 10(1) of the Directive requires that any violation of the rights set forth therein must enjoy effective remedies. On this point, however, the draft of the new Criminal Procedural Act, which is currently being processed, would mean an advance in its current version. It should indeed provide, in its Art 8(4), dedicated to the presumption of innocence as rule of judgment, the following: "The court may not convict the accused if, once the different versions of the facts have been evaluated, reasonable doubts persist as to guilt. Any reasonable doubt as to the facts in dispute that are criminally relevant shall be resolved in favor of the defendant".[34]

Also Art 7(5) of the Directive, establishing that silence shall not be used against the accused, could collide with the current doctrine of the Supreme Court. According to the latter, against the existence of incriminating evidence that requires an explanation from the accused, her silence may be used to strengthen or shore up such evidence.[35] Thus, although in Spain silence evidently has no value as evidence against the accused, it can be used to reinforce

year 1983, then followed by many others judgments, according to which the *in dubio pro reo* principle is a general legal principle, which involves a subjective problem of evaluation of evidence and which, therefore, cannot be subject to appeal or *amparo remedy*, as it is a matter of subjective assessment, in contrast to the presumption of innocence, which is subject to review, as it is based on objective parameters. In the same vein, see the Judgment of the Supreme Court No. 593/2018, of 27 November.

33 Palomares (n 6) 178.

34 As Montserrat de Hoyos Sancho, 'La presunción de inocencia en el anteproyecto de ley de enjuiciamiento criminal de noviembre de 2020 Algunas valoraciones y propuestas con ánimo' (2021) 63 Revista Aranzadi de Derecho y Proceso penal 153, 178, points out, the fact that the legislator expressly recognizes the inseparable relationship between the *in dubio pro reo* principle and the fundamental right to the presumption of innocence has important practical consequences since, in this way, the *in dubio pro reo* principle would be treated as a fundamental right, with all the possibilities of protection and enforceability that are recognized to a right of this nature, through the remedy of cassation and constitutional protection.

35 In this sense, it is remarkable the recent judgment of the Supreme Court No. 298/2020, of 11 June (RJ20/2020; ECLI:ES:TS:2020:1678) according to which silence is not always neutral from the point of view of the evidentiary evaluation, although obviously, in absence of incriminating evidence *stricto sensu*, it can never be the basis for a conviction. Silence can have significance when entails a positive aspect: it implies refusal to offer an explanation that, if it existed, only the accused can offer. From this attitude of the defendant, it is possible to legitimately draw the conclusions that the explanation is not offered, because it does not exist.

existing inculpatory evidence.[36] In this regard, the Spanish Supreme Court seems to follow the controversial interpretative line of the European Court of Human Rights, according to which taking into consideration the passive attitude of the defendant in situations that require an explanation on her part, in order to assess the persuasive force of the incriminating evidence is compatible with the right to remain silent.[37] For its part, also in this sense the draft of the new Criminal Procedural Act seems to seek a revision of this jurisprudential interpretation, by establishing in Art 17(1) that the silence of the accused person or her refusal to testify may not lead to prejudicial consequences (being always possible, in any case, the opportunity to present a reasonable alternative to the version of the prosecution).

Lastly, it should also be highlighted that, sometimes, national jurisdictions have truly taken a *proactive* role in the implementation of defense rights enshrined in the EU Directives. For instance, prior to the transposition of the Directive 2012/13, the Constitutional Court anticipated its formal implementation and clarified certain points on the right to information in criminal proceedings. In this regard, it stated that, since the transposition deadline had expired, the Spanish judicial bodies were obliged to interpret their domestic law in light of the Directive.[38]

Also, the Judgment of the Constitutional Court No. 21/2018, of March 5, established the relevant doctrine on the right of access to the file applicable to the detainee. This ruling is very interesting because it delimited and configured the scope and content of this new right to access to the materials of the case, including the following considerations: relationship with other rights, form of access, timing access, content requirements, determination of accessible documents and possibilities to challenge the police decision before the Courts.

11.4 Concluding Remarks

The harmonization of the criminal procedural laws of the Member States of the Union is a long and complex process, still unfinished, but which undoubtedly conditioned and will continue to influence the Spanish legislative agenda in this area in the coming years, in addition to serving as a binding guide for judicial interpretation. Of course, from the national perspective, there is still a

36 See the Judgment of the Supreme Court No. 450/2007, of May 30, 2007, 16th Legal Basis; see also the more recent Judgment of the Supreme Court No. 474/2016, of June 2.

37 *John Murray v United Kingdom* App no 18731/91 (ECHR, 8 June 1996).

38 Judgment of the Constitutional Court No. 13/2017, of January 20.

long way to go, and not only because of some Directives have a pending transposition, but especially because of the need for Judges and Courts and other legal operators to adapt their actions to the letter and spirit of the European standards also in relation to the Directives already transposed.

The levels of protection provided by the Spanish legal system in relation to certain rights, such as the right to legal assistance, legal aid or the right to be present in court, are sometimes more demanding than those provided for in European legislation. For this reason, especially in view of the forthcoming approval of a new criminal procedure law to replace the nineteenth century Code of Criminal Procedure, it is particularly important to bear in mind the risks of regression in order to try to prevent them.

In this sense, despite the fact that all the Directives include non-regression clauses, there is a risk that the minimum standard of the Directives will be the one applied in future regulations, causing an erosion or reduction in the level of national safeguards. Against this risk, the legislator must avoid mimetically importing European standards, without adaptation or systematic analysis of their integration into the national legal system. Thus, for example, introducing exceptions to the mandatory requirement of legal aid in the terms of Directive 2013/48 or expressly regulating the possibility of prosecuting minors *in absentia* as permitted by Directive 2016/800 would constitute inadmissible legislative actions in Spain.

The non-transposition of some Directives may have their origin in various causes. Thus, from the national perspective, there is a risk of relying excessively on judicial intervention as a way of accommodating the domestic legal system to the European rules, instead of making an ad hoc legislative amendment. This is particularly true where Directives set out general principles or rights, rather than regulating in detail and exhaustively the content and conditions for the recognition of the various rights and procedural safeguards. While it is true that the Courts have the obligation to interpret domestic legislation in accordance with the purpose and the letter of the Directives, it is no less true that judicial activity, by its very nature, is casuistic and therefore mutable in view of the circumstances of the case, so that it does not have the same potential to generate confidence as laws, of a general and abstract nature, and of mandatory compliance for all public authorities, including, obviously, the Judiciary. That is precisely why the Directives provide a plus in the generation of trust, which neither national nor supranational case law (ECtHR and CJEU), by their very nature, are capable of promoting.

CHAPTER 12

The Netherlands

Reluctance and Formalism in the Implementation of EU Defence Rights

Adriano Martufi, Kelly Pitcher, and Jannemieke Ouwerkerk

12.1 Introduction

This Chapter addresses the implementation in the Netherlands of six directives adopted under Article 82(2) of the Treaty on the Functioning of the European Union pursuant to the Stockholm Programme, for the purpose of creating a certain level of harmonization of procedural rights in criminal proceedings (hereafter: 'EU Procedural Directives' and 'Directive'). It is based on an analysis of the legal framework implementing the rights contained therein, as well as relevant case law. The Chapter is built up as follows. First, for a fuller understanding of the implementation of the EU Procedural Directives in the Netherlands, some background information on the protection of fundamental rights in Dutch criminal proceedings is provided in Section 2. In Section 3, the 'state of play' with respect to implementation is briefly set out per Directive, including the main points of concern in this regard. Thereafter Section 4 provides for an overarching critical analysis of the implementation of the EU Procedural Directives in the Netherlands, thereby drawing on the findings set out in the previous section. The Chapter concludes in Section 5 with a brief reflection on the future of fundamental rights protection in Dutch criminal proceedings, in light of the largescale reform of the Code of Criminal Procedure currently underway in the Netherlands.[1]

12.2 Background Information: Fundamental Rights Protection in the Netherlands

With the EU Procedural Directives conferring certain procedural rights on suspects and accused persons in criminal proceedings, in addressing the state of

1 For an overview in the English language of this project, see <https://www.government.nl/topics/modernisation-code-of-criminalprocedure> accessed 9 November 2021.

 | DOI:10.1163/9789004513396_014

play with respect to the implementation thereof in the Netherlands it is important to say something about fundamental rights protection in Dutch criminal proceedings on a more general level. For this purpose, we will briefly describe the constitutional and institutional frameworks for such protection, turning first to the former.

In the Netherlands, the most important sources of fundamental rights in the context of criminal procedure, including criminal investigation and prosecution, are the Constitution of the Kingdom of the Netherlands (*Grondwet voor het Koninkrijk der Nederlanden*; hereafter: Constitution), the European Convention on Human Rights (hereafter: ECHR) and its Protocols, and the International Covenant on Civil and Political Rights (hereafter: ICCPR) – the Netherlands being a signatory to both international treaties[2] – the Charter of Fundamental Rights of the European Union (hereafter: EU Charter) and the EU Procedural Directives.

Fundamental rights play an important role in creating and shaping Dutch criminal procedure, including the rules on criminal investigation and prosecution, the primary source of which is the Dutch Code of Criminal Procedure (*Wetboek van Strafvordering*, hereafter: CCP).[3] However, fundamental rights protection is not always explicit. Indeed, traditionally, such protection has been implicit, through the limitation of the powers conferred on the public authorities in order to investigate and prosecute crime, by attaching conditions to the exercise thereof. Relevant in this regard is that the notion of *'individuele rechtsbescherming'* – the *legal* protection of the individual who has been drawn into the criminal process (which constitutes an important constraint on the pursuit of truth-finding) – is not limited to individual rights protection (indeed, in the doctrine at least, *individuele rechtsbescherming* is a broader concept than individual rights protection, also encompassing other principles and rules than fundamental rights).[4] It has always been the case, though, that the law regulating criminal investigation and prosecution (and providing the aforementioned legal protection) results in subjective rights enforceable before the courts in individual cases.[5] Nowadays, the law of criminal procedure is, in

2 Although regarding the ECHR, it should be noted that the Netherlands has not ratified Protocol No. 7 thereto.

3 The CCP entered into force on 1 January 1926.

4 See in this regard Kelly M. Pitcher, 'Rights-Analysis in Addressing Pre-Trial Impropriety: An Obstacle to Fairness?' in John Jackson and Sarah Summers (eds), *Obstacles to Fairness in Criminal Proceedings. Individual Rights and Institutional Forms* (Hart Publishing 2018).

5 Janneke H. Gerards and Joseph W.A. Fleuren, *Implementatie van het EVRM en de uitspraken van het EHRM in de nationale rechtspraak. Een rechtsvergelijkend onderzoek* (WODC 2013) 230–31.

some areas at least, more explicit in its fundamental rights protection, in that in certain contexts it contains more explicit references to 'rights'. Nevertheless, it is worth emphasizing that traditionally, the CCP has been conceived of as a system of duties and powers of the authorities involved in the investigation and prosecution of crime.

With the CCP being the primary source of law as regards the rules governing the investigation and prosecution of crime – and where most of the rights provided for in the EU Procedural Directives can be found[6] – in practice, it is also the first point of reference in identifying the rules applicable to criminal proceedings. In addition though, the investigation and prosecution of crime must be in accordance with fundamental rights enshrined in the Constitution as well as the international treaties to which the Netherlands is a signatory, most notably, the ECHR and ICCPR, and EU (criminal) law and the Charter and EU Procedural Directives in particular. Of these instruments, the ECHR has thus far been the most influential, a point to which we will return in Section 4. Perhaps surprisingly, the Constitution has been less of a driving force in shaping the law of criminal procedure. There are several reasons for this. Relevant in this regard is that the Constitution does not yet expressly provide for the right to a fair trial.[7] Moreover, the Constitution prohibits courts, including the highest court – the Supreme Court of the Netherlands (hereafter: Supreme Court) – from ruling on the constitutionality of Acts of Parliament, *i.e.* the compatibility thereof with the Constitution.[8] The Supreme Court, then, is not a constitutional court, but rather a court of cassation.[9] It may, however, decline to apply an Act of Parliament on the basis that it is incompatible with a provision of an international treaty to which the Netherlands is a party or a resolution of an international organisation, as may other, lower, courts.[10]

---

6 Although they can also be found in other Acts of Parliament not falling under the law of criminal procedure as such; an example is the Custodial Institutions (Framework) Act.

7 At the time of writing, a bill proposing that the right to a fair trial be incorporated into the Constitution is currently pending before Parliament. For current information on the status of the bill, see <https://www.denederlandsegrondwet.nl/id/vklqnbat9rrv/recht_op_een_eerlijk_proces> accessed 9 November 2021.

8 Constitution, Art 120.

9 There is no constitutional court in the Netherlands.

10 Art 94 of the Constitution provides that: 'Statutory regulations in force within the Kingdom shall not be applicable if such application is in conflict with provisions of treaties or of resolutions by international institutions that are binding on all persons.' (Official translation <https://www.legislationline.org/download/id/4824/file/Netherlands_Const_2008_eng.pdf>).

In describing the constitutional framework in the Netherlands for fundamental rights protection in the context of criminal proceedings, it is worth briefly looking to the courts' approach to the ECHR (the approach to the EU Charter and EU Procedural Directives being further addressed in Section 4 below). In general, courts (including criminal courts) do not hesitate to apply the provisions of the ECHR and corresponding case law of the European Court of Human Rights (hereafter: ECtHR) in concrete cases; this is standard practice.[11] In this context, '[t]reaty-consistent interpretation of national law is a frequently used technique in the Dutch courts to avoid a violation of the ECHR, especially when an act of parliament is at issue.'[12] At the same time, there are areas in which 'attempts … [have been] made to keep the response to ECtHR case law as minimal as possible'.[13] The right of access to counsel at the time of questioning, as provided for in the Grand Chamber's judgment in *Salduz v. Turkey*, is a case in point, a point to which we will return below.[14] The same applies to another procedural right provided for under the right to a fair trial enshrined in Article 6 of the ECHR, namely the right of the accused to examine or have examined witnesses against them – the right to confrontation. Only recently, the Netherlands incurred state liability for violating Article 6 of the ECHR, on the basis that the national court in question, acting pursuant to the relevant legal framework provided for by the Supreme Court, had 'refused to call prosecution witnesses of decisive weight for the trial's outcome due to defence's failure to substantiate its request for their cross-examination'.[15] In matters of criminal procedure it seems, there may be more resistance to the influence of the ECtHR. To an extent this can be explained by the nature of the criminal justice system in place in the Netherlands, to which we now turn in addressing the institutional framework within which fundamental rights are protected in criminal proceedings.

Caution is rightly warranted in using 'ideal types' to depict criminal justice systems, but for the purposes of this chapter it is worth noting that in the literature, the Dutch criminal process is depicted as 'an inquisitorial process with a view to adversarial argument'.[16] Characteristic of the Dutch criminal

---

11 Gerards and Fleuren (n 5) 236.

12 Ibid 234.

13 Ibid.

14 *Salduz v Turkey* [GC] ECHR 2008, (2009) 49 EHRR 19.

15 *Keskin v the Netherlands* App No 2205/16 (ECtHR, 19 January 2021). For a discussion of the Supreme Court's case law following the judgment in *Keskin*, see (in Dutch only) Marieke J. Dubelaar and Kelly M. Pitcher, 'Post-Keskin: enkele reflecties op de nieuwe lijn van de Hoge Raad inzake de uitoefening van het ondervragingsrecht' (2021) 4 Strafblad 139.

16 Berend F. Keulen and Geert Knigge, *Strafprocesrecht* (14th edn, Wolters Kluwer 2021) 40.

justice system is the strong focus on the pre-trial phase of criminal proceedings, while the purpose of the trial itself (*onderzoek ter terechtzitting*) is to 'verify' the results of the criminal investigation, *i.e.* the evidence obtained. In the Netherlands, therefore, trials are short. The Dutch criminal justice system is also characterised by a strong focus on the goal of truth-finding (although, as observed above, the notion of *individuele rechtsbescherming* constitutes an important constraint on this goal) and on efficiency. Indicative in this last regard is the reliance in legal practice on hearsay evidence in the form of witness statements obtained by the police in the pre-trial phase of proceedings.[17] Indeed, witnesses are rarely heard at trial. The focus on the pursuit of truth-finding and efficiency goes some way to explaining the resistance in the Netherlands to the (full) recognition of certain procedural rights of suspects, most notably the right of access to counsel at the time of questioning (a point to which we will return below)[18] and the right to confrontation.

Turning now to the main actors involved in criminal investigation and prosecution, in the Netherlands, criminal investigation is conducted by the police under supervision of the public prosecutor. Indeed, in the Netherlands, the public prosecutor is also considered to be an investigative authority. But given that the Public Prosecution Service also forms part of the judiciary, the public prosecutor is *magistratelijk*, meaning among other things that while they are, in a sense, 'partial' on account of being charged with the investigation and prosecution of crime, they are also expected to fulfil their role with integrity and due regard for the rights of the suspect (and are under a duty to also gather exculpatory evidence and seek an acquittal if the evidence is too thin to found a conviction). Because, however, the Public Prosecution Service falls under the political responsibility of the Minister of Justice and Security, who may issue instructions to the public prosecutor, the public prosecutor cannot be considered to be independent.[19]

---

17 While at the time the CCP was introduced, the legislator appears to have envisaged a more 'immediate' (*onmiddellijk*) form of evidence, almost immediately thereafter the Supreme Court issued a judgment which put evidence in Dutch criminal proceedings on a very different path: HR 26 december 1926, ECLI:NL:HR:1926:BG9435.

18 At the time of the *Salduz v Turkey* judgment (n 14) being handed down, it should be noted, Dutch law did not expressly provide for the former right. As will be explained below, pursuant to the implementation of Directive 2013/48, it is now provided for in the CCP. It should be noted, however, that efforts were already underway to legislate on the matter of access to a lawyer in criminal proceedings without undue delay (pursuant to the *Salduz* judgment) when Directive 2013/48 was adopted; these efforts were then 'overtaken' by the need to implement the newly adopted Directive.

19 The power of the Minister of Justice and Security to issue instructions to the Public Prosecution Service has been the subject of fierce debate in recent years, with critics citing

As to the other members of the judiciary and turning first to the investigating judge, while they have significant powers, it should be noted that they do not have an overall supervisory role in respect of the investigation, a role which is reserved for the public prosecutor. Regarding the trial judge, while on the one hand the aim of the trial is to verify the results of the investigation, on the other hand the trial judge has traditionally played an 'active role', which among other things means that they are responsible for the completeness of the investigation at trial and may in this regard order that further investigations be conducted if they deem it necessary. This role goes some way to explaining why the defence has traditionally had quite a marginal role in Dutch criminal proceedings, the active role of the trial judge (and the *magistratelijkheid* of the public prosecutor) being considered an important safeguard in the prevention of miscarriages of justice. However, with defence rights on the increase and, consequently, more reliance being placed on the defence to raise issues (coupled with higher substantiation requirements in this regard), including those going to the completeness of the investigation, concerns are being raised in the Dutch literature as to just how active the trial judge is nowadays and whether the system is sufficiently protective of the accused.[20]

In setting out the institutional framework for fundamental rights protection in criminal proceedings, it is important to say something about how the violation of standards governing the criminal investigation – including the non-observance of the fundamental rights of the suspect (the term 'suspect' in this chapter may refer to the suspect or the accused, or both, depending on the context, which corresponds to the Dutch legal terminology, in which persons suspected of a crime are called 'suspects' (*verdachten*) both before and after indictment)[21] – is addressed in the Netherlands. Such 'procedural violations' may be raised with the investigating judge in the context of the arraignment/hearing held for the purpose of determining whether the arrest and/or police custody was lawful, or before the trial judge under Article

the (appearance of the) risk of political interference. In the context EU cooperation in criminal matters, it has been problematic in light of the Court of Justice of the European Union's case law on the definition of 'judicial authority' in European arrest warrant proceedings. See in this regard Jannemieke W. Ouwerkerk and others, 'De rol en positie van het openbaar ministerie als justitiële autoriteit in Europees strafrecht. Een verkennende studie naar een toekomstbestendige vormgeving van de rol en de positie van het openbaar ministerie in de EU-brede justitiële samenwerking in strafzaken' (WODC 2021).

20 See, e.g. Leonie van Lent, Annerie Smolders and Marijke Malsch, ' "We kennen allemaal de stukken ...". Pleidooi voor een debat over een onmiddellijker strafproces in Nederland' (2020) 7 Delikt en Delinkwent 528.

21 See CCP, Art 27.

359a of the CCP, the mechanism by which the judge in trial proceedings may attach legal consequences to procedural violations committed in the pre-trial phase of proceedings. Such legal consequences are: a declaration that the prosecution is not admissible, non-use/exclusion of the unlawfully obtained evidence, sentence reduction or a simple declaration that the authorities acted unlawfully. It is fair to say that overall (flagrant procedural violations aside), the framework created for the application of Article 359a CCP is heavily weighted towards *not* attaching legal consequences to pre-trial procedural violations. This has led to concerns being raised over the adequacy of the oversight of the investigation, in which the trial judge now only plays a marginal role.[22]

12.3 The Implementation of EU Directives: State of Play

In this section[23] an overview is provided of the state of play in the Netherlands regarding the implementation of the rights contained in the EU Procedural Directives as well as relevant case law. Formally speaking, all six of the Directives under consideration in this book have been implemented in the Netherlands. For the majority of the Directives, specific implementing legislation was introduced by the Dutch legislator, while only two of the Directives have been dealt with exclusively through implicit or indirect implementation: Directive 2016/343 on the presumption of innocence and right to be present at trial and Directive 2016/1919 on legal aid. The remaining four Directives required to a lesser or greater degree an intervention of the legislator and the adoption of an array of implementing provisions, enshrined through ordinary legislation (principally the CCP), delegated legislation, administrative acts and

22 See, e.g. Mojan Samadi, *Normering en toezicht in de opsporing: Een onderzoek naar de normering van het strafvorderlijk optreden van opsporingsambtenaren in het voorbereidend onderzoek en het toezicht op de naleving van deze normen* (Wolters Kluwer 2020).

23 For the purpose of the analysis underlying this section, use was made of the information provided in the transposition tables attached to the explanatory memoranda to the draft implementing legislation. Such information provided a useful starting point for researching the implementation of the EU Procedural Directives in the Netherlands, but did not prevent further and independent scrutiny of the state of play. As to the analysis of the case law, the focus was on the case law of the Supreme Court, on the basis that such case law may be said to be representative of 'the law in action'. Nevertheless, where necessary, lower case law was included. The selection of cases was based on relevance and is therefore not exhaustive of the case law that can be said to involve the EU Procedural Directives, in particular as regards the decisions of lower courts.

policy guidelines. In the following paragraphs, for each Directive the state of play with respect to implementation and (where instructive) notable developments in the case law are briefly set out, including the main points of criticism in this regard.

As stated above, Directive 2010/64 on the right to interpretation and translation demanded the adoption of specific implementing legislation. As far as the right to interpretation is concerned, the implementing legislation is thought to partially codify existing Dutch practice, previously regulated by means of instructions addressed to the police and the Public Prosecution Service. In addition, the CCP provided for safeguards regarding the right to interpretation before the investigating magistrate and during trial hearings. However, the introduction of some ad hoc provisions into the CCP regarding the right to interpretation contributes significantly to enhance this right in the early stages of criminal proceedings. The newly introduced Article 29b CCP lays down the right to be assisted by an interpreter, thus allowing suspects to request the assistance of an interpreter before police questioning. By contrast, with regard to the right to translation of essential documents, the Act implementing the Directive[24] brings about substantial changes, as national practice in this area has traditionally been more restrictive. In particular, the newly introduced Article 32a CCP stipulates in general terms that the suspect may request the translation of documents they consider 'necessary' for the defence. Among the points of concern with regard to the implementation of the Directive is the lack of effective remedies to challenge a decision refusing the assistance of an interpreter. Further points of contention relate to the possibility of prosecutors to replace a detailed translation of the charges in the indictment with a summary description of the offence in a language the suspect understands.[25] Similarly, Articles 365 and 366 CCP (which regulate the notification of a judgment to suspects who did not attend the trial hearing) do not provide for the translation of parts of a judgment dealing with the evidentiary elements on which a verdict has been based. These provisions were heavily criticised and

24 *Wet van 28 februari 2013 tot implementatie van richtlijn nr. 2010/64/EU van het Europees Parlement en de Raad van 20 oktober 2010 betreffende het recht op vertolking en vertaling in strafprocedures* (*PbEU L 280*) (*Stb.* 2013, 85) (entry into force 1 October 2013, *Stb.* 2013, 268) <zoek.officielebekendmakingen.nl>.

25 If the officer and the suspect disagree about the necessity of obtaining the aid of an interpreter, the matter can be referred to an (assistant) public prosecutor who makes a final decision. See para 3.5 of the Instruction 'on interpreters and translators in the investigation and prosecution of criminal offences'.

have become the subject of increased scrutiny in the case law of the Supreme Court.[26]

Regarding Directive 2012/13 on the right to information in criminal proceedings, while certain rights of the Directive required (some) explicit transposition into national law, others already had a basis in national law. Article 27c of the CCP was introduced into the CCP[27] for the specific purpose of implementing the Directive and is a central provision in this regard. Among other things, it provides for the provision of information to the suspect on the reasons for stopping or arrest, as well as on their rights in which respect it draws a distinction between arrested and non-arrested persons (access to the materials of the case already having been provided for).[28] Prior to its introduction, the CCP did not provide for the right to be informed of certain fundamental rights promptly, and while in practice suspects were provided with information on certain rights, this did not occur in all situations envisaged by the Directive, or in respect of all of the rights stipulated by the Directive in this regard. Points of concern in relation to the implementation of Directive 2012/13 relate to the nature of the information to be provided on arrest (to which the Supreme Court has adopted a somewhat minimalist approach), access to the materials of the case (which the suspect or their lawyer must request) and the remedies cited by the Dutch legislator in respect of 'the possible failure or refusal of the competent authorities to provide information in accordance with this Directive' (which do not provide for the right to an effective remedy *without undue delay*).

Of the six Directives under discussion in this book, Directive 2013/48 has undoubtedly caused the most upheaval in the Netherlands. Prior to the ECtHR's judgment in the case of *Salduz v. Turkey*,[29] Dutch law did not provide for the right to consult a lawyer prior to police questioning, *i.e.* for access to a lawyer without undue delay, while the right to have a lawyer present and participate during police questioning was only recognised in 2015. Pursuant to Directive 2013/48 (and the developments in the ECtHR case law that preceded

26 See *e.g.* Jan Boksem, 'Recht op bijstand door een tolk tijdens verhoor. Commentaar op Art. 29b Sv' (*T&C Strafvordering 2019*, last updated 1 July 2020).

27 Pursuant to the following Act of Parliament: *Wet van 5 november 2014 tot implementatie van de richtlijn nr. 2012/13/EU van het Europees Parlement en de Raad van 22 mei 2012 betreffende het recht op informatie in strafprocedures* (*PbEU L 142*) (*Stb.* 2014, 433) (entry into force 1 January 2015, *Stb.* 2014, 434) <zoek.officielebekendmakingen.nl>.

28 Specifically, the following provisions are cited as implementing Art 7 of the Directive: CCP, Arts 30(1), 33, 34(4), 137, 149a(2) and 149b, and the Decree on case materials (*Besluit processtukken*), Art 7(2).

29 *Salduz v Turkey* (n 14).

its adoption),[30] the CCP now provides for both forms of access to a lawyer in Articles 28 to 28e of the CCP.[31] In addition, the Surrender of Persons Act was amended for the purposes of implementing the Directive; it now declares that relevant provisions of the CCP apply mutatis mutandis to European arrest warrant proceedings. Implementing this Directive required significant changes to existing legislation. The fact that Dutch law did not provide for certain aspects of the right of access to a lawyer in criminal proceedings goes some way to explaining the formalistic nature of some of the legislation expressly transposing the Directive. What is meant by this is that the legislation does not fully capture the protective nature of the right, *i.e.* what stands to be gained in effectuating it in terms of fairness, effective defence and equality of arms.[32] For example, while the CCP provides for a general right of access to a lawyer in criminal proceedings (in Article 28 thereof), the right of access to a lawyer without undue delay, *i.e.* as soon as possible in the investigative stage of proceedings, is not expressed as such – as something from which the suspect stands to benefit and as essential to its effectiveness. We refer to Article 28b CCP. While in certain cases presence of a lawyer is mandatory, otherwise the impression is one of a complicated and technical provision addressed to the authorities rather than the suspect, and setting out when the authorities are required to take active steps to make it possible for the suspect to have access to a lawyer immediately following their arrest. Indeed, the right is only provided for insofar as its exercise is dependent on the authorities taking active steps in this regard. The provision setting out the right to have a lawyer present and participate during questioning – Article 28d – is similarly formalistic in nature. While unlike Article 28c, Article 28d is not limited in scope to suspects to have been deprived of their liberty (seemingly because the right to have a lawyer present and participate during questioning would always seem to require active steps on the part of the authorities), it does make observance of the right dependent on the suspect's request. The uneasiness with this right – again, prior to *Salduz*,

---

30 See (n 18).

31 Through the following Act of Parliament: *Wet van 17 november 2016, houdende implementatie van richtlijn nr. 2013/48/EU van het Europees Parlement en de Raad van 22 oktober 2013 betreffende het recht op toegang tot een advocaat in strafprocedures en in procedures ter uitvoering van een Europees aanhoudingsbevel en het recht om een derde op de hoogte te laten brengen vanaf de vrijheidsbeneming en om met derden en consulaire autoriteiten te communiceren tijdens de vrijheidsbeneming (PbEU L294)* (Stb. 2016, 475) (entry into force 1 March 2017, *Staatsblad* 2017, 66) <zoek.officielebekendmakingen.nl>.

32 We refer in this regard to Recital 12 of the Directive, which gives expression to the constitutional dimension of the right of access to a lawyer, as well as its connection with the notions of fairness and effective defence.

Dutch law did not provide for this right, which was moreover only formally recognised in 2015 – is further apparent from the express reference in Article 28d to the potential for disruption in admitting counsel to questioning, as well as from the delegated legislation further regulating (and restricting) this right. A concern in respect of the implementation of Directive 2013/48 is therefore that the relevant legislation is not evidently 'protective' in nature. In addition, implementation of the right to have a lawyer present and participate *during* questioning in particular is quite minimalistic.[33] A final point of concern is the absence of *timely* remedies in respect of (possible) violations of the right of access to a lawyer in criminal proceedings, Article 359a CCP being the designated 'remedy' in this regard.

Directive 2016/800 on the procedural safeguards for juvenile defendants was implemented into Dutch law through the Act of 15 May 2019.[34] This statute introduced significantly novel provisions, adding to the CCP, the Criminal Code, the Surrender of Persons Act and the Young Offenders Institutions (Framework) Act. The adoption of the implementing legislation has picked up on a debate about the overall lack of adequate safeguards for juveniles in Dutch criminal procedure, most notably with respect to the lack of focus on the 'best interest' of the child in the context of police custody and deprivation of liberty.[35] The implementing legislation introduced specific procedural safeguards to address the particular vulnerability of juvenile suspects. These include the right of such suspects to be informed about their rights and, more generally, about the conduct of the proceedings. Article 488aa CCP lays down a comprehensive implementation of the safeguards provided for under Article 4 of the Directive, stipulating among other things that suspects shall be informed promptly after arrest of their right to be accompanied by parents or guardians and that police questioning may be audio-visually recorded pursuant to the new provision of Article 488ac CCP. In accordance with the Directive, the implementing act introduced several provisions seeking to restrict the use of detention with respect to juvenile defendants.

33 See eg Marianne Lochs, 'Geen coulance maar recht: de actieve raadsman bij het politieverhoor' (2021) 4 Strafblad 129.

34 *Wet van 15 mei 2019 tot wijziging van het Wetboek van Strafvordering en de Overleveringswet ter implementatie van richtlijn nr. 2016/800/EU van het Europees Parlement en de Raad van 11 mei 2016 betreffende procedurele waarborgen voor kinderen die verdachte of beklaagde zijn in een strafprocedure* (*PbEU L 132*) (*Stb.* 2019, 180) (entry into force 1 June 2019, *Stb.* 2019, 181) <zoek.officielebekendmakingen.nl>.

35 See, e.g., 'Kinderombudsvrouw: positie minderjarigen in strafrecht moet beter' [2019] Nederlands Juristenblad 1379.

Directive 2016/1919 was implemented entirely though existing legislation, as apparent from the official notification of implementation published by the Dutch government,[36] although the government does not provide any further explanation as to how the existing legislation in question covers the relevant provision of the Directive, apparently deeming this to be self-explanatory. The rights and provisions of the Directive can be found in various laws, but principally the Legal Aid Act.[37] While the general picture to emerge from the national provisions is that of a legal aid system that complies with the Directive, that legal aid system is also widely perceived to be under financial pressure (as exacerbated by the need to accommodate the ECtHR's judgment in *Salduz v. Turkey*, providing for the right of access to a lawyer without undue delay). This has led to ongoing, critical debate. While to date, the Directive has not featured prominently in this discussion, it is clear that the criticisms being made have the potential to raise issues under the Directive, as relating to the quality of legal aid services in particular.

Finally, Directive 2016/343 was also implemented through existing legislation. This is apparent from the official notification of implementation published by the Dutch government.[38] Once again, while this notification lists a long series of provisions that implement the various articles of the Directive, it is not always clear how (and to what extent) these are covered by the provisions indicated by the government. Even if in many respects the overall system of the CCP can be said to be underpinned by the principle of the presumption of innocence, there are several provisions which may raise questions as to their consistency with the Directive. In particular, it is unclear to what extent the rules of judgment spelled out by the CCP meet the requirements of Article 6(2) of the Directive, pursuant to which doubts regarding the question of guilt shall always benefit the suspect. In the Netherlands, the standard of proof required, as set out in Article 338 CCP, is one of 'judicial persuasion'. In its official notification, the Government relays that a consolidated case law exists on

---

36 *Mededeling van de implementatie van richtlijn (EU) 2016/1919 van het Europees parlement en de Raad van 26 oktober 2016 betreffende rechtsbijstand voor verdachten en beklaagden in strafprocedures en voor gezochte personen in procedures ter uitvoering van een Europees aanhoudingsbevel (PbEU 2016, L 297)* (*Stcrt.* 2017, nr. 59575) <zoek.officielebekendmakingen.nl>.

37 Entered into force on 1 January 1994.

38 *Mededeling van de implementatie van richtlijn (EU) 2016/343 van het Europees parlement en de Raad van 9 maart 2016 betreffende de versterking van bepaalde aspecten van het vermoeden van onschuld en van het recht om in strafprocedures bij de terechtzitting aanwezig te zijn* (PbEU 2016, L 65/1) (*Stcrt.* 29 March 2018, nr. 18991) <zoek.officielebekendmakingen.nl>.

the relevant CCP provisions which states that a court can only come to a finding of guilt if 'beyond any reasonable doubt' that a defendant has committed the offence. In this perspective, if reasonable doubt persists the judge has to acquit. This seems to be in keeping with the underlying rationale of Article 6(2) of the Directive: the principle *in dubio pro reo*. In reality, the interpretation of the objective standard of persuasion seems much more nuanced (and other interpretations of the term 'persuasion' have been proposed).[39] In addition, the current line of the Supreme Court's case law as regards inferences from a suspect's decision to remain silent seems hard to square with the spirit of the Directive. The information provided by the Dutch government is not entirely reassuring in this regard: it only refers to Article 29(1) CCP which lays down a prohibition to put pressure on a suspect during questioning. No mention is made of provisions which might be invoked to avoid courts from drawing on a suspect's silence to prove charges against them. In fact, in some instances (*e.g.* where there is abundance of other incriminating evidence) the silence can be used against the suspect, 'in the sense that the judge may take the silence of the accused into account while weighing other incriminating evidence'.[40] This may influence the appraisal of available evidence[41] and thereby have a bearing on the verdict. In addition, the attitude of a suspect may be taken into account by the judge, in a negative sense, when making a sentencing decision or in other instances during the trial. As for the right to be present at trial, available avenues for appeal do not always secure the suspect's right to a novel determination of the merits of the case.

12.4 Critical Analysis

Having set out the state of play in the Netherlands with respect to implementation of the EU Procedural Directives, the purpose of the current section is to reflect on the nature of implementation of the Directives in the Netherlands in a critical analysis thereof, drawing on and bringing together the various points of concern flagged in the preceding section (12.4.1). We do so against the backdrop of the overall constitutional and institutional framework, as set out in

39 For an overview, see C.P.M. (Tineke) Cleiren, 'De rechterlijke overtuiging. Een sprong met hindernissen' (2010) 171 Rechtsgeleerd Magazijn Themis 259.

40 Jan Boksem 'Zwijgrecht. Commentaar op art. 29 Sv' (*T&C Strafvordering 2019*, last updated 1 July 2020).

41 HR 29 januari 2019, ECLI:NL:HR:2019:97.

Section 2 above. In addition, an attempt will be made to identify current trends in the case law (12.4.2).

12.4.1 *Main Points of Criticism in the Implementation of the Directives*

Admittedly, as some commentators have noted, EU Procedural Directives can be seen as vague,[42] merely repetitive of ECtHR's case law, and largely inadequate to ensure an effective protection of defence rights in both transnational[43] and domestic proceedings.[44] However, as the analysis of implementation in the Netherlands demonstrates, their impact on domestic criminal procedure can hardly be overstated. While some instruments have created a sizeable upheaval with significant repercussions in the public debate well beyond the boundaries of academic and professional discussion (*e.g.* Directive 2013/48 on the right of access to a lawyer), others have produced more subtle and almost invisible tectonic shifts which may nevertheless alter the balance of Dutch criminal procedure (*e.g.* Directive 2010/64 on the rights to interpretation and translation), possibly even more than Strasbourg case law. After all, as correctly pointed out by some commentators, EU Procedural Directives may engage domestic courts in the activity of consistent interpretation of national law (*richtlijnconforme interpretatie*) and may be subject to direct application within national criminal proceedings.[45] What is more, the Court of Justice of the European Union will be gradually called upon to develop autonomous concepts of EU law in the interpretation of the Directives, thus maximising their impact in terms of harmonisation of national law. In other words, the effects of the Directives can be reasonably expected to expand in the future, with a noticeable progression in terms of protecting the rights of the defence across the EU.

In light of the above, it is regrettable that Dutch implementing legislation has not engaged more vigorously with the contents of the Directives and the rights-approach to criminal procedure envisaged thereunder. This

---

42 Joost Nan, 'Richtlijn 2016/343, betreffende de versterking van bepaalde aspecten van het vermoeden van onschuld; iets nieuws onder de zon?' (2016) 9 Delikt en Delinkwent 706, 722.

43 Tommaso Rafaraci, 'The Right of Defence in EU Judicial Cooperation in Criminal Matters' in Stefano Ruggeri (ed) *Transnational Inquiries and the Protection of Fundamental Rights in Criminal Proceedings* (Springer 2013).

44 Lorena Bachmaier Winter, 'The EU Directive on the Right to Access to a Lawyer: A Critical Assessment' in Stefano Ruggeri (ed) *Human Rights in European Criminal Law* (Springer 2018).

45 Michiel Luchtman, 'Kroniek van het Europees strafrecht' (2014) 35 Nederlandse Juristenblad 1082; Jannemieke W. Ouwerkerk, 'Europeanisering van het Nederlandse strafrecht. Blessing in Disguise' (2013) 88 Nederlands Juristenblad 2986.

is somewhat surprising, as some key procedural rights enshrined by the EU legislator were not provided for under Dutch law (the right to have a lawyer present and participate during police interrogation; the right to translation of essential documents; the right to medical examination for juvenile suspects) or were not explicitly recognised by legislation (the right to an interpreter in the pre-trial phase of the proceedings; the right to be informed of procedural rights promptly).[46] A possible explanation for this is that in implementing the Directives, the Dutch legislator was also seeking to ensure continuity. Here it may be observed that Dutch implementing legislation follows a line of linguistic continuity with the terminology employed by the CCP (which refers to the 'powers'). In many instances the language tries to follow closely the terminology previously used by the CCP. This goes hand in hand with an approach to transposition which appears rather formalistic. Save for some exceptions (*e.g.* the relevant parts of Article 28 CCP), the implementing provisions appear at odds with the spirit of the EU Procedural Directives, in that they do not use a language of 'empowerment', but rather convey a sense of unilateral concessions being made to suspects. Indeed, several of the implementing provisions analysed for the purposes of this chapter do not fully capture the protective nature of the rights covered by the Directive, *i.e.* what stands to be gained in effectuating it in terms of fairness, effective defence and equality of arms. This is certainly the case with regard to the right of access to a lawyer, where the right to receive the assistance of a lawyer without undue delay is not expressed as such. In the same vein, the newly introduced provision concerning the right to an interpreter, Article 29b CCP, adopts the terminology traditionally employed by the CCP and seems to address mostly prosecuting authorities, thus demanding that the 'assistance of an interpreter shall be sought'. Similarly, Article 30(1) CCP provides that the public prosecutor may grant access to the materials of the case during the preliminary investigation, adding that access shall in any case be granted as from the interrogation upon arrest. These provisions, far from clearly attributing 'individual rights', are framed and construed as prescriptions addressing the authorities. They suggest that the suspect is regarded as the passive recipient of decisions being made by the prosecutors, judges and police officers. Aside from being at odds with the spirit of the Directives,

46 This right was in fact only partially recognised in practice as the CCP did not provide for the right to be informed of certain fundamental rights promptly, and while in practice suspects were provided with information on certain rights (for example, this was already standard practice in respect of suspects to have been arrested), this did not occur in all situations envisaged by the Directive, or in respect of all of the rights stipulated by the Directive in this regard.

it is also problematic from an internal perspective. As observed in Section 2, in the Netherlands, the effectuation of procedural rights is increasingly being made dependent on the defence taking the initiative in this regard. Yet at first glance the legislation is hardly inviting or accommodating in this regard. This is a matter of some concern, given that the defence has traditionally had a marginal role in the Netherlands and in light of the concerns being raised as to just how active the trial judge is nowadays and therefore whether the system is sufficiently rights-protective.

A further concern from a rights-perspective is the lack in some areas of effective and timely judicial remedies. What is particularly noticeable in this regard is the choice not to implement specific remedies that may provide immediate and effective redress, *i.e.* redress 'without undue delay', to violations of rights taking place in the pre-trial or early stage of criminal proceedings. The apparatus of remedies identified by the Dutch legislator, largely drawing on existing provisions in the CCP, seems to revolve around mechanisms which can only be activated during trial (*e.g.* the exclusionary remedies for unlawfully obtained evidence). To a large degree, decisions concerning the effective implementation of procedural rights in the early stage of proceedings remain firmly in the hands of prosecuting authorities. Apart from the lack in some areas of prompt and timely remedies, this raises questions with respect to the independence of those handling complaints or challenges filed by the suspect given the lack of external judicial review of decisions (*e.g.* by an investigating judge).[47] It is noticeable that challenges against decisions to refuse the assistance of an interpreter made by a public prosecutor, can be dealt with by an assistant public prosecutors (in practice, a senior police officer), thus casting serious doubts with regard to compliance with the requirements of an 'effective judicial remedy' under Article 47(1) of the EU Charter.

Finally, aside from the issue of framing and approach to remedies, another hurdle to a fuller and more effective exercise of procedural rights is caused by the somewhat minimalistic approach to certain rights of the Directives. Worth mentioning in this respect is the manner in which the right of access to a lawyer and to have a lawyer present and participate during questioning in particular, is regulated. The delegated legislation which, within the framework of what has been provided for by the CCP, further regulates and restricts this right

---

47 See however CCP, Art 30(4), in case of refusal or partial access to the case file the suspect may submit a notice of objection to the investigative judge within fourteen days after the date of the notification referred to in paragraph 3, and thereafter each time after periods of thirty days. The investigative judge shall hear the public prosecutor and shall give the suspect the opportunity to present his views before taking a decision.

(*e.g.* by preventing the counsel from replying to questioning on behalf of their clients) reveals a certain uneasiness with this right. This legislation may therefore be criticised on the basis that it potentially undermines the effectiveness of the right. Similarly, while Directive 2012/13 compels Member States in no uncertain terms to ensure that case materials 'are made available', Dutch provisions regarding access to case materials (including Article 30(1) CCP) express a system in which the defendant or their lawyer must first submit a request for that purpose.

12.4.2 *Current Trends in Dutch Case Law*

What transpires from the above is that the national legislation may at the very least be criticised on the grounds that while it was introduced for the specific purpose of implementing the Directives, it does not speak for itself in terms of the rights-protection envisaged by the Directives.

Many of the implementing provisions analysed reflect a rather conservative approach, aimed at drawing to the largest extent possible on existing procedural provisions and mechanisms. It is therefore unfortunate that in ruling on matters falling within the scope of the Directive, the Dutch Supreme Court appears reluctant to expressly engage with the Directives.[48] To elaborate, as stated in Section 2, in legal practice the CCP is the first point of reference in identifying the rules applicable to criminal proceedings. While the CCP provides for a number of rights covered by the EU Procedural Directives, sometimes as a result of explicit transposition thereof into the CCP, courts, including the Supreme Court, do not always refer to the underlying Directive in applying the relevant provisions of the CCP. When the Supreme Court does refer to the Directives, this is often only *ad adiuvandum*, and national provisions are rarely interpreted in light of the corresponding Articles in the Directive. Meanwhile, the Dutch Supreme Court remains rather loyal to its reliance on the ECHR, even when some safeguards expressed in the Strasbourg case law are codified in the Directives.

In the literature, concerns have been raised as to whether courts (and other actors) are sufficiently 'clued-up' as to when it is that EU law is involved, with all that this entails.[49] While it is difficult on the basis of the case law examined

48 See in this regard Jannemieke W. Ouwerkerk and Pieter A.M. Verrest, 'De struisvogel voorbij. Pleidooi voor een actieve participatie in de Europese rechtsontwikkeling inzake fundamentele rechten in de strafrechtspleging' (2021) 7 Delikt en Delinkwent 585.

49 See, e.g. Michiel Luchtman and Rob Widdershoven, 'Het Nederlandse strafrecht in de ban van het Unierecht' (2018) Ars Aequi 873; Sjarai M.A. Lestrade, 'Spetsializirana prokuratura (verstekzitting), (HvJ EU C-688/18) -het recht van verdachte aanwezig te zijn op de

for the purposes of this chapter to ascertain why courts do not always refer to the Directives, it seems likely that a more 'open attitude' on the part of Dutch courts towards EU law is to be expected as knowledge of and familiarity with EU secondary law and, importantly, the EU Charter increase. None of this is to say, however, that Dutch courts are unwilling to engage with and apply EU (criminal law) law. Indeed, there are cases in which courts have made use of the instruments available them to give precedence to EU law in circumstances in which (a provision of) an EU Procedural Directive has not been properly converted into national law: the instrument of consistent interpretation and the instrument of direct effect. Regarding the former instrument, in tax and private law cases the Supreme Court has held that it is the wording of the national legislation, and not the explanations provided, or comments made during the legislative process (as set out in the drafting history), that is decisive in this regard. Only where such explanations or comments unequivocally give expression to an intention on the part of the legislator to deviate from the Directive in question, may they be taken into account in this regard (a situation which is unlikely to occur in the Netherlands, it has been argued).[50] In the literature, this principle is assumed to apply to criminal cases also.[51] There have also been cases in which the courts have given direct effect to the relevant directive.[52] Finally, courts make use of the preliminary ruling procedure, although overall it is fair to say that courts, including the Supreme Court, are reluctant to do so, seemingly because it would impact on the efficiency of proceedings.[53]

12.5 Concluding Remarks

The overall picture to emerge from the analysis underlying this chapter is that of a pragmatic approach to the implementation of the six Directives. Where

---

terechtzitting' (*EHRC Updates*, 31 March 2020) <https://www.ehrc-updates.nl/commentaar/209278?skip_boomportal_auth=1> accessed 10 November 2021.

50 See Luchtman and Widdershoven (n 49) 887–88. See further Jannemieke W. Ouwerkerk, 'Indirect Effect of EU Law after *Kolpinghuis Nijmegen* (C-80/86): Consistent Interpretation in Dutch Criminal Courts' in Valsamis Mitsilegas, Alberto di Martino and Leandro Mancano (eds), *The Court of Justice and European Criminal Law. Leading Cases in a Contextual Analysis* (Hart Publishing 2019).

51 See, e.g., Luchtman and Widdershoven (n 49) 888.

52 See, e.g., HR 30 mei 2017, ECLI:NL:HR:2017:968.

53 See in this regard Marc de Werd, 'Europees strafrecht vraagt om méér regie van rechters' (2017) Nederlands Juristenblad 1894, referring to the Supreme Court's judgment in HR 22 mei 2015, ECLI:NL:HR:2015:3608.

possible, the legislator has relied on existing legislation. Where the legislator has had to introduce new legislation, the relevant Directive-provisions have been framed in such a way as to ensure continuity within the consolidated version of the laws into which they were being implemented. As a result, the national implementation of the Directives is quite formalistic in nature, in that it does not always give expression to the protective dimension of the Directives in terms of fairness, effective defence and equality of arms, or empower suspects in this regard. It is also quite minimalistic in nature, the national provision on the presence and participation of a lawyer during police questioning being particularly illustrative in this regard. A further, more general, point to emerge concerns the right to an effective remedy and the absence in certain areas of *timely* remedies in respect of (possible) rights violations. The thinking in this regard appears to be that unfairness in the pre-trial stage can be remedied at the trial and appeals stages of the proceedings.

With largescale reform of the Dutch Code of Criminal Procedure on the horizon, however, the current state of affairs may be subject to transformation in the months and years to come. We refer to the 'modernisation project' currently underway in the Netherlands. The most recent proposals of reform pledge to achieve a 'a future-proof, accessible workable ... [Code of Criminal Procedure] that provides a balanced system of safeguards'.[54] One of the driving forces behind this proposed reform is the need to reduce the gap of the current text (which entered into force in 1926) with the overarching and right-centred case law of the ECtHR.[55] It is therefore plausible that some of the key points of concern brought to light in this chapter (reflecting as they do the historical development of Dutch criminal procedure with its strongly inquisitorial attitude and focus on truth-finding) may give way to a more rights-based and adversarial narrative in the texture of the forthcoming code. In our view, such a transformation would be welcome, in light of more participatory conceptions of the criminal process.[56] From this perspective, construing key procedural safeguards as fundamental rights of the suspect, *i.e.* as something from which they stand to benefit in terms of fairness, effective defence and equality of

54 Sven Brinkhoff, Joeri Bemelmans and Maarten Kuipers, 'Criminal Procedure Law' in Piet Hein van Kempen, Maartje Krabbe and Sven Brinkhoff (eds), *The Criminal Justice System in the Netherlands* (Intersentia 2020) 106.

55 See in this regard page 29 of the official, consolidated of the proposal published in July 2020 in the context of the large-scale reform referred to in the introduction to this chapter; see (n 1).

56 See generally John D. Jackson and Sarah J. Summers, *The Internationalisation of Criminal Evidence: Beyond the Common Law and Civil Law Traditions* (CUP 2012).

arms – whether through legislation or case law – is important. This is particularly so in the Netherlands, where the defence has traditionally had a marginal role, while the effectuation of procedural rights is increasingly dependent on the defence itself raising issues (and higher substantiation requirements) in this regard. At the same time, we acknowledge that a more rights-based approach to criminal procedure is dependent on more than the 'law in books' alone. Legal culture plays a significant role in this regard.

There are, moreover, drawbacks to construing procedural guarantees solely or predominantly in terms of individual rights, among other things given its 'reductive' potential and the risk of other values being overlooked.[57] To be clear, that is not what is being advocated here. But in our view the EU Procedural Directives calls for more explicit acknowledgement in the legislation and case law of the rights-dimension of the safeguards provided for therein, alongside the duties and powers of the authorities involved in the investigation and prosecution of crime and other written and unwritten rules and principles of law.

---

57 The hearing of witnesses at trial may be framed as a right of the defence, but it may also be construed in terms of the principle of immediacy (*het onmiddellijkheidsbeginsel*), which in the Dutch doctrine at least is tied up with the notion of judicial responsibility for the completeness of the inquiry at trial. See Van Lent, Smolders and Malsch (n 20). See more generally Jackson and Summers (n 4).

PART 3

Comparative and Transnational Analysis

CHAPTER 13

Comparative Remarks

Michele Caianiello and Giulia Lasagni

13.1 Introduction*

The objective of this Chapter is to give a concise report on some of the most relevant trends emerging from a comparative analysis on national legal frameworks concerning the procedural safeguards of the suspected or accused in criminal proceedings. In particular, the analysis focuses on those rights included in the six Directives issued in the aftermath of the Stockholm Programme,[1] and encompasses nine Member States, namely Bulgaria, Croatia, France, Germany, Italy, Poland, Portugal, Spain, and the Netherlands (hereinafter generally referred as 'Member States').

Such legal systems have been examined in the course of the research under a twofold perspective.

The first methodology is a transversal legal comparative approach. Due to the limited remit of this contribution, the analysis does not aim at listing all incongruencies among Member States in the implementation of the six procedural Directives;[2] on the contrary, it rather focused on identifying different normative approaches that seem to generate or incentivize divergent solutions in the level of protection for defence rights throughout the EU. In this perspective, the comparison seems to point out how it is more difficult than it appears at first glance to find a normative approach able to ensure by default a high level of compliance at the national level (§13.2).

---

* Although the Chapter is a joint reflection of the authors, its drafting is broken down as follows: Caianiello, § 13.4 and 13.5; Lasagni §§ 13.1, 13.2 and 13.3. A special thanks for their precious suggestions to Isadora Neroni Rezende, Karolina Kremens, Wojciech Jasiński, Alessandra Santangelo and Antonio Pugliese. The national reports mentioned in this Chapter have been drafted in the course of the CrossJustice projects and can be freely accessed at: <https://site.unibo.it/cross-justice/en>.

1 Directive 2010/64/EU of 20 October 2010; Directive 2012/13/EU of 22 May 2012; Directive 2013/48/EU of 22 October 2013; Directive (EU) 2016/343 of 9 March 2016; Directive (EU) 2016/800 of 11 May 2016; Directive (EU) 2016/1919 of 26 October 2016.

2 Largely analysed in legal doctrines and at the same EU level, see for all, the precious activity carried out in this field by the European Judicial Network.

 | DOI:10.1163/9789004513396_015

The second perspective adopted in the research originates from an innovative multi-disciplinary approach, that combined legal and computer science expertise. Through the elaboration of "harmonization indexes" and "heat maps" based on Artificial Intelligence (AI) technology, this analysis highlighted similarities and lacunas in the recognition of defence rights across domestic systems, thanks to a semantic and textual examination of legal texts. This method, therefore, allowed to cross-check the results of traditional legal analysis, trying to bypass, by way of automated assessments, some problematic features typical of comparative studies, such as linguistic discrepancies and ontological divergencies (§ 13.3).

The results of this combined effort, as it will emerge, highlight several critical profiles that, on one side, show the difficulties in reaching effective harmonization in the field, and, on the other, may help tracing a potential way forward towards a higher level of safeguard for defence rights throughout the EU.

Pointing the finger against gaps and lacunas, however, should not let us forget how much has actually been accomplished in the last few years. This is even more so, considering that the harmonization had been carried out via legal acts, like directives, which as such do not have a generalized direct effect on national law and which, in the specific matter, are almost unanimously criticized for having lost much of their mandating strength during the negotiations that preceded their approval.[3]

Just to mention some of the major achievements, reference could go to the extension of the right to a lawyer also during police questioning;[4] the strengthening of client-attorney confidentiality; the establishment of communication rights with consular authorities;[5] the focus on juvenile specific needs as

3 See, for all, Silvia Allegrezza, 'Toward a European Constitutional Framework for Defence Rights' in Silvia Allegrezza and Valentina Covolo (eds), *Effective Defence Rights in Criminal Proceedings. A European and Comparative Study on Judicial Remedies* (Wolters Kluver/CEDAM 2018) 3 ff; Andrè Klip, *European Criminal Law* (4th edn, Intersentia 2021) 299 ff.

4 For instance, in Germany (cf. Anna H. Albrecht and Anne Schneider, 'German National Report', 32) and in Croatia (cf. Zlata Đurđević, Elizabeta Ivicevic Karas, Marin Bonacic, and Zoran Buric, 'Croatian National Report', 36). On the contrary, the rule still remains unapplied in Portugal, on the basis that "in any event […] statements [before the police] may virtually never serve as evidence later in trial", cf. Miguel João Costa and Pedro Caeiro, 'Portuguese National Report', 35.

5 Although only in some States the accused who benefits from multiple nationalities is explicitly granted the right to choose which consular authorities to communicate with, as requested by Art 7(1), Directive 2013/48. This is the case of Bulgaria (cf. Miroslava Manolova, 'Bulgarian National Report', 44), Portugal (Costa and Caeiro (n 4) 39); Spain (Ana-María Neira-Pena, 'Spanish National Report', 39).

defendants; the adoption of a more systemic perspective on the right to interpretation and translation;[6] or the recognition of the right to information since the early phases of the proceedings.

Indirectly, the implementation of the Directives also brought to a partial harmonization of investigative measures, for instance by pushing for the establishment of identity parades, confrontations, and reconstructions of the crime scenes in many States where such measures had not before any legal basis or practice.[7]

Lastly, even aspects that do not find yet a satisfactory regulation in most countries, such as the audio video recording of interviews of the suspected or accused, or the need to attach effective legal consequences to violations of the presumption of innocence in its notion as rule of treatment, or the urgency to find a satisfactory regulation of the intertwine between procedural safeguards and privacy violations,[8] started to be transnationally considered as problematic profiles that require to be addressed, precisely thanks to such EU legislative acts.

All this, though at times unsatisfactory in terms of foreseeability of the applicable procedural norm, contributes to the slow creation of a common culture on the defence needs and standards of protection among Member States.

The comparative analysis indeed shows how, besides for legislative technical limitations and transposition inaccuracies or lacunas, it is the fragmentation of Member States' legal culture the main factor that, in the end, substantially impairs an effective recognition of defence rights throughout the EU. With its innovative approach, the present study tries to contribute to fill this gap, increasing the level of mutual knowledge and understanding for legal operators.

6 For instance, in most examined Member States (all, but in Spain – cf. Neira-Pena (n 5) 14 – and Portugal – cf. Costa and Caeiro (n 4) 16), the transposition of the Directive brought to the creation of official registers for interpreters and translators. See however, below (n 75).

7 As it is the case of the Netherlands with regard to confrontation (cf. Jannemieke Ouwerkerk, Kelly Pitcher and Adriano Martufi, 'Dutch National Report', 64); Germany, at least explicitly, with regard to reconstruction of the crime scene (cf. Albrecht and Schneider (n 4) 32).

8 As requested, respectively, for juvenile defendants, in only partially mandatory terms, by Art 9, Directive 2016/800 and for the presumption of innocence, by the combined reading of Arts 4(2) and 10, Directive 2016/343. For the intertwine between procedural safeguards and privacy, see below Mariavittoria Catanzariti, Chapter 14, § 14.1 ff.

13.2 Common Trends and Lacunas in the Protection of Procedural Safeguards

This comparative analysis cannot but start from the observation that, in the examined Member States, most Directives had been implemented only indirectly, that is, by identifying and sometimes re-interpreting national provisions that pre-existed their entry into force.

Only in few cases, however, the misalignment between EU and national standards is blatant also at a formal glance – the most evident example certainly being Portugal, where, out of six Directives, only one found some form of explicit transposition.[9]

Most frequently, substance hides in nuances. In this sense, the analysis moved beyond the official assessments of national governments, that tend to overestimate, purposefully or by way of tradition, the adequacy of indirect implementation techniques against explicit transposition.[10]

This phenomenon forces legal operators, both practitioners and scholars, to extend the inquiry also over the ontological dimension of concepts, as illustrated in national regulation and developed by national courts. Exemplificative, in this sense, is the definition of "suspect". Against the use of a single term across jurisdictions, for instance, in Poland the notion has such a narrow scope that substantially deprives of its meaning most of the transposing regulation, despite of a level of formal compliance that, on paper, appears comparable with that of other States.[11] The impact of such discrepancies and alike becomes disruptive in transnational proceedings, but of course significantly affects also domestic jurisdictions, where the innovative reach of the Directives struggles to find fertile soil.

This analysis identified at least four main situations, partially even contradictory with each other, that contribute to slowing down harmonization or impeding it from becoming effective.

In some cases, the phenomenon seems to derive from the vagueness or ambiguity of the Directives' provisions. In others, from lacunas in the EU

9 That is, Directive 2016/800, see above Miguel João Costa and Pedro Caeiro, Chapter 10, § 10.3.

10 Especially if compared to the same assessment often made by legal doctrine and the same Commission.

11 See below, § 13.2.1. A partially similar reflection could be extended, again with regard the same country, about the definition of *juvenile* defendant: In Poland, indeed, persons who are 17- to 18-year-olds do not enjoy the protection of the Directive (cf. above, Karolina Kremens, Wojciech Jasiński, Dorota Czerwińska and Dominika Czerniak, Chapter 9, § 9.2).

legislation related to profiles that the Directives aim at harmonizing, but that are substantially left to national discretion as far as their regulation is concerned. However, the significant divergence among national regimes may be also observed with regard to norms established in detail by the Directives. Lastly, a notable role seems also to derive from a general underestimation of the concrete contexts and structures required to make certain procedural safeguards operational.

13.2.1 *Vagueness or Ambiguity within the Directives: The Right to an Effective Remedy*

A major ground to identify the misalignment of procedural safeguards throughout the EU certainly relies on the vagueness or ambiguity of certain rights contained in the different Directives. One of the most obvious examples in this regard may be found in the definition of "effective remedy". Explicitly present in all Directives,[12] but in Directive 2010/64,[13] this right clearly appears as one of the most crucial and, at the same time, least defined aspects of the notion of due process that the Stockholm Programme aimed at ensuring.[14] Several issues can be identified as causes of this situation.

Firstly, the Directives do not outline what a remedy is or should be. For instance, it remains unclear whether it should be limited to a right to appeal, or whether other mechanisms, such as exclusionary rules, should be encompassed too.[15]

---

12 Art 8(2), Directive 2012/13; Art 12, Directive 2013/48; Art 10, Directive 2016/343; Art 8, Directive 2016/1919; Art 19, Directive 2016/800.

13 Where it however emerges from the combined reading of Recital (24): "should ensure control can be exercised"; Recital (25): "should have the right to challenge"; and Recital (27): "taking appropriate steps to ensure those rights are guaranteed"; as well as by Art 2(5) and Art 3(5) "shall ensure [...] the possibility to complain that the quality of the interpretation/translation is not sufficient".

14 Also defined as the Convention's "darkest" provision. See Judges Matscher and Pinheiro Farinha in *Malone v United Kingdom* App No 8691/79 (ECHR, 2 August 1984).

15 On which see, for all, Sabine Gless and Thomas Richter (eds), *Do Exclusionary Rules Ensure a Fair Trial? A Comparative Perspective on Evidentiary Rules* (Springer Open, Cham 2019) and John A.E. Vervaele, 'Lawful and Fair Use of Evidence from a European Human Rights Perspective' in Fabio Giuffrida and Katalin Ligeti (eds), *Admissibility of OLAF Final Reports as Evidence in Criminal Proceedings* (University of Luxembourg, June 2019) 56 ff. Concerning the right to effective remedy with specific regard to Directive 2013/48, cf. also Anneli Soo, 'Article 12 of the Directive 2013/48/EU: A Starting Point for Discussion on a Common Understanding of the Criteria for Effective Remedies of Violation of the Right to Counsel' (2017) 25 European Journal of Crime, Criminal Law and Criminal Justice 1, 31 ff.

Secondly, the Directives do not define what a remedy should include to be considered "effective". Unfortunately, the question does not find a much clearer answer in the jurisprudence of the European Courts.[16] The issue becomes even trickier once read in combination with those provisions requiring rights to be granted "without delay"[17] or, even more ambiguously, "without undue delay".[18] In this sense, it can be inquired whether a remedy, in order to be effective, should necessarily be granted just after the act against which a complaint is lodged has been performed or whether broader timing can also be tolerated.[19]

---

16 In the case-law of the Strasbourg Court, a remedy can be regarded as effective only if available both on the books and in action, that is, only if it can prevent an alleged infringement from persisting or an at least provide an adequate response for past infringements (cf. *Kudła v Poland* App No 30210/96 (ECHR, 26 December 2000) §§ 157–58). Thus, it is not sufficient for a remedy to be established in national law: Its effectiveness should be concretely assessed, as by considering the time it takes for the corrective action to be taken or the applicant's effective ability to activate the remedy in light of the specific circumstances of the case (even though the ECtHR has controversially affirmed that the lack of a suspensive effect does not necessarily undermine the effectiveness of a remedy, in *Umoru v Italy* App no 37442/19 (ECHR, 8 June 2020) §43). According to the ECtHR, it is not strictly necessary for the appeal to be lodged with a judicial authority; however, the empowered authority shall comply with the independence and impartiality requirements set forth in Art 6(1) ECHR. On this point, a difference may be observed between Art 13 ECHR and its analogue in Union law. Indeed, Article 47(1) CFR expressly requires that any violation of the fundamental rights enshrined in the Charter itself be effectively challengeable before a court. Most importantly, in the criminal matter, both European courts require that decisions imposing a punitive measure shall be granted a full judicial review. Thus, it is necessary to identify at least one authority with the power to rule both on questions of fact and of law (*Umlauft v Austria* App No 15527/89 (ECHR, 23 October 1995) § 37; *Oztürk v Germany* App No 8544/79 (ECHR, 21 February 1984) § 56; *Menarini Diagnostics S. R. L. v Italy* App No 43509/08 (ECHR,, 27 September 2011) §§ 59-63-67; *Schmautzer v Austria* App No 15523/89 (ECHR, 23 October 1995) § 36; *Gradinger v Austria* App No 15963/90 (ECHR, 23 October 1995) § 44); on the EU law side, cf. *e.g.* Case C-222/84 *Marguerite Johnston v Chief Constable* (CJEU, 15 May 1986); Case C-222/86 *Union nationale v Georges Heylens and O*, (CJEU, 15 October 1987); Case C-97/91 *Oleificio Borelli SpA v Commission* (CJEU, 3 December 1992). See also, Zlata Đurđević, 'Judicial Control in the Pre-trial Criminal Procedure Conducted by the European Public Prosecutor's Office' in Katalin Ligeti (ed), *Towards a Prosecutor for the European Union*, Vol I (Hart Publishing 2013).

17 Cf. Recital (18) and Art 2, Directive 2010/64.

18 Cf. Art 13, Directive 2012/13; Recitals (19-30-35-36-46) and Arts 3, 5, 6, 7, 10 Directive 2013/48; Recital (27) and Arts 6, 8, 10, Directive 2016/800; Recitals (19, 24) and Arts 4, 6 Directive 2016/1919.

19 Cf. on the issue Valentina Covolo, 'Ensuring the Effectiveness of Defence Rights: Remedial Obligations under the ABC Directives' in Silvia Allegrezza and Valentina Covolo (n 3) 92–93, to whom the second hypothesis seems preferrable: "While the preamble of Directive 2013/48/EU explicitly states that 'the temporary derogation can be assessed by a court, at least during the trial stage', according to Directive 2012/13/EU the right to challenge

Indeed, if effective remedy should be understood as the possibility to challenge – at a certain point – the potential violation of a right, most Member States could be considered as compliant with EU requirements just relying on the regimes already into force before the advent of the Directives.

In this perspective, only a few profiles appear as immediately problematic.

Among them, the basically complete lack of protection for suspects who are not already officially presented with charges (*osoba podejrzana*), in Poland, which can suffer important restrictions of their rights without any substantial form of protection; and, to a lower extent, of suspects in the *inquiry* phase in France.[20]

Equally critical appears the absence of specific rules regarding potential violations of the presumption of innocence meant as a rule of treatment, especially concerning the presentation of the accused to the public. In most Member States, indeed, these breaches do not find any remedy within the realm of criminal proceedings; the only legal consequences usually taking the form of potential disciplinary sanctions, or civil requests for reparation. Such

---

a decision denying access to documents 'does not entail the obligation for the Member States to provide for a specific appeal procedure, a separate mechanism, or a complaint procedure in which such failure may be challenged'. From this perspective, national law complies with the ABC Directives so far as decisions delaying legal assistance, or refusing access to certain materials, are adopted by a non-judicial authority but subsequently scrutinized by the court competent for reviewing the merits of the accusation. Hence, a Member State may grant sufficient judicial protection through the review undertaken by a judge at the trial stage of criminal proceedings on the admissibility and use of evidence collected in breach of defence rights [...] It thus follows that depending on the structure of the national criminal justice system and the judicial remedies available to the defendant, the effectiveness of the judicial protection afforded may vary from one Member State to another".

20 "Polish law provides for a formal procedure by which the person is preliminarily charged with a crime (Art 313 k.p.k.). This takes place by issuing a formal charging decision against her, promulgating it, which is followed by mandatory interrogation, unless the person has fled. In theory, the investigative authorities are obliged to bring charges as soon as they have sufficient data indicating the crime was committed by a specific person. Delaying formal charging is impermissible. Only if the charges are formally presented does the individual gain the status of *podejrzany* and becomes a party to the proceedings with a possibility of fully exercising defence rights [...] As a consequence, Polish law makes a very strict distinction between the status of *podejrzany* and *osoba podejrzana* [...] The latter term has no legal definition, although it is understood as referring to a person who is in fact suspected of committing a crime, but who has not yet been initially charged with an offence" – cf. Kremens *and o* (n 11) § 9.3.1 – but might, for instance, has already been subjected to investigative acts, like searches or seizure, without enjoying any procedural safeguards. For France, cf. Eleonora Cervellera and Raphaële Parizot, Chapter 6, § 6.3.4.

legal actions, however, both for their theoretical design and their concrete application, are widely considered to be fairly ineffective.[21]

Moreover, remedies that are available in national laws significantly vary from country to country: requirements to trigger appeal tools, for instance, as well as the powers of the courts in charge to examine them.[22]

The situation is also quite fragmented with regard to exclusionary rules. Firstly, not all States provide for them with regard to the rights recognized in the six Directives.[23] Even where such rules are established, approaches towards them vary: in some countries they are implicitly derived from a balancing of constitutional values (France, Germany),[24] while in others they are provided for straightforwardly by the legislative provision in relation to specific breaches (Croatia, Portugal), or in rather broad terms, *i.e.* for the general violation of procedural safeguards (Bulgaria, Spain).[25] Some countries present a hybrid form (Poland and, to some extent, Italy)[26] while in other systems the possibility to apply exclusionary rules, *per se* existing as a remedy, is totally left to the discretion of the court, in a case-by-case assessment about the concrete impact of the breach (the Netherlands).[27]

The picture gets however sensibly more critical if the "effectiveness" of the remedy is read in light of the need for a timely response, as from this angle only few cases could be considered to match the requirements of the Directives.

This is, for example, the possibility to trigger a judicial review before the investigating judge in case of limits to the right of access to file in the

21 This is clearly the case in Bulgaria (see above, Manolova, Chapter 4, § 4.3.1); Germany (Albrecht and Schneider (n 4) 65); Croatia (cf. Đurđević *and o* (n 4) 81); Laura Bartoli, Marianna Biral, Cosimo Emanuele Gatto, Giulia Lasagni, Vanessa Maraldi, Irene Milazzo, Isadora Neroni Rezende, Antonio Pugliese and Alessandra Santangelo, 'Italian National Report', § 6.4.1.

22 For an overview on the different remedies across Europe, see Silvia Allegrezza (ed), *Criminal Appeals in Europe: A Comparative Study* (forthcoming publication); raising the issue on a cross-border dimension Vania Costa Ramos, Michiel Luchtman and Geanina Munteanu, 'Improving Defence Rights Including Available Remedies in and (or as a Consequence of) Cross-Border Criminal Proceedings' (2020) 3 Eucrim 230 ff.

23 Though they might provide them for other violations, as it is in the case of Germany.

24 Cf. Albrecht and Schneider (n 4) 8; and above, Cervellera and Parizot (n 20) § 6.3.3.

25 Cf. Đurđević *and o* (n 4) 8 ff; Costa and Caeiro (n 4), 13 ff; Manolova (n 5) 47–48; Neira-Pena (n 5) 41.

26 For Poland, cf. Marcin Wolny and Małgorzata Szuleka, 'Right to defence v. evidence procedures. Admissibility of evidence in the light of EU law and national legal standards. Country report: Poland' (2021) Helsińska Fundacja Praw Człowieka < https://www.hfhr.pl/27220-2/> 19 ff.; for Italy, cf. Bartoli *and o* (n 21), *e.g.* § 4.5.1.

27 Cf. above, Adriano Martufi, Kelly Pitcher and Jannemieke Ouwerkerk, Chapter 12, § 12.2.

Netherlands,[28] or the wider possibility in Bulgaria to appeal decrees of investigative bodies directly before the prosecutor (or, if the decree is issued by the prosecutor, before her hierarchical superior).[29]

Against this general background, what could be overall observed is that remedies, although pivotal for the successful application of the rights enshrined in the Directives, passed almost unchanged through the implementation of the Stockholm programme.[30]

13.2.2 *Specific Rights, Undefined Parameters: Access to File, Trial* in Absentia, *Role of the Lawyer*

Sometimes, the lack of a fully harmonizing effect may be traced back not to the vagueness of the right in itself, but rather to the absence of a common approach in defining the parameters that constitute such safeguard.

This is for instance the case of the grounds allowing restrictions to the right of access to file. The reference to "prejudice to ongoing investigation or seriously harm the national security of the Member State" included in Art 7(4), Directive 2012/13, is indeed so broad to seriously risk inverting the relation between rule and exception in favour of the latter.[31] This causes a broad array of solutions at the national level, where legislation range from systems in which access to files is always fully granted (Bulgaria),[32] to models in which full access may be requested only after one year from the start of the inquiry (France),[33] passing through most other models, in which the matter is *de facto* left to the discretion of the investigating authorities, with limited possibilities for the defendant to challenge such decision until an advanced stage of the proceeding.

Similarly, the possibility to carry out a trial *in absentia* where the suspected or accused, "having been informed of the trial", is represented by a lawyer (Art 8(2), Directive 2016/343), leaves rather undefined the tangible level of

28 Ouwerkerk *and o* (n 7) 50.

29 Art 200 of the Bulgarian Criminal Procedure Code, on which cf. Manolova (n 5) 46 ff, raising issues about effectiveness of such remedy.

30 Interestingly enough, perhaps because of its common placement outside of criminal procedure codes, a tendency towards relatively specialized remedies can be found more easily with regard to the legal aid regimes, although their effectiveness or timing is often put in question, see, *eg*., Albrecht and Schneider (n 4) 60, highlighting the lack of direct impact of potential violations on the admissibility of evidence.

31 Regardless of the invitation to interpret such exceptions "strictly" contained in Recital (32), Directive 2012/13.

32 Cf. Manolova (n 5) 29.

33 Cf. Eleonora Cervellera and Raphaële Parizot, 'French National Report', 22.

awareness that the authorities should grant to the defendant to be sure she has knowledge of the schedule of the hearing. This becomes especially problematic where the lawyer is appointed by the court. Also in this sense solutions are thus doomed to be highly varying.

They range from cases in which formal notification is considered enough to comply with the Directive (Poland, the Netherlands),[34] to countries where instead a specific attention is put on the substantial awareness of the hearing schedule (Spain and, arguably, Italy),[35] to countries in which the issue is partially underestimated or otherwise given for granted, as presence at trial is mostly mandatory (Croatia, France, Germany, Portugal),[36] or may be made so (Bulgaria).[37]

This inhomogeneous picture becomes particularly problematic in light of Directive 2016/343 but has also a direct impact on transnational proceedings. Conditions of trial *in absentia* indeed represent a rather common ground for refusing the execution of a European Arrest Warrant.[38] To make matters worse, the EAW Framework Decision on the subject is arguably not entirely overlapping with those of the Directive.[39] The lack of clear European parameters in this regard, therefore, incentivises national authorities to rely rather on

---

34 Cf. Karolina Kremens, Wojciech Jasiński, Dorota Czerwińska and Dominika Czerniak, 'Polish National Report', 82; Ouwerkerk *and o* (n 7) 123.

35 Cf. Neira-Pena (n 5) 61 and for Italy, Bartoli *and o* (n 21), §§ 6.6.2 – 6.6.4, at least in the more recent interpretation of the Supreme Court, Sez. un., no 23948 of 17 August 2020.

36 Đurđević *and o* (n 4) 88–89; Cervellera and Parizot (n 33) 70 ff; Albrecht and Schneider (n 4) 65 ff; Costa and Caeiro (n 9) § 10.4.3.2. Even in those countries, however, the existence of exceptions may put at risk the very core of the right, see the case of Croatia, where if "proceedings are conducted for an offence punishable by imprisonment up to twelve years, and the accused who was duly summoned did not appear, or the summons cannot be served to him because he changed the address and did not notify the court thereof, or if it is obvious that he avoids to receive the summons, the court may decide to conduct the trial in the absence of the accused if the accused was warned previously that he may be trailed in absence and if he has already given his statement regarding the charge in the presence of the defence counsel (Article 404(3) CPA)" (cf. Đurđević *and o* (n 4) 88).

37 Only with regard to serious crimes or if otherwise ordered by the court, cf. Manolova (n 5) 84.

38 Cf. Art 4a, Council Framework Decision 2002/584/JHA of 13 June 2002 on the European arrest warrant and the surrender procedures between Member States, as amended by Council Framework Decision 2009/299/JHA of 26 February 2009.

39 Cf., *e.g.*, Hannah Brodersen, Vincent Glerum and André Klip, *Improving Mutual Recognition of European Arrest Warrants for the Purpose of Executing Judgments Rendered Following a Trial at which the Person Concerned Did Not Appear in Person* <https://www.inabsentieaw.eu/wp-content/uploads/2020/02/InAbsentiEAW-Research-Report-1.pdf> 54–56.

domestic standards, which do not necessarily ensure the best level of protection to the rights of the accused.

Another major right which highly suffers from the lack of precise definition of its constituting elements in the Directives is access to a lawyer, and in particular the distinction among the right for the lawyer to "be present", to "attend" and to "participate effectively" to certain investigative acts.[40]

No clear definition of such terms is provided for in Directive 2013/48, but for a hint in Recital (25), where, referring to the last expression, it is recommended that "lawyer may, inter alia, in accordance with [national law procedures], ask questions, request clarification and make statements".[41] The ambiguity of the wordings, and the non-binding value of the few interpretative reported criteria, leave several profiles subject to different regulations across the EU and, reportedly, offer some back-up to those systems which traditionally see the role of the defence lawyer as a rather passive one.

In the Netherlands, for instance, where the right to assistance during police questioning was introduced only in 2015 after *Salduz*, the possibility for the lawyer to participate can be excluded if considered "disruptive" by police.[42] In Germany, where the same right was recognized only thanks to the transposition of the Directive, lawyers can intervene, but only after the interrogation and not during it.[43] In France, the intervention of the lawyer is also in principle admitted at the end of the interview, but her questions may be objected by the police, and the only remedy against such an opposition is the possibility to demand including comments in the recordings of questioning.[44]

Other systems show a broader approach. In Croatia, for instance (where questioning of the defendant is also always audio-recorded) the accused,

40 Cf. Art 3(3)(b) and (c), Directive 2013/48, on which see Teresa Armenta Deu and Lisa Urban, 'The Right of Access to a Lawyer under Directive 2013/48/EU' in Allegrezza and Covolo (n 3) 74 ff.

41 On which see, *e.g.*, Anna Ogorodava and Taru Spronken, 'Legal Advice in Police Custody: From Europe to a Local Police Station' (2014) Erasmus Law Review 195; Jacqueline Hodgson and Edward Cape 'The Right to Access to a Lawyer at Police Stations. Making the European Union Directive Work in Practice' (2014) New Journal of European Criminal Law 467 ff; Lorena Bachmaier Winter and Stephen C. Thaman, 'A Comparative View of the Right to Counsel and the Protection of Attorney-Client Communications' in Lorena Bachmaier Winter, Stephen C. Thaman and Veronica Lynn (eds), *The Right to Counsel and the Protection of Attorney-Client Privilege in Criminal Proceedings. A Comparative View* (Springer 2020), 20.

42 Cf. *Salduz v. Turkey* App no 36391/02 (ECHR, 27 November 2008), cf. Martufi *and o* (n 27) § 12.2).

43 Cf. Albrecht and Schneider (n 4) 32.

44 Cf. Cervellera and Parizot (n 33) 32.

having given her statement, may be requested for clarification by the police: in this phase, the lawyer cannot consult with the accused, but can suggest her not to answer to one or more questions. After the conclusion of this first part, questions can then be posed directly by the lawyer.[45] Greater margins of intervention are also recognized in Bulgaria, Italy, Spain and Poland, where lawyers may make requests, comments and raise objections also during the questioning.[46]

Practical circumstances not considered by the Directives can also significantly hamper the possibility for the lawyer to exercise an "effective participation". Exemplificative in this case is, for all, the timeframe (of ca 30 min) that several States introduced to limit the communication between the counsel and the accused before questioning (Croatia, France, the Netherlands).[47]

13.2.3 *When Details Do Not Necessarily Make It Easier: A Scattered Supranational Picture*

In some cases, the reason behind misalignments between EU and domestic systems are clearly attributable to a general political programme, that in all sectors of law, including criminal justice, tend to reduce or rebut the impact of the EU over national law. Blatant, in this sense, is the case of Poland, where some fundamental rights have never been transposed in accordance to the Directives, and some, though initially implemented, have undergone a process of progressive limitation. Significant are for instance the clear limitations of the right of access to a lawyer, that, contrary to Art 3(2), Directive 2013/48, do not generally allow the accused to confer with the lawyer before questioning; of the right to be present at trial, in a system where the defendant may be prohibited to attend trial hearings even when willing to do so, and regardless of potential public order reasons; of the right of access to file, first correctly implemented and then significantly restricted in 2016.[48]

In other situations, however, reasons for non-compliance with the EU *acquis* seems harder to grasp and rather scattered if observed through transnational lenses.

This is the case of Directive 2016/800, whose provisions are actually quite detailed and relatively rule-based. Despite that, the Directive still does not

---

45 Cf. Art 276(4) and 208.a(7) of the Croatian Criminal Procedure Code, cf. Đurđević *and o* (n 4) 38.

46 Cf. Manolova (n 5) 37; Kremens *and o* (n 34), 42 ff; Bartoli *and o* (n 21) § 5.4; Neira-Pena (n 5) 35. In Portugal, on the other side, no right to a lawyer is recognized before police questioning, cf. Costa and Caeiro (n 4) 35.

47 Đurđević *and o* (n 4) 59; Cervellera and Parizot (n 33) 35; Ouwerkerk *and o* (n 7) 79.

48 Kremens *and o* (n 34) 4 ff.

find application in Member States where the pre-existent discipline of juvenile criminal proceedings only in small part reflects the rights enshrined in the EU standards (Spain)[49] or is largely diverging, either due to complete lack of transposition (Bulgaria)[50] or because of a substantial inadequacy of safeguards for vulnerable accused, starting from the very setting of the age threshold (Poland).[51]

Also some limitations to the right of access to a lawyer appear difficultly explainable in a systematic perspective. For instance, in Portugal the transposition of Directive 2013/48 was not deemed necessary; however, the right is not extended to police questioning, confrontations, identity parades of reconstructions of the crime scene, which are without margin of doubt clearly listed in its scope.[52] According to Art 8(1)(c), moreover, derogation to the rights of the Directive cannot be "based exclusively on the type and seriousness of the alleged offence". Nonetheless, exceptions grounded on the severity of some crimes, especially terrorism or organized crime, do represent the basis for a derogatory regulation in several countries, such as in Spain (*incommunicado* regime),[53] and Portugal,[54] (where the presence of a lawyer is always ensured, though appointing a person different from that chosen by the accused), or Italy[55] (where the derogation is broader, as it encompasses a real postponing of accessing to the lawyer as such).

The absence of uniform transposition of facsimiles, such as the indicative model Letter of Rights attached to Directive 2012/13, also emerges as significant in this regard. The model, though not strictly binding in its form,[56] was indeed provided for with a complete list of the rights to be included *and* a translation in all EU languages.

Despite this easing, in several countries the adopted "model Letters" differ, in the sense that one or more of the mandatory information rights are missing, or substantial limitations may anyway be observed. In Poland, for instance, no

49 Cf. above, Neira-Pena, Chapter 11, § 11.3.1.2.

50 Where a proposal to transpose the Directive is pending since 2020, though with no outcome so far, cf. Manolova (n 21) § 4.2.

51 Kremens *and o* (n 11) § 9.3.1.

52 Art 3(3), Directive 2013/48; cf. Costa and Caeiro (n 4) 34 ff.

53 Cf. Neira-Pena (n 49) § 11.3.2.

54 Cf. Costa and Caeiro (n 4) 40 ff.

55 Cf. Bartoli *and o* (n 21) § 5.6.

56 Cf. Directive 2012/13, Annex 1: "The sole purpose of this model is to assist national authorities in drawing up their Letter of Rights at national level. Member States are not bound to use this model. When preparing their Letter of Rights, Member States may amend this model in order to align it with their national rules and add further useful information".

warning is given about the right to free legal aid and access to file;[57] in Croatia, information is lacking on remedies and again on legal aid.[58] In France, the letter is used in domestic proceeding, but does not have an EAW equivalent.[59] In Bulgaria, it is substituted with a prosecutorial decree, which however does not encompass the rights to medical examination and does not indicate the maximum number of hours or days the suspect or accused may be deprived of liberty before being brought before a judicial authority.[60] Portugal, again, did not provide any explicit transposition for the Directive, and does not, therefore, make use of the Letter or of any national surrogate.[61] Against this background, the situation in Italy and in the Netherlands appears more linear, as in both countries Letters of Rights have been created, by following more closely the wording of the Directive.[62]

In Germany, the model Letter was partially amended, substituting the right to be informed of the accusation with the more safeguarding direct communication on charges. This, however, was not extended to the first interrogation before police; a caveat which seems to go quite against the spirit that animated the whole EU legislation on information rights. A loophole to the protection of this right during police questioning may be observed also in Italy, where information about the rights listed in Directive 2012/13 is provided to the accused in cases of questioning before the prosecutor, or before the police when the latter is delegated by the prosecutor, but only partially in case of questioning before the police that acts on its own initiative.[63]

In Spain, the transposition of the list of information rights is relatively complete. Spain is also the only country that seems to have incorporated the effort towards the "comprehensibility" requested by Art 4 of the Directive, as it explicitly requires to deliver the information rights in an "accessible language,

57 Kremens *and o* (n 34) § 31.

58 Đurđević *and o* (n 4) 29.

59 Cervellera and Parizot (n 33) 22 ff.

60 In case of detention not disciplined by the criminal procedure code, a document similar to the Letter of Rights is issued to the detainee, but it does not contain all the rights lsited in the Directive, cf. Manolova (n 5) 30–31.

61 And where information of rights is limited to a narrower list of rights, cf. Costa and Caeiro (n 4) 19, 25.

62 Alessandra Santangelo, Isadora Neroni Rezende and Marianna Biral, Chapter 8, § 8.2; Ouwerkerk *and o* (n 7) 47, though in the latter case according to a model different from that of the Directive.

63 Cf. for Germany: Albrecht and Schneider (n 4) 22–24; and for Italy: Bartoli *and o* (n 21) § 4.2.1.1.

adapted to the age, degree of maturity, disability and any other personal circumstance".[64]

However, the Spanish system is clearly deficient against one of the most crucial information rights, that is the obligation to inform the accused of the "nature and legal classification of the criminal offence, as well as the nature of participation", as well as of "any relevant changes in the object of the investigation and of the alleged facts".[65] In Spanish law, these elements are indeed substituted with the milder reference to a general description of the facts attributed to the accused, and information of subsequent changes will only "be provided with sufficient detail to allow the effective exercise of the right of the defence" – of course, according to the determination of the investigators.[66]

Derogations concerning the right to be informed of the accused, even in clear violation of the Directive, may be found also in other legal orders. In Germany, as anticipated, where no information about legal qualification is given in case the person is interviewed by police, such information is replaced by a "rough description of the accusation";[67] in Croatia, the right to information does not extend also to subsequent "changes".[68] On the other side, Bulgaria, Italy, France, Portugal and Poland appear more in line with the Directive under this profile, though sometimes only thanks to substantial interventions of the case-law, that subsequently brought the necessary statutory amendments.[69]

13.2.4 *Underestimating Practical Contexts and Structures: Training, Costs, and Qualitative Assessments*

Lastly, detrimental effects to a coherent application of procedural safeguards throughout the EU may also be observed with regard to some practical or structural profiles that, although mentioned in the Directives, do not find any specific discipline at the supranational level. They remain, therefore, openly left to national discretion in their concrete implementation.

The first reference, in this sense, are training obligations, established in all Directives but for 2013/48 and 2016/343.

---

64 Cf. Neira-Pena (n 5) 28. A proposal is this sense was also raised by the Polish Ombudsman in 2019 with regard to juvenile defendants, but without success, cf. Kremens *and o* (n 34) § 52.

65 Art 6(3) and (4), Directive 2012/13.

66 Cf. Neira-Pena (n 5) 29.

67 Cf. Albrecht and Schneider (n 4) 24–28.

68 Cf. Đurđević *and o* (n 4) 31.

69 As in the case of Italy, thanks to *Drassich v Italy* App. no. 25575/04 (ECHR, 11 December 2007), cf. Alessandra Santangelo *and o* (n 63) § 8.2. For the other mentioned countries, cf. Costa and Caeiro (n 4) 27; Kremens *and o* (n 34) 34; and Cervellera and Parizot (n 33) 21.

These pieces of EU legislation, indeed, clearly affirm the need to establish training programmes for all different actors involved of criminal proceedings (judges, prosecutors, law enforcement, defence counsels). Nonetheless, they do not spare wording on how such programmes should be structured, or financed, in order to ensure an acceptable quality threshold. In practice, this brought to a situation in which, after the entry into force of the Directives, nothing, or very little, has changed at domestic level concerning remedies.

Currently, the field where these obligations seem to be taken less seriously is Directive 2012/13, for which some training is reported only in France, and just for magistrates.[70] It follows Directive 2016/1919, where programmes are established, in very different forms, only in Italy, Poland and the Netherlands.[71] Very fragmented is the situation concerning Directive 2010/64: in this context, sometimes no training programme is provided at all (Italy, Poland, Spain); sometimes it is foreseen only for magistrates, though in quite a superficial way (France);[72] in other cases it exists, but is limited to interpreters (Portugal, Croatia, the Netherlands).[73] Better is the situation in juvenile justice, where the need for specific training is generally more recognized, though still far from being unanimous: in some cases, specific programmes are not established yet (Portugal, the Netherlands); or are limited to court-appointed lawyers (Croatia, Italy).[74]

For Directive 2010/64 and Directive 2016/1919, such criticalities then naturally merge with the problematic lack of provisions for a dedicated budget, at the national or EU level, to support the costs deriving from interpretation and translation, as well as from legal aid services. In some countries the implementation of Directive 2010/64 was explicitly subjected to the obligation not to increase costs for the state (Spain).[75] The underestimation of such structural

70 Cervellera and Parizot (n 33) 24.

71 Cf. Ouwerkerk *and o* (n 7) 108; Kremens *and o* (n 34) 73; Santangelo *and o* (n 63) § 3.3.1.

72 *I.e.* half a day programme, cf. Cervellera and Parizot (n 33) 15.

73 And in the Netherlands only to registered interpreters, cf. Ouwerkerk *and o* (n 7) 38.

74 Cf. Đurđević *and o* (n 4) 72; Santangelo *and o* (n 63) § 3.3.1.

75 Cf. Neira-Pena (n 5) 18. Regarding Directive 2010/64, the underestimation of structural profiles touches also upon the organization itself of the interpretation services. Indeed, in most examined Member States (all, but in Spain – cf. Neira-Pena (n 5) 14 – and Portugal – cf. Costa and Caeiro (n 4) 16), the transposition of the Directive brought to the creation of official registers for interpreters and translators. Nonetheless, the concrete ways in which such a measure brought to an effective improvement on the quality of this form of assistance remains highly diverging. In Croatia, interpreters and translators are part of courts' permanent staff and are registered in lists kept in county courts (Đurđević *and o* (n 4) 18–21). In France, the list is centralized before the Court of Cassation (Cervellera and Parizot (n 33) 14). In some cases, besides for linguistic skills, further competence is required: in Croatia, general and legal knowledge is necessary (Đurđević *and o* (n 4) 18–21); in the

and financial requirements has been unsurprisingly identified as a significant element undermining the effective implementation of these two Directives.

Moreover, to a certain extent, this situation also plays as a counterbalancing factor against the broader scope of application of the right of access to a lawyer pursued by Directive 2013/48:[76] Indeed, if cases of assistance are expanded, but nothing is done to financially support legal aid budget, the effectiveness of such right cannot but be drastically reduced for a large part of the population.

A similar consideration also partially explains the widespread trend to consider the right to interpretation and translation as alternative options, rather than two autonomous safeguards, both necessary to the defendant who does not understand the language of the proceedings.[77]

Such an approach may be observed in some Member States, where the possibility to provide an oral instead of written translation is drafted in terms so broad as to make it the rule.[78] In Germany, despite the CJEU landmark decision *Covaci*, the right to translation is always performed orally if the accused is assisted by a lawyer;[79] a similar conclusion finds application also in France, where a combination of interpreter and lawyer assistance is clearly preferred to the need of providing written translation.[80] This restrictive interpretation does not however find application in all Member States: in Bulgaria, Croatia, and Italy, for instance, oral translation is allowed only in exceptional circumstances.[81]

Peculiar, is again the case of Portugal, where oral translation remains an exception; however, in that system the recognition of the right to translation does not follow the criteria established by the Directive (essential/non-essential document), and it is rather based on a "necessity/unnecessity" assessment, which adds vagueness to the already limited foreseeability of the precise scope of this right.[82]

Netherlands, the register is organized in different sections in which interpreters are classified according to their sectorial expertise (*eg.* criminal law, civil law cases), cf. Ouwerkerk *and o* (n 7) 38.

76 Cf. Ouwerkerk *and o* (n 7) 102 ff.

77 Ibid 40–41; James Brannan, 'Identifying written translation in criminal proceedings as a separate right: scope and supervision under European law' (2017) 27 Journal of Specialised Translation 43.

78 Contrary to what established by Art 3(7), Directive 2010/64, for which such cases should remain exceptions.

79 Cf. Albrecht and Schneider, Chapter 7, § 7.4.

80 Cf. Cervellera and Parizot (n 33) 14 ff.

81 Cf. Manolova (n 5) 13; Đurđević *and o* (n 4) 19; Bartoli *and o* (n 21), § 3.4.

82 Though according to the requests made by the defendant, cf. Costa and Caeiro (n 4), 16.

Dealing with underestimation of structural mechanisms, also the lack of rules and guidelines referring to how certain "assessments" should be carried out within criminal proceedings should be mentioned. The reference here goes to the evaluation of the capacity of the suspect or accused to "speak and understand the language of the criminal proceedings", to ascertain the need for interpretation and translation.

Despite the statement that "Member States shall ensure that a procedure or mechanism is in place", and that the latter should require "that competent authorities verify in any appropriate manner, including by consulting the suspected or accused persons concerned" the existence of such needs,[83] the provision indeed remained a little more than a recommendation.

Therefore, it is not surprising to observe a whole variety of practices at the national level, that differ under all relevant profiles, starting from the definition of which authority is in charge of the assessment. In some States, the power is conferred to police officers, with a possibility to appeal their decision to the prosecutor or the judge, depending on the phase of the proceeding (the Netherlands);[84] in others, the decision is made by judicial authorities (Germany, Italy);[85] in most cases, however, the matter is not clearly regulated and rather decided on a case-by-case basis (Poland, Portugal, Croatia, Spain, Bulgaria).

Moreover, none of the examined Member States has established a formal test to ascertain the linguistic skills of the accused. The procedure usually remains highly informal, which makes its results often quite difficult to challenge for the defendant. In Spain, in particular, it is explicitly affirmed that the burden of proof over the lack of sufficient linguistic understanding shall be borne by the accused.[86]

Against this background, the Dutch and Croatian systems appear more safeguarding. In the Netherlands, it is prescribed that the accused shall not only "understand", but also "master" the language not to trigger the need for interpretation and translation.[87] In Croatia, though missing any formalization, the domestic jurisprudence considers it sufficient to ask the defendant about her skills, without attaching any presumptive value to parameters such as being resident or a worker in the country. In case of doubt, the person shall be recognized the right to interpretation.[88]

83 Cf. Art 2(4) and Recital (21), Directive 2010/64.

84 Cf. Ouwerkerk *and o* (n 7) 26 ff.

85 Cf. Albrecht and Schneider (n 4) 15; Bartoli *and o* (n 21), § 3.2.

86 Cf. Neira-Pena (n 5) 24.

87 Cf. Ouwerkerk *and o* (n 7) 26.

88 Cf. Đurđević *and o* (n 4) 22.

13.3 Beyond Legislative Texts: The Role of Judicial Interpretation

Undoubtedly, the substantial level of protection of procedural rights shall be measured also in light of the case law, that has a direct impact on the matter, especially in its domestic dimension. The examined case law included decisions making reference to the Directives explicitly, and such that simply referred to the rights – often already provided for at the national level – that the Directives insisted onto.[89]

In this regard, a first observation is, that despite a legislative apparatus composed of six Directives, in all Member States national courts are reportedly tending not to make explicit reference to EU legislation, and mainly refer to domestic frameworks or, at most, to the jurisprudence of the Court in Strasbourg.

On one side, this phenomenon was to be expected due to historical reasons; being the Directives relatively more recent compared to the Convention, and the case law of the CJEU on the criminal matter still rather limited. Not always, however, the ECtHR case law provides for the highest standards of protection at the European level. In these situations, "overreliance" on the Conventional system may bring to the unintended consequence of "neutralizing" the innovative capacity of the Directives. A greater level of reference to the EU legislation, therefore, could have been expected at least with regard to those rights that find in this context a higher protection, for instance the privilege against self-incrimination in criminal proceedings, or the right to interpretation and translation.[90] Against these profiles, the sensitiveness of national courts, and especially of courts of last resort, seems still quite below its potential.

89 To this end, it shall be clarified that, in order to adopt a more rational approach, the present research took into account national judicial decisions referring to the procedural safeguards recognized by the six Directives issued only after the expiration of the transposition deadlines of each Directive they referred to. Only where such case law was too scares, the research was extended to previous jurisprudence.

90 For instance, the right to silence within criminal proceedings, as the wording of Art 7, Directive 2016/343 provides for a higher level of protection than that of the ECtHR case law, *e.g.* in *Ibrahim and o. v UK* App Nos 50541/08, 50571/08, 50573/08 and 40351/09 (ECHR, 30 March 2016), especially concerning the prohibition to use the choice to remain silent against the defendant. A similar trend may be noticed to a certain extent also with regard to the already mentioned distinction between the right to interpretation and translation. As noticed by Ouwerkerk *and o* (n 7) 41: "the Strasbourg court has extracted this right from Article 6(3)e, which merely provides for the right to obtain the assistance of an interpreter in court. What is more the ECtHR has often admitted that, as the text of the relevant provisions in the ECHR refer to an 'interpreter', not a 'translator', oral linguistic assistance may satisfy the requirements of the Convention, see *Husain v Italy* App no 18913/03 (ECHR, 24 February 2005)".

The increasing number of preliminary requests filed by first instance judges in criminal matters in the last few years, gives hope for a slow change of perspective. To date, however, the effort is certainly not equally distributed among Member States, and often does not reach its purpose due to the divergent number of interventions of distinct highest courts. Examining the relevant case law of the CJEU, it can be noticed how requests tend to originate from a relatively close group of Member States (Italy, Bulgaria, Germany, Poland, Spain), while others appear so far totally absent from the circuit (Croatia, France, Portugal, the Netherlands).[91]

The jurisprudence of the Court in Luxembourg, however, is far from being overreaching when it comes to the criminal matter, and to procedural safeguards of the defendant in particular. In this sense, it seems worth to briefly recall the areas that have already emerged as more critical even in this transitional phase of the harmonization process. At the moment, still relatively few final decisions of the Court have been issued, and not with regard to all six Directives. Yet, the situation is hopefully destined to change in the near future.

13.3.1 *The Case-Law of the Court of Justice and National Approaches: Overview*

Only some of the rights recognized in the Directives have been so far brought before the attention of the Court, and even less have already been the target of final decisions. Regardless, the preliminary request ratio has notably increased in the last couple of years, and the picture could therefore quickly become much broader than the current one.

At the time of writing, however, with regard to Directive 2010/64, the Court has mainly focused on clarifying (or trying to clarify) the notion of "essential documents" for which a translation is required, and on whether substantial terms to appeal a decision should run from the moment of formal notification or of rather from the actual communication of the act in a language that the persons understand.[92]

Decisions on Directive 2012/13 also appear so far relatively narrow in scope and mostly concerned the right to information (how or where to notify the accused of her rights, and especially the information about the accusation, particularly critical in case of simplified proceedings, like penal decrees).[93]

91 See the case law referred to in § 13.3.1.

92 Case C-216/14 *Criminal proceedings against Gavril Covaci* (CJEU, 15 October 2015); Case C-278/16 *Criminal proceedings against Franck Sleutjes* (CJEU, 12 October 2017); Case C-338/20 *DP* (*Prokuratura Rejonowa Łódź-Bałuty*) (CJEU, 6 October 2021).

93 Case C-612/15 *Criminal proceedings against Nikolay Kolev and Others* (CJEU, 5 June 2018); Case C-646/17 *Criminal proceedings against Gianluca Moro* (CJEU, 13 June 2019); *Covaci*

Critical and relevant issues, however, already emerged also with regard to transnational cooperation, in particular about the application of information rights within EAW proceedings.[94] The right of access to file, on the other side, has been raised only to a lesser extent.[95]

Issues concerning the scope of application of the rights emerged also with regard to Directive 2013/48,[96] together with significant questions concerning potential limitations for the accused to choose a lawyer of her own choice,[97] or the boundaries of temporary derogation to the right to a lawyer.[98]

Much broader, in terms of evolving themes, are the decisions issued or pending about Directive 2016/343, starting from the very scope of the presumption of innocence as such,[99] and of the privilege against self-incrimination in particular.[100] Specific questions have then been proposed with regard to the presumption as a rule of treatment,[101] or to the standards related to the burden of proof. Still limited, on the contrary, is instead the jurisprudence on the right to be present at trial.[102]

The same goes for Directive 2016/800, which so far has come to the attention of the Court only in relation to the execution of a European Arrest Warrant.[103] No case law, finally, is reported yet with regard to Directive 2016/1919.

The right to an effective remedy, transversal to most Directives, has been so far touched by CJEU decisions only to a limited extent, in a case concerning the right to a lawyer and to information.[104]

(n 92); Joined Cases C-124/16, C-188/16 and C-213/16 *Criminal proceedings against Ianos Tranca and Others* (CJEU, 22 March 2017); Case C-615/18 *UY v Staatsanwaltschaft Offenburg* (CJEU, 14 May 2020); Case C-467/18 *Criminal proceedings against EP* (CJEU, 19 September 2019). See also the pending cases C-769/19 *Spetsializirana prokuratura* and Case C-282/20 *ZX* (both preliminary references from Bulgaria).

94 Case C-649/19 *Criminal proceedings against IR* (CJEU, 28 January 2021).

95 *Kolev and Others* (n 93).

96 *EP* (n 93); Case C-659/18 *Criminal proceedings against VW* (CJEU, 12 March 2020).

97 *Kolev and Others* (n 93).

98 *Criminal proceedings against VW* (n 96).

99 Case C-439/16 PPU *Criminal proceedings against Emil Milev (I)*, (CJEU, 27 October 2016); Case C-310/18 PPU *Criminal proceedings against Emil Milev (II)*, (CJEU, 19 September 2018); *EP* (n 93).

100 Case C-481/19 *DB v Commissione Nazionale per le Società e la Borsa (Consob)* (CJEU, 2 February 2021).

101 Case C-8/19 PPU *Criminal proceedings against RH* (CJEU, 12 February 2019); Case C-377/18 *Criminal proceedings against AH and Others* (CJEU, 5 September 2019).

102 On the standard of proof, see *RH* (n 101); Case C-653/19 PPU *Criminal proceedings against Spetsializirana prokuratura* (CJEU, 28 November 2019); on the right to be present at trial, cf. Case C-688/18 *Criminal proceedings against TX and UW* (CJEU, 13 February 2020).

103 Case C367/16 *Dawid Piotrowski* (CJEU, 23 January 2018).

104 Directive 2013/48 and 2012/13, cf. *EP* (n 93).

Against this significant, but overall limited case law, it may be observed that approaches of national courts are quite diverging throughout the EU and also within the same Member States, depending on which procedural safeguard they refer to.

Naturally, this can be explained at least partially with the persistence of some structural differences among legal orders, which heavily influence the interpretation and concrete application of the same rule (even where semantically identical) across jurisdictions.

Fundamental systemic divergences include, for instance, the degree of relevance given to evidence collected in preliminary investigation at trial, or the more proactive or passive role conferred to the defence lawyer, or the legislative tendency to conceive procedural safeguards more as provisions limiting public authorities' prerogatives, than conferring rights to the privates involved.[105]

Structural differences, however, seem to emerge also beyond traditional discrepancies attributed to the influence of inquisitorial or accusatorial models. For example, the scope of the right to a lawyer at the national level seems to depend to a significant extent also on the choice, made by the legal system, to have or not have a complete overlapping between mandatory defence and free legal aid. Indeed, in some countries (all but Italy and Spain) the necessary presence of the lawyer also implies that costs are paid by the State,[106] which has relevant implications on the sustainability of the right in practical terms.

Given such a complex structural scenario, some national courts, especially those of last resort, reportedly tend to promote a minimalist approach towards EU law, that limits its effects in favour of national standards. This may reportedly be observed even where the former entails a higher level of protection for its citizens, and even where the national legal bases would actually allow for a broader interpretation of the rights at stake. Examples in this sense maybe found in the Netherlands, where a narrow interpretation of the "participation" of the lawyer during questioning is developed;[107] in Bulgaria and Spain, concerning the interpretation of "essential documents", or again in Bulgaria about the scope of the right to be present at trial for juvenile defendants.[108] In some cases (France,[109] Portugal),[110] the position of higher courts is even reportedly

105 Cf. *e.g.*, in the Netherlands, Ouwerkerk *and o* (n 7) 129.

106 Given the possibility, in some States, to recover costs from the accused if she gets convicted, *e.g.* in Germany.

107 Cf. Ouwerkerk *and o* (n 7) 62 ff.

108 Cf. Neira-Pena (n 5) 15 ff; Manolova (n 5) 17, 62.

109 Cf. Cervellera and Parizot (n 33) *e.g.* 26–27.

110 Cf. Costa and Caeiro (n 9) §10.4.

that of an explicit and net rejection of EU standards, showed by a constant refusal to make reference to the CJEU regardless the requests coming from first instance judges.

On the other hand, national courts are also increasingly playing an essential role in pushing towards harmonization beyond the limits of the Directives' texts or of their official transpositions.

This occurred, for instance, in Italy, Bulgaria and the Netherlands with regard to the extension of certain procedural rights also to the so-called punitive administrative matter;[111] in Poland, where the jurisprudence, at least to a certain extent, tries to limit the severe lacunas for instance with regard to the right to assistance by a lawyer;[112] again in Bulgaria and in Spain, where the case law strengthened the burden of proof rules in light of the presumption of innocence.[113] Particularly significant is the Spanish case, where the Constitutional court recognized some Directives' provisions a direct effect, anticipating their safeguarding value before the transposition into national law.[114]

13.3.2 *Hints from Automated Analysis*

Against this background, the research adopted also a different perspective to analyse the state of play of procedural safeguards in the EU through the lenses of harmonization.

This innovative point of view grows upon a semantic analysis and annotation of the legal provisions contained in the six Directives. The methodology, developed by computer scientists in cooperation with legal experts, takes its cues from the "translation" of legal text into a numerical text representation, following a computational approach that exploits Natural Language Processing (NLP) techniques, which is an application of AI technologies. According to this methodology, text excerpts, such as legal provisions, have been transformed into a vector, by which words are represented by numbers. The main aim of such semantic analysis was the tracking of significant frequency of occurrences from mere counts or redundancies.[115]

---

111 Right to silence in Italy (cf. Santangelo *and o* (n 63) § 8.3), right to interpretation and translation in the Netherlands and in Bulgaria (Ouwerkerk *and o* (n 7) 39 ff; Manolova (n 5) 13).

112 Kremens *and o* (n 11) § 9.3.1.

113 Neira-Pena (n 5) 65; Manolova (n 5) 82.

114 Cf. Neira-Pena (n 5) 32. A more limited attempt in this sense could be seen also in Portugal, with regard to Directive 2010/64, cf. Costa and Caeiro (n 4) 18.

115 For further illustrations on the methods and result of this research see below, Luigi Di Caro, Llio Humphreys, Emilio Sulis and Rohan Nanda, Chapter 16, § 16.5 ff.

The result of such analysis allowed the development of a "harmonization index", that enables to compare the level of harmonization among Member States in an automatic way. This task is usually based on single assessments made by national legal experts (as in traditional legal comparative analysis). In the present analysis, also an automated perspective was added, thanks to an examination of the scores directly emerging from the legal texts at the different levels (national/European).

In other words, the semantic automated analysis provided a significant alternative examination of the level of harmonization of procedural safeguards throughout the EU, that allows to countercheck whether the conclusions derived from a human-based and traditional legal analysis find adequate match in the legislative texts. This also allows, on a further level, to inquiry on whether implementation into national legislation resulted in modifications of the notions contained in the supranational texts.

Thus, this method became especially relevant in the given playfield, where the level of explicit definitions of terms is generally quite low, the linguistic divergences between Member States is high and judicial interpretation is also rather divergent.

On a basic level, the analysis pointed out how some of the differences in the application of the procedural safeguards may derive from different linguistic versions of the six Directives.[116]

116 "For instance, the English version of Article 2(1) of Directive 2010/64 states that "[m]ember States shall ensure that suspected or accused persons who do not speak or understand the language of the criminal proceedings concerned are provided, without delay, with interpretation during criminal proceedings before investigative and judicial authorities, including during police questioning, all court hearings and any necessary interim hearings." The Italian version of the same states: "Gli Stati membri assicurano che gli indagati o gli imputati che non parlano o non comprendono la lingua del procedimento penale in questione siano assistiti senza indugio da un interprete nei procedimenti penali dinanzi alle autorità inquirenti e giudiziarie, inclusi gli interrogatori di polizia, e in tutte le udienze, comprese le necessarie udienze preliminari." There is a structural difference in the way the concepts are related to one another. In the English version, the concept "criminal proceedings before investigative and judicial authorities" has three examples, namely "police questioning", "all court hearings" and "any necessary interim hearings." However, in the Italian version, the third concept is an example of the second concept. The French and German versions follow the conceptual structure of the English version. Conversely, linguistic comparison can also help resolve uncertainties and ambiguities. For instance, according to Recital 28 Directive 2010/64, "[w]hen using videoconferencing for the purpose of remote interpretation, the competent authorities should be able to rely on the tools that are being developed in the context of European e-Justice (e.g. information on courts with videoconferencing equipment or manuals)." It seems strange that "information" should be an example of a "tool". However, in light of the comparison between

More in-depth analysis can be derived from this approach.

It was possible, for instance, to rank the level of transposition, highlighting implementation lacunas in a systemic way, taking into account not just explicit transposition, but also rules already present in the legal framework even before the advent of the EU legislative package. Namely, the analysis showed that the Directive that by far presents more non-transposed provisions is Directive 2016/800 (182 lacunas), followed at a large distance by Directive 2013/48 (69), Directive 2016/1919 (56); Directive 2012/13 and 2016/343 (respectively: 49 and 41), and finally by Directive 2010/64 (only 32 lacunas).[117]

Such data may be interesting from several perspectives. For instance, they seem to clearly exclude a direct link between the level, or quality of the transposition and the amount of time elapsed since each piece of EU legislation became binding.

On a different viewpoint, it shall be considered that lacunas may have a different impact depending on which of norms they refer to. Accordingly, bare high numbers do not *per se* entail a level of infringement necessarily more severe than a lower one. Also, as already argued, Directives differ in terms of their structure, some being more prescriptive than others, and therefore containing more provisions that might be "forgotten" in the transposition.

From this consideration, one might suppose that more "rule-based" Directives are more likely to have implementation loopholes, while Directives with a vaguer, or more "principle-based" nature might be less subject to this phenomenon. This explanation, however, does not result satisfactory in all cases. For instance, while it could fit for Directive 2016/800, it does not make sense if referred to Directive 2016/1919. The latter Directive, indeed, presents a relatively high level of transposition lacunas, while showing a nature more "principle than rule-based".

---

linguistic versions, it is clear that this is the intended meaning. For instance, the Italian version of the recital is: "Quando si utilizza la videoconferenza per l'interpretazione a distanza, le autorità competenti dovrebbero poter utilizzare gli strumenti sviluppati nel contesto della giustizia elettronica europea (ad esempio informazioni sui tribunali che dispongono di materiale o di manuali per la videoconferenza)". Linguistic comparison also clarified that Recital 28 provides only one instance of tools, "information on courts with videoconferencing equipment or manuals", rather than two examples, "information on courts with videoconferencing equipment" and "manuals" – an alternative reading that is only possible in the English version", cf. Emilio Sulis, Davide Audrito, Luigi Di Caro and Llio Humphreys, CrossJustice Project, Deliverable 3.2, 'Rule ontology, user's guide' <https://site.unibo.it/cross-justice/en> § 9.2.

117 Data extrapolated from Emilio Sulis, Llio Humphreys, Davide Audrito and Luigi Di Caro, CrossJustice Project, Deliverable 3.5, 'Report on semantic analysis and annotation of legal data', Table 2.

Therefore, it can be observed how the normative legislative technique seems to produce dissimilar effects on the of level implementation, which do not necessarily follow easily predictable explanatory paths and depend to different extents on the specific profile touched upon the EU legislation.

"Harmonization indexes" and "heat maps" can also be interestingly used to reflect upon the method chosen at the national level to implement each Directives.

Ranking the latter according to the level of explicit transposition, and thus on the direct impact they brought into national systems, Directives 2016/800 and 2013/48 emerge again on top (respectively, with 236 and 181 explicit transpositions), this time followed by Directive 2012/13 (162), Directive 2010/64 (124), Directive 2016/1919 (52) and finally Directive 2016/343 (only 10 cases of explicit transposition).[118]

The misalignment between the two proposed dataset confirms therefore, from a different perspective, that a major role in assessing the status of procedural safeguards in the EU relies in the notion and interpretation of pre-existing norms, rather than on the explicit introduction of new provisions.

It is at this point that the semantic analysis, which will be further illustrated in the volume, brings its most relevant contribution, allowing – on the basis of the text analysis – to draw "heatmaps", that describe for each article of the Directives the level of similarities between pairs of Member States.[119]

To this end, NLP techniques may thus provide a significant contribution in identifying systems which, in relation to certain provision, present a higher level of affinity.

This might have significant impact, for instance, in transnational proceedings including EAW or EIO, which already involve usually only two Member States at the time.

13.4 The (Ir?) Relevance of the Type of Legal Bases at the EU Level

The picture that emerges from the analysis carried out shows that the path of harmonisation in the field of criminal justice is rather complicated. It

118 Ibid.

119 See Di Caro *and o* (n 115) § 16.7, pointing out that "for instance, the following 'heat map' about "Art_5" of Directive 2016/1919 clearly describes how three pairs of States (Italy and Germany, Germany and Spain, Poland and Germany) have more similar text (light color) than other States. On the contrary, Italy's and Poland's cases seem very different".

is particularly so in the field of criminal procedure, and specifically in the extremely sensitive area of respect for the rights of the accused.

In the light of these considerations, it would seem natural to conclude that, theoretically, the most suitable instrument, and perhaps the only one, to obtain satisfactory results in this sector is a regulation.

Thanks to such legislative tools, the EU could achieve vertical unification without having to wait for all the Member States to correctly transpose the provisions adopted at Union level.

Obviously, this route is not *per se* feasible, as is often the case with purely theoretical hypotheses developed by scholars.

On the one hand, it is the Treaty that precludes this option. Indeed, Art 82(2) TFEU allows the EU legislator only to adopt directives, and not regulations, on the rights of the accused. Moreover, as well known, in Art 82(2), the purpose that justifies recourse to EU legislation is promoting better functioning of judicial cooperation and the principle of mutual recognition. In other words, the European legislator may adopt directives on the defendant's safeguards only when they are instrumental in producing added value in judicial cooperation, by harmonising certain aspects of the criminal justice systems so as to increase mutual trust among Member States. Regulations could therefore be considered incompatible with the principle of subsidiarity.

On the other hand, even besides for such limitations, perhaps the use of regulations in this area would not be anyway able to produce definitive effects in terms of system unification. As we have seen, most of the inequalities among Member States are not related to what is written in the law, *i.e.* they are not due to the legislative wording in the strict sense. Rather, they are caused by different basic legal cultures, which produce different interpretations and applications even against legal texts formally expressed in homogeneous ways.

13.5 Which Effective Protection?

It is therefore necessary to work with the tools that are available on the ground: Directives, the final version of which is evidently non-linear and characterized by some gaps in the definition of concepts.

This is due to a large extent to the strong jealousy[120] that Member States show when it comes to ceding part of their sovereignty to standardise criminal procedure systems. The fact, politically speaking, is easily understandable.

120 Cf. above, Michele Caianiello, Chapter 1, § 1.2.

Criminal procedure is one of the most obvious forms – naturally not the only one – of state sovereignty, since it is only through it that the power to punish individuals in a community is regulated. Precisely because it touches on the relationship between the sovereign power and the citizen, criminal procedure is also strongly linked to constitutional law (so much so that some scholars have described it as a form of 'applied constitutional law').[121] It is therefore inevitable that each State tends to act as a protective guardian of the way in which it administers the rules that are laid down in this very sensitive area.

We must therefore accept that, in the area of defendants' rights, the harmonisation process will proceed slowly, in a partial way, and through a set of interventions that will be able to produce effective results only in the long run (and thanks to adequate training of stakeholders).

In particular, there are three ways in which harmonisation is taking shape.

The first is vertical (top-down model) and is achieved thanks to the binding value of EU legislation (the directives adopted) and the judgments of the Court of Justice. Both these instruments, although of great importance, have limitations. Specifically, as illustrated also above, some regulatory provisions lack precision (and therefore leave too much freedom to the Member States).[122] CJEU decisions, in turn, are still scarce in number[123] and do not always intervene in key areas in the matter (because they are left to the impetus of the national courts, which make, or refuse to make, requests of preliminary references).

The second method follows the opposite direction, proceeding from the lowest level (the State), to the supranational one (therefore in a bottom-up movement). It is constituted by preliminary rulings made by national courts, whose intrinsic structure does not ensure a homogeneous coverage of all the critical issues that would be potentially relevant in the interpretation of the Directives. Moreover, a limitation to this method also derives from the narrow number of Member States whose judges currently decide to make a reference to the Court of Justice.[124] In short, this is a structurally non-homogeneous and

121 Daniele Negri, 'Diritto costituzionale applicato: destinazione e destino del processo penale' (2019) 2 Processo penale e giustizia 553. The author referred to (and examined) the definition adopted originally by Walter Sax, 'Grundsätze der Strafrechtspflege' in Karl August Bettermann, Hans Carl Nipperdey, Ulrich Scheuner (eds), *Die Grundrechte*, III-2, (Duncker & Humblot 1959) 966–967.

122 See above, § 13.2.

123 See above, § 13.3.1.

124 See above, § 13.3.

incomplete mode of operation, both *ratione materiae* (not all potentially relevant matters are involved) and, so to speak, *ratione personae* (not all "persons" – the judges of the Member States – operate with the same diligence).

The third way in which harmonisation takes place is horizontal, and operates through judicial cooperation among Member States. Limits to mutual recognition of judicial decisions, and thus to cooperation, act as threats for those systems whose standards of protection are not compliant with EU directives and principles. This is a way of implementing harmonisation which certainly has some practical limitations (it is entirely left to the initiative of the individual national courts and lawyers), but which may be effective in some cases, at least where non-cooperation imposes too high a cost on the non-compliant State, either economically or, more frequently, politically.

All the three methods identified require considerable effort on the part of the legal operators.

Firstly, besides for the ECHR, justices and defence counsels need to be familiar also with the relevant EU law and jurisprudence, in order to understand which aspects require clarification (and which can be relied on/can find a solution in established case law).

This task is however problematic, given the multifarious nature of such supranational system. EU law is integrated in national systems, as well as strongly intertwined with the normative corpus of the ECHR (which, in turn, is in continuous dialogue with national systems). Furthermore, in both the EU and the ECHR systems, case law is a fundamental source, and probably the most important. This in turn implies that interpreters have to be familiar with two quite different methodological approaches (interpretation and application of statutory sources and capacity to find the *rationes principii* of the judicial decisions) to which their legal tradition is still not always ready providing adequate training.

Secondly, professionals dealing with this branch of law need to have a minimum level of knowledge of the other Member States legal systems.

Within such basic knowledge one must include the main principles of the criminal matter, the essential scheme on how national criminal proceedings is regulated, and some understanding on how in practice works the interaction among police, prosecutors, defence counsels and judges. Eventually, some familiarity with how legal reasoning is expressed by national court may help in understanding strengths and weaknesses of a given criminal justice system.

Only this way one can adequately appreciate the magnitude of potential lacunas in procedural safeguards and whether to refer a case before the CJEU for a preliminary ruling, and on which points: Indeed, as shown by the analysis of single national systems,[125] despite national Governments' claims of having complied with the requirements of a Directive, in practice things often work out rather differently.

For the reasons already expressed above, against this background AI systems may be of significant help, as they allow an integrated analysis of the different levels in a relatively quick and effective manner.[126]

Of course, their impact heavily depends on the quality of the data that is fed into the system.[127] As long as they are accurate and constitute the result of research conducted with a high level of professionalism and precision, AI systems can however provide a significant added value in the speed and accuracy of learning a different legal orders.

It is therefore conceivable that, by continuing along this path, the complex process of harmonising State criminal procedures, in particular with regard to the rights of the defence, could be speeded up and could lead to the integration of national systems, which has been the ultimate objective of the EU since the inception of the Area of Freedom, Security and Justice.

125 Cf. above, Part II of the volume.

126 Cf. above, Caianiello (n 120) §§ 1.4 and 1.8.

127 See Giuseppe Contissa and Giulia Lasagni, 'When it is (also) Algorithms and AI that decide on Criminal Matters: In Search of an Effective Remedy' (2020) 28 European Journal of Crime, Criminal Law and Criminal Justice 295; Michele Caianiello, 'Dangerous Liaisons. Potentialities and risks deriving from the interaction between Artificial Intelligence and preventive justice' (2021) 29 European Journal of Crime, Criminal Law and Criminal Justice 21.

CHAPTER 14

Procedural Rights through the Lenses of Data Protection

The Case of Data Subjects' Rights

Mariavittoria Catanzariti

14.1 Introduction

The Chapter explores how the different legal frameworks related to the Directive 2012/13 on the right to information in criminal and EAW proceedings and the Directive (EU) 2016/680 (Data Protection Law Enforcement Directive, hereinafter "LED") intertwine, with special focus to data subjects' rights. It aims to investigate whether the level of protection granted to suspects and accused persons can be increased or be shrunk by the trigger of data protection safeguards. Although the rationales of procedural safeguards and data protection are apparently different in scope, the Chapter argues that both affect the level of individual rights' protection depending on how data is used for combating crimes, and that data protection may have an impact on some procedural rights as a standard setter for access to justice. This paper in fact does not argue that data protection acts as a duplication of some of the procedural rights laid down by the Directive 2013/12, such as the right to information and the right to access to the materials of the case, rather that it may be a trigger to activate a better protection for suspects, because an indirect violation of data subjects' rights may imply a violation of procedural rights.

The use of the Internet of Things (IoT) technology in police work and Big Data Analytics as well as smart surveillance and predictive policing techniques[1] put at the forefront the concern of this paper, moving from the idea that if evidence is based on data, data usage itself plays a key role in depicting the destiny of people who happen to be involved in a criminal proceeding.[2]

---

1 On these related aspects I rely on my chapter 'Enhancing Policing through Algorithmic Surveillance' in Luisa Marin and Stefano Montaldo (eds), *The Fight Against Impunity* (Elgar 2020) 239–257.

2 As correctly pointed out by Angela Aguinaldo and Paul de Hert, 'A leading role for the EU in drafting criminal law powers? Use of the Council of Europe for policy laundering' (2019) 10 New Journal of European Criminal Law 99: "Within [...] Council of Europe, member states are now enabled to stretch the extraterritorial powers exercised by their law enforcement

 | DOI:10.1163/9789004513396_016

The purpose limitation principle in the field of law enforcement is extraordinarily large in scope and the main priority for someone whose data is processed for preventing crimes and possibly to build up the accusation is to know which data has been processed and for what specific purposes and regarding the scope.

14.2 Blurring of Legal Boundaries

Datafication has blurred legal boundaries of data protection and procedural rights. Large scale-data gathering is becoming one essential way of how public sector data access and process data on a regular basis.[3] Law enforcement authorities are increasingly processing personal data during investigations in a manner that becomes most relevant in scope if considering the targeted individuals involved in criminal proceedings. This represents then a trend that blurs together operational, technical, and informal aspects of the way in which law enforcement authorities use huge amounts of data that they have at their disposal in a way or another. It has then been correctly observed that "Procedural law needs to be de-individualized".[4] On the one hand, this need highlights the urgence to understand the procedural remedies within the context of the challenges presented by information societies that involve group dimensions rather than individual centred positions;[5] on the other hand, the use of data to conduct investigations, detection and prosecution of crimes completely disrupts the criminal categories related to evidence that are peculiar of each national legal system. Is it then arguable that in a globalized and

---

authorities in obtaining electronic evidence through a controversial Guidance Note and soon, a Second Additional Protocol. Interestingly, throughout these developments, the EU remained passive but as of late, has come up with proposals for the European Production and Preservation Orders, among others. The mixture of alarm and astonishment among civil liberties representatives about the decision-making procedures at the level of the Council of Europe can be best understood in a broader regulatory context of policy enterpreneurship, rent-seeking behaviour and, overall, rational choice institutionalism".

3 Ira Rubnistein, Greg Nojeim, Ronald Lee, 'Systematic Government Access to Personal Data: A Comparative Analysis', November 13, 2013, https://cdt.org/wp-content/uploads/2014/11/government-access-to-data-comparative-analysis.pdf, accessed 25 January 2022.

4 Bart van der Sloot and Sascha van Schendel, 'Procedural law for the data-driven society' (2021) 30 Information & Communication Technology law 304, 305.

5 Alessandro Mantelero, 'From Group Privacy to Collective Privacy: Towards a New Dimension of Privacy and Data Protection in the Big Data Era' in Linnet Taylor, Luciano Floridi and Ban van der Slot (eds), *Group Privacy New Challenges of Data Technologies* (Springer 2017) 139–158.

interconnected world, it is a matter of national law to lay down the rules on the admissibility of evidence in criminal proceedings?

The issue here is broader than the fact if EU law can or not interfere in the procedural autonomy of Member States. It is rather a conceptual problem that arise from the data maximization of bulk collection and how the evidence's requirements can be affected by it. Although the legal framework of data processing for law enforcement purposes is laid down by a directive that needs implementing instruments at national level, the trend of the EU has been in the last decade to push the data protection safeguards laid down by the European Charter of Fundamental Rights as a standard setter of individual rights in other areas of the law that indirectly affect the right to an effective judicial remedy.[6] This has been the case, for example, in the field of justice criminal cooperation through the application of the principle of mutual trust.[7]

In legal terms, what is interesting is not only the fact that evidence is of course typified in each national legal system and much depends on the procedural legal system itself, but to what extent data can be transformed into evidence and how this affects life and better or worst chances for suspected and accused persons. In practical terms, it entails considering that if personal data processed for investigation, prevention and detection of crimes is used to reach a binding judicial decision, the right to an effective judicial remedy of suspected or accused persons who are also data subjects inevitably impacts on their procedural rights.

In the European context, the ongoing controversial debate on the proposed *e-evidence* regulation related to orders for the production and storage of electronic evidence in the context of criminal proceedings, is justified by the application of the principle of mutual recognition.[8] It would be implemented substantially by virtue of the issue or of the validation of an order by a competent judicial authority of the country where the recipient of the order is located. Such orders can be notified directly to hosting service providers and internet infrastructure providers such as the address IP and domain name registries. The proposed regulation aims to maintain the distinction between access data and data of content. In case of data contents, it would be possible to issue

6 Anu Bradford, *The Brussels Effect: How the European Union Rules the World* (OUP 2019) 131 ff.

7 See on the deficiencies of justice systems Case C-216/18 PPU *Minister for Justice and Equality v LM* (CJEU, GC 25 July 2018).

8 See Sergio Carrera and Marco Stefan, 'Access to Electronic Data for Criminal Investigations Purposes in the EU' (2020) 1 CEPS 1 <https://www.ceps.eu/wp-content/uploads/2020/02/LSE20120-01_JUD-IT_Electronic-Data-for-Criminal-Investigations-Purposes.pdf> accessed 15 November 2021.

orders only for specific crimes that are punishable with detention measures. Furthermore, it would only concern stored data, excluding the applicability to wiretapping in real time.

It is interesting, in light of the present analysis, that the proposal contemplates the possibility of exercise a right to object to data processing on the basis of the protection of fundamental rights, and moreover, that when the order is about matters that affect national security, the state issuing must take into account (albeit at its discretion) the interest in the national security of the recipient state as if he were evaluating interest in "its own" national security.

When we deal with data, then the idea of legal boundaries becomes even more rarefied from a semantic perspective as it may be sectoral, jurisdictional, substantial, procedural, individual and collective.

14.3 The Context of the Law Enforcement Directive

Although the specific instrument ruling on data processing for detection, prevention and investigation of crimes is the Law Enforcement Directive, GDPR generally sets up the general rules applicable to data subjects' rights in these cases. Art 23 GDPR in fact restricts the scope of obligations and rights of data subjects when the restriction respects the fundamental rights and freedoms and it is proportionate and necessary in a democratic society to safeguard the the prevention, investigation, detection or prosecution of criminal offences or the execution of criminal penalties, including the safeguarding against and the prevention of threats to public security. This provision needs to be "de-codified" in practice. It is in fact not clear whether, according to these restrictions, an individual may be under investigations without knowing it because her data is processed. There is not a clear indication such as the one included in the amended Italian *Codice della privacy* (D. lgs. 96/2003) which forbids to use evidence unlawfully gathered by means of data processing.

At a closer glance, in terms of effective rights of data subjects, Art 13 LED only provides that the controller – that could be a police authority – provides information rights to the data subject on: (a) the identity and the contact details of the controller; (b) the contact details of the data protection officer, where applicable; (c) the purposes of the processing for which the personal data are intended; (d) the right to lodge a complaint with a supervisory authority and the contact details of the supervisory authority; (e) the existence of the right to request from the controller access to and rectification or erasure of personal data and restriction of processing of the personal data concerning the data subject. In addition, the data subject shall be informed about (a) the legal basis for the processing; (b) the lenght of data storage and the criteria used to determine it; (c) where applicable, the categories of recipients of the personal data, including in third countries or international organisations; (d) additional information, where the personal data is collected without the knowledge of the data subject. This last case is instructive of the fact that information rights, as a matter of facts, have not any inhibitory function regarding effects on individuals that may have been produced irrespectively of criminal proceedings where the same subjects find themselves involved.

In the context of criminal proceedings, the right to information can be restricted for various reasons: avoiding obstructing official or legal inquiries, investigations or procedures; prejudicing the prevention, detection, investigation or prosecution of criminal offences or the execution of criminal penalties; protecting public security; protecting national security; protecting the rights and freedoms of others.[9]

The fact that the right of information as well as the access rights are mandatory means that data processing, undertaken while infringing these guarantees, is not lawful and therefore may give rise to the activation of legal remedies. If data processing occurs infringing these guarantees in the context of criminal proceedings, for example where data processing may be in substance an integral part of the materials of the case (Art 7), then access to data potentially may consists of an effective access to the materials of the case, especially if evidence is based on that data. In fact, if data processing is undertaken in the absence of these guarantees, the arrest or detention should be unlawful. Given this assumption, it is arguable that if par. 1 is not respected – providing it that "where a person is arrested and detained at any stage of the criminal proceedings, Member States shall ensure that documents related to the specific case in the possession of the competent authorities which are essential to challenging effectively, in accordance with national law, the lawfulness of the arrest or detention, are made available to arrested persons or to their lawyers" – then par. 2 should apply *in concreto*, meaning that "Member States shall ensure that access is granted at least to all material evidence in the possession of the competent authorities, whether for or against suspects or accused prepare the defense".

9 On the implementation of the right of information in practice, see Fundamental Rights Agency (FRA), *Rights in Practice: Access to a Lawyer and Procedural Rights in Criminal and European Arrest Warrant Proceedings* (2019) 26 <https://fra.europa.eu/sites/default/files/fra_uploads/fra-2019-rights-in-practice-access-to-a-lawyer-and-procedural-rights-in-criminal-and-european-arrest-warrant-proceedings.pdf> accessed 15 November 2021.

This interpretation would abide by the basic principle based on which compromising the right to access to information, as well as the right to access to the documents of the case also affects the right to an effective judicial remedy as well as the right to defense.

In this respect, the data protection guarantees laid down by LED seem to be broader than the Directive 2012/13, because they expressly mention the right of data subjects to be granted with an effective remedy against controllers or processors if data processing has been conducted not according to the provisions included in the Directive (Art 54 LED), meaning that data subjects' rights have been infringed as a result of an un-lawful processing. If we instead compare the right to information in criminal proceedings, there is not a specific mention of a right to redress against the public authorities that did not have provided the right of information.[10]

When Art 14 LED stipulates that Member States shall provide for the right of the data subject to obtain from the controller confirmation as to whether or not personal data concerning him or her is being processed, and, where that is the case, access to the personal data and the following information, also the parallel with the right to receive information about the accusation is easy.[11] Whether or not the accusation is based on a lawful data processing is relevant not only in terms of strategic defense but also in terms of transparency of data use. In particular, according to the ECHR case law, the concept of "criminal charge", must be interpreted with reference to the substantial rather than the formal situation (*Casse v. Luxembourg*, § 71). Moreover, receiving full and detailed information on the charges, the nature and the cause of the accusation as well as on the legal characterisation that the court might adopt in the matter, is quintessential to the right to a fair trial (*Pélissier and Sassi v. France* [GC], § 52 & 54; *Sejdovic v. Italy* [GC], § 90; *Varela Geis v. Spain*, § 42; *Dallos v. Hungary*, §§ 47 and 52).

Moreover, the Letter of Rights including under Art. 4(2) § a) the right of access to the materials of the case, is strictly linked to the data protection rights, without which the right to a fair trial is not adequately respected. The Letter of Rights in fact shall also contain basic information about any possibility, under national law, of challenging the lawfulness of the arrest; obtaining a review

10 See Steven Cras and Luca De Matteis, 'The Directive on the Right to Information. Genesis and Short Description' (2013) 1 EUCRIM 22.

11 See Alessandra Calvi & Juraj Sajfert, 'How to exercise data subject rights under the Law Enforcement Directive (EU) 2016/680?' (2021) *Brussels Privacy Hub workshop summaries*, https://cris.vub.be/ws/portalfiles/portal/74718602/20210305_Enforcing_Europe_summary_final.pdf, accessed 25 January 2022.

of the detention; or making a request for provisional release. If materials of the case encompass certain data records regarding the suspected persons, then access to the materials of the case easily becomes also a right to access by data subjects. The right to access, under Art 14 LED, requires Member States to ensure the right of the data subject to obtain from the controller confirmation as to whether or not personal data concerning him or her is being processed, and, in addition (a) the purposes of and legal basis for the processing; (b) the categories of personal data concerned; (c) the recipients or categories of recipients to whom the personal data have been disclosed, in particular recipients in third countries or international organizations; (d) where possible, the data storage time and the criteria used to decide it; (e) the existence of the right to rectification, erasure of personal data or restriction of processing of personal data concerning the data subject; (f) the right to lodge a complaint with the supervisory authority and the contact details of the supervisory authority; (g) communication of the personal data undergoing processing and of any available information as to their origin.

The right to access by data subjects has a parallel with the access to the documents of the case the fact that the suspect is informed to have the right to access the documents of the case.[12] The Letter of Rights shall also contain basic information about any possibility, under national law, of challenging the lawfulness of the arrest; obtaining a review of the detention; or making a request for provisional release.

It is interesting to notice that, as well as in the data protection framework (Art 15 LED), the access to the materials of the case may be refused in case of a serious threat to the life or the fundamental rights of another person or if such refusal is strictly necessary to safeguard an important public interest, for example being in prejudice to an ongoing investigation or determining a serious harm to the national security of the Member State in which the criminal proceedings are instituted. In addition, a decision to refuse access should be taken by a judicial authority or at least be subject to judicial review.[13] The reasons for restriction of the right to access under Art 15 LED are almost similar, although more detailed (Art 15 (1) a-e).

---

12 See *Previti v Italy* App No 1845/08 (ECHR, 12 February 2013) § 208.

13 For an overview, see Anna Pivaty and Anneli Soo, 'Article 7 of the Directive 2012/13/EU on the Right to Information in Criminal Proceedings: A Missed Opportunity to Ensure Equality of Arms in Pre-Trial Proceedings?' (2019) 27 European Journal of Crime, Criminal Law and Criminal Justice 126.

From the comparison between the two instruments, it is clear enough that if data processing is not lawful, this should mean that any detrimental criminal consequence arising from this should not affect in any way individuals, in a context inspired by the rule of law.

According to FRA Opinion 8, the right to access materials of the case is not absolute and has to be balanced with other interests, although Member States should proactively make arrangements to ensure that limitation to access to information is not unjustified or protracted for a long time. They should also facilitate individuals or their lawyers to obtain copies with the use of digital technology, including mobile devices, to avoid or minimize any indirect costs of accessing case materials.[14] This may be the case of access to digital files having as an object their personal data.

Art 18 Law Enforcement Directive and Art 6 Directive 2012/13 then need to be considered together. While Data protection safeguards grant that Member States may provide for the exercise of the rights referred to in Arts 13, 14 and 16 to be carried out in accordance with Member State law where the personal data are contained in a judicial decision or record or case file processed in the course of criminal investigations and proceedings, the right to be informed about the accusation under Art 6 stipulates that Member States shall ensure that suspects or accused persons are provided with information about the criminal act they are suspected or accused of having committed. That information shall be provided promptly and in detailed form to ensure the fairness of the proceedings and the effective exercise of the rights of the defense and should also include the reasons of the arrest or detention, including the criminal act they are suspected or accused of having committed, as well as the accusation, including the nature and legal classification of the criminal offence, as well as the nature of participation by the accused person. Member States shall ensure that suspects or accused persons are promptly informed of any changes in the information where this is necessary to safeguard the fairness of the proceedings.[15]

14 *Rasmussen v Poland* App No 38886/05 (ECHR, 28 July 2009) §§ 48–49; *Moiseyev v Russia* App No 62936/00 (ECHR, 9 October 2008) §§ 213–218; *Matyjek v Poland* App No 38184/03 (ECHR, 24 April 2007) § 59; *Seleznev v Russia* App No 15591/03 (ECHR, 26 June 2008) §§ 64–69.

15 Sometimes a court may be required to adjourn a hearing of its own motion in order to ensure the right to defence (*Sadak and Others v. Turkey (no. 1)* App Nos 29900/96, 29901/96, 29902/96 and 29903/96 (ECHR, 17 July 2001) § 57; *Sakhnovskiy v Russia,* App No 21272/03 (ECHR, GC, 2 November 2010) §§ 103 and 106).

What provided by Art 25 LED is also interesting to offer an overview of available forms of accountability and transparency in the field of law enforcement data processing. The logs of consultation and disclosure shall make it possible to establish the justification, date and time of such operations and, as far as possible, the identification of the person who consulted or disclosed personal data, and the identity of the recipients of such personal data. However, logs are functional to the design of a form of technical transparency rather than of substantial transparency. The logs are only functional to verify the lawfulness of processing, the self-monitoring, the integrity and security of the personal data, and for criminal proceedings. In any event, the supervisory authority always keeps a right of access to logs that shall be granted by controllers and processors.

What emerges from the analysis is a lack of harmonization between two instruments that results in a reduced protection prompted by the directive on procedural rights outside the context of data processing.

14.4 What Is Substantial of Procedural Rights?

The CJEU has developed a consolidated case law on data retention that substantiate in data processing for law enforcement purposes. This case law represents the *trait-d' union* between data protection regime, privacy-related topics in the field of electronic communications and data retention for law enforcement purposes.[16] In light of this interconnected framework, the need for a modernization process aligned with GDPR, has led EU to engage in the reform of a proposal of a e-privacy regulation to protect personal data in electronic communications. This instrument will replace Directive 2002/58/EC. In the words of EDPB "the ePrivacy Regulation cannot derogate from the application of the latest CJEU case law, which notably provides that Articles 7, 8, 11 and 52(1) of the Charter must be interpreted as precluding legislative measures, which would provide, as a preventive measure, the general and indiscriminate retention of traffic and location data. Therefore, providing a legal basis for anything else than targeted retention for the purposes of law enforcement and safeguarding national security is not allowed under the Charter, and would anyhow need to be subject to strict temporal and material limitations as well as review by a Court or by an independent authority".[17]

16 See Marek Zubik, Jan Podkowik and Robert Rybski, *European Constitutional Courts towards Data Retention Laws* (Springer 2021).

17 Statement 03/2021 on the ePrivacy Regulation Adopted on 9 March 2021, <https://edpb.europa.eu/system/files/2021-03/edpb_statement_032021_eprivacy_regulation_en_0.pdf>.

The most relevant principles common to this case law basically provide that the limitations on right to privacy and data protection must constitute a necessary, appropriate and proportionate measure within a democratic society to safeguard national security, defense and public security, and the prevention, investigation, detection and prosecution of criminal offenses or of unauthorized use of the electronic communication system; must be provided for by law (meaning that the scope of limitation of the exercise of individual rights should be provided by the same legal basis '*which permits the interference with those rights must itself define the scope of the limitation on the exercise of the right concerned*'[18]); must respect the essence of those rights and comply be proportional (generally related to other potentially equal general interest recognized by the EU or the need to protect the rights and freedoms of others). This means that Member States shall lay down specific binding rules governing the scope and application of the limitation or restriction of individual rights and imposing minimum safeguards, in order to ensure sufficient guarantees against the risk of abuse of data. In other terms, what must be included in the provision of law authorizing a limitation or restriction of data subjects' rights is the indication of what circumstances and under which conditions a measure providing for data processing non in compliance with data subjects' rights may be adopted.

The leading case *Digital Rights Ireland*[19] has declared Directive 2006/24/EC on data retained by providers of publicly available electronic communications services or of public communications networks invalid under EU law, affirming specific criteria to assess the legitimacy of data gathering: the presence of a serious crime; strictly necessary measures to combat serious crimes; judicial or independent administrative authorization; information rights of data subjects; data retention located in Europe.

In particular, the Court underlined the need to interpret the territorial scope of data protection and privacy in a broad manner, declaring the Data Retention Directive invalid as non-compliant with Arts 7 and 8 of the Charter of Fundamental Rights. Since the directive does not require data to be stored on the territory of the Union, consequently the control by an independent authority, explicitly required by Art 8, paragraph 3, of the Charter, cannot be considered fully guaranteed according to EU law (§ 68).

After the delivery of the judgement *Tele 2 Sverige / Watson*,[20] the compliance of Directive 2002/58 on the use of electronic communications by law enforcement authorities with Arts 7 and 8 of the Charter has determined in practice

---

18 Schrems II, § 175 and Privacy International, § 65.

19 Cases C-293/12 and C-594/12 *Digital Rights Ireland Ltd.* (CJEU, GC, 8 April 2014).

20 Joined Cases C-203/15 and C-698/15 *Tele 2 Sverige AB* (CJEU, 21 December 2016).

the obligation for Member States to adopt national laws that do not allow, as a preventive measure to combat only serious crimes, the storage of targeted traffic and location data, unless data storage is limited to what is strictly necessary, the categories of data, the media concerned, the data subjects and the storage time.

This means that national legislation cannot permit, for the purposes of the fight to crime, the general and indiscriminate retention of all traffic and location data of all subscribers and users.

In addition, the access by competent national authorities to the stored data for the purpose of fighting crime, must be prohibited when it is not limited exclusively to the fight against serious crime, if access is not subject to prior judicial control by a court or by an independent administrative authority and whereas there is no obligation to keep data within the European Union. In the field of data retention, the Court of Justice has reached important conclusions in the context of the algorithmic analysis of data collected through mass-surveillance programs, leading up to the *Opinion 1/15 on the PNR Agreement EU-Canada*.[21] Legislative measures must be subject to adequate safeguards. Therefore, they must establish clear and precise binding rules that indicate under what circumstances and under what conditions the service providers shall hand over data to public authorities on request. To ensure that access is limited to cases of strict necessity, national legislation must also establish the substantive and procedural conditions governing the access by competent national authorities to stored data.[22]

General access to all stored data cannot be regarded as limited to what is strictly necessary. Therefore, national legislation must be based on objective criteria to define the circumstances and conditions based on which national competent authorities should have access to the data. Access can only be granted to the data of persons suspected of having planned or having committed a serious crime or being implicated in one way or another in this crime. Access to data of other people can also be justified where there is objective evidence that the data could, in a specific case, effectively contribute to fight against such activities. Access, as a rule, except in cases of verified emergency, is subject to preliminary review carried out by a court or by an administrative independent body.

21 *Opinion 1/15 of the Court* (CJEU, 26 July 2017).

22 See EDPB, Recommendations 02/2020 on the European Essential Guarantees for surveillance measures, adopted on 10 November 2020, https://edpb.europa.eu/sites/default/files/files/file1/edpb_recommendations_202002_europeanessentialguaranteessurveillance_en.pdf, accessed 25 January 2022.

A person whose data has been accessed must be informed as soon as such notification is no longer likely to jeopardize any investigations. Such notification is required to allow the persons concerned to exercise, among other things, their right to a legal remedy.

National legislation must provide for data to be retained within the EU and for the irreversible destruction of data at the end of the data retention period. Member States are also required to ensure control by an independent authority on the compliance with the level of protection guaranteed by the EU law. In a following case, *Ministerio Fiscal*,[23] the CJEU ruled on a preliminary reference submitted by a Spanish court to obtain clarifications on the interpretation of the definition of "serious crime" in the case *Tele 2*. The Court of Justice found that public authorities' access to the data aimed at identifying holders of SIM cards activated with a telephone stolen mobile phone, through surname, first name and, if applicable, address of such subjects, represents an interference with fundamental rights of the latter, sanctioned by the aforementioned articles of the Charter of Rights fundamental, which is not sufficiently serious to limit the aforementioned access, given the purpose of prevention, investigation, detection and prosecution of crimes, to the fight against serious crime.

Recently, the Grand Chamber of the CJEU ruled again on data retention in four judgements concerning the Joined Cases C-511/18 (*La Quadrature du Net and Others*), C-512/18 (*French Data Network and Others*) and C-520/18 (*Ordre des barreaux francophones et germanophone and Others*), as well as in the case Privacy International, reaching disruptive conclusions.[24]

In all these cases, the Court excluded the national security exemption (Art 4(2) TEU),[25] based on the fact that the general and indiscriminate retention of traffic and location data relies on data processing by service providers and therefore falls under the scope of the Directive 2002/58, which should be interpreted in a consistent manner with GDPR, regardless the fact that it involves protecting national security and combating crime.[26] In fact, the exclusion of the scope of application of GDPR provided by Art 2 (according to which, GDPR does not apply to processing operations carried out "by competent authorities" for the purposes of, inter alia, the prevention and detection of criminal offences, including the safeguarding against and the prevention of threats to public security), in fact only applies to data processing carried

23 Case C-207/16 *Ministerio Fiscal* (CJEU, GC, 2 October 2018).

24 Joined Cases C-511/18, C-512/18 and C-520/18 *La Quadrature du Net and Others* (CJEU, GC, 6 October 2020); Case C-623/17 *Privacy International* (CJEU, 6 October 2020).

25 See *La Quadrature du Net and Others* (n 20) § 99 and *Privacy International* (n 20) § 75.

26 Thomas Wahl, 'CJEU: data Retention allowed in Exceptional Cases' (2020) 3 EUCRIM 184.

out by competent authorities for same purposes rather than by service providers. Consequently, either national legislation which requires providers of electronic communications services to retain traffic and location data for the purposes of protecting national security and combating crime and national legislation enabling a State authority to require providers of electronic communications services to forward traffic data and location data to the security and intelligence agencies for the purpose of safeguarding national security fall within the scope of Directive 2002/58.[27] Moreover, the restriction of data subjects' rights provided by Art 23 GDPR in fields such as, for example, national security, defense, public security, law enforcement – cannot justify any indiscriminate and generalized data retention by providers of access to online public communication services and hosting service providers. Therefore Directive 2002/58 must be interpreted in compliance with GDPR and Arts 7 and 8 of the European Charter of Fundamental Rights.

In la *Quadrature du Net and Others*, the Court develops its reasoning on the concept of procedural autonomy, equivalence and effectiveness (§ 223, 224, 225), holding that "procedural rules for actions intended to safeguard the rights that individuals derive from EU law", cannot be less favourable than the rules governing similar domestic actions (in light of the principle of equivalence) in order not to render "impossible in practice or excessively difficult the exercise of rights conferred by EU law (the principle of effectiveness)" (§ 223). This means that rights laid down by the directive on information rights does not prejudice data protection safeguards. In fact, based on the principle of equivalence, if information or evidence is gathered in contravention of the Directive 2002/58, national law governing those proceedings cannot lay down "less favorable rules on the admissibility and use of such information and evidence than those governing information and evidence obtained in breach of domestic law" (§ 224). The third point developed by the Court deserves particular attention as it focuses on the principle of effectiveness, by virtue of which "the objective of national rules on the admissibility and use of information and evidence is, in accordance with the choices made by national law, to prevent information and evidence obtained unlawfully from unduly prejudicing a person who is suspected of having committed criminal offences. That objective

27 Xavier Tracol, The two judgments of the European Court of Justice in the four cases of *Privacy International, La Quadrature du Net and Others, French Data Network and Others* and *Ordre des Barreaux francophones et germanophone and Others*: The Grand Chamber is trying hard to square the circle of data retention, Computer Law & Security Review, Vol. 41, July 2021, https://www.sciencedirect.com/journal/computer-law-and-security-review , accessed 25 January 2022.

may be achieved under national law not only by prohibiting the use of such information and evidence, but also by means of national rules and practices governing the assessment and weighting of such material, or by factoring in whether that material is unlawful when determining the sentence" (§ 225). These three elements are the core of the adversarial principle and of the right to a fair trial "entailed by the admissibility of such information and evidence" (§ 226). This may imply in fact that a court must disregard "information and evidence obtained by means of the general and indiscriminate retention of traffic and location data in breach of EU law, in the context of criminal proceedings against persons suspected of having committed criminal offences" (§ 227) on facts on which a party is not in a position to comment effectively on and that consequently on "evidence pertaining to a field of which the judges have no knowledge and is likely to have a preponderant influence on the findings of fact" (§ 226).[28] This lack of knowledge, impairing the right of defense, must entail the exclusion of the evidence from that proceeding in order to avoid the violation of the right to defense.

In conclusion, stating that "national criminal courts must disregard information and evidence obtained by means of the general and indiscriminate retention of traffic and location data in breach of EU law" (§ 229) – this judgement upholds that data processed unlawfully cannot be used as information or evidence in criminal proceedings.

La Quadrature du Net & Others case has been more recently coupled by another important judgement, *Prokuratuur*,[29] which has confirmed that the adversarial principle cannot be undermined by national rules on the admissibility and use of information and evidence that permit that information and evidence are obtained unlawfully and unduly prejudice a person who is suspected of having committed criminal offences (§ 43). This judgement not only joins the conclusions of *La Quadrature du Net & Others* in pointing out that national criminal courts cannot use information and evidence obtained by means of the general and indiscriminate retention of traffic and location data

---

28 See on this ECtHR case law on the right to understand fully the extent of the charges in order to prepare an adequate defence (*Mattoccia v Italy* App No 23969/94 (ECHR, 25 July 2000) § 60). This right may be exemplified if offences are sufficiently listed; the place and the date of the offence is stated; there is a reference to the relevant Articles of the Criminal Code, and the name of the victim is mentioned (*Brozicek v Italy* App No 10964/84 (ECHR, 19 December 1989) § 42). On the right to comment on the accusation, see *Öcalan v Turkey* App No 46221/99 (ECHR, GC, 12 May 2005) § 140; on the adversarial principle, see *Rowe and Davis v the United Kingdom* App No 28901/95 (ECHR, GC, 16 February 2000) § 59; *Leas v Estonia* App No 59577/08 (ECHR, 6 March 2012) § 76.

29 Case C-746/18 *Prokuratuur* (CJEU, GC, 2 March 2021).

in breach of EU law, but also extends to data access by competent authorities in breach of EU law. In this sense, it confirms the previous case-law in limiting data access by public authorities only to procedures and proceedings to combat serious crime or prevent serious threats to public security.[30] However, it specifies that the access to electronic communication or regarding the location of the terminal equipment of individuals, for the purposes of the prevention, investigation, detection and prosecution of criminal offences, is prohibited regardless of the length of data access' and of the quantity or nature of the data available (§ 45).

In extending the prohibition of a generalized and indiscriminate data access to data access by public authorities, this case does not consider the public prosecutor as an independent judicial authority enabled to carry out a preliminary review authorizing access of a public authority to traffic and location data for the purposes of a criminal investigation. In fact, it holds that "national legislation that confers upon the public prosecutor's office, whose task is to direct the criminal pre-trial procedure and to bring, where appropriate, the public prosecution in subsequent proceedings, the power to authorise access of a public authority to traffic and location data for the purposes of a criminal investigation" is in contrast with EU law (§ 59).

Concurrently, in the case *Privacy International* the Court applies the conclusions achieved in *La Quadrature du Net* not only to data retention but also to handovers and disclosures of traffic and location data in a generalized and indiscriminate way to the security and intelligence agencies (§§ 79, 82, 83). The fact that such a transmission is conducted in an indiscriminate way, meaning that it applies to all persons, does not provide any specific link with the objective of safeguarding national security (§ 80).

14.5 Conclusions

This Chapter has offered a preliminary overview of a parallel analysis of data subjects' rights – including the right to information and the right to access – and the right to information and access to the materials of the cases laid down by the Directive 2012/13.[31]

30 For a detailed overview and comment on the judgement, see Chiara Greco, 'Quest'acquisizione non s'ha da fare: ennesimo 'no' della Corte di Giustizia alla data retention indiscriminata in campo penale. Nota a CGUE 2 marzo 2021, Prokuratuur' (2021) 2 Diritto dell'Informazione e dell'Informatica 235.

31 See Report from the Commission to the European Parliament and the Council, on the implementation of Directive 2012/13/EU of the European Parliament and of the Council

From the previous paragraphs, it emerges that a lawful data processing may be potentially a trigger of other substantial safeguards such as for example the right to an effective judicial remedy.

Although a clear disconnection between legal regimes related to criminal proceedings and data processing for law enforcement purposes has been observed, the unifying role of CJEU case law has been essential in the past years to draw a common line between various sectoral regimes of protection touched by data processing's operations. Data, in this sense, requires many levels of protection but is also capable to bridge the gaps between different areas of the law. In its function of crossing the boundaries – literally, if we think in terms of its borderless character and metaphorically, if we consider the common aspects of data processing regardless of who is the controller and what are the purposes – data compels the law to be creative enough in offering new paths for protection of traditional legal principles – such as the adversarial principle.

The Chapter showed how data protection safeguards have been the object of a meta-reasoning by the European Court of Justice and acted as collectors of a set of guarantees that pervade other fundamental rights and core democratic principles.

On the one hand, this can be interpreted as an expression of the European legal culture that elaborates on the connection between rights and principles; on the other hand, this is the result of a tension, often political and institutional, which is sorted out by a courageous attitude of the Judiciary. The risk could be on a large scale to charge of too many expectations the approach to data governance as a 'data protection zone', even whereas concerns and priorities may be different. In the last decade data protection safeguards have been generally used by the Court of Justice to align the interpretation of secondary law with the Charter of Fundamental Rights, globally expanding its outreach.[32] The law should be then always aware enough of the instrumental use of technicalities to preserve those principles and rights that technicalities address.

of 22 May 2012 on the right to information in criminal proceedings, Brussels, 18.12.2018 COM(2018) 858 final.

32 Federico Fabbrini, Edoardo Celeste and John Quinn, *Data Protection Beyond Borders: Transatlantic Perspectives on Extraterritoriality and Sovereignty* (Bloomsbury 2020).

PART 4

Developing a Computable Approach to Defence Rights

CHAPTER 15

Logic Representation of Legal Norms

Marco Billi, Giuseppe Contissa, and Galileo Sartor

15.1 Legal Knowledge Representation: An Introduction

In our increasingly pervasive and interconnected world, the application and enforcement of the law makes it necessary to take into account the interplay of multiple normative systems, especially when dealing with international or European matters, contracts, and other commercial and social interactions involving different countries.

The different normative systems that interact in a legal case may introduce conflicts, or differing consequences. This makes it harder for the legal expert to know which sources of law he must consider in order to prepare for a case. This increase in complexity is true of both national legal systems and of trans-national or international laws and conventions. All these sources of law need to be considered to properly reason about the law.

The system of EU and national rules in particular is a multilevel one, in which determining the legal provisions applicable to a specific case can be an extremely challenging task due to the existence of numerous international conventions, bilateral agreements and national instruments, with the overlapping of different rules. This issue renders necessary a careful legal analysis of the subordination between various legal sources and their temporal and territorial legal effect.

Assistance in this can come from legal representation of rules, in order to assist legal professionals in understanding the ever-increasing legal corpus.

The computable representation of legal norms has a considerable history, going back to the 70's and 80's, with the first breakthrough provided by the use of logic programming. New topics of research in the area are primarily based on the developments of well-structured rule-based systems, the application of new different reasoning models, and the implementation of argumentation frameworks.[1]

1 Francesca Toni and Marek Sergot, 'Argumentation and Answer Set Programming' in Marcello Balduccini and Tran Cao Son (eds), *Logic Programming, Knowledge Representation, and Nonmonotonic Reasoning: Essays Dedicated to Michael Gelfond on the Occasion of His 65th Birthday* (Springer 2011).

 | DOI:10.1163/9789004513396_017

There is also the question of how to deal with judgements of the EU Court of Justice and the national jurisdictions that, although at a slow pace and depending on the specific issues presented by the national courts, still add to the legal corpus. Another interesting matter that adds to the complexity of the problem is the global dimension of today's information society that generates new complex issues.

The computable representation of legal norms can be a solution to many of the aforementioned issues, by building a machine-readable version of the law, on which an expert system can be made to reason. By translating legal norms into rules written in a programming language, the system is able to apply legal reasoning to the rulebase. The objective of the modelling is therefore the creation of a reasoning platform that can assist any user in finding and applying the relevant rules, by understanding which conditions have been met and which factual elements are needed in the decision.

To properly reason with the law it is necessary to define what requirements are needed, both from a legal and technical standpoint.

Let us now consider the main legal requirements[2] that have been observed while modelling the different legal sources:

- Isomorphism (one to one correspondence between norms in the formal model and natural language)

  In Karpf[3] we find five main rules, listed also in Bench-Capon and Coenen[4] as the following: (i) Each legal source is presented separately; (ii) The representation preserves the structure of each legal source; (iii) The representation preserves the traditional mutual relation, references and connections between the legal sources; (iv) The representation of the legal sources and their mutual relations (...) is separate from all other parts of the model, notably representation of queries and facts management; (v) If procedural law is part of the domain of the model then the law module will have representation of material as well as procedural rules and it is demanded that the whole system functions in accordance with and in the order following the procedural rules. Following these rules greatly help to satisfy the main concerns of well-engineered knowledge systems, namely verification, validation, and maintenance.

2 Thomas F Gordon, Guido Governatori and Antonino Rotolo, 'Rules and Norms: Requirements for Rule Interchange Languages in the Legal Domain' in Lecture Notes in Computer Science (Springer 2009).

3 Jurgen Karpf, 'Quality assurance of legal expert systems' (1989) Artificial Intelligence and Law.

4 Trevor JM Bench-Capon and Frans P Coenen, 'Isomorphism and legal knowledgebased systems' (1992) Artificial Intelligence and Law 1(1) 65.

- Reification: rules representing legal norms need to be treated as object with properties by other rules, in order to deal with the following aspects of legal systems and norms:
  - Jurisdiction: that is the limits within the rules are authoritative and binding.
  - Authority: that is the property specifying who produced the rule, and its ranking within the sources of law (e.g. constitutional provision, statutory law, regulation, administrative, etc.).
  - Temporal properties: rules may be qualified by temporal properties, one is the external time of a legal norm, i.e. the answer to the question: during what time-interval(s) has the norm been included in the legal system? This includes rule validity, which is also related to the annulment of a norm (the effect applies ex tunc), and its abrogation (the effect applies *ex nunc*). The other time is the internal time of a legal norm, which includes all temporal issues which are involved in the application of a valid norm. In particular, it deals with the answer to the question: what time-interval(s) was the norm intended to cover? This question concerns the interval in which the conditions contemplated by the norm should happen in order that they will produce the norm's effect, i.e. the subsumption interval or the norm.
- Defeasibility: when the antecedent of the rule is satisfied by the facts of the case, the conclusion of the rule presumably holds, but this presumption can be defeated.[5] The defeasibility of the legal rules comes down to the following issues:
  - Conflicts: rules may lead to incompatible legal effects, that can be resolved through rule priorities, such as: lex specialis (which gives priority to the most specific rule), lex superior (which gives priority to the rule from the higher authority), lex posterior (which gives priority to the rule enacted later).
  - Exclusionary rules: rules that provide a way to explicitly undercut other rules, making them inapplicable.
- Ways to handle vagueness: the interpretation of rules may refer to factors that cannot be strictly expressed in logic form, so they may be assumed as true to handle their vagueness. Let us for example consider Art 3(1) of Directive 2010/64, where it is stated that "Member States shall ensure that

5 Guido Governatori, Antonino Rotolo and Erica Calardo, 'Possible WorldSemantics for Defeasible Deontic Logic' in Thomas Agotnes, Jan Broersen, and Dag Elgesem (eds), *Deontic Logic in Computer Science* (Springer 2012).

suspected or accused persons [...] are, within a reasonable period of time, provided with a written translation of all documents" or the Art 3(9) of the same Directive, where it is stated that "Translation provided under this Art shall be of a quality sufficient to safeguard the fairness of the proceedings [...]".

In this case the concepts of reasonable period of time, or the quality of the proceedings, are not defined in the legal source.

- Normative effects (obligations, permissions etc.), and their persistence over time.
  - Qualificatory. It ascribes legal quality to a person or object (e.g. x is an EU citizen if x is an Italian citizen)
  - Definitional or constitutive rules.
  - Deontic (imposes obligations or permissions).
  - Potestative (attributes power).
  - Evidentiary. It establishes the conclusion to be drawn from certain evidence, taking also into account legal presumptions.

The legal requirements described above can help identify the technical requirements of a reasoning system. In particular the following have been identified.[6]

- *Tractability and reasonable computational complexity*

  Although decidability and computability are important to an understanding of computation, the tractability criterion is needed to explore and evaluate problems and the amount of computation needed to solve instances. A problem is called intractable if the time required to solve instances grows exponentially with the size of the instances. It is important because exponential growth means that even moderately large instances cannot be solved in any reasonable time. Therefore, one should strive to divide the overall problem of generating intelligent behaviour into tractable subproblems rather than intractable ones. This is a general issue that is handled differently by different reasoners. The computational complexity also derives from the language the engine is built in. We will analyse this aspect in more depth with regard to the following criteria.
- *Procedural order of inference rules*

  Two types of rules are common in AI: knowledge and inference. Knowledge rules, or declarative rules, state all the facts and relationships about a problem. Inference rules, or procedural rules, on the other hand, advise on how to solve a problem when certain facts are known. Knowledge

6 Kasper Van Den Berg, Tom Van Engers, and Patries Kordelaar, 'Requirements for Legal Knowledge Representation' (2009) *Law, ontologies and the semantic web: channelling the legal information flood* 188, 21.

rules go in the knowledge base, whereas inference rules become part of the inference engine. Knowledge rules may look like the following:

RULE 1: IF the person does not understand a language AND the Person is on trial in that language THEN the person is granted the right to interpretation in the trial.

Inference rules contain rules about rules and thus are also called metarules. They pertain to other rules (or even to themselves). Inference (procedural) rules may look like the following:

RULE 1: IF there is an exception to a certain rule THEN that rule is not valid.

This kind of inference rule is useful since a rule that is considered invalid can be excluded from the computation process.

– *Semantic values of the expressions*

While both the values "true" and "false" are the basic values propositions may have, other formal theories may introduce more values for particular purposes, i.e. "unknown" and "uncertain".

In decision-making under certainty (where values can be true or false), it is assumed that complete knowledge is available so that the decision-maker knows exactly what the outcome of each course of action will be (as in a deterministic environment). It may not be true that the outcomes are 100 percent known, nor is it necessary to really evaluate all the outcomes, but often this assumption simplifies the model and makes it tractable.

In decision-making under uncertainty (where values can be either "unknown" or "uncertain"), it is necessary to consider situations in which several outcomes are possible for each course of action. In this case, the probability of occurrence of the possible outcomes is unknown or cannot be estimated. Decision-making under uncertainty is more complex because of insufficient information. Instead of dealing with uncertainty, one possibility is to obtain more information so that the problem can be treated with certainty (because it can be "almost" certain). If more information is not available, the problem must be treated under a condition of uncertainty, for example by using abductive reasoning.

Engines may present different built-in solutions when dealing with "unknown" and "uncertain" values. A further aspect that may be relevant and should be considered is the possibility of engine customization and/or alteration.

– *Control strategies*

Given an implementation of a rule system, we must consider how the rules are used, which introduces an important procedural component. These issues apply to implemented rule systems, where the execution of the rules in a program implies a sequence of order of application of the rules.

There are several sub-issues: the chaining of rules to reach a goal, the resolution of conflicts between rules, procedures to clean or filter the rule set, the order of evaluation of rules and terms, and any side effects which may arise as a result of the execution of a rule. One way to see the issue is that while each individual rule may be well-formed, we may have issues related to the interactions among the rules which then require higher-level or more abstract rules to be imposed over the sets of rules.

Rule chaining concerns how the rules are used in order to obtain a goal. One general strategy is forward chaining, where base facts are used to infer goal expressions, which become further input as sub-goals in the determination of a further goal. Another strategy is backwards chaining, which proceeds from a goal to the sub-goals that support it. For every sub-goal, we pursue any further supporting sub-goals until we attain base facts, from which we may infer up the chain whether the first goal holds or not.

For either strategy, we should consider whether the chaining follows depth first or breadth first searches for base facts. We can also use a mixed strategy, where we first start backwards chaining to base facts, use our results of base facts with forward chaining to determine what else may follow, and once the chain is exhausted, return to backwards chaining with respect to the next goal.

– *Explanation and justification*

Explanation in rule-based systems is usually associated with a way of tracing the rules that are fired during the course of a problem-solving session. This is about the closest to a real explanation that today's systems can provide, given that their knowledge is usually represented almost exclusively as bare rules and do not include basic principles necessary for a human-type explanation. Explanation is an extremely important function because understanding depends on explanation, and makes it easier to implement proposed solutions easier. Constructing explanations can become a very complex task, especially when undertaken by machines.

There are two main methods for generating explanations, the static explanation method and the dynamic explanation method. In order to generate a static explanation it is sufficient to preinsert pieces of English text (scripts) into the system, thus, each question that may be asked is associated with a textual answer. Several problems are associated with static explanations. For example, all questions and answers must be anticipated in advance, and for large systems this is very difficult. Also, the system essentially has no idea what it is saying. In the long run, there is a danger that the program might be modified without changing the text, thus causing inconsistency.

Conversely, the dynamic explanation is reconstructed according to the execution pattern of the rules. The system reconstructs the reasons for its actions as it evaluates rules. This second method of explanation is the better solution to avoid possible inconsistency issues.

An additional aspect that needs to be taken in to account is how to design a decision report, i.e. a report that can be viewed when the outcome of a goal is known, outlining the reasons for that specific decision. The value of every base level and intermediate attribute relevant to the final outcome should be displayed in the decision report. Justifications should be provided in human readable and understandable form, ensuring that the logic in the rules is presented sensibly to the user.

15.2 Modelling Criminal Procedure Law in Logic Form

The CrossJustice project studies the rights of defendants in criminal matters according to the laws of several EU Member States and provides a decision support system, accessible by professionals and citizens alike. The system provides assessments concerning specific cases, and moreover determines the level of harmonisation of national legislations, namely the extent to which national legal frameworks and regulatory acts are in line with the EU acquis and relevant legislative acts of the European Union.

The aim is to help legal practitioners in their daily activities, through a platform that supports interoperability and communication between the several legislative measures that single member states have adopted, by showing how these laws interact, and the extent to which they comply with EU law.

The main objective of the project is the creation of a rule-based expert system including a computable representation of the Directive 2016/343, Directive 2010/64, Directive 2016/800, Directive 2016/1919, Directive 2012/13 and Directive 2013/48, related to the rights of suspects and accused persons in criminal proceedings and the national articles concerning the same subject matter.[7] The system shall inform the users of all the applicable rights according to both European and national acts.

Furthermore, the system includes a representation of the national implementations from four EU Countries, namely Italy, the Netherlands, Poland, and Spain (although with regard to the latter, only the articles concerning the

7 The platform is currently available online at the website <https://legalmachinelab.unibo.it/crossjustice/>.

right of the suspect and accused to be assisted by an interpreter and to be provided a translation have been modelled).

This has made it possible to focus on the interaction between the different legal sources, and to identify possible conflicts or inconsistencies in the different national implementations.

The particular relationship between directives and national laws presents a high level of complexity. In fact, differently from EU Regulations, Directives are meant to provide only a baseline, that each Member State can apply differently, to better serve the national legal system, and tradition.

As single Member States have (a limited) discretionary power in implementing these provisions, it is easy to understand how there can be discrepancies that may in certain cases give rise to complex legal issues, especially when the matter at hand involves multiple states.

These differences often regard the applicability of a law, and may stem from a) differences in the used terminology, possibly referring to diverse legal concepts, and b) the omission or addition of certain legal requirements by national laws.

For instance, under the EU Directive 2013/48 any accused has the right to consult a lawyer, while under the Dutch transposition the accused must also be deprived of their liberty, as they assume that persons not under such restrictive measures are already free to do so, and thus do not need special protection.

```
%% has_right(_art3_1, PersonId, _right_to_translation, _document_
translation)
%
% Article 3
%
% Member States shall ensure that suspected or accused
% persons who do not understand the language of the criminal
% proceedings concerned are, within a reasonable period of time,
% provided with a written translation of all documents which are
% essential to ensure that they are able to exercise their right
% of defence and to safeguard the fairness of the proceedings.
has_right(art3_1, PersonId, right_to_translation, essentialDocument):-
  proceeding_language(PersonId, Language),
  essential_document(_, PersonId, documents),
  \+ person_understands(PersonId, Language).

%% essential_document(_art, PersonId, _documents)
%
```

```
% Article 3.2
%
% Essential documents shall include any decision depriving a
% person of his liberty, any charge or indictment, and any
% judgment.
essential_document(art3_2, PersonId, documents):-
  person_document(PersonId, document_deprives_liberty).

essential_document(art3_2, PersonId, documents):-
  person_document(PersonId, charge).

essential_document(art3_2, PersonId, documents):-
  person_document(PersonId, indictment).

essential_document(art3_2, PersonId, documents):-
  person_document(PersonId, judgement).

%% essential_document(_art3_3, PersonId, _documents):
%
% Article 3.3
%
% The competent authorities shall, in any given case, decide
% whether any other document is essential. Suspected or accused
% persons or their legal counsel may submit a reasoned request to
% that effect.
essential_document(art3_3, PersonId, documents):-
  authority_decision(PersonId, essential_document),
  person_request_submitted(PersonId, essential_document).
```

This is not the only issue in the modelling of such laws. Another common issue arising from the computable representation of the law consists in how to accurately deal with open ended clauses without excessively restricting the scope.[8] For example, Art 3, paragraph 1, of Directive 2010/64 states that *suspected or accused persons shall be provided with a written translation of all documents which are essential to ensure that they are able to exercise their right of defence*

8 Herbert Lionel Adolphus Hart and Leslie Green, *The concept of law* (Oxford The Clarendon Press ed, 1961); Bench-Capon, Trevor JM and Pepijn RS Visser, 'Open texture and ontologies in legal information systems' (1997) Database and Expert Systems Applications. 8thInternational Conference, DEXA '97. Proceedings.

and to safeguard the fairness of the proceedings. The legislator does not describe what exactly constitutes an essential document, but leaves the decision up to the judge, who may be required to intervene on a case-by-case basis depending on the subject matter.

This is further illustrated in the second and third paragraph of the same article. While the former gives a brief example of what forms an essential document, the latter states that the final decision shall always be left to the judge.

For the transposition of this article we have decided to represent both examples as described by the directive, as well as a rule stating that the judge may declare any document to be essential for the proceedings. In our codebase we have explicitly stated, through the use of a single predicate to indicate that a document has been deemed essential (i.e., *essential_document*), which is successfully instantiated (thus found to be true) either by the application of the second or third paragraph of the same article.

The second paragraph presents a list of documents that fulfill the conditions/examples set out by the Directive, while the third paragraph is translated through the use of a predicate (*authority_decision*) which symbolizes that the judiciary has already taken a decision to that effect, in our case it has declared that a document is essential to the proceedings and therefore falls within the scope of the Directive.

Moreover, the fact that the decision is based either on the second or the third paragraph is registered by the system, and will be presented in the final result as a reference to the article. This is useful in terms of explainability and clarity, and can aid in understanding why a document has been declared as essential.

This does not limit the discretionary power of the judge, as the solution given by our system is either one of the examples already covered by the Directive or it is due to an explicit decision of the legal authority. If we did not have an article as a reference for the applicability of a norm, the final decision would be up to the judge, and our system would require the authority's opinion before presenting the user with a positive solution.

```
%% has_right(_art37_1, PersonId, _right_to_be_visited,
%        _relatives)
%
% Article 37(1) Decree no 230 of the President of the Republic
% of 30 June 2000
%
% 1. Visits of convicted persons, inmates and defendants after
% the verdict of the first stage
```

```
% are authorized by the Head of the institute. Visits with
% persons different from relatives and
% cohabitees are authorized when sensible reasons occur.
has_right(art37_1, PersonId, right_to_be_visited, relatives) :-
   (person_status(PersonId, convicted);
   person_status(PersonId, inmate)),
   authority_decision(PersonId, authorized).
```

For example, let us now take a look at Art 37, paragraph 1, Decree n. 230 of the President of the Republic of the Italian legal system. The article states that any visit to convicted person needs to be authorized by the Head of the Institute. As the legislator has not given any indication regarding what conditions are needed to allow the person to be visited, but has left the decision to the authority, it has been decided to use the predicate (*authority_decision*) to indicate that such authorization has been granted to the person.

Finally, the system does not give any indication to the scope of the documents. Reading the final part of the first paragraph of Art 3, we can see that the European legislator requires that they are needed *to ensure that they are able to exercise their right of defence and to safeguard the fairness of the proceedings*. This is related to the issue of vagueness, in which concepts that are not defined in the legal corpus, for which instead we rely on concepts that are mostly agreed on. If we speak about the "good character", "reasonable amount of time", and other such vague conditions, we are addressing concepts that the system does not have, so we have decided to ignore them, de facto considering them as true.[9]

In this particular case, another possibility would have been to ensure that, under every rule that required the judge to ensure that the fairness of the proceedings has been respected, an additional condition would have been inserted, depending on the confirmation by the authority. We considered such a requirement to be too lacking in information to be added to the system.

```
%% has_right(_art4, PersonId, _right_to_legal_aid, _free)
%
% Article 4
% Legal aid in criminal proceedings
%
```

9 Marek J Sergot, Fariba Sadri, Robert A. Kowalski, Frank Kriwaczek, Peter Hammond and H. Terese Cory, 'The British Nationality Act as a Logic Program' (1986) Communications of the ACM 29(5) 370.

```
% 1. Member States shall ensure that suspects and accused persons who lack sufficient resources to pay for the
% assistance of a lawyer have the right to legal aid when the
% interests of justice so require.
%% 2. Member States may apply a means test, a merits test, or
% both to determine whether legal aid is to be granted in
% accordance with paragraph 1.
has_right(art4, PersonId, right_to_legal_aid, free) :-
  ( person_status(PersonId, suspect)
  ; person_status(PersonId, accused)
  ),
  authority_decision(PersonId, lack_resources).

authority_decision(PersonId, lack_resources) :-
  proceeding_matter(PersonId, means_test);
  proceeding_matter(PersonId, merits_test).
```

Another issue we have encountered in our transposition, slightly related to the former, is how to manage those cases where the European legislator has not established a minimum standard for the application of a norm. Guidelines arranged by the European Union are not immediately applicable, they are subject to implementation in the Member States. Therefore, whenever the European legislator has not given any precise information regarding concrete requirements, we have elected to use the aforementioned predicate "*authority_decision*" to indicate that the judge, or another legal authority, has the final say on that particular matter, regarding both the form and substance of the proceeding.

For example, let us consider the transposition of Art 4, Directive 2016/1919, which grants the right of a person to legal aid. The only parts explicitly transposed have been paragraphs 1 and 2, describing that a person shall have the right to legal aid if he or she is a suspect or accused in the proceedings, and the authority has successfully performed a means or merits test, verifying that the person lacks the resources to pay for the lawyer. Since paragraph 3 of the same article does not indicate any concrete requirements, but only introduces concepts in need of further implementation, the transposition of this paragraph does not include any definition of what exactly constitutes a means or merits test.

With regard to each national legislation, the situation is quite different. As Member States describe in more detail what the conditions for accessing legal aid are, it has been necessary to translate them in a computable form. For example, the Polish legislator has decreed that any person who cannot bear the costs may request the appointment of a defense counsel (Art 78(1) code of criminal procedure). In this case it has been decided to represent the article has having two requirements, the first that the person cannot bear the costs, and the second that the person has requested the appointment of a lawyer.

In this case, there is no need to insert an additional predicate stating that the legal authority is required to confirm the circumstances of the person and appoint a defense counsel, as that is already implied for all proceedings. Furthermore, at least as far as the literal interpretation of this article is concerned, the discretionary power of the judge is limited to accepting the proof of the status of the person.

```
%% has_right(_art78_1, PersonId, _right_to_legal_aid,
_appoint_ex_officio)
%
% Article 78(1-1a) code of criminal procedure
%
% 1. An accused, who does not have a defence counsel of his own
% choice, may request the appointment of a defence counsel ex
% officio,
% if he can duly prove that he is unable to bear the costs of
% defence without prejudice to the necessary maintenance of
% himself, or his family.
has right(art78_1, PersonId, right_to_legal_aid, appoint_ex_officio) :-
  person_status(PersonId, cannot_bear_costs),
  person request_submitted(PersonId, appoint_lawyer).
```

Both the Dutch (Art 28 Legal Aid Act) and Italian (Art 76 Presidential Decree n. 115/2002) legislator, on the other hand, establish more stringent and practical conditions on the access to legal aid. The legislators require the person to fall under a certain threshold of income, thus we have used the predicate person_income(PersonId, X), where X stands for the limit required by the national source.

```
%% art34Applies(PersonId)
%
% Article 34 legal aid act
%
% Legal aid as per the provisions of this statute shall be
% granted to those whose annual income is 21800 Euros [as of 1
```

```
% January 2020: 27900 Euros]
% or less if they are a single householder, or, if they share a
% household with one or more persons, does not exceed 31000 Euros
% [as of 1 January 2020: 39400 Euros].
art34Applies(PersonId) :-
  person_event(PersonId, single_householder),
person_income(PersonId, X),
  X < 27900.

art34Applies(PersonId) :-
  person_event(PersonId, share_householder),
person_income(PersonId, X),
  X < 39400.

%% art76Applies(PersonId)
%
% Article 76 Presidential Decree no 115/2002
%
% Conditions for admission to legal aid
% 1. Anyone who has a taxable income, resulting from the last tax return,
not exceeding 11,746.68 euros, may be admitted to legal aid.
art76Applies(PersonId) :-
  person_income(PersonId, X),
  X < 11746.68.
```

The lack of a uniform minimum standard for providing legal aid to person in the Member States results in different scenarios that may arise, especially if the user is looking to compare several national legislations between themselves. An effort has been made in keeping the original structure as isomorphic as possible, and at the same time leaving the European transposition as an open-ended clause under the discretion of the legal authority. Therefore, this tool can be of use to both a citizen looking for an answer regarding the law in a specific Member State, as well as legal professionals who are more interested in verifying the conformity between the legal sources, and how those relate to the original article referenced in the Directive.

```
%% has_right(_art3_2, PersonId, _right_to_access_lawyer, _)
%
% Article 3.2
%
```

```
% 2. Suspects or accused persons shall have access to a lawyer
% without undue delay.
% In any event, suspects or accused persons shall have access to
% a lawyer from whichever of the
% following points in time is the earliest:
% (a)
% before they are questioned by the police or by another law
% enforcement or judicial authority;
% (b) upon the carrying out by investigating or other competent
% authorities of an investigative or
% other evidence-gathering act in accordance with point (c) of
% paragraph 3;
% (c) without undue delay after deprivation of liberty;
% (d) where they have been summoned to appear before a court
% having jurisdiction in criminal matters,
% in due time before they appear before that court.

has_right(art3_2_a, PersonId, right_to_access_lawyer, questioning) :-
  (  person_status(PersonId, suspect)
  ;  person_status(PersonId, accused)
  ),
  proceeding_matter(PersonId, questioning).

has_right(art3_2_b, PersonId, right_to_access_lawyer, evidence_gathering_act) :-
  (  person_status(PersonId, suspect)
  ;  person_status(PersonId, accused)
  ),
  proceeding_matter(PersonId, evidence_gathering_act).

has_right(art3_2_c, PersonId, right_to_access_lawyer, deprived_of_liberty) :-
  person_status(PersonId, deprived_of_liberty),
    \+ exception(has_right(art3_2_c, PersonId, right_to_access_lawyer, deprived_of_liberty), _).

has_right(art3_2_d, PersonId, right_to_access_lawyer, summoned_court) :-
  proceeding_matter(PersonId, summoned_court).
```

```
%% has_right(_art5_1, PersonId, _right_to_information, _inform_
person)
%
% Article 5.1
%
% The right to have a third person informed of the deprivation of
liberty
% 1. Member States shall ensure that suspects or accused persons who
are deprived of liberty have
% the right to have at least one person, such as a relative or an employer,
nominated by them, informed
% of their deprivation of liberty without undue delay if they so wish.
has_right(art5_1, PersonId, right_to_inform, PersonId2) :-
  ( person_status(PersonId, suspect)
  ; person_status(PersonId, accused)
  ),
  person_status(PersonId, deprived_of_liberty),
  person_nominate(PersonId, PersonId2),
  \+ exception(has_right(art5_1, PersonId, right_to_inform, PersonId2), _
).
```

Another critical feature of any reasoning system is the indication of the temporal succession of events. As can be seen in representation of Art 3, Directive 2013/48, it is stated that the right shall be granted at the first possible moment in time.

The issue that arises from the computable translation is related to the fact that the following events do not follow a strictly chronological order but they can either be present or not at different times during the proceedings. It is not possible to state that a right is to be granted unless another event has already occurred.

Therefore, it has been decided to identify each article with the phase of the proceedings it is granted on, and if the user, at the moment he queries the system, finds himself in a situation in which more than one of the events has occurred, he shall find that the same article applies more than once. It shall be up to the user to identify which moment in time was the earliest and accurately verify the correct (or mistaken) procedure.

An advantage of identifying the relevant phase of the proceedings only once, instead of comparing it to the others, is that it results in a more comprehensive overview of the solutions adopted by the legislator. This feature is particularly useful for comparing an article with each national implementation, as the system's results can more easily be compared to their national counterparts. Whenever two or more events have occurred, and the user is looking for a similar article granting the same right in the national sources of law, verifying when that right has been granted may lead to a deeper understanding of the issue. For example, if the Directive returns two results, while the Dutch legal system only one, looking at which right is missing from the national sources is immediately an indication of a wrong, or partially lacking, transposition of the Directive.

Furthermore, another issue related to a lack of temporal succession of events consists in the missing transposition of the expression "without undue delay". This can be seen in Art 3, letter c, and Art 5, paragraph 1, of the aforementioned Directive.

Such a requirement is absent in our computable representation, as it is assumed that a user of the system is looking for an indication of which rights he is entitled to, or of which rights he has been deprived of. Knowing that a right shall be granted immediately, without undue delay, at the first possible instance or in due time before an event, is beyond the scope of our reasoning system.

While in practice the judge may exert a greater degree of control over the proceedings, our transposition is, for now, limited to the dictates of the written source of law. Therefore, whenever there is a reference to the "manner provided for by the law" the system shall only reason based on the characteristics of the article itself, and does not include common practice or the jurisprudential opinion.

Another feature of the law that has not been included in our code is the transposition of the legal effects of the application of a norm. For example, Art 16(1) of the Polish code of criminal procedure states that there are no adverse consequences for breaching the right of the defendant to be informed of his rights. Such a declaration would not make any difference in our code, as the ultimate goal of the system is to inform the person of his rights, not the occurrences beyond the granting of such right. The only exception to this is the right to remedy to a legal decision, which is granted to the person in case of a violation of a right (when provided for by the law).

Future developments may include widely accepted judicial opinions, which could work towards clarifying the interpretative issues that arise within the predicates in the code, as well as practices, customs and legal traditions. This could lead to the development of a system able to reason between multiple interpretations of a rule, by using either the logic transposition or the judge's opinion.

We propose in fact that such a system should be kept up to date with the relevant legal corpus, and an effort should be made to add further parts to the knowledge base, to enable the continued support to citizens and professionals alike.

15.3 Rules and Exceptions

The language used for the development of the CrossJustice rulebase is SWI-Prolog.[10] This is a logic programming language with which the development team is familiar, and that has a certain number of advantages. It is well documented, and readily available on most systems; it is deeply extensible, both with premade tools, and custom ones, as we will see. SWI-Prolog is a partly standard compliant language, and this enables the use of other implementations of the Prolog base language, to add new features to the system.

The decision has been made to separate the legal texts in a folder structure, resembling the one available on the CrossJustice portal, with the Directive in a single file, and the relevant national articles in another file, one for each state. This will probably be changed in the future, to separate also the different national legal texts.

There are a certain number of main goals, that can be called as entry levels for the different legal sources, and that are mostly common to the different national implementations.

One example of this from Directive 2010/64/EU is the following:

For the result of the EU directive:

directive_2010_64(Right, dir, Article, PersonId, Matter)

For the national implementations:

directive_2010_64_it (Right, it, Article, PersonId, Matter)

directive_2010_64_es (Right, es, Article, PersonId, Matter)

directive_2010_64_pl (Right, pl, Article, PersonId, Matter)

This simple change facilitates a clear distinction, both in the code, as well as the logic structure, of the different national documents.

In each representation, the top-level goal is followed by exceptions and main rules (the assessment of the applicability of the law). This process is similar to the representation used in the Interlex Project,[11] with a number of differences, given the new field of application.

---

10 <https://www.swi-prolog.org/>.

11 INTERLEX – Advisory and Training System for Internet-related private International Law (JUST-JCOO-AG-2017, Proposal Number 800839), available at <https://interlex-portal.eu/en/index.html>.

The following text box contains an example of the initial predicates pertaining to Directive 2010/64/EU, and its immediate division in conditions: the necessary facts for the application of the Directive (in this case mainly implemented in Art 1), and a predicate related to any right contained in that Directive (i.e. whether *Person* has the right to interpretation with regards to the lawyer, the trial, certain documents, etc.). Therefore, it will state that the person has a right when the requirements for the application of the Directive are satisfied and there is at least one right granted to the person in the same source of law.

```
has_right(Right, dir, Article, PersonId, Matter) :-
  once(directive_2010_64_applies(PersonId)),
  has_right(Article, PersonId, Right, Matter).

directive_2010_64_applies(art1_2, PersonId, personalData) :-
  (  person_status(PersonId, suspect)
  ;  person_status(PersonId, accused)
  ),
  person_made_aware(PersonId, personStatus),
  proceeding_status(PersonId, started),
  \+ proceeding_status(PersonId, concluded).
```

15.3.1 *The Rule-Modelling Process*

The process of converting the rules has been largely inspired by the work done in the InterLex project. In the InterLex project the main focus was on the representation 3 main legislative EU instruments: Regulation (EU) No 1215/2012 on jurisdiction and the recognition and enforcement of judgments in civil and commercial matters (recast) (Brussels Regulation); the Regulation (EC) No 593/2008 on the law applicable to contractual obligations (Rome I); and the Regulation (EC) No 864/2007 on the law applicable to non-contractual obligations (Rome II). Regulations, in Member States, have direct application and do not have to be transposed into national laws. For this reason, the modelled rules were self-contained, in both the necessary definitions and conditions, as well as the legal effects. In these three regulations there is a limited number of references to national laws, and instead take a higher-level approach, with the allocation of jurisdiction and applicable law, leaving the judgement in the merit of the case itself to the national judge. There is no room for the national legislator to interpret or modify what the Regulations entail. For example, the general rule of jurisdiction states that the courts of the EU Member State in which the defendant is domiciled will have jurisdiction in the case, regardless of the defendant's nationality. The expert system developed in the InterLex project could, given a set of facts, find the applicable laws and inform of the jurisdiction and applicable law.

In the CrossJustice project the EU directives chosen can show a further degree of complexity, given their nature and the necessity of being altered and implemented in the specific legal system of each Member State. The aim of the Directive is not to provide a direct solution, but to instead guarantee the applicability of these laws in compliance with the internal legal system of the different states.

The process used to model the rules can be identified as follows:

1. Identify an article and all its dependencies

   Article 2(7).

   In proceedings for the execution of a European arrest warrant, the executing Member State shall ensure that its competent authorities provide persons subject to such proceedings who do not speak or understand the language of the proceedings with interpretation in accordance with this Article.

2. The article is then divided in its logic structure, in "pseudo-code", attempting to maintain isomorphism with the original rule, while making a number of changes to model the rules:
   a. the connectives (or, and) have been developed by repeating the relevant part of sentence or creating a new sentence, the relatives (which, who, etc.) have been developed and explicated;
   b. pronouns have been replaced by their referred nouns or lexical expressions;
   c. irrelevant terms and repetitions have been suppressed;
   d. when necessary, sentences have been modelled to get simpler syntax sentences;
   e. whenever possible, use has been made of equivalent terms to minimize the number of derived predicate names;
   f. sequences of words have been replaced by single terms whenever compound words were found.

   IF proceeding is european arrest warrant
   AND person language is NOT proceeding language
   THEN person has right to interpretation.

3. The logic structure is written in Prolog, following a set of guidelines and ontology build while modelling the system.

```
has_right(art2_7, PersonId, right_to_interpretation,
        europeanArrestWarrant):-
    proceeding_type(PersonId, europeanArrestWarrant),
    proceeding_language(PersonId, Language),
    \+ person_language(PersonId, Language).
```

The predicates were selected to enhance the isomorphism between the legal source and the Prolog code, and to avoid conflicts between unlinked legal sources (i.e. laws from different States), a *class:attribute* or *class:relation* model was chosen. The predicates are thus nested in "containerized" environments (classes), and the programmer can expose them explicitly when needed. One example of this are the user-insertable facts, that all belong to the "user" class, and as such are written explicitly as *user:<predicate>* (ex. user:personDomicile(john, italy, rome))

This enables us to have a uniform approach to representation across different legal systems (see point c in the list above, on irrelevant terms and repetitions).

The mapping between the formal rules and source text (structural elements in the rules) is guaranteed by explicitly identifying the specific article and comma that are translated. For this reason, the rules are in the form *<predicate>(<article>, <person>, <other>)*, with the arguments representing the article of the source text, the person subject of the sentence, and other relevant information.

15.3.2 *The Structure of the Directives*

The directives are fairly general in scope, and do not add too many requirements for a certain right. For example, most rules related to the right to a translation rely only on the condition of being a suspect or accused. For example, one of the first articles of Directive 2010/64 states that:

> Article 2 (1):
>
> Member States shall ensure that suspected or accused persons who do not speak or understand the language of the criminal proceedings concerned are provided, without delay, with interpretation during criminal proceedings before investigative and judicial authorities, including during police questioning, all court hearings and any necessary interim hearings.

This can be modelled as follows:

```
has_right(art2_1, PersonId, right_to_interpretation, trial) :-
    proceeding_language(PersonId, Language),
    \+ person_language(PersonId, Language).
```

A similar approach has been made to model the national implementations, as we can see in the following sections, where we modelled the articles corresponding to 2 (1) of the Directive.

Italian Implementation

Art 143 (1) (1) of the Italian Criminal Procedure Code states that:

> The accused who does not know the Italian language is entitled to be assisted by an interpreter – free of charge and regardless of the outcome of proceedings – to understand the accusations against him and follow the actions and hearings in which he participates.

Following the same method described for the Directive we have the following formal representation:

```
has_right(art143_1_1, PersonId, right_to_interpretation, trial):-
    proceeding_language(PersonId, italian),
    \+ person_language(PersonId, italian).
```

Polish Implementation

Art 72(1) of *the Polish Code of Criminal Procedure* states that:

> An accused, who does not have a sufficient command of Polish, is entitled to the gratuitous help of an interpreter (translator).

```
has_right(article72_1, PersonId, right_to_interpretation, trial):-
    proceeding_language(PersonId, polish),
    \+ person_language(PersonId, polish).
```

To enable the expression of specifications related to a right granted by the Directives, we have introduced two additional predicates, with a different meaning.

These express two high level categories of specifications, as identified by the legal experts in analysing the different articles.

```
auxiliary_right(Article, PersonId, Right, Matter)
right_property(Article, PersonId, Property, Value)
```

In the first rule, we express the relation between a *primary right* and the further rights that expand the meaning or the implementation of the first one.

We use the expression *auxiliary right* to highlight the relation that exists between the two. Primary rights are the basis of the defence of the defendant, they are generally always applicable and concern multiple stages of the proceeding (such as the right to an interpreter during the trial phase). The EU adds to these rights several instances and characteristics that only come into effect when the general right has been recognized and granted to the defendant (such as the existence of appropriate assistance for vulnerable persons).

Auxiliary rights do not directly regulate the legal sphere of the defendant but are depending upon or reasonably linked to a main right.

This link can either be a temporal one, so that a right exists only after the main one has been applied (for example, the right to remedy to a previously taken decision), or a subjective one, which implies that the defendant has particular needs, must explicitly submit a request or must act in order to have a right recognized (for example, the right to have the costs of the interpreter be paid by the state).

This division is also necessary to develop a cleaner transposition of national laws. As the transposition of directives is a prerogative of Member States, it often happens that there are multiple sources of laws that can be said to transpose a single article, as each legal source is applicable only to a specific stage of the proceeding. The result is usually that a single EU right is transposed in three or four national articles, each of which relates to a different subject matter of the proceedings. Our system shall thus be able to identify the relevant general rights, as well as the secondary rights that the person has according to the relevant circumstance.

The second rule is used to explicitly define certain properties, or details, of a right.

The difference between auxiliary rights and properties consists in the fact that the latter exists irrespective of the presence of the defendant, or is up to the general authority to decide. A property of a right, in our ontology, implies that the person has either a marginal advantage from that characteristic (for example, the fact that any lawyer shall be appointed from a list of lawyers, or the fact that investigation procedures shall be recorded), or it is the duty of the national authority, be it the police or the judge, that shall verify the respect of the correct procedures (for example, the fact that the training of the lawyers shall be of a sufficient quality to ensure the respect of the principle of fair proceedings, or the limits on the presentation of arrested persons, such as on the application of restrictive measures).

In modelling the different legal sources these specific predicates have been useful both to understand and visualize the relation between general and procedural rights.

```
1. has_right(interpretation, art2_1, PersonId, trial) :-
2.   proceeding_language(PersonId, Language),
3.   \+ person_language(PersonId, Language).

4.  auxiliary_right_scope(art2_3, [art2_1, art2_2, art2_7]).

5.  auxiliary_right(art2_3, PersonId, assistance, vulnerable):-
6.     person_condition(PersonId, hearingSpeechImpediments).

7. right_property_scope(art2_6, [art2_1, art2_2, art2_7]).

8.  right_property(art2_6, PersonId, means, technology) :-
9.     \+ physical_presence_required(PersonId, interpreter,
                    safeguard_fairness).
```

In this snippet of code we can easily identify the three articles, starting respectively in lines 1, 5, and 8.

Art 2(1) is the *general rule*, to which the other are related. The associations between articles can be seen in the *auxiliary_right_scope* and *right_property_scope.*

Art 2(3) has been modelled as an *auxiliary right*, since it is an additional right granted after the general one (Art 2(1)).

Art 2(6) has instead been modelled as a *right property*, since it defines a specific detail (property) of Art 2(1), namely the way in which that right should be granted.

In the example at hand, it is easy to identify the relation between the articles, and thus the representation is clear. It can however be more complicated to separate general and auxiliary rights.

This representation style has been used also in the national legislations, and can help identify the different rights granted by the national legislator.

The following is an example of the *auxiliary right* and *right property* related to the presented articles, as the Spanish (lines 10-14) and Italian (lines 15–17) legislators respectively have transposed those articles into their own legal systems, and how it is connected to our computable system.

```
1. auxiliary_right_scope(art119_criminalProcedureCode,
            [art143_1_1_criminalProcedure,
```

```
                art143_1_2_criminalProcedure]).

2.auxiliary_right(art119_criminalProcedureCode, PersonId,
        assistance, mute) :-
3. person_condition(PersonId, speechImpediment).

4. auxiliary_right(art119_criminalProcedureCode, PersonId,
        assistance, deaf) :-
person_condition(PersonId, hearingImpediment).

5. right_property_scope(art143_3bis,
            [art143_1_1_criminalProcedure,
             art143_1_2_criminalProcedure]).

6. right_property(art143_3bis, PersonId, means, technology) :-
7.  \+ physical_presence_required(PersonId, interpreter,
                correct_exercise_right).
```

15.4 Justification and Explanation

In order to be able to effectively challenge a decision, the affected individual needs to have access to all the information relevant to such a decision, including the explanation.[12] Anyone aiming to challenge an automated decision should be able to identify the legal elements the decision can be grounded on, as well as the inference process that leads the system to its conclusion. The judge (as well as other actors involved) needs to comprehend the logic of the system, including the conditions that have led the machine to that result.

Furthermore, the use of explainable systems may provide insights into the law itself, making it possible for the policy makers to identify and analyse possible conflicts and issues in drafting and implementing laws.

Legal professionals, besides verifying whether a particular right is recognised under a national jurisdiction, are also interested in the conditions under which that right is granted, and on the measures available for its protection.

The main non-ISO structure in the rule-base built for the CrossJustice Project is the meta-interpreter. A Prolog meta-interpreter is a Prolog program that takes a Prolog goal and another Prolog program, then proceeds to attempt

12 Katie Atkinson, Trevor Bench-Capon and Danushka Bollegala, 'Explanation in AI and law: Past, present and future' (2020) Artificial Intelligence.

to prove the goal against the second Prolog program, according to the rules given by the first program.

At a simple level, the meta-interpreter could be simply prove(Goal):- call(-Goal), but this instruction would not add much information, since it would simply tell the main Prolog interpreter that to prove a goal it must call and verify that goal.

Below we present a revised version of the prototype meta-interpreter, that is used as a basis for the explanation method.

```
solve((A,B), Result) :- !,
  solve(A, ARes),
  solve(B, BRes),
  append(ARes, BRes, Result).

solve((A;_), Result) :-
  solve(A, Result).

solve((_;B), Result) :- !,
  solve(B, Result).

solve(member(A, B), [system_predicate]) :- !,
  call(member(A, B)).

solve(\+(A), [not(A)]) :- !,
  call(\+(A)).

solve((A)\=(B), [doNotUnify(A, B)]) :- !,
  call((A)\=(B)).

solve(A, [system_predicate]) :-
  predicate_property(A, built_in), !,
  call(A).

solve(A, [A|[Res]]) :-
  clause(A,B),
  solve(B, Res).
```

This simple (but expandable) meta-interpreter is used to generate a proof tree tracing the execution of the program by printing the sequence of evaluated predicates. In its simple form it will add metadata to some predicates, e.g., adding a “fact” tag to the user-input data (asserted predicates) used in the evaluation. It will then present the user with the relation between the data used, and the rules present in the rulebase. This functionality can be useful to legal experts and other users alike, who want a detailed answer. Moreover, it allows further integration with other systems by exposing the output with a stable API that can be integrated in / or communicate with other platforms.

In the CrossJustice project, this integration has been obtained via a graphical web-based platform that is more user friendly, providing a simple form that a non-expert user can easily fill.

Therefore, the end-result is decorated with extra data, and can be formatted according to the need. For example, the data could be used to automatically generate documents useful in the proceedings.

More experienced users could also interact with the system at a lower level, by modifying rules at runtime, and comparing the results with the new changes. This functionality could be used by the European or national legislator, when deciding on an amendment to an existing rule, or on the introduction of a new one.

Let us consider the transposition of Art 5, paragraph 1, of Directive 2013/48 and the relative articles transposing such article in the Italian legal system, which are Art 387 of the Italian Code of Criminal Procedure, Art 29 of Law n.354/1975 Implementing Provisions and Art 62, paragraph 1 of Decree n.230/2000.

The European legislator states that a person deprived of liberty has the right to inform a third person, nominated by them, of their status. The computable representation of this article is the following:

```
%% has_right(_art5_1, PersonId, _right_to_information,
%         _inform_person)
%
% Article 5.1
%
% The right to have a third person informed of the deprivation of
% liberty
% 1. Member States shall ensure that suspects or accused persons
% who are deprived of liberty have
% the right to have at least one person, such as a relative or an
% employer, nominated by them, informed
% of their deprivation of liberty without undue delay if they so
```

```
% wish.
has_right(art5_1, PersonId, right_to_inform, PersonId2) :-
    ( person_status(PersonId, suspect)
    ; person_status(PersonId, accused)
    ),
    person_status(PersonId, deprived_of_liberty),
    person_nominate(PersonId, PersonId2),
    \+ exception(has_right(art5_1, PersonId, right_to_inform,
PersonId2), _).
```

The result of the reasoning step will inform the user of the fact that he has the right to inform another person, who has been nominated, according to Art 5, paragraph 1. Secondly, the explanation provided by the meta-interpreter will show that the conditions for the application of that rule were: 1) the person is an accused 2) the person is deprived of liberty 3) the person has nominated another person and 4) there is no exception found for the article.

The Italian legal sources do not include such a widely applicable article but are divided into several smaller scoped norms. Art 387 of the Italian Code of Criminal Procedure states that family members shall be informed of the arrest or temporary detention of a person. Art 29 of Law n. 354/1975 Implementing provisions states that relatives shall be informed of the entrance in the institute of detainees and inmates, a principle remarked upon in Art 62 paragraph 1 of Decree n.230/2000 with regard to penitentiary institutes. The conditions for applying these Arts are different from the ones present in the Directive: it is necessary to either state that the person has been arrested, or that the person is in a state of detention.

At first glance it could seem that the Italian implementation is a correct transposition of the Directive, as both legal systems grant the same right to the same person. However, looking more in depth at the data provided to us by the meta-interpreter, it is evident that, according to the Italian legislator 1) the person cannot nominate someone to be informed; 2) only arrest or detention are considered as requisites, while the Directive speaks more broadly of *deprivation of liberty*, of which the formers are just used as examples.

directive_2013_48 – art5_1

Article 5.1
The right to have a third person informed of the deprivation of liberty
1. Member States shall ensure that suspects or accused persons who are deprived of liberty have the right to have at least one person, such as a

relative or an employer, nominated by them, informed of their deprivation of liberty without undue delay if they so wish.

Explanation:

```
has_right(right_to_inform, dir, art5_1, mario, luigi)
 has_right(art5_1, mario, right_to_inform, luigi)
  person_status(mario, accused) [FACT]
  person_status(mario, deprived_of_liberty) [FACT]
  person_nominate(mario, luigi) [FACT]
  not(exception(has_right(art5_1, mario, right_to_inform,
                   luigi), _))
```

In the example above it is shown, with the different levels of indentations, that a person named Mario has the right to inform another person (named Luigi), of his deprivation of liberty.

This is true because of the facts that: 1) Mario is accused of a crime; 2) Mario is also deprived of his liberty in the proceedings; 3) Mario nominates Luigi as his relative/employer to be informed; and 4) there is no reason why this should not be allowed (i.e. there is no exception to this rule that is valid).

With the explanation module of the platform, it is possible to compare the answers given by the Directive and the national implementation, and verify the conformity between legal systems. Even if both rights are granted, it may be that the requirements are different, thus leading to discrepancies in the transposition or application of a norm. Thus, it is possible to identify discrepancies or issues in the different legal systems.

This comparison has been enhanced through the use of argumentation,[13] to enable features such as rule hierarchy and conflictual relations between rules and predicates. It has been implemented into the system a preference between the nature of the sources of rules, such as the fact that all European Directives should be given priority over the national legislation. This supports explainability by comparing the two results and identifying significant discrepancies based on the different conditions between the applicability of two or more significant articles, and visualizing how the national legislation differs from the European law.

---

13 Giuseppe Pisano, Roberta Calegari, Andrea Omicini and Giovanni Sartor, 'Arg-tuProlog: a tuProlog-based Argumentation Framework' (2020) CEUR Workshop Proceedings, CEUR-WSorg, vol 2710.

15.5 Reasoning: Deductive and Abductive Approach

It is commonly agreed that legal reasoning is defeasible reasoning.[14] In the EU corpus, defeasibility occurs by means of expressions such as: "unless proved otherwise"; "unless otherwise agreed"; "unless ..."; "except in those cases"; "with the exception of"; "subject to ..."; "notwithstanding"; etc.

In Prolog, defeasibility is usually managed by using negation by failure, making logic programming a non-monotonic logic.[15] Hence, each of the above expressions has to be accounted for by using negation by failure.

There are however different methods of approaching this issue, that have been considered while modelling the rules. Unfortunately, the existing solutions were not up to the standard needed, but it may be considered in future expansions of the platform.

There are in fact multiple methods of reasoning, namely deductive, inductive, and deductive.

Douglas Walton states that deductive (and inductive) reasoning starts from a "hypothetical state of things", and looks for the available solutions that it can derive from those statements. Abductive reasoning, on the contrary, looks for what may be true: *Abductive arguments, and plausible arguments generally, tend to be presumptive, resulting in conclusions that are hypotheses or supported guesses.*

While abductive reasoning is not commonly used in legal reasoning, in our case it might be of use. One should not take for granted that the users (not necessarily legal experts) are able to answer every question, giving the system all the necessary facts. This is an issue also in human interactions, where there is the possibility that a person in good faith is not able to provide all the information needed.

Let us imagine a lawyer, tasked with organizing the defence for a person who is currently in another country. The lawyer might not know with certainty whether the person is capable of speaking fluently the language needed in the trial.

He might therefore leave that information as *unknown* in the system, and receive two separate possible solutions: one valid if the person speaks the language, and another if that is false.

14 Henry Prakken and Giovanni Sartor, 'Argument-Based Extended Logic Programming with Defeasible Priorities' (1997) Journal of Applied Non-Classical Logics 7(1), 25.

15 Robert Kowalski, *Computational logic and human thinking: how to be artificially intelligent* (Cambridge University Press 2011).

In complex systems, with different rulebases that interact with one another, this could be very useful in making the platform useful.

Another possibility is to write the rules in a language as close as possible to natural language (i.e., English), to make it not only easier to read/write the rules legal experts not comfortable with a programming language such as Prolog, but also to transform the statements that are part of the rulebase in questions it could pose the user.

For instance, if the interpreter were to find an unverified statement "a right is granted if the person speaks the language of the trial", the system could ask "does the person speak the language of the trial?" in an automated way.

15.6 Conclusions

The complexity of the legal norms modelled in the CrossJustice platform, both internally and in relation to others, has sometimes limited the isomorphism of the representation, in particular when dealing with exceptions or open concepts.[16] However, the issue has been adequately solved with the solutions proposed in this chapter. The selected field of application is one more complex than others, more traditionally explored as applications of knowledge-based systems in law, such as tax legislation, administrative regulations, provision of benefits, etc. On the one hand, tax legislation is often considered "complex" because of the high number of exceptions and requirements to be verified to reach a conclusion, but tax rules are nevertheless quite easy to be represented because they generally lack the high number of differing interpretations or implementations. Another problem that is more typical of a field such as that selected for the rule modelling is the number of concepts which lack a precise definition set by the lawmakers, or in which there are multiple such definitions in the national implementations. These are the so-called "open texture" concepts discussed in Paragraph 15.3, whose meaning should be identified by searching in a multiple domain context and taking into account case law and doctrinal interpretations. Despite the high difficulty and complexity of representation, the results of our work show how potentially any field of the law may be represented in the form of rules, using the adopted methodology – with the opportune adaptations – and transposed into a platform for broader use.

16 Robert Kowalski, 'Logical English' in Proceedings of Logic and Practice of Programming (LPOP) (2020).

An important point for further development of this or similar platforms is the process of keeping the platform, and the rulebase up to date with the normative changes, and to enhance it in the future by adding other sources of law. In this way the system will continue to grow in its usefulness to citizens and legal experts alike.

CHAPTER 16

EU Directives Implementation

Automated Analysis of Complexity and Harmonization

Luigi Di Caro, Llio Humphreys, Emilio Sulis, and Rohan Nanda

16.1 Introduction

The work presented in this Chapter was designed for the purposes of a specific European project, named "CrossJustice" (hereinafter CJ). The first part of the Chapter focuses on the modelling of definitions within the six procedural European Union Directives, which were the focus of the research project. The goal is that of illustrating the steps and the challenges towards the construction of a lightweight ontology representing this information. The process of building the ontology revealed a number of aspects that present opportunities for further research.

In the second part, an automatic experimentation concerning the harmonization of EU directives is presented, built on top of an automatic analysis of national implementations for each pair of states to investigate the similarity of the corresponding texts. The applied text mining and natural language processing techniques then culminate in the computation of the cosine similarity between vectors associated with legal texts. On that basis, an aggregated index approximates the degree of harmonization within the six EU Directives.

16.2 Analogical Lightweight Ontology

In this section a description of the creation of a lightweight ontology is presented, that translates and implements criminal procedural rights and contributes to improving the use of judicial cooperation instruments as set out in national law and EU Directives. The ontology is intended to help legal practitioners understand the precise contextual meaning of terms, as well as helping to inform a rule ontology for modelling rules. While the focus is on a specific domain, this Chapter may be used as a reference to guide the creation of lightweight ontologies in other domains.

The sources for the definitions are: the six European Directives, the legal sources referenced by the Directives, and judgments from the Court of Justice

 | DOI:10.1163/9789004513396_018

of the European Union (CJEU). Enforcing the law necessarily involves applying abstract rules and concepts to specific scenarios. A term-based legal ontology can provide a useful reference to find the meaning of terms and their interrelationship, which can in turn help with search functionalities and rule ontologies.

16.2.1 *Background*

Ontologies can vary in their level of specificity. For instance, the LKIF Core Legal Ontology[1] is jurisdiction neutral, the LOIS ontology framework[2] has separate entries for EU and legal national terms, and the ELTS ontology framework[3] uses a bottom-up approach which allows multiple definitions of terms explicitly linked to the source of the definition. The classical definitions used for the ELTS ontology often derive from a specific article dedicated to definitions. They often follow formulaic wording such as "*X means Y*", "*X has the meaning of Y*" or "*X refers to Y*".

A general study of the nature of definitions[4] found that most classic definitions contain hypernyms (usually general rather than direct hypernyms), meronyms, synonyms and purpose-related information. In the framework of the CrossJustice project, we faced the unusual problem that in the six relevant Directives, only two of them contain an article dedicated to definitions. Art 3 of Directive 2016/800 contains 3 definitions, for the terms "child", "holder of parental responsibility" and "parental responsibility". Art 3 of Directive 2016/1919 contains only one definition, for the term "legal aid".

There are some classical definitions to be found elsewhere (and we do use them in the ontology). For instance, Recital 15 of Directive states that "[t]he term 'lawyer' in this Directive refers to any person who, in accordance with national law, is qualified and entitled, including by means of accreditation by an authorised body, to provide legal advice and assistance to suspects or

1 Rinke Hoekstra, Joost Breuker, Marcello di Bello and Alexander Boer, 'The LKIF Core Ontology of Basic Legal Concepts' (2007) 321 CEUR Conference Proceedings 43.

2 Daniela Tiscordia, 'The LOIS Project: Lexical Ontologies for Legal Information Sharing' (2006) Proceedings of the V Legislative XML Workshop, European Press Academy < https://citeseerx.ist.psu.edu/viewdoc/download?doi=10.1.1.474.9540&rep=rep1&type=pdf> accessed 2 November 2021.

3 Ajani Gianmaria, Boella Guido, Di Caro Luigi, Robaldo Livio, Humphreys, Llio, Praduroux Sabrina, Rossi Piercarlo and Violato Andrea, 'The European Legal Taxonomy Syllabus: A multi-lingual, multi-level ontology framework to untangle the web of European legal terminology' (2006) 11 Applied Ontology 325.

4 Luigi di Caro, 'What's in a Definition? An Investigation of Semantic Features in Lexical Dictionaries' (2020) Proceedings of the 16th International Conference on Web Information Systems and Technologies (WEBIST 2020) 225.

accused persons." However, there are not many of these, and apart from not being in the expected place, they also have different connecting keywords to those usually used for classical definitions.

This is an opportunity to explore a phenomenon typically neglected in the construction of domain specific legal ontologies. Whether classical definitions are present or absent, laws or, more in general, legal sources, are typically peppered with a number of hidden (in the sense that they are not clearly marked out as definitions) and incomplete definitions, which may nevertheless help legal practitioners (and legal reasoning systems) to reason on the basis of analogy or teleology. Such definitions can be found not only in articles but also recitals, which play an important role in the legal interpretation of the CJEU.

Different types of such definitions were identified and described as follows:

- *Example Definitions*: A concept is explained in terms of typical examples. This class of definition in particular invites reasoning by analogy. There is a sense of completeness, that the instances must belong either to the examples or something similar;
- *Include or Exclude Definitions*: Include/example definitions are often used to emphasize the inclusion or exclusion of certain items where this would otherwise be uncertain or even surprising. Include/exclude definitions are incomplete as there may (or may not) be other items that are included or excluded;
- *Definitions by Reference*: Some legislation explicitly refers to other legislation for definitions of certain concepts. Those definitions apply also to the referring legislation by virtue of the explicit reference. The scope of a definition may be expanded to cover another legislation where there is explicit reference to the definition from that other legislation.[5]

In this Chapter, a report on the work of collecting and representing such definitions in the domain of criminal procedural rights is illustrated.

16.2.2 *Types of Definitions*

In the work of collecting and representing definitions for the purpose of the lightweight ontology, it is useful to start with and refine the abovementioned classes.

The *Sense Definition* is what we typically imagine when we consider definitions and often have formulaic phrases to link the *definiens* with the 90
definiendum, such as X means Y, X is understood to mean Y. Di Caro found that

5 Llio Humphreys, Guido Boella, Leendert van der Torre, Livio Robaldo, Luigi Di Caro, Sepideh Ghanavati and Robert Muthuri, 'Populating legal ontologies using semantic role labeling' (2021) 29 Artificial Intelligence and Law 171.

Sense Definitions typically contain synonyms, hypernyms, meronyms and/or purpose-related information.[6] For our purposes, what distinguishes Sense Definitions from the other definition types described below is that they have a sense of completeness. As an example, Art 1(1) of Directive 2010/64 states "This Directive lays down rules concerning the right to interpretation and translation in criminal proceedings and proceedings for the execution of a European arrest warrant." From this we obtain the following Sense Definition for the Directive: "EU legal act providing rules concerning the right to interpretation and translation 100 in criminal proceedings and proceedings for the execution of a European arrest warrant".[7]

The *Part Definition* consists of components or elements of a concept such as procedures or rights, where the meaning is best understood by the sum of its parts. For example, in Art 4(2) of Directive 2012/13, we can consider each numbered item as a component of the information to be provided in a Letter of Rights: "2. In addition to the information set out in Art 3, the Letter of Rights referred to in paragraph 1 of this article shall contain information about the following rights as they apply under national law:

(a) the right of access to the materials of the case;
(b) the right to have consular authorities and one person informed;
(c) the right of access to urgent medical assistance; and
(d) the maximum number of hours or days suspects or accused persons may be deprived of liberty before being brought before a judicial authority".

The *Essential Part Definition* consists of components or elements of a concept that are crucial for the existence of that concept. For example, in Recital 33 of Directive 2016/800, "Confidentiality of communication between children and their lawyer is key to ensuring the effective exercise of the rights of the defence and is an essential part of the right to a fair trial." The connecting key phrases "is key to" and "is an essential part of" are suggestive of an Essential Part Definition in this instance, but there are other such keywords, as illustrated below sub (i) to (x).[8]

(i) The *Purpose Definition* seeks to explain a concept by its purpose. For example, there are two legitimate purposes for refusing access to certain materials in Art 7(4) of Directive 2012/13: "By way of derogation from paragraphs 2 and 3, provided that this does not prejudice the right to a fair trial, access to certain materials may be refused if such access may lead to a serious threat to the life or the fundamental rights of another person or if such refusal is

6 Di Caro (n 4).
7 Hoekstra (n 1).
8 Tiscornia (n 2).

strictly necessary to safeguard an important public interest, such as in cases where access could prejudice an ongoing investigation or seriously harm the national security of the Member State in which the criminal proceedings are instituted". As such, we put as secondary concepts the following purposes: 1) to avoid prejudicing an ongoing investigation and 2) to avoid seriously harming the national security of the Member State in which the criminal proceedings are instituted.[9]

(ii) The *Parameter Definition* contains one or more parameters that are taken into account in the application of a legal concept and that helps to understand that concept more clearly. Art 8(2) of Directive 2016/800 provides a good example of a Parameter Definition where we have a parameter for multiple legal concepts: "The results of the medical examination shall be taken into account when determining the capacity of the child to be subject to questioning, other investigative or evidence-gathering acts, or any measures taken or envisaged against the child".[10]

(iii) The *Ratione Temporis Definition* is constituted by the timeframe of application of a legal concept, such as a principle, right, obligation or even the whole directive. For example, Art 2(1) of Directive 2016/800 enshrines two *ratione temporis* Definitions, in that it states that "This Directive applies to children who are suspects or accused persons in criminal proceedings. It applies until the final determination of the question whether the suspect or accused person has committed a criminal offence, including, where applicable, sentencing and the resolution of any appeal".[11]

(iv) The *Ratione Persone Definition* identifies the subjects of a legal concept, such as a principle, right, obligation or even the whole directive. For instance, Art 2 of Directive 2016/343 enshrines that "This Directive applies to natural persons who are suspects or accused persons in criminal proceedings. It applies at all stages of the criminal proceedings, from the moment when a person is suspected or accused of having committed a criminal offence, or an alleged criminal offence, until the decision on the final determination of whether that person has committed the criminal offence concerned has become definitive".[12]

9 Ajani (n 3).

10 Di Caro (n 4).

11 Humphreys (n 5).

12 Víctor Rodriguez-Doncel, Cristiana Santos, Pompeu Casanovas and Asunción Gómez-Pérez, 'A Linked Term Bank of Copyright-Related Terms' in Rinke Hoekstra (ed) *Proceedings of the 28th Int. Conf. on Legal Knowledge and Information System* (*JURIX*) (IOS Press 2015).

(v) The *Typical Example Definition* (a subclass of the Example Definition) is based on a typical example of a wider concept in order to provide the latter's definition. For instance, in Article 2(3) of Directive 2010/64: "The right to interpretation under paragraphs 1 and 2 includes appropriate assistance for persons with hearing or speech impediments".

(vi) The *Atypical Example Definition* (a subclass of the Example Definition) is based on a specific example of a wider concept that is not commonly included in the wider concept. For instance, in Recital 16 of Directive 2016/800 the conclusion of the proceedings "is understood to mean the final determination of the question whether they have committed the offence, including, where applicable, sentencing and the resolution of any appeal". The legislature decided to clarify that the conclusion of the proceedings includes the resolution of any appeal, which is not commonly conceived as a stage of the proceedings and therefore represents an atypical example. Note that the connecting keyword "include" can be indicative of a Typical or Atypical Definition, depending on the context.

(vii) The *Important Example Definition* (a subclass of the Example Definition), like the Typical Example Definition, provides an example of a wider concept in order to provide the latter's definition. However, in this case, while it invites wider analogy, it determines that at least the inclusion of this particular case must be respected. For instance, in Recital 13 of Directive 2013/48, the duty of care towards suspected or accused persons who are in a potentially weak position is emphasised "in particular" towards those who have "any physical impairments which affect their ability to communicate effectively".

(viii) The *Parameter Example Definition* is both a subclass of the Example Definition and of the Parameter Definition. Just like the Parameter Definition, it adopts examples of parameters to clarify a concept. However, like the various Example Definitions described here, the list of parameters is not exhaustive and therefore invites reasoning by analogy. This can be seen in the following example from Recital 4 of Directive 2013/48: "The extent of the mutual recognition is very much dependent on a number of parameters, which include mechanisms for safeguarding the rights of suspects or accused persons and common minimum standards necessary to facilitate 220 the application of the principle of mutual recognition".

(ix) The *Non Example Definition* (a subclass of Example Definitions) is based on an example that is excluded from a wider concept in order to provide the latter's definition. For instance, Recital 13 of Directive 2013/48 excludes two specific proceedings for the wider concept of "criminal proceedings", and in so doing, provides a clearer definition of that concept. The norm states that "proceedings in relation to minor offending which take place within a prison and proceedings in relation to offences committed in a military context which are dealt with by a commanding officer should not be considered to be criminal proceedings for the purposes of this Directive".

(x) The *Definition By Reference* represents the fact that not every piece of legislation contains a definition for every concept, and some legislation explicitly refers to other legislation for definitions of certain concepts. For example, Recital 49 of Directive 2016/343 states that "the Union may adopt measures in accordance with the principle of subsidiarity as set out in Art 5 TEU (Treaty on the European Union). In accordance with the principle of proportionality, as set out in that article, this Directive does not go beyond what is necessary in order to achieve those objectives." The definitions for the principle of subsidiarity and the principle of proportionality apply explicitly to Directive 2016/343.[13]

16.2.3 (*Continues*) *Classes and Relationships*

The work described in this Chapter is influenced by European Legal Taxonomy Syllabus[14] in the following ways:

- it is assumed that the scope of a definition is the legislative source itself, unless its scope has been explicitly restricted or expanded. In our work, restriction of scope is identified by phrases such as "for the purposes of paragraph X", while expansion of scope is identified by an explicit citation to the definition from another piece of legislation;
- it is assumed that definitions are specific to the jurisdiction of the legislation concerned. In the context of the EU, it is expected that transposition of legislation (and the concepts defined therein) may result in modification to the definition of the concepts, such that it is necessary to define the relationship between related concepts.

The implementation of the ontology, on the other hand, is based on the Linked Term Bank of Copyright-Related Terms.[15] This ontology is also domain-specific, multilingual and multi-jurisdictional. The Copyright Term Bank in turn is built on Lemon and SKOS classes. For the CJ lightweight ontology, the following classes from the Copyright Term Bank have been used:

- *Concept*: the *definiens;*
- *LexicalEntry*: the words or phrases used to represent the context;

---

13 Robert van Kralingen, 'A Conceptual Frame-based Ontology for the Law' in Pepijn R. S.Visser and Radboud Winkels (eds) *Proceedings of the First International Workshop on Legal Ontologies (LEGONT '97)* (University of Melbourne 1997).

14 Ajani (n 3).

15 Rodriguez-Doncel (n 12).

- *LexicalSense*: represents the lexical meaning of a lexical entry, and when linked to a Concept, implies that the lexical entry can be used to refer to that Concept;
- *SenseDefinition*: the *definiendum*, along with the legal source of the definiendum.[16]

To this, the following classes have been added:
- *PartDefinition;*
- *EssentialPartDefinition;*
- *PurposeDefinition;*
- *ParameterDefinition;*
- *RationeTemporisDefinition;*
- *RationePersoneDefinition;*
- *TypicalExampleDefinition;*
- *AtypicalExampleDefinition;*
- *ImportantExampleDefinition;*
- *ParameterExampleDefinition;*
- *NonExampleDefinition;*

There is no specific class for a Definition by Reference. Instead, all definitions have one or more Scope fields. So in the example described above, the principle of proportionality defined in Art 5 of TEU has as its scope not only the TEU itself but also Directive 2016/343, due to the Definition by Reference in Recital 49 of that Directive.[17]

Since the above-mentioned new definition types necessarily involve a relationship between concepts, it is also important to model the relationship between concepts with the following properties:
- *IsPartOf;*
- *HasPart;*
- *IsPurposeOf;*
- *HasPurpose;*
- *IsParameterOf;*
- *HasParameter;*
- *IsRationeTemporis;*
- *HasRationeTemporis;*
- *IsRationePersone;*

16 Emilio Sulis, Llio Humphreys, Fabiana Vernero, Ilaria Angela Amantea, Davide Audrito and Luigi Di Caro 'Exploiting co-occurrence networks for classification of implicit inter-relationships in legal texts' (2021) Information Systems 101821.

17 Bernard Steunenberg and Mark Rhinard, 'The transposition of European law in EU member states: between process and politics' (2010) 2 European Political Science Review 495.

- *HasRationePersone;*
- *IsTypicalExampleOf;*
- *HasTypicalExample;*
- *IsAtypicalExampleOf;*
- *HasAtypicalExample;*
- *IsImportantExampleOf;*
- *HasImportantExample;*
- *IsParameterExample;*
- *HasParameterExample;*
- *IsNonExampleOf;*
- *HasNonExample;*
- *IsEssentialPartOf;*

This duplication has the following advantages:

- It enables the original source text to be easily accessed in the *Definition* instances;
- It enables users to visualise the relationship between different concepts (from the point of view of the relevant legal source).

16.3 Ontology Creation

Below, the structure of a possible ontology is reported, together with some examples.

The first step is of the importing of the Linked Term Bank of Copyright-Related Terms into WebProtégé. The Term Bank was available as an N-Triples file,[18] which can be then converted into the Resource Description Framework (RDF) format using an online conversion tool.[19] The RDF file can be then imported into WebProtégé.

Here is a summary of the structure of the Linked Term Bank of Copyright-Related Terms:

- *Owl:Thing* has 4 direct subclasses: *Concept*, *Lexical Entry*, *Lexical Sense* and *SenseDefinition;*
- Concepts have one or more of the following AnnotationProperties:
  - *rdfs:label*: the most common term for this *Concept* as a *plainLiteral* value;

18 Víctor Rodríguez-Doncel, 'A Linked Term Bank of Copyright-Related Terms' (*Home Page of Víctor Rodríguez-Doncel* 2015) <http://www.cosasbuenas.es/blog/copyright-term-bank> accessed 2 November 2021.

19 See <https://www.easyrdf.org/converter> accessed 2 November 2021.

  - *skos:definition*: a link to an instance of *SenseDefinition*, which provides the definition, source and other relevant data;
  - *isSenseOf*: a link to one or more *LexicalEntry* instances, which provide the terms used to express the *Concept;*
  - *jurisdiction*: a link to a DBPedia entry which provides information about the jurisdiction;
  - *reference* (value: *link* [*dbpedia entry*]);
  - *closeMatch*: a link to a similar concept in the IATE EU terminology database;
  - *narrower*: a link to an instance of a narrower *Concept*;
  - *rdfs:comment*: as a *plainLiteral* value.

The AnnotationProperties *rdfs:label, skos:definition* and *isSenseOf* appear in all Concepts.

- *LexicalEntries* have the following Annotation properties:
  - *rdfs:label*: a term used to express a *Concept* in a *plainLiteral* value;
  - *denotes*: a link to one or more *Concept* instances denoted by the term in the *LexicalEntry;*
  - *language*: the language of the term, in a *plainLiteral* value;
  - *sense* (value: *owl:NamedIndividual* of class *LexicalSense*).

The AnnotationProperties *rdfs:label, skos:denotes* and *sense* appear in all LexicalEntries.

- LexicalSenses have the following Annotation properties:
  - *reference*: to one or more instances of the class Concept);
- SenseDefinitions have the following properties:
  - *source*: the name of the glossary of terms from where the definition came from, as well as an URI for the glossary;
  - *value*: a definition as a plainLiteral value, with the value property itself having a "lang" property;

For the ontology, all the above classes and properties have been kept, being interested in representing (classical) sense definitions. However, in addition to SenseDefinitions, a number of other definitions have been created, so that the overall class structure is as follows:

- *Concept;*
- *LexicalSense;*
- *LexicalEntry;*
- *Definition;*
  - *SenseDefinition:*
    - *PartDefinition;*
    - *EssentialPartDefinition;*

  - *PurposeDefinition;*
  - *ParameterDefinition;*
  - *RationeTemporisDefinition;*
  - *RationePersoneDefinition;*
- *AnalogicalDefinition:*
  - *TypicalExampleDefinition;*
  - *AtypicalExampleDefinition;*
  - *ImportantExampleDefinition;*
  - *ParameterExampleDefinition;*
  - *NonExampleDefinition;*

Here is an example of a Typical Example Definition from Art 2(3) of Directive 2010/64:

> The right to interpretation under paragraphs 1 and 2 includes appropriate assistance for persons with hearing or speech impediments.

In the ontology, the Concept "*the right to interpretation*" is linked to a Typical Example Definition, which has a field for the definition, as well as a comment field providing the original article for reference. There is another Concept for "*appropriate assistance for persons with hearing or speech impediments*".

The Copyright TermBank relies entirely on Annotation Properties for showing links among concepts, their lexical senses, lexical entries and sense definitions. On the other hand, in our ontology we also have classifications that are defined in terms of their relationship between other concepts. As such, we use Relationship Properties to explain such relationships. This has the benefit of enabling the viewer to visualise the relationship between different concepts, as can be seen in the screenshot below.

Here is an Important Example Definition from Directive 2010/64, at its Recital 27.

> The duty of care towards suspected or accused persons who are in a potentially weak position, in particular because of any physical impairments which affect their ability to communicate effectively, underpins a fair administration of justice. The prosecution, law enforcement and judicial authorities should therefore ensure that such persons are able to exercise effectively the rights provided for in this Directive, for example by taking into account any potential vulnerability that affects their ability to follow the proceedings and to make themselves understood, and by taking appropriate steps to ensure those rights are guaranteed.

16.4 Observations for Semi-Automated Ontology Population

The automatic extraction of definitions, as well as the population of the ontology has been carried out manually to be able to develop and verify both the methodology and the model, given the small dataset available. Future work could envisage automatic approaches following and exploiting the results of this experimentation. This approach, indeed, created a working model potentially applicable via automation, and also capable to be successfully applied in other contexts and to other data sets. Data collected in preparation for creating the ontology within this research can contain identifiable factors that may be useful for developing such systems in the future. One such factor is the source of the definition. For example, judgments normally provide real examples of what counts as a particular legal concept. The fact that a CJEU hearing is needed to establish such a relation suggests that the definitions extracted are Atypical Example Definitions.

More often, we envisage that a definition classification system might put significant weight on certain keywords (or key phrases) connecting a *definiendum* with its *definiens*. This factor has been used extensively in the manual identification and classification of definitions carried out for this project. For example, in Art 4 of Directive 2013/48, the connecting keyword "include" precedes typical examples:

> Member States shall respect the confidentiality of communication between suspects or accused persons and their lawyer in the exercise of the right of access to a lawyer provided for under this Directive. Such communication shall include meetings, correspondence, telephone conversations and other forms of communication permitted under national law.

Here are some examples of connecting keywords (and key phrases) and the definition class they normally indicate:
- "*based on*" can indicate a Part Definition (but not always as it can also mean "*reasons for*");
- "*cornerstone*", "*essential part*" or "*presupposes*" indicate an Essential Part Definition;
- "*for example*" or "*such as*" indicate a Typical Example Definition;
- "*in particular*" and "*at least*" indicate an Important Example Definition;
- "*include*" or "*including*" indicate a Part Definition or a Typical, Atypical or Important Example Definition. "*Could include*" indicates a Typical Example Definition. "*Should include*" and "*including as a minimum*" indicate an Important Example Definition;
- "*excludes*" or "*does not include*" indicate a Non Example Definition.

However, the relationship is not always straightforward, and real-world knowledge or contextual analysis can help to resolve classification difficulties.

Recital 55 of Directive 2016/800 provides a difficult example with the connecting keyword "including".

> Children should be treated in a manner appropriate to their age, maturity and level of understanding, taking into account any special needs, including any communication difficulties, that they may have.

Our rules of thumb for the keyword "*including*" are as follows:

1. if "*including*" is followed by a list of items, these are, by default, typical examples;
2. if "*including*" is followed by just item, that item is an atypical example that might otherwise be excluded from inclusion in the broader concept;
3. if the item is clearly not an atypical example, then it must be an important example.

According to this reasoning, "*communication difficulties*" should be classed as an important example of "*special needs*". But our real-world knowledge strongly suggests that what we have here is in fact a very typical example, and nothing else in the Recital suggests that particular attention must be given to this example. And so, we conclude that in this case, we have a Typical Example Definition. Our real-world knowledge reasoning overrides syntactic reasoning.

There are hard cases that require not only real-world knowledge, but also contextual understanding. Recital 44 of Directive 2013/48 contains the text:

> Requested persons should have the right to communicate with the lawyer representing them in the executing Member State. It should be possible for such communication to take place at any stage, including before any exercise of the right to meet with the lawyer. Member States may make practical arrangements concerning the duration, frequency and means of communication between requested persons and their lawyer, including concerning the use of videoconferencing and other communication technology [emphasis added] in order to allow such communications to take place.

Normally, videoconferencing would be considered an atypical means of communication between persons subject to proceedings and their lawyer, but the norm concerns European Arrest Warrant proceedings that often imply geographical distance between the accused person and their lawyer. In this context, videoconferencing is not considered atypical but rather important.

There are also cases where alternative classifications are possible. For example, Recital 55 of Directive 2013/48 contains the following text:

> This Directive promotes the rights of children and takes into account the Guidelines of the Council of Europe on child friendly justice, in particular its provisions on information and advice to be given to children. This Directive ensures that suspects and accused persons, including children, are provided with adequate information to understand the consequences of waiving a right under this Directive and that any such waiver is made voluntarily and unequivocally.

The extracted definition of "*suspects and accused persons*" could reasonably be classified as either an Atypical or Important Example Definition. Children are atypical examples of suspects, but they are also an important example in the context of this particular norm, because it is especially important for this group to receive information. An option could be to represent this as an Atypical Example Definition.

It is unclear at this point how much the classification may require a deeper analysis than can be obtained simply with syntactic rules. However, given the challenges described above, we envisage that any system for extracting and classifying definitions will require manual post-editing in the foreseeable future.

16.5 Similarity and Harmonization: An Automated Approach

In this section, a description of an automatic approach for capturing the harmonization of national law with respect to EU Directives is reported. Harmonisation is the process of adopting regulations in a common way across the different Member States, aiming to have the same rules apply to each country. A Directive comes into effect only after it has been transposed into national law via the so-called National Implementing Measures (NIMs). This section focuses on legal texts officially adopted by the Member States to transpose the provisions of EU Directives.

Two main methods have been used for transposing EC law into national law:[20]

i. 'Copy-out': implementing legislation adopts the same, or mirrors as closely as possible the original wording of the Directive;

20 Steunenberg (n 17).

ii. 'Elaboration': choosing a particular meaning according to what the draftsperson believes the provision to mean, with the aim of working a provision into something clearer (this is an UK practice).

The typical method for transpositions is 'copy-out'. In this case, texts of NIMS are expected to be similar. As European Directives provide national legislators of each Member State some discretion in the choice of methods and forms for implementation, the corresponding legal texts (transpositions) are different. Nevertheless, a certain degree of similarity is expected, by comparing the English versions of the implementation of six European Directives examined in CJ. In particular, legal experts annotated in the Transposition Tables (TT) of the CJ project four types of annotations:

- *Explicitly transposed* [*Exp*]*:* either via new legislation or via amendments to existing legislation;
- *De facto/indirectly implemented* [*Ind*]: transposition unnecessary because the right already existed in previous legislation;
- *No national implementation* [*NoN*]: lack of transposing national norm or non-conformity of the national norm with the requirements of the EU provision;
- *Specific transposition is not required* [*Not*]: transposition may be unnecessary because 1) the legal provision lacks deontic or constitutive value e.g. Arts 1 and 2 of the Directives usually define only the scope of the Directive, or 2) Member States may derogate from a particular provision (e.g. Art 6(3) of the Directive 2016/800).

To investigate the similarity of transpositions into the national law, a typical computational approach in Natural Language Processing and in Information Retrieval use to represent text as vectors of terms frequencies (Bag-of-words, BoW representation). Legal texts have to be processed, for instance, by considering fixed-length vectors of words (n-grams).

Related works on similarity and harmonization proposed various automatic techniques in legal domain: i) The analysis of legal texts by using both bag-of-n-grams and the frequency of terms with TF-IDF; ii) Word2Vec implementation as an improvement over traditional bag-of-words; iii) A network analysis to describe the dataset; iv) graph embedding approaches (e.g. Node2Vec) on the network, as a state-of-the-art algorithm for learning embeddings of nodes in a homogeneous network (a network having the same type of nodes). This library aims to map the vertices/nodes of the graph to a vector space such that nodes having similar neighbourhoods in the network have similar embeddings/representations; v) Similarity metrics computation, analysis of results and visualisation.

16.6 Methodological Framework

In this section, a 'text analysis' pipeline as presented in a similar work is reported.[21] The text of NIMs is preprocessed to remove less useful information with the following four main steps:

- [Step 1] By adopting two *regular expressions* to remove some particular cases from the original JSON file, i.e. some "Camel cases" of terms (this kind of error appears when a term is followed by a new line wrap and then a term with upper case) as well as cases of digits in the form of numbered list (1°, 2°, etc.);
- [Step 2] *Text preprocessing* according to the following passages:
  - lower case reduction;
  - stop words and punctuation removal;
  - pos-tagging (to consider only: nouns, verbs, and adjectives);
  - stemming (reduce terms in their root form according to Porter stems);
- [Step 3] *Bag-of-words model.* This step transforms each NIM/article to a fixed-length vector of terms (model). With *Bag-of-ngrams* models, by considering n-grams (bigrams and trigrams include respectively two and three words) and obtaining different representations of the same text . Most frequent features can be selected to reduce sparsity.

Here the focus is on the collection of six EU procedural Directives made by individual documents *d* (the TT parts/articles of an EU Directive) in Step 3, assuming that the corpus is the entire set of NIMs (by considering 'Explicitly transposed' articles) for each Directive.

Bag-of-words technique aims to represent the text of each document in numbers, based on a vocabulary from all the unique words. Bag-of-ngrams is a more sophisticated approach to create a vocabulary of grouped words of length *n* (i.e., *n*-grams). The corresponding vector of numbers counts the occurrences of terms in the document. A fine-grained measure considers different frequency metric, i.e. Tf-Idf.

Term frequency–inverse document frequency (Tf-Idf) is a numerical statistic for reflecting how important a word is to a document in our collection. The measure implies two parts: Term Frequent (TF) simply describes how frequently a term appears in each document. Inverse Document Frequency (Idf) computes the importance of the term in the complete collection. The Tf-Idf metric is the fraction of the total number of documents over the number of documents which includes the term of interest, by computing the logarithm of the whole fraction to obtain a more compact measure.

---

21 Sulis (n 16).

- [Step 4] *Document-Term matrix*. Further, the cleaned data need to be converted into a numerical format where each word is represented by a matrix (word vectors). In language processing, the assumption on vectorisation is that similar text must result in closer vectors (i.e., the vectors derived from textual data to reflect various linguistic properties of the text).

In particular, for each individual NIMs the aim was to obtain a vector of the corresponding Document-Term Matrix (DTM). In the resulting matrix, every row is a NIM (here, a single TT part/article) and every column is a term/stem/n-gram. The values in the matrix are the frequencies of each term in a document.

The columns can be too many, so a Dimensionality Reduction strategy must be applied, e.g. Multi-Dimensional Scaling (MDS) and Principal Component Analysis (PCA).

Notes on computer programming. The *scikit-learn* python library is used, recording results on SQL database tables, and exploiting several methods of interest, e.g.:

- *count_vectorizer*: the method converts a collection of text documents to a matrix of token counts. Two parameters of interest are: *ngram_range*, able to consider n-grams in the text (for bigrams: ngram_range = (2,2); and *max_features* considers the top-ranked features (e.g., max_features = (100));
- *fit_tranform*: the combination of *fit* and *transform* methods. While *fit* method is calculating the mean and variance of each of the features present in our data, the *transform* method is transforming all the features using the respective mean and variance.

16.7 Similarity

Traditionally, the 'similarity' of two legal documents used to be assessed "manually" by legal experts. As anticipated, the challenge here is to automate this similarity computation.[22] Existing automatic methodologies for finding similar legal documents can be classified into two categories:

- (i) network-based methods, which rely on citations to prior case documents;
- (ii) text-based methods, which use the content/textual information of the documents.

22 Paheli Bhattacharya, Kripabandhu Ghosh, Arindam Pal, Saptarshi Ghosh, 'Methods for Computing Legal Document Similarity: A Comparative Study' (LDA 2019 Workshop, JURIX 2019 Conference, Madrid) <https://arxiv.org/pdf/2004.12307.pdf> accessed 2 November 2021.

As mentioned, in this Chapter we report an experimentation of the (ii) approach on 'similarity' in legal informatics concerning the comparison between the EU Directive and the transposition into the national law. In a similar recent work, text mining and natural language processing (NLP) techniques have been explored to assist the Commission and legal professionals in studying and evaluating the transposition of directives at a fine-grained provision level.[23]

The metric adopted is Cosine Similarity (CS), a measure to compare the vectors of two NIMs (V1 and V2). CS includes the dot product of the vectors V1 and V2. The denominator is the product of their lengths, given by the Euclidean distance. The effect of the document length is compensated by the denominator which normalizes the similarity value. The range of values that the CS can vary is {-1, 1}.

The CS values can be computed between the Member States implementations at the level of each NIM article in the TT (e.g., for a predefined EU Directive, making a comparison of the corresponding "Explicit transpositions" of Art 1 both in Italy and in Bulgaria, and so on). Finally, the most similar NIMs for each EU Directive is reported.

Notes on computer programming. We adopted the *cosine_similarity* method from the *scikit-learn* python library (*sklearn.metrics.pairwise*).

Finally, to synthesize the results, a visualization technique has been employed to describe the similarity between pairs of states on each Directive item. As in Figure 16.1, a colored table (or heat map) can describe for each article the degree of similarity between pairs of member states. Dark colors (e.g., green or blue) imply no similarity, while lighter colors (e.g., white/yellow) indicate a certain degree of text similarity.

For instance, the following 'heat map' about "Art_5" of Directive 2016/1919 clearly describes how three pairs of States (Italy and Germany, Germany and Spain, Poland and Germany) have more similar text (light color) than other States. On the contrary, Italy's and Poland's cases seem very different. The diagonal is null (black color in our case), because the relationship between the text of a State and itself is not considered.

23 Rohan Nanda, Giovanni Siragusa, Luigi Di Caro, Guido Boella, Lorenzo Grossio, Marco Gerbaudo, Francesco Costamagna 'Unsupervised and supervised text similarity systems for automated identification of national implementing measures of European Directives' (2019) 27 Artificial Intelligence and Law 199.

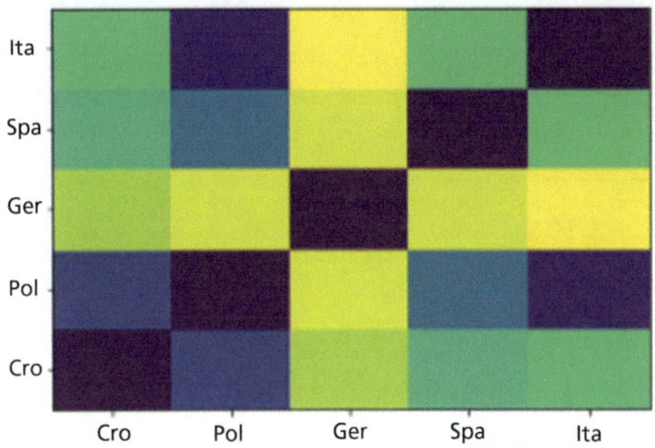

FIGURE 16.1 A heat map for similarity scores of Art 5 (directive 2016/1919)

16.8 Harmonization Index

On the basis of similarity indices, the idea is to obtain an aggregated index to describe the degree of similarity of NIMs with respect to a certain EU Directive. Such a 'harmonization index' can be compared across States and the six EU Directives studied in the project to investigate how the automatic analysis of legal texts may help to identify the different degree of implementations. Finally, exploiting the similarity among pairs of States, a proposal of a Harmonization Index is obtained by the following three steps: (i) select only the texts (provisions) with the label "Explicitly Transposed" for each Directive and for each article (grouping them in case there are more than one for each article); (ii) on these processed texts, calculate the *cosine similarity* (so for each article we obtain the similarity of the texts between the pairs of states at textual level – represented with heat maps); (iii) the average of *cosine similarity* values (AVG(CS)) of the normative texts gives an idea of how similar or not all these parts "Explicitly Transposed" are. These values are continuous, so in addition to the numerical value (multiplied by 100 to be more readable) one proposal is to use three classes: "*High*" if above 30, "*Low*" if below 20, and "*Medium*" if in between.

These measures provide an idea about how to address the issue of obtaining an automatic value of a Harmonization Index. It is not possible to calculate the index when the occurrences of the label "Explicitly Transposed" are not significant (for example, in the Directive 2016/343 there are very few cases in the TT). When it is high, it indicates that – looking only at the legal texts – the States are likely to be "aligned" among themselves in applying a certain EU Directive.

TABLE 16.1 Harmonization index (H-I) and the average values of similarity in directive 2013/48

Article	AVG(CS)%	H-I
art_2	31,02	High
art_3	21,59	Medium
art_4	21,01	Medium
art_5	18,11	Low
art_6	16,59	Low
art_7	21,92	Medium
art_8	20,68	Medium
art_9	21,37	Medium
art_10	38,11	High

16.9 Concluding Remarks

This Chapter described both human and computational efforts towards the analysis and the modeling of the complexity of a specific legal domain (that of the CJ project) within a European context. In particular, it is focused on the key concepts of "Ontology creation" and "Harmonization in EU Law", having value not only for the CJ project, but also for the whole legal informatics community.

Conclusion

or rather … Charting a Way forward for New Forms of Integration

Giuseppe Contissa and Giulia Lasagni

After thirty months of research, it is hard to summarise in a few final words all the road that has been undertaken.

National legislative and case law analyses, legal reasoning on complex normative frameworks, developing automated forms of semantic analysis and creating a freely accessible online platform: all these activities required the greatest commitment from all research members. We hope that this volume has brought forth these efforts to the readers.

In these very final pages, we wish to move our gaze beyond what has been accomplished, to look towards what stands before us. The results of a research, indeed, rarely represent an end point, but rather move forward the starting line for the studies about to come.

In this regard, there are several profiles that immediately reveal themselves as potentially relevant for further investigations.

First, the integrated analysis and reasoning methodology experienced in the CrossJustice project could find application to other aspects of criminal procedure law. For instance, it could be used to examine the rights of the victim, also influenced by EU harmonization, thanks to Directive 2012/29. A research line, partially already touched in the present study, could then consider the transnational application of all these safeguards within the mutual cooperation mechanisms (European Arrest Warrant, European Investigation Order, Regulation (EU) 2018/1805).

Second, the approach developed in Crossjustice may be useful for the objective of evidence-based policy-making, as it provides ways to analyse the impact of the law, supporting the legislator in understanding gaps, inconsistencies and interpretative issues that may hamper the effort of harmonisation. Such approach may be extended to other areas of the law influenced by EU harmonization.

Third, the symbolic-logic approach to the development of Legal AI technologies, adopted in Crossjustice, provides a decisive advantage over data-driven approaches: the system grounds its reasoning into an explicit model of the law, and this ensures transparency and explainability of the outcomes, enabling the human user to integrate such outcomes in its decision-making activity.

 | DOI:10.1163/9789004513396_019

Other relevant research lines have then been only partially examined in the present study, but are acquiring a growing weight in shaping the effectiveness of procedural safeguards on a national and supranational dimension.

For instance, the increasing deployment of digital technology does require a much deeper reflection on the integration between criminal procedure rules, remedies, and potential violation of the rights to privacy and data protection. The widespread use of digital data also for punitive purposes, indeed enlarges the issue to a dimension which today cannot clearly be fairly and effectively regulated any longer with the limited set of procedural norms currently available in most national jurisdictions.

All these developments, however, represent only a part of what needs to be done to ensure a better and more substantial implementation of fundamental rights throughout the EU.

The other side lays in practical, but essential aspects: financial support to the institutional framework and adequate training for all actors involved in the proceedings, from lawyers, to judges, to prosecutors, to law enforcement and linguistic operators.

Training programs, in particular, often struggle today to keep pace with the technological development and the globalized context in which jurists need to take their own steps. We hope that this research, beyond all its limit, could contribute to change such educational paradigm, providing for a methodological paradigm that allows to better navigate the difficult waters of the increasingly complex, integrated, multidisciplinary, but also exciting environment that is our society.

Index